Cuba

IN THE AMERICAN

IMAGINATION

Cuba

IN THE AMERICAN

IMAGINATION

METAPHOR AND THE

IMPERIAL ETHOS

LOUIS A. PÉREZ JR.

The
University
of North
Carolina
Press
Chapel Hill

© 2008 The University of North Carolina Press

All rights reserved

Designed by Richard Hendel

Set in Arnhem and Scala Sans types

by Tseng Information Systems, Inc.

Manufactured in the United States of America

The paper in this book meets the guidelines for permanence
and durability of the Committee on Production Guidelines
for Book Longevity of the Council on Library Resources.

Library of Congress Cataloging-in-Publication Data

Pérez, Louis A., 1943–

Cuba in the American imagination : metaphor and the
imperial ethos / by Louis A. Pérez, Jr.

p. cm.

Includes bibliographical references and index.

ISBN 978-0-8078-3216-5 (cloth : alk. paper)

1. United States—Relations—Cuba. 2. Cuba—Relations—
United States. 3. Cuba—Foreign public opinion, American.
4. Metaphor—Political aspects—United States—History.
5. Imperialism—History. 6. Popular culture—United States—
History—19th century. 7. Popular culture—United States—
History—20th century. 8. Political culture—United
States—History—19th century. 9. Political culture—United
States—History—20th century. 10. Public opinion—
United States—History. I. Title.

E183.8.C9P4653 2008

327.7307291—dc22   2008000078

A Caravan book. For more information, visit
www.caravanbooks.org.

12 11 10 09 08   5 4 3 2 1

To the memory of

Francisco Pérez Guzmán

(1941–2006)

Always Panchito—

colleague and friend

Somehow we can not speak of or deal
with Cuba with composure and without
becoming extravagant.
—Senator Stephen Benton Elkins
   (June 30, 1902)

Contents

Acknowledgments

It is perhaps a truism that the completion of a book is itself the culmination of successful collaboration between an author and, on one hand, the staffs of libraries and archives and, on the other, a host of friends and colleagues. In regard to the former, I am grateful for the assistance provided by the reference and interlibrary loan staffs of Davis Library at the University of North Carolina at Chapel Hill. I am especially appreciative of the tireless efforts made in my behalf by Tommy Nixon and Teresa Chapa, who for all the years this project was in progress, during the research and writing, made available to me their vast knowledge and experience. I was also the beneficiary of the assistance provided by the staffs at the U.S. National Archives, the Library of Congress, the Biblioteca Nacional "José Martí," the New York Public Library, the Pennsylvania Historical Society, the Butler Library at Columbia University, the P. K. Yonge Library at the University of Florida, and the Princeton University Library.

I am also grateful to Lizabeth Martínez Lotz, Robert Cooper Nathan, Virginia M. Bouvier, and Luis Martínez Fernández for providing assistance with research materials and bibliography. Susan Fernández offered early constructive comments on various portions of the manuscript, raising questions and offering suggestions that prompted reconsideration—and reformulation—of some of the arguments advanced in the book, for which I am grateful. Lars Schoultz gave careful reading to long sections of the manuscript and graciously provided me with important materials he found in the course of his own research. Long discussions and spirited disagreements over the years have in no small way informed this book: it has been a fruitful—and enjoyable—collaboration. Robert P. Ingalls subjected several manuscript chapters to a rigorous reading. He provided substantive comments and stylistic suggestions and in the process strengthened the content and improved the reading of the book. I have also benefited greatly from the reading of the manuscript by Amy Kaplan, whose insightful suggestions helped to sharpen the analytical framework of the book. And to Walter LaFeber a special thanks for his thoughtful comments and helpful advice on all facets of the manuscript.

I am especially appreciative of the assistance of Elaine Maisner at the University of North Carolina Press, who from the inception to the completion of this book has provided continuing supportive guidance. In her capacity of senior editor at UNC Press, she has brought to fruition a magnificent corpus of scholarship on Cuba at North Carolina.

In the course of the last several years, as this book has taken final shape, over countless repeated miles along Bolin Creek, Deborah M. Weissman listened patiently to ideas both forming and formed. Her thoughtful insights have worked their influence throughout the book.

Chapel Hill, North Carolina
September 2007

Cuba

IN THE AMERICAN

IMAGINATION

Introduction The Idea of Cuba

Cuba occupies a special place in the history of American imperialism. It has served as something of a laboratory for the development of the methods by which the United States has pursued the creation of a global empire. In the aggregate, the means used by the United States in Cuba constitute a microcosm of the American imperial experience: armed intervention and military occupation; nation building and constitution writing; capital penetration and cultural saturation; the installation of puppet regimes, the formation of clientele political classes, and the organization of proxy armies; the imposition of binding treaties; the establishment of a permanent military base; economic assistance—or not—and diplomatic recognition—or not—as circumstances warranted. And after 1959, trade sanctions, political isolation, covert operations, and economic embargo. All that is American imperialism has been practiced in Cuba.

But it is also true that, for all the ways that Cuba stands as an embodiment of American imperial practice, it is at the same time different—so different, in fact, that it must be considered as a case apart. Cuba seized hold of the North American imagination early in the nineteenth century. What made awareness of Cuba particularly significant were the ways that it acted on the formation of the American consciousness of nationhood. The destiny of the nation seemed inextricably bound to the fate of the island. It was impossible to imagine the former without attention to the latter.

All through the nineteenth century, the Americans brooded over the anomaly that was Cuba: imagined as within sight, but seen as beyond reach; vital to the national interest of the United States, but in the possession of Spain. To imagine Cuba as indispensable to the national well-being was to make possession of the island a necessity. The proposition of necessity itself assumed something of a self-fulfilling prophesy, akin to a prophetic logic that could not be explained in any way other than a matter of destiny. The security and perhaps—many insisted—even the very survival of the North American Union seemed to depend on the acquisition of Cuba. The men and women who gave thought to affairs of state, as elected leaders and appointed officials; as newspaper editors and magazine publishers; as entrepreneurs, industrialists, and investors; as poets and playwrights; as lyricists, journalists, and novelists; and an ever-expanding electorate—almost all who contemplated the future well-

But that spontaneity must itself be understood to possess a history, socially determined and culturally fixed. To engage the logic of metaphor is to gain access to the normative sources of power.

★ ★ ★

It is perhaps impossible to take the full measure of the character of public support accorded to the imperial project. It was sometimes active; at other times, passive. At least as often it was a matter of indifferent acquiescence. Perhaps, as Steel suggested, Americans did not even know that an empire existed. But if Steel was only partially correct, it would be a remarkable corroboration of the discursive capacity of self-representation to conceal the existence of empire from the imperial body politic. It also raises complicated issues bearing on the pathology of power and, more specifically, the capacity of Americans to propound—and persuade themselves of—purpose utterly unconnected to practice.

The analysis of the relationship between language and power necessarily involves the examination of the ways that metaphor produced knowledge and thereupon enabled power to shape a consensus about the nature of reality. This is, as historian Michael Hunt has persuasively suggested, on one hand, to take stock of "the need for greater sensitivity to language and especially to the meaning embedded in key words" and, on the other, "to look beneath the explicit meanings texts convey to the deeper structures of language and rhetoric that both impart and circumscribe meaning."[3]

Americans embraced imperialism principally by way of an accumulated stock of metaphorical constructs, mostly as a set of figurative depictions arranged in the form of a narrative to represent national purpose. This was metaphor as the principal means through which a people persuaded themselves of the beneficence of their purpose and the propriety of their conduct, that is, the wherewithal to sustain the self-confidence and moral certainty so central to the maintenance of systems of domination. The ideological function of metaphor was contained in its use as a source of normative truths, to represent the exercise of North American power as a matter of moral purpose.

★ ★ ★

For almost all of the nineteenth century, the Americans stood vigil over the future of Cuba. The perception of Cuba as profoundly relevant to North American well-being meant that almost everything that happened on the island somehow implicated U.S. interests. Certainly the Americans thought so. And on the matter of the future of sovereignty over Cuba, the Americans were as unequivocal as they were unyielding. "The American Government,"

U.S. minister to Spain Alexander Everett pronounced as early as 1825, "could not consent to any change in the political situation of Cuba other than one which should place it under the jurisdiction of the United States."[4] This meant first and foremost, of course, the determination to prevent the transfer of Cuba from Spain to any other European power. But it also meant opposition to the succession of sovereignty of Cuba by the Cubans. First during the years 1868–78 and 1879–80, but especially 1895–98, Cubans embarked upon wars of liberation explicitly with the objective of seizing control of their own future. These were popular mobilizations, imbued with a sense of destiny radically different from what the Americans had imagined for Cuba. The Cuban independence war of 1895–98 in particular challenged North American designs on Cuba's future, and indeed in 1898—in what subsequently passed into U.S. history books as the "Spanish-American War"—the Americans acted in defense of their interests.

The consequences of the U.S. intervention were far-reaching and complex and assumed many forms. The claim to have committed to war in 1898 in behalf of Cuba was subsequently celebrated as acting on those qualities that Americans most admired about themselves: support for Cuban liberty and sympathy for Cuban suffering, from which developed easily enough the disposition to propound the defense of freedom as a matter of discharge of amour propre, and eventually the conviction that righteous motive and moral purpose were sufficiently compelling reasons to deploy power as a means of self-fulfillment.

The perception of the "Spanish-American War" as—in the words of Nelson Miles, the commanding general of the army in 1898—"America's war for humanity"[5] was commonly shared and widely held at the time and passed fully into realms of received wisdom. That American political leaders and military planners in 1898 prosecuted the war as a matter of disinterested purpose is, however, far less certain. The men charged with decision-making authority were eminently conscious of the strategic implications of war, and especially of the degree to which control of Cuba involved issues of vital national interests. To ignore recourse to war in 1898 as a matter of realpolitik—Carl von Clausewitz's war as the "continuation of politics by other means"—is to disregard the meaning of nearly a century of fixed North American purpose the singular objective of which was control of Cuba.

There is no gainsaying, however, that popular belief in the deployment of power as a matter of moral discharge gained discursive ascendancy in the narratives of the national purpose in 1898. Few Americans then—or thereafter—would have disagreed with Secretary of War William Howard Taft's characterization that the United States had been inspired in 1898 by "pure altruism," and "that the real ground for the war was the sympathy that the Americans had with a people struggling against an oppressive and misguided rule."[6] No one at the time seemed to doubt the generosity of purpose that was 1898. The pronouncement of essayist A. D. Hall captured the sense and essence of the emerging popular consensus on the meaning of the war:

> If ever there was a war that was entered into purely from motives of humanity and with no thought whatever of conquest, it is this one. The entire people of the United States were agreed that their purpose was a holy one. . . . War is justifiable, when waged, as the present one unquestionably is, for purely unselfish motives, simply from a determination to rescue a people whose sufferings had become unbearable to them and to the lookers-on. The United States, by its action, has set a lesson for the rest of the world, which the latter will not be slow to learn and for which future generations will bless the name of America.[7]

★ ★ ★

The view of 1898 as an undertaking for humanity served to fix the moral calculus by which the Americans thereafter imagined the purpose of their power and celebrated the virtue of their motives. The war produced a "decisive change in the consciousness of the Americans themselves," pronounced historian Archibald Cary Coolidge ten years after the end of the conflict, who thereupon concluded that they were "called upon to play a part in the broader affairs of mankind."[8]

The proposition of power exercised as generous purpose was celebrated as an attribute of character—national character, to be precise: what made Americans American. This was to act out self-identified attributes of national character both as means of internal consensus and mode of international conduct: more specifically, as cultural source of a foreign policy in which self-proclaimed national virtues served as the principal formulation with which to propound national interests. Prior to 1898, historian Norman Graebner discerned, "the foreign policies of the United States were rendered solvent by ample power to cover limited, largely hemispheric, goals." Everything changed after 1898: "By contrast, moral purpose embodied in the quest for universal peace, democracy, and justice, operating in a supposedly rational world, created endless expectations among those who claimed the selfless obligation to serve mankind. After 1900 the country's official phraseology gradually embraced global abstract objectives which no traditional power could achieve."[9]

The claim of generosity of purpose as motive and the sacrifice of life and treasure as means subsequently developed into the principal discursive representation by which the Americans advanced their interests in the world at large. These notions must be viewed as the formative pronouncements of the American purpose abroad. They suggest in form and function a creation myth, that is, the "birth" of a new international entity, charged with salvation of the world. The rationale of American imperialism was inscribed in a master narrative that propounded unabashedly a stance of moral superiority: Americans given to selfless service to mankind, without ulterior motive, without selfish intent. The formidable power of the United States, Americans persuaded themselves, would be placed at the service of the well-being of humanity. The logic of this conviction served to shape the dominant ideological formations of the twentieth century.

Precisely because the pursuit of national interest was imagined as enactment of moral purpose, the Americans could plausibly demand the world to acquiesce to the purity of their motives. Having persuaded themselves that they acted entirely out of disinterested motive and selfless intent, in the service of humanity, as agents of order, progress, and liberty, they concluded that other people had no cause to doubt their intentions or oppose their policies. Power thus exercised with the certainty of beneficent purpose could not readily admit the plausibility of opposition. Indeed, to oppose noble intent could only suggest ignoble motive. Those who would challenge the authenticity of American altruism, those who opposed the goals of American generosity, were necessarily evildoers and mischief-makers, misinformed or else malcontents given to doing bad things, and by definition deemed to be enemies of humanity. So fully were Americans in the thrall of the moral propriety of their own motives as to be unable to recognize the havoc their actions often wrought on the lives of others.

The Americans thus assigned themselves the role of a moral force in defense of those inalienable rights with which they had invented themselves. The undertaking was assumed as a duty of destiny—as a matter of providential design—celebrated in hymns and prayer, in song and poetry as well as fiction and film, in political discourse and historical scholarship. Men and women both of means and of modest social origins; essayists, poets, and lyricists; civic associations and women's organizations—all in varying degrees and at different times, by way of aesthetic production and scientific pronouncements, as religious conviction and philosophical musings—contributed to the moral environment in which imperialism flourished.

The proposition of beneficent intent and benign motive in defense of freedom and liberty in the world at large, very much derived from the experience of 1898, served to ascribe moral purpose to political conduct. It was a powerful self-confirming proposition, from which to defend empire as a matter of principle and expand power as a defense of virtue. The notion resonated as a public discourse. The felicity of the imagery sat well with the popular imagination, disposed to celebrate its virtues, and especially when those virtues constituted the principal attributes of a nation new in the history of the world. Americans were smitten by their self-constructed selves: a people providentially chosen to bring light to a dark world. "We have expanded into an empire," exulted naval analyst H. C. Taylor in 1899, "and are now the imperial republic of the world. . . . Plans for the future must be made by minds willing to acknowledge that imperial resources may be needed to preserve these possessions that have fallen to us, to protect their feeble peoples, and to aid them in the their efforts to secure a political happiness and freedom hitherto denied them."[10] Those who opposed the imperial project, scoffed Indiana senator Albert Beveridge the following year, were "either insincere, or else unbelievers in the soundness of American institutions, the purity of the American heart, and the noble intention of the American mind."[11] President William McKinley rebuked critics who opposed imperialism for having "no confidence in the virtue or capacity or high purpose or good faith of this free people as a civilizing agency."[12] Certainty of purpose was always more important than consideration of consequences. This was foreign policy propounded explicitly as a faith in national character, where motive mattered more than means and outcomes mattered less than intentions. This was the making of the American sublime.

The proposition of discharge of moral duty as enactment of national character in 1898 imbued Americans with a sense of righteous purpose. Woodrow Wilson was among the many Americans deeply moved by the moral use of power abroad as a means of political coercion. The future president himself would later propound a foreign policy very much derived from the moral purpose of power associated with the intervention in Cuba in 1898.[13] Indeed, no president did more to define the purpose of American power as a matter of moral responsibility and righteous duty than Woodrow Wilson. Writing even as the war of 1898 was still in progress, Wilson celebrated the intervention in Cuba as "an impulse of humane indignation and pity—because we saw at our very doors a government unmindful of justice or of mercy, contemptuous in its every practice of the principles we professed to live for."[14] Reflecting later on 1898 in his *History of the American People* (1902), Wilson imagined the war in behalf of Cuba as an expression of the noblest instincts of the American people: "It was a war of impulse," he repeated. Writing the history of a period through which he himself had lived, Wilson wrote with moral certitude: "Intervention had come, not for the material aggrandizement of the United States, but for the assertion of the right of the government to succor those who seemed hopelessly oppressed."[15] The propriety of power in behalf of beneficent purpose,

Wilson insisted, constituted the principal virtue of U.S. foreign policy. "We [are] the apostles of liberty and of self-government," he proclaimed. "We have given pledges to the world and must redeem them as we can." The "very principles of life" and "sense of identity" were derived from the new place of the United States in the world: "to serve, not subdue the world." Concluded Wilson, "No war ever transformed us quite as the war with Spain transformed us. No previous years ever ran with so swift a change as the years since 1898. We have witnessed a new revolution. We have seen the transformation of America completed."[16]

Belief in moral discharge as national purpose developed into an enduring legacy of 1898 and passed into the master narrative of historical scholarship. The historiography developed into another site for self-confirmation of national virtue, and through much of the twentieth century historians engaged unabashedly in a celebration of the selfless magnanimity with which the United States went to war in 1898 and subsequently attended to the well-being of the world at large. This was a narrative point of reference, a framework through which the historiography acted to set the limits to the historical and in the process established its affinity to the political. Journalist, historian, and later Michigan senator Arthur Vandenberg gave early voice to what was to develop into a salient tenet of American historiography. The American intervention in Cuba was "one of the loftiest purposed acts in the history of civilization," Vandenberg exulted in 1926, one that complimented "the altruism of a nation which . . . is prepared to serve human-kind in its own way and on its own initiative with a purity of dedication unmatched in any other government on earth."[17] This perspective held sway through much of the twentieth century. "Peoples of primitive or retarded cultures," Julius Pratt wrote in 1950, "thrust into the currents of advanced international politics and economics, may need guardians to guide and direct their development and to give them government and protection while they learn to care for themselves in the modern world," and to the point, "those who have fallen under the guardianship of the United States have fared well in the main. . . . American imperialism has, on the whole, been benevolent."[18] The rise of the United States "toward world power and participation in international events," historian H. Wayne Morgan repeated the received wisdom of 1898 fifteen years later, "carried in it potent ideas and ideals that captured the allegiance of most Americans. It promised to carry the dream of freedom to all the corners of the world. . . . It fed pride in America's greatness [and] in the goodness of her institutions. . . . Honest indignation at the thought of misery in other lands, and the earnest desire to end cruelty and oppression, fortified the general public's belief in the American mission."[19]

The meaning of 1898 played deeply into the ways that Americans constructed a sense of themselves and their place in the world. The war that the Cubans inaugurated in 1895 and into which the Americans inserted themselves in 1898 served as the occasion in which the idea of moral conduct was first enacted as rationale for the exercise of U.S. power overseas, subsequently to shape the terms by which the Americans represented themselves at home and abroad. As historian Paul McCartney has correctly suggested, the war of 1898 contributed in "decisive ways to the development of American national identity."[20] Much changed after 1898.

★ ★ ★

The place of Cuba in this transformation was decisive. Empire came easily to the Americans in 1898, in part because it was not all their own doing. In fact, they received vital assistance from the Cubans. For more than three years, Cuban insurgent armies had effectively battled Spain, at a frightful cost to themselves, of course, but with desolating effect on the Spanish army and the Spanish treasury. The Cubans had brought the Spanish ever closer to defeat, whereupon the Americans intervened and claimed the victory. Cubans played a decisive part as unwitting allies of American imperialism, enabling the Americans to launch a global empire at comparatively small cost to life and treasure. "It is to [the Cubans'] ragged army," the *New York Journal* would acknowledge only weeks after the conclusion of the war, "that we owe the acquisition of Porto Rico, the Philippines and all the glory that our troops have garnered in this war. If it had not been for their unconquerable spirit we should never have interfered in Spain's colonial affairs, and the curtain that is rising on our new destiny would have stayed down."[21] That the Cubans were, as it happened, also among the first people to fall victim to the North American imperial sway was an outcome of no small irony. The Cuban war to end one empire precipitated an American war that begat another.

Beyond facilitating the U.S. military defeat of Spain, however, the Cubans also contributed—unknowingly—to enhancing the North American sense of self-righteous hubris. The ease of victory served to confirm the American certainty of destiny, and thereupon to consecrate the sense of moral purpose and to increase the military confidence with which the United States subsequently engaged the world.[22] The narrative certainty was set in place early—and endured, certainly in the popular imagination. Its origins came naturally enough from success in war, and quickly the celebration of victory developed into the exaltation of the victors. President William McKinley set the tone early as he heaped praised on "the heroes of Santiago," who distinguished themselves in a war "unequaled in its completeness and the quick succession with which victory followed victory," and added, "Our troops sailed to Cuba and achieved a glorious triumph." He was exultant as he celebrated the victories at "Santiago, the charge of San Juan hill and El Caney," the "intrepid valor and determination of our gallant troops," in short, all the qualities that made U.S. military forces "illustrious and invincible."[23] That Cubans were party to and part of the "glorious triumph" passed unacknowledged.

The war of 1898 as the first postbellum national war effort—North and South together in a common cause against an overseas adversary—fixed permanently how Americans came to think of themselves: a righteous people given to the service of righteous purpose. These sentiments did not originate with 1898, of course. They were in fact deeply inscribed in the national myth. But the belief in an exalted manifest destiny as a matter of a logic for an international presence was confirmed in 1898, in what the Americans understood as a victory achieved—unaided—with such ease and complete success. The empire that followed was providential, proof that Americans had been called upon to discharge their duty to mankind. "In the providence of God," President William McKinley proclaimed in 1899, "who works in mysterious ways, this [territory] was put into our lap, and the American people never shirk duty."[24] The idea of humanitarian mission served as a source of enduring moral subsidy throughout the twentieth century and beyond, as a means of self-representation and a mode of representation to others. The people who readily endorsed the proposition of beneficent duty as motive for armed intervention in Cuba in 1898 would henceforth exercise power abroad as duty of beneficence. It was the American way.

1

Metaphor between Motive and Meaning

*Midway between the unintelligible and the commonplace,
it is a metaphor most which produces knowledge.*
—Aristotle, Rhetoric, 3:10

*There is a very different tradition associated with the notion of
metaphor, . . . one which treats metaphor as central to the task
of accounting for our perspectives on the world: how we think
about things, make sense of reality, and set the problems we
later try to solve. In this . . . sense, "metaphor" refers both to a
certain kind of product—a perspective or frame, a way of looking
at things—and to a certain kind of process—a process by which
new perspectives on the world come into existence.*
—Donald A. Schön, "Generative Metaphor: A Perspective on
Problem-Solving in Social Policy" (1979)

*The astute and the designing may make a skillful use of a
metaphor to mislead an easily led public. The mind naturally
likes to note resemblances, delights in generalizations and
simplifications. The unthinking . . . are content with the crudest
generalizations and will readily accept a picture for an argument.
Counting on this, [many] . . . will tacitly assume that such and
such a resemblance or analogy is complete in all points and will
begin to draw arguments therefrom.*—Stephen J. Brown, The
World of Imagery: Metaphor and Kindred Imagery (1927)

*Human beings do not live in the objective world alone, nor
alone in the world of social activity as ordinarily understood, but
are very much at the mercy of the particular language which
has become the medium of expression for their society. . . . The
fact of the matter is that the "real world" is to a large extent
unconsciously built up on the language habits of the group. . . .
We see and hear and otherwise experience very largely as we
do because the language habits of our community predisposes
certain choices of interpretations.*—Edward Sapir, Culture,
Language, and Personality (1962)

*It is not only capital, in the strict economic sense, which is
subject to appropriation, manipulation, and exploitation, but
also cultural capital in the form of symbolic systems through
which man may extend and change the boundaries of his
experience.*—Basil Bernstein, "Social Class, Language, and
Socialization" (1972)

Language is as it is because of its function in the social structure.
—Michael Halliday, Explorations in the Function of Language
(1973)

Paradigms of power dwell in the realm of metaphors. Power seeks moral subsidy and social validation within those representations of higher purpose so readily provided by metaphorical depiction, those figurative constructs where the terms of representation are arranged to provide the perspective desired. Metaphor serves principally as a hortatory device, to persuade and to prevail upon, a way to mediate perception of reality: to see something as other than what it is, and thereby enable conduct for a purpose other than what is professed.

The concept of metaphor insinuates itself into virtually all facets of the culture: in aesthetic production and popular vernacular, in religion, philosophy, and science, to mention only a few. Metaphors constantly evolve; their meanings change; sometimes they become literal; sometimes they get lost altogether. As a mode of discourse in the service of power, metaphors discharge a special function to enable domination and induce submission. That is, they act to articulate the premise of power and therein offer insight into the larger logic of imperial paradigms.

The depictive efficacy of metaphor is contained within the larger moral system from which it originates, whereby the exercise of power deemed proper and proclaimed appropriate in one domain obtains validation by association with another. The exercise of power derives normative plausibility best by way of everyday forms, principally from familiar cultural models represented as a matter of the commonplace and common sense: that is, metaphor as a means of cognitive access to conceptual realms in which the premise of power assumes the guise of propriety. "Figurative language," psychologist Catarina Cacciari correctly suggests, "is arguably the most powerful source for meaning creation and sense extension." Indeed, Cacciari argues, metaphors "force us to see things in a different perspective and to reconceptualize them accordingly."[1]

But it is also true that the purpose of power informs the function of metaphor: it is intrinsic to the very act of selecting one figurative depiction and not another. Metaphor creates new knowledge by way of old information and thereby shapes perceptions, precisely the circumstances under which decisions are made and actions are taken. Once situated within a moral system, with its attending codes of cultural conduct and social convention, metaphor transforms moral-to-live-by into prescription-to-act-upon. Its very use must be understood as a matter of intent and purpose, for to choose to mediate reality by way of one set of cultural representations is also and at the same time necessarily to prompt a culturally determined—and politically desired—course of conduct. It suggests the condition of possibility. The options are inscribed in the very production of metaphor; it is meant to imply intent of purpose as a condition intrinsic to its selection. Metaphor does not necessarily reveal similarities as much as it creates them, and thereupon suggests a range of reasonable inferences intended to inform opinion and influence behavior. "Metaphors bring about changes in the ways in which we perceive the world," philosopher Earl MacCormac observes, "and these conceptual changes often bring about changes in the ways in which we act in the world."[2]

That metaphor works at all, that the premise of its representational reach provides a plausible basis of justification for action, is itself a function of a self-confirming logic. Figurative representations, linguist Raymond Gibbs argues persuasively, "are not linguistic distortions of literal mental thought but constitute basic schemes by which people conceptualize their experience and the external world," which in turn "underlies the way we think, reason, and imagine."[3] In proposing a point of view, metaphor propounds a course of action. Indeed, the cognitive power of the metaphor must be understood to lie in its capacity to predispose attitude as a condition to dispose conduct, or acquiesce to the conduct of others. "We define our reality in terms of metaphors," linguists George Lakoff and Mark Johnson suggest, "and then proceed to act on the basis of the metaphors. We draw inferences, set goals, make commitments, and execute plans, all on the basis of how we in part structure our experience, consciously and unconsciously, by means of metaphor."[4] Meaning and moral converge on each other in dialectical engagement: indeed, the interaction is intrinsic to the conceptual efficacy of metaphor. To paraphrase anthropologist Edward Sapir, as soon as the image is available and readily accessible, the concept becomes easy to handle.[5] It remains only to expand its implications into accessible domains—and to act upon it. Metaphorical representation depicts a condition for which the desired response assumes the appearance of self-evident plausibility.[6]

The use of metaphor is more than a matter of rhetorical flourishes and stylistic embellishment. Metaphors have consequences. They are supposed to. And never more than when they are summoned in the service of power. They serve to fix more than perspective and point of view. They also possess causal properties. Metaphorical representations are instrumental in shaping the cognitive context in which people apprehend the world about them, the way they arrive at an understanding of their time and place, often the very reason they choose one course of action among others. "Metaphorical activity occurs in sites of difference," linguist Gunther Kress has written, "whenever there is contention of an ideological kind, whenever an attempt is made to assimilate an event into one ideological system rather than another," and adds, "The ubiquitous action of metaphor is one force in the discursive and ideological process of 'naturalising' the social, of turning that which is problematic into the obvious."[7] To confront metaphor is not only to engage a mode of thought but also to contend with a means of moral validation, specifically the way that systems of domination normalize the internal moral logic of power.

★   ★   ★

Metaphor has been central to the premise of empire. It has served as a source of plausible purpose by which the colonial polity imagines the creation of empire as self-explanatory and self-confirming, thereupon transacting the exercise of power as an obligation of duty and a deed of disinterest. To invoke the figurative was to assemble a stock of usable imagery of power hierarchies, usable in the sense that it propounded the rationale of domination as a matter of self-evident propriety. Metaphor concealed the ideological content of language, a process that purported to persuade without the need to explain and validate the propriety of power as a premise of normality, what anthropologist Christopher Tilley suggested metaphors "utilized as vehicles of power in the sense of social domination and control."[8] The very raison d'être of colonialism was inscribed within pretension to plausibility, derived from time-honored representations of *mission civilatrice*: with domination depicted as deliverance, self-interest represented as selfless purpose, and subjugation rendered as salvation.

The choice of metaphor hence offers insight into political purpose. Metaphorical constructs as modes of representation were intrinsically self-confirming and provided normative plausibility to the exercise of power. Insofar as the use of metaphor involved choice, it necessarily implied purpose and suggested means, and more: to choose one metaphor—and not another—was to propound a perspective on the nature of the world, to call attention to some attributes and ignore others, not as a matter of serendipity but as a function of intent. Metaphors have their politics, and their politics consist of either disguising differences or suggesting similarities. That is their purpose. The use of figurative representations, sociologist Mary Douglas notes, acts to "create to some extent the realities to which they apply."[9] It thus becomes necessary to approach metaphor as a function of its political meaning, that is, from the perspective of the implications it was designed to suggest and the inference it sought to invite, purposefully, as a cognitive process by which it acted to narrow the choice of perception to the one desired. Point of view was inscribed within the metaphor, which is to suggest that the politics was embedded within the image.

There were discernible elements of surreptitious purpose associated with the production of metaphor and its development as a discursive framework within systems of domination. The relationship between metaphor and the exercise of power was drawn by philosopher Gemma Corradi Fiumara, who observed that "attention could be profitably directed away from the classic instruments of social control" and to "the everyday workings of our linguistic and educational tradition." This implies a new emphasis on what Fiumara characterized as "the unnoticed indoctrinating influence of the ongoing discourses, which necessarily reverberate in life-shaping experiences more secretly and surely than any form of overt authority," something akin to George Lakoff and Mark Johnson's suggestion that metaphor "by virtue of what it hides, can lead to human degradation."[10] Metaphorical constructs served to inscribe the logic of power within established cultural models as a means to create the normative plausibility of empire. It was to draw upon what Wallace Stevens identified as "the familiar world of the commonplace" through "sense of the analogy."[11]

The depictive resonance of metaphor lay in its capacity to shape a narrative of moral validation in the service of power. This is not to suggest, of course, that power holders were averse to the use of violence as a means through which to exact submission to their will. Attention to the function of metaphor does not imply a disregard for the use of force. Nor does it reduce the importance of economic, political, cultural, and psychological forms of coercion. To call attention to the activity of metaphor, rather, is to argue that power functioned best within systems of domination in the form of moral suasion and normative inducement, where the logic of authority obtained legitimacy from those cultural models through which the powerful and the powerless together derived more or less their understanding of the rightful order of the world. It is to argue for the need to understand the circumstances in which the use of metaphorical representation acts explicitly as a function of power, and thereupon situate its role within symbolic systems and value networks as a factor in the social production of knowledge. It is, lastly, to suggest that the premise of power was transmitted within established social practice in which representation conveyed ideological perspective and point of view, and thereupon proceeded to shape the political function of knowledge. Power sustained itself best in the interaction between domination and subordination with only minimal—and infrequent—need to resort to force and violence as a means by which to exact compliance.

Metaphor in this instance must be seen as a function of social arrangements, culturally derived and ideologically driven that, when turned in on itself, can be made to reveal the normative premise of power and yield insight into the moral assumptions by which systems of domination acquired logic and legitimacy.[12] This was a process of choice, and the discursive context in which that choice functioned provides perspective on the moral pretensions by which empire sustained itself. The observations on language offered by linguists Robert Hodge and Gunther Kress have particular relevance to metaphor: that is, to contemplate metaphor "as the medium of consciousness for a society," the study of which offers insight into "consciousness and its ideological bases."[13]

That metaphorical depiction was at once self-confirming and self-serving does not, of course, reduce its usefulness as a source of insight into the larger ideological purpose for which it was summoned. On the contrary, precisely because metaphor involved both process and product, because it often acted to arrange an otherwise incongruous proposition into a plausible premise, it offers a means with which to examine the workings of domination as a moral system. Integral to this scheme of things was the need to create discursive realms deemed appropriate to the purpose of power, which meant, too, the need to articulate new representations of social relationships and the development of new sources of cultural knowledge.

The prerogative of power was enacted most typically by way of figurative depictions derived from normative models. Metaphors of gender relations, for example, imputed strength to male and weakness to female, further differentiating between the rational and the emotional, between virility and vulnerability, and always asserting patriarchy as rationale to protect and pretext to rule. Racial hierarchies offered another readily comprehensible set of discursive markers with which to represent civilization and barbarism, with white people depicted as modern and black and brown people portrayed as primitive, with the duty of the former to uplift the latter as rationale to exercise power. Age differentials provided still another usable model to validate a hierarchy of power, with wisdom associated with adulthood and innocence assigned to childhood, creating dichotomies of maturity and immaturity, independence and dependence, and always the authority of adults over children understood as right and proper. These were not mutually exclusive categories, of course, and indeed they were often interchanged and exchanged as circumstances warranted and needs dictated.

The plausibility of power was thus inscribed in those cultural arrangements otherwise deemed normal and normative. Metaphorical constructs were put to political use through social practice, as in those arrangements, for example, in which women were expected to submit to the authority of men, where blacks were presumed to be subordinate to whites, and where children were subject to the authority of adults, thus providing the normative models that validated systems of domination as a matter of the rightful order of things. They shared a common vernacular of hierarchical role-specific functions, readily inferred and easily understood. Metaphorical representations served as a means of persuasion: that is, to create categories of meaning and arrange them into patterns of purpose. It could hardly be otherwise. The depictive credibility of metaphor was due precisely to its origins within shared cultural assumptions, situated within the context of value systems, as a matter of custom and convention from which to intuit or otherwise infer the moral intended.[14] Metaphor derived the power of moral suasion from the value system from which it originated, which was also the one to which it appealed for normative validation.

★ ★ ★

Cuba came to the attention of the world at large principally by way of figurative depiction, more precisely, in the form of metaphors imbued with colonial meanings: in the sixteenth century as "the Key of the New World" ("*la Llave del Nuevo Mundo*"), "the Key to the Gulf" ("*la Llave del Golfo*"), and "the Bulwark of the West Indies" ("*el Antemural de las Indias Occidentales*"); in the nineteenth century as "the Queen of the Antilles," "the Pearl of the Antilles," "the Gem of the Antilles," and "the richest jewel in the royal crown," by which time, too, it had earned the designation of "the Ever Faithful Isle" ("*la Siempre Fidelísima Isla*").[15]

Metaphorical representation also developed into the principal mode by which the Americans propounded the possession of Cuba as a matter indispensable to the future well-being of the United States. To advance a plausible claim to a territory governed by Spain, and to which its inhabitants presumed rightful succession to rule, required the Americans to create a parallel reality by which they persuaded themselves—and sought to persuade others—that Cuba rightfully belonged to them, not only, however, and indeed not even principally, as a matter of self-interest but as a function of providential purpose and moral propriety. Metaphorical constructs were central to the process by which national interest was enacted as idealized purpose: at once a combination of denial and dissimulation, a source of entitlement, and a means of empowerment.

To understand the North American use of metaphor is to gain insight into the use of cultural models and social relationships in which the U.S. imperial project was conditioned. Metaphors of Cuba served to advance U.S. interests and were, in turn, mediated by racial attitudes and gender hierarchies, on one hand, and prescience of destiny, on the other. They worked best within those belief systems from which Americans obtained their cues concerning matters of civic duty and moral conduct and, indeed, were the principal means by which intent of purpose and reception of meaning were transacted. Figurative depiction drew into complicity all who shared a common cultural system from which collectively to receive the meaning desired of metaphor, what Herbert

Clark and Catherine Marshall described as "mutual knowledge based on community membership."[16]

That this process was at the same time a source of knowledge further invites attention to the role played by metaphor in the maintenance of systems of domination, and more: it is to be sensible of the cognitive determinants by which the propriety of power was inferred. This was knowledge with consequences, for it was assembled as a function of North American needs, that is, interests, and acted upon as a matter of North American normative systems, that is, culture.

The importance of metaphor in this context is related directly to its capacity to facilitate moral accommodation to empire, as a way to think about the exercise of power and thereby make sense—indeed, to make common sense—of the imperial project. Metaphor provided the means by which Americans came to an understanding of the world around them, the way, psychologist C. C. Anderson suggested, by which metaphors generally make "the unfamiliar, the incongruous, and the inexplicable" comprehensible.[17]

To understand the ways that Americans engaged the Cuba of their imagination is thus to obtain insight into the moral dimension of power, as both a model for conduct and a mode of knowledge.[18] This necessarily involves, first, the examination of the cultural representations by which power insinuated itself into the normative order of daily life. But it also requires attention to the character of information with which Americans assembled their knowledge of Cuba, as well as its form and function—neither of which should be presumed to be a matter of happenstance—and always with the understanding that this information arrived principally in the form of culturally conditioned depictions. But most of all it requires attention to the ways that these representations themselves were a product of power. This was knowledge assembled as the ideological framework in which the exercise of power was transacted in the form of presumed propriety, whereupon it passed into realms of conventional wisdom and received truths.

The efficacy of the metaphor as a medium of representation was contained in its capacity to suggest a moral context into which to inscribe the normative logic of American hegemony. It was to refer the imagination to those shared culturally determined behaviors that, when summoned into the service of political purpose, ratified the premise of imperial practice. Metaphor reached deeply into those semiconscious realms of sentiment and sensibility, there to arouse strong feelings that often propelled Americans to act because they "felt" it was the right thing to do: to manipulate emotions and foster predisposition toward some matters and prejudice to others.[19] This was to draw

Cuba into domains of North American awareness by way of culturally coherent models, derived from familiar experience, thereupon to serve as source for complex narratives by which the logic of domination was validated.[20] Anthropologists Deborah Durham and James Fernandez posit "a sense of complicity of language" between the author and audience, as one person "making of a metaphor, readily grasped by another, can become an instrument of consensus and thus community between them." Philosopher Ted Cohen suggests another level: metaphor as a means "to form or acknowledge . . . community and thereby to establish an intimacy between the teller and the hearer."[21]

Metaphorical representations were essential to the claim of moral intent with which Americans presumed to insert themselves into the lives of Cubans. It was not sufficient that Americans persuade themselves of the generosity of their purpose; it was also necessary to persuade Cubans of the beneficence of American motives. Therein lay the moral sources of North American hegemony in Cuba. The process by which power was exercised—and experienced— had everything to do with the capacity to advance a version of reality to which both peoples more or less willingly subscribed.

It was within the meaning drawn inferentially from a larger normative logic, and the corresponding conduct prescribed as a matter of cultural practice, that metaphor acted to ratify the propriety of power. Self-interests served to shape U.S. conduct toward Cuba, of course. But it was necessary, too, that the presumption of beneficent purpose, so very central to the ways that Americans were given to represent themselves, appear as the intent for which power was exercised. It was to this function that metaphor was put: political purpose inscribed within moral practice. The degree to which metaphorical depictions act on the senses, psychologist Robert Rogers suggests, is related to the fact that "we take them in without suspecting the forces they contain."[22] That metaphor possessed the capacity to propound normative credibility meant, too, that it could ascribe moral plausibility to political purpose.

The presumption of beneficent intent toward Cuba captured the North American imagination as purpose writ large. The exercise of power, the Americans persuaded themselves, was in behalf of Cuban well-being, as a duty to discharge as a matter of disinterested obligation and selfless intent. "All that I have done," President William McKinley assured President of the Cuban Republic in Arms Salvador Cisneros early during the first intervention (1899–1902), "was for your own good."[23] A field agent of the Commerce Department in Cuba in 1905 similarly insisted that the U.S. military occupation had been "undertaken solely in order to protect the Cubans from molestation from outside while they were recovering from the wounds and ravages of war, and to assist them in putting their new house in order."[24] The Americans explained their purpose during the second intervention (1906–9) in similar terms. "We are here only to help you on," Secretary of War William Howard Taft assured a University of Havana audience in 1906. "With our arm under your arm, lifting you again on the path of wonderful progress that you have traveled, we shall, I am confident, be again able to point with pride to the fact that the United States is not an exploiting nation, but only has that deep sympathy with the progress of popular government as to be willing to expend its blood and treasure in making such government in the world successful."[25] Even the North American seizure of Cuban territory to establish a naval base in Guantánamo Bay—Article VII of the Platt Amendment—was depicted as an act "to enable the United States to maintain the independence of Cuba, and to protect the people thereof."[26]

What was especially striking about North American narratives of Cuba was their capacity to sustain all through the nineteenth century, and deep into the twentieth, an enduring consensus around the beneficent purpose of North American power. The propriety of power was validated principally through metaphors of such commonplace representation as to make domination assume the form of readily recognizable attributes of "normal." "There is also the experience," psychiatrist Paul Lieberman correctly observes, "that what is imagined has an inevitability, a logic of its own: even when we recognize that something is an image or imaginary, it still has a power; 'it' leads us along."[27] This was metaphor as mode and model, of course, but also as a discursive device through which to facilitate the exercise of power as a matter of commonplace normality. The Americans presumed to exercise power over Cuba as a matter of moral entitlement, properly discharged as a function of providential purpose and beneficent mandate: they never questioned the propriety of this arrangement, never doubted the legitimacy of this authority.

Metaphorical representation fashioned a particular narrative mode into which to inscribe surreptitious cognitive content; that is, it was as a means to create sufficient discursive space to accommodate self-deception and minimize self-doubt. It transmuted conceit into conviction, transformed self-deception into self-righteousness, and disguised the exercise of self-serving power as an act of selfless moral purpose. In the end, metaphor served as a means with which to confer utter moral certainty on the exercise of power.

The North American relationship with Cuba expanded around norms of duty and codes of conduct and was inevitably enacted in forms that appeared at once self-explanatory and self-evident. To decipher figurative meaning in this instance involves more than understanding the literal relationship from which the metaphor was derived. Moral was transmitted and meaning was transferred without the need for explanation, intuitively inferred precisely because its logic possessed normative plausibility. The representational efficacy of metaphor was in its capacity to efface the signs of its presence. Metaphor inscribed into the imperial purpose those representations so normatively conditioned, so experientially derived, so culturally shared, as to enable the exercise of power to pass wholly as a reasonable discharge of North American moral conduct. That Americans rarely questioned the exercise of power over Cuba as either inappropriate or improper was itself powerful corroboration of the capacity of metaphor to reproduce premise as proof. The inferential structure of the metaphor enabled the premise to propound plausibility of purpose. Indeed, the inference was determined a priori as a function of the premise: the appearance of similitude was in fact structurally contrived. Metaphors, Londa Schiebinger has correctly suggested, "function to construct as well as describe—they have both a hypothesis-creating and a proof-making function."[28]

The dominant and indeed the enduring metaphorical representations of Cuba were derived from readily accessible models. They obtained depictive relevance as a function of their capacity to expand commonly shared and widely held normative truths into readily inferred political meanings. They serve as markers, in that as products of a historical moment they can be made to yield insight into the desires, hopes, and fears that informed the North American relationship with Cuba. Metaphors passed into the realms of conventional wisdom and received truths precisely because they offered ready cognitive validation to the premise of North American power. They developed as the stock-in-trade of political vernacular and popular idiom and entered the public imagination by way of printed text and spoken language; through mainstream newspapers and magazines; as news stories, feature articles, and editorials; from church pulpits to theater stages. Metaphorical representations gained currency through film and fiction, by way of the lyric of music, travel accounts, and tourist guidebooks. They assumed visual forms and pictorial depictions, principally as editorial cartoons and caricatures. They also served as an explanatory device and medium of historical knowledge and were subsequently consecrated in what passed for scholarship, whereby the discourse of power was ratified in the practice of the scientific method.

Cuba occupied multiple levels within the American imagination, often all at once, almost all of which functioned in the service of U.S. interests. The North American relationship with Cuba was above all an instrumental one. Cuba—and Cubans—were a means to an end, to be engaged as a means to fulfill North American needs and accommodate North American interests. The Americans came to their knowledge of Cuba principally by way of representations entirely of their own creation, which is to suggest that the Cuba that the

Americans chose to engage was, in fact, a figment of their own imagination and a projection of their needs. Americans rarely engaged the Cuban reality on its own terms or as a condition possessed of an internal logic, or Cubans as a people possessed of an interior history or as a nation possessed of an inner-directed destiny. It has always been thus between the United States and Cuba.

2

Imagining

Self-Interest

Cuba is the Gibraltar of the New World
—United States Democratic Review *(1852)*

Cuba is to become the Constantinople of America.
—*Representative Otho Robards Singleton (1854)*

Cuba is a natural fortress at our very doors.
—*Senator Stephen Mallory (1859)*

Cuba is our Armenia.
—Atlanta Constitution *(September 15, 1895)*

Cuba is the Turkey of transatlantic politics.
—Harper's New Monthly Magazine *(June 1898)*

The possession of Cuba has been the dream of American statesmen ever since our government was organized. Cuba is at our doors—at the gateway of the Panama canal—a few hours distant from our southern coast. Our title to it is as good as that of anybody. We have as righteous a claim to it as the people who are now occupying it.—Chicago Tribune *(September 19, 1906)*

Cuba is the Guardian of the Gates of the American Mediterranean, the Key to the Gulf of Mexico, the Sentinel of the Caribbean Sea.
—*Howard B. Grose*, Advance in the Antilles: The New Era in Cuba and Porto Rico *(1910)*

A powerful metaphor may complete its work so effectively as to obliterate its own traces.
—*Gemma Corradi Fiumara*, The Metaphoric Process: Connections between Language and Life *(1995)*

How auspicious the future must have seemed at the time. A people given un-abashedly to joyful triumphalism of new nationhood, self-confidently expand-ing their borders, as if in discharge of providential purpose. Louisiana was ac-quired in 1803, then Florida in 1821, and once at the water's edge, the national gaze fixed on the southern horizon. That Cuba came into view, figuratively speaking—"almost in sight of our shores," John Quincy Adams exaggerated to make the point[1]—was to claim the Gulf of Mexico as waters of paramount importance to the well-being of the North American Union.

Territorial consolidation also brought realization of maritime vulnerability. To enter the logic of the geostrategic calculus of the nineteenth century is to readily understand how the Americans persuaded themselves of the need to possess Cuba. Lying astride the principal sea-lanes of the middle latitudes of the Western Hemisphere, on one side commanding the entrance to the Gulf of Mexico and the outlet of the vast Mississippi Valley and on the other fronting the Caribbean Sea, the island assumed commercial and strategic significance of looming proportions. It became all but impossible for the Americans to contemplate their future well-being without the presumption of possession of Cuba.

So it was that Americans developed a sense of nationhood that almost from the outset envisioned the inclusion of Cuba as part of the national territory, a sense, too, that Cuba was vital to the fulfillment of the destiny of the United States. The national community that shared a common sense of destiny could not but in part purchase that solidarity by sharing a common sense of vulnera-bility.

The fixation thus began early: an island "almost in sight" yet out of reach and, as long as it remained out of reach, a source of deepening disquiet. The solvency—perhaps even the very survival, some brooded—of the North Ameri-can Union seemed to depend on possession of Cuba. "An object of transcen-dent importance to the political and commercial interests of our Union," John Quincy Adams insisted, and more: "The annexation of Cuba to our fed-eral republic will be indispensable to the continuance and integrity of the Union itself."[2] For James Buchanan, "the acquisition of Cuba would greatly strengthen our bond of Union" and "insure the perpetuity of our Union," and for Secretary of State William Marcy possession of Cuba was a matter "of the highest importance as a precautionary measure of security" and "essential to the welfare . . . of the United States."[3]

The nineteenth-century premise of American nationhood was fully imbued with the presumption of possession of Cuba, anticipated with the supposi-tion of certainty and awaited with the expectation of fulfillment. Awareness of Cuba in the United States developed at formative moments of national development, and the timing fixed permanently the place that Cuba would occupy in the American imagination. It inscribed itself into the emerging national consciousness and thereupon insinuated itself into the North American sense of self. From the moment that Americans began to imagine themselves as a nationality, as a people with common — that is, "national" — interests, they dwelled on the need to possess Cuba. A sense of national completion appeared to depend upon Cuba, without which the North American Union seemed unfinished, perhaps incomplete, maybe even slightly vulnerable. "We must have Cuba. We can't do without Cuba," James Buchanan insisted.[4]

Cuba, a place deeply implicated in the American sense of security and survival, loomed large in North American meditations on the future of the nation. It developed fully into a national preoccupation, one that reached deeply into the ways that the Americans contemplated the defense of their interests and the definition of their well-being. "The instincts of the American people," Louisiana senator Judah Benjamin affirmed at midcentury, "have already taught them that we shall ever be insecure . . . until [Cuba] is placed under our protection and control."[5] "There is a well fixed and almost universal conviction upon the minds of our people," editor J. D. DeBow insisted in 1850, "that the possession of Cuba is indispensable to the proper development and security of the country."[6] The *United States Democratic Review* was categorical: "Cuba is so situated, that we have the right to say [that] our comfort, happiness, and existence depends . . . on a union with [the island]."[7] If possession of Cuba was to have made the United States stronger and more secure — and indeed, in Buchanan's words, "insure the perpetuity of our Union" — that Cuba remained outside the Union cast a pall over the sense of the national well-being. In 1854, U.S. ministers to Spain, France, and Great Britain — Pierre Soulé, John Mason, and James Buchanan, respectively — convened in Ostend, Belgium, and provided one of the most clearly distilled statements of North American thinking on Cuba. The central point was advanced unambiguously: "The Union," the Ostend Manifesto warned pointedly, "can never enjoy repose, nor possess reliable security, as long as Cuba is not embraced within its boundaries."[8]

Knowledge of Cuba developed as a function of North American interests: Cuba principally as a place deemed vital to the realization of all that was associated with the promise of American nationhood. To have imagined the island as essential to the endurance of the nation — "indispensable to the continuance and integrity of the Union itself" — was to have implicated Cuba in the North American sense of future, which meant, too, that the future of Cuba was a matter over which the Americans laid claim as a function of their interests. "To protect our lives, our liberty, our institutions, our homes and families," Texas senator Roger Mills pronounced outright, "we have the right to control the destiny of the Island of Cuba [and] in the exercise of these rights we have fixed the destiny of the people of Cuba."[9] The future of Cuba was imagined indissolubly linked to the needs of the United States. "The intercourse which its proximity to our coasts begets and encourages," the Ostend Manifesto insisted, "has, in the progress of time, so united [the] interests [of Cubans and Americans] and blended their fortunes that they now look upon each other as if they were one people and had but one destiny."[10]

★ ★ ★

Cuba entered the North American imagination as coveted territory: possessed of purpose and informed by point of view, and almost always as figurative representation. It revealed itself as metaphor and metaphysical depiction, a mingling of allegory and analogy and mixing of allusion and affinity, arranged in a generally coherent narrative order around the proposition of Cuba as indispensable to the well-being of the United States. Cuba mattered principally because of its location, and it was location to which the Americans assigned multiple metaphorical representations.

Consciousness of Cuba developed around what was available, what was within reach and at hand, and indeed in this instance, out of what was perceived to be within sight. An imagined field of vision reached deeply into the emerging North American sense of nationhood. The claim to be able to "see" Cuba had far-reaching implications: it was to cast a possessive eye toward the island, a way to expand the reach of vision as a means to reduce the view of distance. To have situated Cuba within North American view—"almost in sight of our shores"—was to arrange the cognitive framework of possession around an imagined field of sight and space. The representation of knowing as seeing was turned on its head: seeing was knowledge. To claim to see what was beyond the range of sight was to diminish distance between the island and the mainland and thereby propound proximity as basis for a proprietary claim to Cuba. Martin Van Buren explained North American "deepest interest" in Cuba as a result of the "geographical position which places it almost in sight of our southern shores." The location of Cuba "almost within sight of the coast of Florida," James Buchanan insisted, meant that "the fate of this island must ever be deeply interesting to the people of the United States."[11]

There was a geography at work here, of course, but it was a geography construed as a proof of destiny and imagined as divine handiwork. Cuba "belongs to us geographically," Kentucky senator John Crittenden insisted in 1859, from which he deduced that "it must come to us; it must become ours before very long."[12] "To cast the eye upon the map was sufficient to predict [Cuba's] destiny," pronounced the Senate Committee on Foreign Relations at midcentury.[13]

Geography did indeed seem to suggest destiny, and about destiny there was unanimity: it was manifest. "Judging from . . . the geographical position of Cuba," mused poet Walt Whitman, "there can be little doubt that . . . it will gradually be absorbed into the Union. . . . It is impossible to say what the future will bring forth, but 'manifest destiny' certainly points to the speedy annexation of Cuba by the United States."[14]

But it was also true that the proposition of proximity was itself both premise and product of subjective vision and indeed serves in part to explain the process by which a fiction of the imagination obtained the plausibility of fact. As an imagined circumstance the proposition of proximity advanced plausibility by way of figurative constructs of other kinds. Proximity acquired depictive currency in the form of virtual contiguity. Secretary of State Hamilton Fish described Cuba as "almost contiguous to the United States," while U.S. minister to Spain Caleb Cushing insisted outright the island was a territory "contiguous to our shores."[15] Louisiana representative Miles Taylor similarly insisted that Cuba "lies contiguous to our territory," from which he concluded that "the geographical position of the island is such that it seems to be marked out by nature to become, at no distant day, part of the Union."[16]

The notion of contiguity conflated both location and distance into a usable premise for possession. The Americans could plausibly advance claim to Cuba because it was properly "part" of the United States. Cuba was "by nature . . . connected with the United States," Hamilton Fish pronounced.[17] As a matter of fact, argued Montana senator Thomas Carter, Cuba was "practically part of our territory."[18] "This island forms properly an appendage of the Floridas," U.S. minister to Spain Alexander Everett argued, and Secretary of State Edward Everett pronounced Cuba a "natural appendage to our Continent."[19] This led easily to the next leap of faith. "Cuba is a mere extension of our Atlantic coast line," Indiana senator Albert Beveridge insisted, "a geographical annex of Florida" and "a prolongation of the Florida Peninsula." Affirmed Beveridge, "That Cuba should be American is the highest example of manifest destiny in history. Geography makes her American—she is geographically part of Florida. Her position in the Gulf makes her American. . . . No island so small ever maintained a separate existence near a country so great and a government so powerful."[20]

Proximity was reiterated and ratified—and indeed reified—through a series of metaphorical depictions and none perhaps as prominent as the representation of Cuba "at the door" of the United States, and hence rightful to claim and proper to possess. "Cuba [is] situated, as it were, at our very door," U.S. minister to Spain Augustus Dodge insisted in 1858. Edward Everett invoked similar imagery, commenting that "Cuba lies at our doors" and, because it "bars the entrance" of the Mississippi River and "keeps watch at the doorway" of the isthmian route to California, must "in the natural order of things" belong to the United States.[21] Texas senator Roger Mills delighted in metaphorical flourishes to make the same point: "Here at our doors is an island which our fathers called the key to the Gulf of Mexico. It locks and unlocks the door to that great inland sea. . . . Cuba is not only the key that locks and unlocks that door, but it is the fortress that defends it."[22]

To propound proximity as the basis to claim possession of Cuba was to invite inference of providential purpose. The notion of proximity was inscribed with metaphysical meaning, accepted as a prophetic imperative, which meant, too, that North American possession of Cuba was commonly understood as fulfillment of a divinely ordained destiny. "It is because Cuba has been placed by the Maker of all things in such a position on earth's surface as to make its possession by the United States a geographical and political necessity," insisted Kentucky representative James Clay at midcentury, that "we must have Cuba, from a necessity which the Maker of the world has created."[23] Geography was a matter of providential agency, insisted New York representative Townsend Scudder, for Cuba was a "territory that God and nature intended to be a part of the United States."[24] Nature and the natural order had revealed their design through geography. "Cuba seems placed," mused writer Richard Kimball, "by the finger of a kindly Providence, between the Atlantic and the Mexican seas . . . to serve as the center of exchange for a domestic commerce as great as the territory of the Union."[25] The Ostend Manifesto proclaimed outright that Cuba "belongs naturally to that great family of States of which the Union is the Providential nursery,"[26] and *DeBow's Review* asserted that Cuba was "but part of our own South, unnaturally and arbitrarily separated."[27] New York senator William Seward—Lincoln's future secretary of state—transformed the metaphysical argument of providential geography into a literal case of geology. "Every rock and every grain of sand in the island were drifted and washed out from American soil by the floods of the Mississippi, and other estuaries of the Gulf of Mexico," Seward insisted. "The island has seemed to me . . . to gravitate back again to the parent continent from which it sprang."[28]

The metaphor of gravitation further propounded possession of Cuba as a matter of physics and assumed a place of prominence in the nineteenth-century narratives of Cuba. "The natural, God's law," U.S. consul general in Havana Ramon Williams insisted, "forces [Cuba] to gravitate to the United States."[29] With regard to the "final destiny of Cuba," predicted *Boston Globe* editor Maturin Ballou in 1888, the "natural laws" were as certain "in their operation as are those of gravitation," adding, "[Cuba's] home is naturally within our own constellation of stars."[30] Cuba "belonged naturally in the orbit of the Northern Republic," writer Isaac Ford insisted in 1893, "and sooner or later will be drawn into its place by the law of economic gravitation. . . . Cuba belongs in the Union. Nature intended it to be there."[31]

Secretary of State John Quincy Adams configured geographical imagery around the idea of Cuba as a "natural appendage" of the United States and thereupon concluded that the "interests" of Cuba and the United States were "formed by nature." Writing to the U.S. minister in Spain Hugh Nelson in 1823, Adams invoked the apple as a metaphor to make the case for the incontrovertible logic by which the laws of gravity would act to bring Cuba into the North American Union: "There are laws of political as well as of physical gravitation; and if an apple, severed by the tempest from its native tree, cannot choose but fall to the ground, Cuba, forcibly disjoined from its own unnatural connexion with Spain, and incapable of self-support, can gravitate only towards the North American Union, which, by the same law of nature, cannot cast her off from its bosom."[32]

The representation of Cuba as "ripe fruit," an object whose fate was to "gravitate" to the United States as a matter of a "law of nature," acquired enduring metaphorical resonance.[33] The idea alluded to the temporal dimensions of a destiny foretold, a matter of passage of time during which ripening would occur, whereupon the inexorable forces of nature—gravity, in this instance—would act with predictable certainty. "The acquisition of Cuba," Senator William Seward surmised in 1859, "is a question of time, of necessity, and of opportunity."[34] The metaphor also allowed for the possibility of "picking" the fruit when ripe. More than a quarter of a century after Adams first used the apple metaphor, the Senate Committee on Foreign Relations returned to the image: "The fruit that was not ripe when John Quincy Adams penned his despatch to [Hugh Nelson] . . . is now mature. Shall it be plucked by a friendly hand, prepared to compensate its proprietor with a princely guerdon? Or shall it fall decaying to the ground?"[35] Nineteenth-century historian Parke Godwin predicted that "Cuba will be ours," and added, "The fruit will fall into our hands when it is ripe, without an officious shaking of the tree."[36] Annexation was inevitable, Kentucky senator John Crittenden predicted in 1859, for "Cuba will fall, like the ripe fruit, into our lap."[37] Missouri senator Trusten Polk argued for annexation entirely within the logic of ripened fruit: "Let us bear in mind . . . that the ripe apple requires to be plucked from its native tree; and it must be plucked so soon as it is ripe. If deferred beyond maturity, the rich fruit will have lost its value; the golden opportunity will have passed away forever. This Cuban fruit, I trust, is even now ripe for the gathering."[38] Journalist Alexander Jones used the pear as a metaphor for Cuba at midcentury—"At present the pear is ripe neither for the Cubans nor ourselves"—and historian

"Patient Waiters Are Not Losers."
Uncle Sam: "I ain't in a hurry; it'll drop in my basket when it gets ripe."
From *Puck*, January 13, 1897.

. . . .

James Ford Rhodes imagined Cuba as a plum—"The plum was ready to drop into America's mouth."[39]

Through the power of their own metaphors, the Americans had rendered the need to possess Cuba as essential to the well-being of the North American Union. Possession of Cuba was perceived to be as inevitable as it was indispensable. Cuba had become for the Americans the most important place in the world. It could hardly have been otherwise. The idea of Cuba as vital to the security of the United States—"indispensable to the continuance and integrity of the Union itself"—could not but have made the island a matter of abiding national preoccupation. "I know of no portion of the earth that is now so important to the United States of America as the Island of Cuba is," Georgia senator Robert Toombs pronounced at midcentury. Kentucky representative James Clay agreed: "There is no subject of our foreign relations whatever at all to compare with [the acquisition of Cuba]. . . . No one has for a moment doubted the vital necessity to us of the acquisition of Cuba."[40] The island "lies in the gateway of the Gulf," pronounced Nevada senator William Stewart almost fifty years later; "she lies where she is absolutely essential to the preservation of the peace of the United States."[41]

National purpose obtained its rationale by notions of position and proximity: place as imagined implied possession as necessary. A consensus of enduring vitality formed around the need to possess, in the words of Senator Toombs, that "portion of the earth" that engaged the attention of almost every presidential administration of the nineteenth century and thereafter. The need for the "ultimate acquisition of Cuba," the Senate Committee on Foreign Relations pronounced at midcentury, was "recognized by all parties and all administrations, and in regard to which the popular voice has been expressed with a unanimity unsurpassed on any question of national policy that has heretofore engaged the public mind. . . . All agree that the end is not only desirable but inevitable. The only difference of opinion is to the time, mode, and conditions of obtaining it."[42]

★ ★ ★

The notion of proximity expanded into multiple figurative domains throughout the nineteenth century: proximity not only as a matter of distance but also inscribed with moral meaning. To imagine proximity as a spatial condition—depicted variously as "almost within sight" and "at our very door"—was to confer on Cuba the attributes of "neighbor" and thereupon posit a relationship conceived as a matter of moral engagement. "Cuba is so near to us in point of geographical location that she is our neighbor in actual, physical fact," New York representative William Sulzer pronounced.[43] The proposition of proximity enabled the Americans to imagine a spatial condition from which to infer a social contract as a function of "neighborhood." "Nature has placed that island in our immediate neighborhood," insisted Hamilton Fish, "and has established the foundations of the relations of business, commerce, and material interests."[44]

The imagery transmitted more than spatial information, of course. It also arranged the normative framework in which knowledge implied purpose. This was metaphorical construct as cultural model, possessed of meaning within domains of shared knowledge of the world; its purpose was to mediate per-ception of reality, to influence dispositions, and to induce conduct. This was metaphor as discourse. It possessed its own internal logic, capable at once of shaping cognitive perspectives and validating behavioral responses: metaphor as a way to propound a self-explanatory moral from which prescribed duty was intuitively understood and acted upon as a matter of time-honored conven-tions. The figurative became factual; the representation passed for reality.

The metaphor of Cuba as neighbor evoked a complex ensemble of moral meanings in the service of North American interests. To imagine Cuba as neighbor, sufficiently near as to be "at our very doors," was to situate Cuba within a value system governed by established normative protocols associated with the etiquette of neighborliness. The metaphor of Cuba as neighbor had far-reaching implications, for it derived specific meaning from a larger moral order by which neighbors were presumed to be bound to one another. The premise—and practice—of neighborliness implied a relationship drawn around established covenants by which neighborhood assumed form. Ameri-cans could render aid and assistance the way that good neighbors attended to the well-being of one another. But it was also true that this was a neigh-borhood in which the Americans declared their interests paramount. Because "neighbor" was a construct informed with notions of charity, duty, and respon-sibility, and because these were notions upon which only the Americans could reasonably act, the metaphor served to disguise power exercised as a matter of self-interest.

The proposition of neighbor thus acted to inscribe Cuba into the North American imagination less as an object of national interest than as a subject of beneficent concern. To envisage a relationship as a matter of neighborli-ness implied reciprocal obligations, of course. But it also served to propound moral sanction for—presumptively—beneficent intervention in the affairs of another people that, given the vast power differential between Cuba and the United States, privileged the North American moral claim to exercise power. Indeed, as writer David Rieff commented in another context, "One should not talk about neighborliness without conceding that this neighborliness is also a form of hegemony."[45]

That the depiction of Cuba as neighbor served to disguise self-interest in the form of selfless intent was not always apparent, but its absence should not conceal the fact that the efficacy of the metaphor was derived entirely from its capacity to provide moral purport to political purpose. This had to do with those internal dialogues by which Americans stylized narratives of national interest to conform to ideals of self-representation. That this involved in vary-ing degrees a discourse of self-deception matters less than the way it facilitated the pursuit of self-interest as a matter of disinterested purpose, which thus admitted the appearance of self-righteous motive to inform the pursuit of national interest. These were not disinterested constructs. They were, in fact, inscribed in purpose and point of view: policy, in a word, but so normatively synchronized as to utterly disguise political design as a matter of moral conduct.

The depiction of Cuba as neighbor enabled the Americans to persuade themselves of the moral propriety of their interest in Cuba. President Franklin Pierce insisted in 1853 that North American interests were derived from "the proximity of that island to our shores," interests that were related "to our neighborhood to the island of Cuba."[46] The island was "wretchedly governed," lamented James Buchanan, and "the inhabitants were oppressed in every way, under an unmitigated, irresponsible, and distant despotism." And to the point: "It was just at our doors, and the people of the United States could not fail to feel a deep interest in its fate."[47] The presence of an Old World colonial regime as a New World neighbor was represented as anathema to American sensibilities. Florida senator Stephen Mallory in 1859 denounced Spanish rule in Cuba "as the most appalling instance of mis-government on the face of the earth, . . . a despotism within almost hearing distance of our own shores, which has existed under our own eyes."[48] During the Cuban Ten Years War (1868–78), President Ulysses Grant referred to the "protracted struggle in such close proximity to our own territory" as reason to offer to mediate the conflict, "in the interest of a neighboring people."[49] Secretary of State Hamilton Fish similarly expressed concern for Cuba by way of multiple metaphorical representations of proximity: Cuba as a "near neighbor of ours"; Cuba as a matter of U.S. interest because of a conflict "in progress on our very borders" and "by reason of its immediate neighborhood . . . lying within sight of our coast"; Americans as troubled by a "scene of strife . . . at the very threshold [of the United States] . . . in an island lying at our door" and "a conflict in a contiguous territory."[50] For Fish it was "the proximity of the Island of Cuba" that "awaken[ed] earnest interest in our people in what concerns its inhabitants," and hence the source of "our sympathy for the Cubans, who are our neighbors."[51] The United States, Fish explained, was "horrified and agitated by the spectacle, at our very doors, of war."[52]

The metaphor of neighbor expanded fully into a paradigm and thereupon implicated Cuba in time-honored social compacts by which the well-being of a "neighborhood" was maintained. If neighborliness implied duty, it also conferred rights. The standard of conduct was not difficult to divine. The metaphor of neighborhood served as a device through which to set the limits of

Cuban autonomy: that all neighbors shared common interests did not mean that all neighbors shared equal power to defend their interests. This was a neighborhood in which the Americans proclaimed their interests paramount, and, of course, they possessed the power to act on their claim. "Cuba, whatever be its political condition, whether a dependency or a sovereign State, is, of necessity, our neighbor," Secretary of State William Marcy affirmed in 1853, adding, "It lies within sight of our coast. . . . Standing in that geographical relation, it is imperative upon us to require from it . . . all the observances imposed by good neighborhood."[53] Cuba was expected to conduct its affairs in a manner respectful of the interests of its neighbor the United States, always with the understanding that the protocols of neighborliness conferred on the northern neighbor the moral authority to put an end to whatever annoyances—real or imagined—disturbed the tranquility of the neighborhood. Cuba was the Gibraltar of the Gulf of Mexico, pronounced Ohio senator George Pugh at mid-century, who proceeded to expand his metaphorical reach: "We own the Gulf of Mexico, practically, and are entitled to the key which locks and unlocks it." The presence of Spain "in the neighborhood" posed a constant threat to the interests of the United States, Pugh insisted, and drew the moral of the argument: "No man, and therefore no nation, has any right to retain a cause of injury at the door of a neighbor, without having there also immediately at hand, the means of precaution and redress." Pugh invoked Deuteronomy 22:8: "'When thou buildest a new house,' said the law of Moses, 'then thou shalt make a battlement for thy roof, that thou bring not blood upon thine house, if any man fall from thence.'"[54] The House of Representatives Committee on Foreign Affairs outlined the U.S. position explicitly during the Ten Years War: "The immediate proximity of Cuba to the United States gives to these grave events an importance which cannot be fully appreciated by any other state. . . . The Cuban question becomes, therefore, an American question."[55]

Cuba as neighbor implied the idea of spatial proximity as source of a social covenant from which to infer binding moral obligations between neighbors. The Americans could thus intervene in Cuban internal affairs during times of adversity in the guise of one neighbor assisting another. They could also assert authority to intervene in Cuba the way that one household could properly claim the right to seek to end the disorderly conduct of a neighboring one. Abolitionist projects in Cuba during the 1850s, for example, were denounced in the United States as a threat to the internal tranquility of the United States. "It would call into existence, in immediate proximity to our southern shores," warned writer John Thrasher, "a negro community . . . which would be dangerous to us as a neighbor." Mississippi representative O. R. Singleton protested that the abolition of slavery—at the "gateway to the United States . . . [and] at the very doorway of the nation"—threatened to create "an African colony upon our very hearth-stone, with its blighting and devastating effects upon our commerce and institutions."[56] James Buchanan agreed and warned, "This Island is within sight of our shores, and should a black Government like that of Hayti be established there, it would endanger the peace and domestic security of a large and important portion of our people."[57] The abolitionist project in Cuba, the Ostend Manifesto warned in 1854, "seriously endangers our internal peace and the existence of our cherished Union." American political leaders would be guilty of committing "base treason against our posterity," the manifesto pronounced, "should we permit Cuba to be Africanized and become a second St. Domingo [Haiti], with all its attendant horrors to the white race, and suffer the flames to extend to our own neighboring shores, seriously to endanger or actually to consume the fair fabric of our Union."[58] Mississippi governor John Quitman contemplated the prospects of the abolition of slavery in Cuba with apocalyptic despair. "The erection of a strong negro or mongrel empire opposite to the mouth of the great outlet of the commerce of the Southwestern States," Quitman warned in 1854, "would forever put a stop to American progress and expansion on this continent, and very probably [bring] about a dissolution of this Union. . . . Such a result would be fatal to us." What happened in Cuba mattered greatly in the United States, Quitman insisted: "Our destiny is intertwined with that of Cuba. If slave institutions perish there they will perish here."[59]

Almost two decades later, the Americans would reverse themselves and denounce the continued existence of slavery on the island, for which they invoked again the proposition of proximity as the rationale for new demands. "Four millions of the same race as those now held in slavery in Cuba," minister to Spain Daniel Sickles insisted after the U.S. Civil War, "had become citizens of the United States, enjoying all civil and political rights, and forming an element of popular opinion having peculiar claims to respect in relation to a question touching so large a number of colored people dwelling almost within sight of our southern boundary."[60]

★ ★ ★

It would be unduly facile, of course, to attribute mischievous intent to the use of figurative depiction. In fact, it is far more complicated. That metaphorical representations responded to national interests can hardly be disputed. They were not deployed randomly; perspective and purpose were the sources of their production. Metaphorical constructs provided a normative grounding for a version of reality and validation of conduct. The imagery fixed the coordi-

"More Trouble for Uncle." Depiction of Cuba negotiating
trade arrangements with European countries, thereby creating
a "disturbance" in the neighborhood. From
Minneapolis Journal, November 18, 1902.

. . . .

nates in which to situate Cuba, certainly as a geography but also within a belief
system, that is, the context in which to fashion appropriate cultural forms by
which to represent—and act upon—political purpose.

But it is also true that the efficacy of metaphor resided precisely in its capacity to obscure its function. To have produced metaphor around ascribed
resemblance was to create usable knowledge, loaded with normative implications. There was an epistemology at work here: a way to knowledge, intrinsic

to which was the development of an ideology grounded in national myths as a mode of perception. This was political purpose in the form of cultural practice: the creation of a discursive method by which to inscribe moral imperative into new cognitive realms. If philosopher Max Black was only partially correct in his argument that the good metaphor produces "shifts in attitudes,"[61] it is necessary to understand the larger implications of nineteenth-century metaphorical representations of Cuba. In fact, they possessed the capacity to fashion the premises upon which reality was apprehended and in the process arranged the determinants by which prescriptive modes of conduct were enacted. Figurative usage—neighbor, in this instance—propounded the presence of a relationship, and once that possibility gained currency as plausible, the "work" of the metaphor was completed. To have accepted the metaphor as credible was to be implicated in its premise and inevitably complicit in its purpose. Embedded within the metaphor was a version of reality and a model for its engagement. Representation of the island as neighbor contributed to a narrative ordering of reality in which knowledge of Cuba served an instrumental function. It provided, too, a sense of meaning and suggested a code of conduct as the frame of reference in which to proclaim a relationship whose very existence was an invention of North American interests in the first place.

★ ★ ★

North American designs served easily enough to dismiss Cubans' pretensions to agency. Insofar as the Americans acknowledged at all the presence of Cubans in Cuba, it was to presume their acquiescence to a supporting role in the fulfillment of North American destiny. The idea of a people possessed of an internal history and the thought of Cubans endowed with proper aspirations to independence and sovereignty were prospects that the Americans rarely considered plausible and never deemed tenable.

North American views on the prospects of Cuban nationhood were fashioned around complex and often contradictory sentiments. On one hand, the Americans could hardly repudiate the proposition of sovereign nationhood, particularly as it involved a New World colony of an Old World monarchy. The ideal of self-government, so very much at the heart of the discourse by which the Americans celebrated the sources of their own nation, could not easily be suppressed from the national narrative or denied moral authenticity.[62]

On the other hand, the Americans contemplated the possibility of sovereign nationhood for Cubans with a mixture of fear and foreboding. John Quincy Adams dismissed the idea peremptorily, describing Cubans as "not competent to a system of self-dependence."[63] Henry Clay attributed Cuban incapacity for self-government to "the population itself," which was deemed "incompetent

at present, from its composition and amount, to maintain self-government."[64]
Simply put, Cuban self-rule was not a plausible proposition. Cuba contained a
large population of Africans and people of African descent, free and enslaved,
and of white descendants of Spaniards, in the aggregate a mixed racial population that had become emblematic of Latin American people everywhere,
a people that Americans presumed generally unprepared for if not intrinsically incapable of successful self-government.[65] Not only were there too many
Cubans of color. White Cubans themselves were found wanting—both in
number and in character. U.S. minister to Spain Alexander Everett insisted
that "the white inhabitants form too small a proportion of the whole number
to constitute of themselves an independent State."[66] South Carolina representative William Waters Boyce scorned the "Spanish Creole race of Cuba" as "the
worst kind of materials with which to build up republican institutions. . . .
They are utterly ignorant of the machinery of free institutions."[67]

The North American aversion to Cuban independence was based on a set
of assumptions central to which was an understanding of history as a moral
system. It drew freely upon dichotomies of civilization and progress, on one
hand, and barbarism and backwardness, on the other. The history of the Latin
American republics was viewed as a sorrowful chronicle of disorder and endless instability, of a mixed-race population incapacitated by centuries under
the yoke of Spanish colonial rule. It was a history from which the Americans inferred certain truths, namely, that Latin Americans were a people without the
aptitude and lacking the attributes necessary for successful self-government.
"This unfortunate Hispano-American race is incompetent to self-government,"
affirmed Louisiana senator Judah Benjamin in 1859. "Wherever they have tried
it, they have had revolution, strife, and civil disorders. The people do not know
how to yield to the will of a majority."[68]

These traits were readily ascribed to Cubans. "The most intelligent of the
Creoles," the U.S. consul in Havana insisted in 1848, "have an abiding conviction of their utter incapacity for self government, a conviction which must
be felt by any one who has had opportunities of studying or even observing
their character. Any government administered by them would soon rival
that of Mexico or the other Republics of the Spanish race."[69] U.S. minister to
Spain Caleb Cushing did not disguise his dim view of political conditions in
nineteenth-century Latin America and what these circumstances portended
for Cuba. He brooded on the "bad news from Mexico . . . and recent similar
events in Ecuador, Colombia, Peru, the Argentine Confederation, and other
countries of Spanish America, their frequent revolutions, pronunciamentos,
and civil wars, and the apparent incapacity of the Spanish-American Republics to manage republican institutions or to maintain domestic peace, and the

question whether Cuba was capable of self-government, it being [apparent] that the Spanish-Americans inherit all the vices, but not the virtues, of their parent race in Europe." Concluded Cushing, "The semi-insane spirit of chronic rebellion which has so long prevailed in Cuba, and which whatever pretexts or even plausible reasons it may allege in the want of wisdom of the superior government, has its real causes in the character, conduct, and mode of life of the Cubans themselves."[70] All of which, Cushing insisted, pointed to "the absolute nonexistence in Cuba at the present time of the essential elements of an independent state."[71] Essayist Edmond Wood argued that "neither Spanish colonists nor their descendants, whether of pure or mixed blood, have ever developed the constructive faculty and executive capacity that are necessary in order to establish stable government." Good government had "never been successfully exercised [by] any people of Spanish origin or training," Wood wrote, adding that "the truth is that these countries are making a ghastly play at government." And to the point: "As every one of the fifteen Latin American republics has had many domestic revolutions, the conclusion is reasonable that Cuba is not free from the same tendency."[72] Michigan senator Zachariah Chandler addressed his colleagues "from personal knowledge": "I spent a winter in the interior of the Island of Cuba. . . . [They] are one million of the refuse of the earth. . . . They are ignorant, vicious, and priest-ridden. . . . The people are superstitious and vicious; and they are bigots as well. They are devout Catholics. . . . They are anxious for plunder; they are anxious for positions where they can get bribes. True patriotism does not exist on the Island of Cuba. They love the very chains that bind them."[73]

Notions of civilization and attitudes toward race were conflated and circulated as the currency of conventional wisdom. A premise was transformed into a principle and thereafter passed into domains of popular knowledge from which the Americans drew to inform their understanding of Cuba. The specter of Haiti loomed as an unstated but understood moral and, indeed, served as one of the dominant metaphors of the nineteenth century, used variously to represent the lawlessness and the chaos surely to overtake Cuban efforts at self-government. Independence "could only be nominal," warned the Senate Committee on Foreign Relations in 1859; "it could never be maintained in fact." The committee added, "Civil and servile war would soon follow, and Cuba would present, as Hayti now does, no traces of its former prosperity, but the ruins of its once noble mansions."[74] Essayist Edward Bryan alluded to the "geographical proximity" of the island to warn of dire consequences attending Cuban independence. "Cuba would become another Hayti," Bryan predicted, "if not in form, at least in point of fact. The ultimate question, then, to be laid before the American people is, are you prepared to see another Hayti spring up at your doors and command the entrance into the interior of your continent?"[75]

These were matters of deep concern for the Americans, who were fearful that political disorder and social turmoil in Cuba threatened to transform the "neighborhood" into a source of regional instability and international conflict, and hence a menace to U.S. strategic and commercial interests. The presumption of Cuban ineptitude as a threat to the well-being of the United States all but precluded the possibility that the Americans would readily acquiesce to the establishment of a sovereign Cuban republic. The Americans were loathe to permit control of a territory deemed of such vital importance to national self-interest—"indispensable to the continuance and integrity of the Union itself"—by anyone other than themselves. Cuba could not be allowed to pass under the control of a people judged variously as ill-suited and unfit for self-government. The Cubans could not be trusted to govern the island in the best interests of the United States.

That Cuba would ultimately pass under North American control was an article of faith, and hence a matter of conviction. The island was perceived to be populated by a people ill-fit to govern themselves and ruled by a country ill-equipped to govern anyone else. All through the nineteenth century, the Americans pursued the acquisition of the island with resolve if without results. James Polk and Franklin Pierce attempted to purchase Cuba, but without success. These efforts were followed by other, more discreet overtures, and these, too, came to nothing. In the meantime, defense of the colonial status quo in Cuba developed into the principal strategy for eventual acquisition of Cuba, but always with the understanding that the only admissible alternative to Spanish sovereignty was North American rule.[76] The fate of Cuba, insisted California representative Milton Latham, due to "its proximity to our shores," was of "vast importance to the peace and security of this country." To the point: "We cannot allow it to pass from its present proprietors into other hands."[77] South Carolina senator John Calhoun urged "resort to the hazard of war with all its calamities" to prevent Cuba from passing "into any other hands but ours," and added, "This, not from a feeling of ambitions, not from a desire for the extension of dominion, but because that island is indispensable to the safety of the United States."[78] The "whole power of the United States would be employed to prevent . . . Cuba from passing into other hands," Secretary of State John Clayton warned at midcentury. He continued, "This Government is resolutely determined that the Island of Cuba shall never be ceded by Spain to any other power than the United States."[79]

The succession of sovereignty from Spain to the United States was imagined as straight and direct. Received wisdom admitted no other possibility.

"The ultimate acquisition of Cuba," pronounced Pennsylvania senator Donald Cameron in 1896, "has been regarded as the fixed policy of the United States — necessary to the progressive development of our system. All agree that [it] is not only desirable but inevitable."[80] Texas senator Roger Mills summarized a century of U.S. policy in 1896: "It has been the settled policy of our country, of all parties, at all times, that this all-important key shall never pass out of the feeble hands of Spain to any other Government except that of the United States."[81]

★ ★ ★

The Cuban war for independence (1895–98) changed everything. For more than three years, the Cubans waged war against Spain, in the name of *Cuba Libre*, in behalf of Cuba for Cubans, for an independent sovereign nation. In fact, the success of the Cuban insurrection threatened more than the propriety of Spanish colonial rule; it also challenged the presumption of American succession to rule. Certainly the cause of *Cuba Libre* had aroused widespread popular enthusiasm across the United States. But the administrations of Grover Cleveland and William McKinley, as custodians of a national policy with antecedents early in the nineteenth century, viewed Cuban independence warily and never wavered in their opposition to sovereign nationhood for the island. Even the "most devoted friend of Cuba," Secretary of State Richard Olney warned in 1896, and even the "most enthusiastic advocate of popular government" could not look at developments in Cuba "except with the gravest apprehensions." Olney feared that the "struggle that is raging almost in sight of our shores" would result in the Spanish "abandonment of the island to the heterogenous combination of elements and of races now in arms against her." He added,

> There are only too strong reasons to fear that, once Spain were withdrawn from the island, the sole bond of union between the different factions of the insurgents would disappear; that a war of races would be precipitated, all the more sanguinary for the discipline and experience acquired during the insurrection, and that, even if there were to be temporary peace, it could only be through the establishment of a white and black republic, which, even if agreeing at the outset upon a division of the island between them, would be enemies from the start, and would never rest until the one had been completely vanquished and subdued by the other.[82]

President Grover Cleveland contemplated purchasing the island — not, however, to concede independence to Cubans. On the contrary: "It would seem absurd for us to buy the island," Cleveland made clear, "and present it to the people now inhabiting it, and put its government and management in their hands."[83] Cuba was "an integral portion of the territory of the United States," writer William Mills insisted in 1898, which required "that the unnatural relation [with Spain] should be broken and that the natural relation [with the United States] should be assumed." Mills wrote what many were saying:

> We have in all time maintained that by virtue of her geographical position, the incorporation of Cuba into our territorial system was natural and right, and even indispensable to our safety. Any sovereignty other than that of the United States, whether claimed and exercised by an Old World monarchy or established by the people of the island themselves, will in all essentials be at issue with the inherent evolutionary force of our development, and . . . a foe to our safety and an obstacle to our progress. The independence of Cuba is, therefore, an historical absurdity. . . . Nothing but her complete incorporation into our territorial system will allay the menace of her geographical position.[84]

North American disquiet deepened as the Cuban insurgency expanded. "I do not believe that the population is to-day fit for self-government," U.S. minister Stewart Woodford warned from Madrid in early 1898. Woodford characterized the insurgency as "confined almost entirely to negroes," with "few whites in the rebel forces." And once more the allusion was made to Haiti: "Cuban independence is absolutely impossible as a permanent solution of the difficulty, since independence can only result in a continuous war of races, and that this means that independent Cuba must be a second Santo Domingo [Haiti]."[85]

★ ★ ★

The antecedents of the war between Spain and the United States in 1898 had been set in place early in the nineteenth century. They were inscribed within the very figurative representations with which the Americans had made Cuba relevant to themselves. War in 1898 was understood to promise something of a consummation of territorial integrity and fulfillment of a prophetic imperative. This is not to suggest, of course, that the war with Spain over Cuba was inevitable. It is, rather, to argue that the imagery employed to represent the meaning of Cuba during the nineteenth century decisively shaped the disposition for war.[86] The determinants of war had long served as the logic of the very discursive forms by which Cuba had gained entree to the American imagination: as reason and rationale, as purpose and policy. It was with a sense of a fate foretold that the *New York Times* explained the coming of war with Spain in April 1898. "We go to war with Spain," the *Times* pronounced, "not for the accomplishment of an ambition, but in obedience to the laws of nature. It is

"The Duty of the Hour: To Save Her Not Only from Spain but from a Worse Fate."
From *Puck*, May 11, 1898.

. . . .

time this thing were done and we do it, as the ripened fruit drops from the tree."[87]

War with Spain was foretold also by the long-standing North American vow that the United States would resist the transfer of sovereignty of the island to a third party. All through the nineteenth century, the Americans had unabashedly threatened war to prevent, in John Calhoun's words, Cuba from passing "into any other hands but ours." Secretary of State John Clayton's midcentury warning that the United States was "resolutely determined that the Island of Cuba shall never be ceded by Spain to any other power than the United States" must be presumed to have included the Cubans themselves. The prospects that Spain would cede Cuba to a "foreign power," Clayton had warned, would "be the instant signal for war."[88]

Spanish sovereignty in Cuba was coming to an end—or so it appeared. And it was indeed perceptions that shaped policy and influenced conduct, the basis upon which political decisions were made and military action taken.[89] Whether Cubans would have, in fact, gone on to defeat Spain, in 1898 or thereafter, or even at all, cannot be demonstrated, of course. This is something that can be argued but cannot be proven. What can be determined and documented, however, is that all parties involved—Cubans, Spaniards, and

Americans—had arrived at the conclusion that the days of colonial rule over the island were numbered, and that the days were few indeed.

The administration of President William McKinley contemplated the prospects of war with a sober sense of purpose, mindful of the need to intervene in Cuba in order to broker an outcome compatible with U.S. interests. But it was also true that the proposition of national interests had been fully inscribed into metaphorical constructs of selfless intent. The United States could thus proceed to make war by way of a discourse so wholly derived from figurative representations as to preclude the need to make national interests the explicit rationale for war.

Figurative depictions of Cuba were modeled from cultural practice, derived from the very moral systems by which Americans obtained their own sense of self-worth and self-identity, almost all of which served a priori to implicate Americans in normatively scripted codes of conduct. Metaphors of Cuba were both a mode of allusion and a model of action. To accept the premise of the former was to be implicated in the practice of the latter. Images wholly of North American origins, that is, the depictive forms by which Cuba had entered the North American imagination, could not but have confronted the Americans with the need to act on the moral imperatives prescribed within the very metaphors of their own creation.

Multiple metaphorical representations of proximity arranged the discursive logic by which the Americans forged the consensus for war. The idea of Cuban proximity seemed to enmesh the Americans in an inexorable logic, one construed almost entirely from the duty of neighbor. That Cuba "lies so near to us as to be hardly separated from our territory," President Grover Cleveland insisted, required the United States to concern itself in the affairs of "the neighboring island."[90] The American people, U.S. minister to Spain Hannis Taylor affirmed, could not contain their indignation at "the tragic and inhuman scenes enacted almost in sight of their very shores," on "an island so near to our coast line as to be almost a part of our territory."[91] The "spectacle of distress and misery in the neighboring community," Assistant Secretary of State William Day decried, had "deeply moved" the United States.[92] Secretary of State John Sherman denounced the excesses of a war "in the neighboring island of Cuba," demanding that "a war, conducted almost within sight of our shores . . . at least be conducted according to the military codes of civilization." The "sight" of the misfortunes of "a neighboring country," Sherman warned, in the face of "a devastating internal conflict at [U.S.] doors," could not but compel the United States to act in Cuba.[93] Sherman prepared his instructions to the new U.S. minister to Spain Stewart Woodford in 1897 by way of a narrative rich with allusions to proximity as the source of North American concern for Cuba. The U.S. government "beholds the island suffering" as a result of an "internecine warfare at its very doors," explained Sherman, and warned that the United States as "a neighboring nation," and "keenly sympathetic with the aspirations of any neighboring community in close touch with our own civilization," could not long remain passive at the spectacle of "a devastating internal conflict at its doors."[94] The "trouble commenced in [Spain's] house," Ohio senator Joseph Foraker insisted. "She made it a general nuisance, and persisted in so maintaining it long after she had been notified that it had become insufferable." That the "island lies at our door," Foraker reasoned, rendered "our relation special and our duty is special." He concluded, "The American people naturally sympathize with all who struggle for liberty and independence, but especially with . . . our immediate neighbors."[95]

The now familiar metaphor of Cuba as neighbor thus gained discursive ascendancy in the deliberations leading to war and indeed was central to the logic by which Americans persuaded themselves of the moral propriety of war. A righteous people could not remain indifferent to the suffering of neighbors. The United States, exhorted Congregationalist minister Washington Gladden, could not "stay at home and look out of the window while the robbers are breaking into our neighbor's home." He added, "Because the Nation has a conscience and a moral life of its own it must recognize the fact that it has neighbors, and must behave itself neighborly. . . . We have responsibility for sufferers beyond our frontiers."[96] In the weeks and days leading to war, the *New York Times* invoked almost daily the proposition of duty to neighbor as rationale for intervention. "Our only desire respecting Cuba," the *Times* pleaded editorially, "is to see it . . . in a condition of good neighborhood." It was Spain, insisted the *Times* on another occasion, "which has prevented the United States and Cuba from being as good neighbors." The *Times* denounced "the awful situation at our doors" and the "abhorrent conditions which had existed . . . so near our own borders."[97] "The island is our neighbor," the *New York Times* pronounced, a relationship that required the United States "to remove the menace of an endless warfare carried on at our very doors."[98]

Other newspapers joined the *New York Times*. "How much longer," the *New York World* asked editorially, "shall we consent to the extermination of our neighbors and friends?"[99] "For years," protested the *Baltimore Morning Herald*, "we have borne patiently the existence of a slaughterhouse at our very doors."[100] The *Cleveland Plain Dealer* rendered the matter of proximity in terms of local distance:

> When the people of Cleveland realize that Cuba is no farther away from the United States than Put-in Bay is from Cleveland or than Crestline or

Canton are from Cleveland they will appreciate potently how shameful has been our national policy of non-interference. We are blind to suffering that is almost within our sight; we are deaf to voices that almost reach our ears; we are dumb to supplications at our very feet. . . . The Cubans are habitats of our national domain, for the little island is as much a part of us geographically as a state. And yet to these brothers by location we deny succor. . . . Would any other enlightened nation in the world have tolerated for this length of time such a reign of carnage and pillage within sight of its shores? It is inconceivable.[101]

To imagine Cuba as neighbor was to deploy metaphor as argument, to propound real obligations derived from a figurative relationship as the basis for actual conduct. The notion of neighbor was rendered in two different depictive forms, and both implied one course of action. In one version, Cuba was represented as a neighbor in distress and dire need. "No honorable-spirited people," insisted Illinois senator Shelby Moore Cullom, "can afford to sit silently by and see tens and hundreds of thousands of people helpless and starving to death at the nation's door."[102] Virginia senator John Daniel insisted that the United States had a "moral obligation" to Cuba: "one of equity, one of fraternity, one of neighborship."[103] "We can not, in my opinion," insisted Massachusetts senator Henry Cabot Lodge in April 1898, "allow that fire to burn longer at our doors." Lodge continued: "They say that they are not our own people. They are just outside the walls of the house we call our own. Ah, when they say to me, 'Are you your brother's keeper?' I respond, 'Yes; we are the keeper of those people in Cuba,' for we announced fifty years ago to the whole world that the Cuban question was an American question."[104]

The "good Samaritan" metaphor provided the second depiction of the national purpose. For writer Andrew Draper, the issue of 1898 had to do with the country conducting itself like "the good Samaritan, [which] feels it has a duty to its suffering neighbor who has fallen among thieves."[105] Illinois senator William Mason evoked the image with passion: "We take Cuba as the good Samaritan did, and bind up her wounds, furnish her people with something to eat, and clothes to wear; and the nations of the world will say at last, in the beginning of the new century, there is one nation not seeking conquest, not seeking power, but one nation following the Nazarene, that has learned the sublime thought, 'Bear ye one another's burdens.'"[106]

The implications of the "good Samaritan" were subsequently drawn to their logical conclusion and served later to justify the U.S. military occupation of Cuba. To relinquish control of Cuba, insisted essayist John Kendrick Bangs at the end of the war, "would be a complete shirking of the responsibilities we

"I Guess the Powers Won't Interfere if I Stop That."
From *New York Journal*, April 17, 1898.

. . . .

assumed by our intervention." Bangs added, "It does not suffice to help a man who is half dead, from injuries he has received, up out of a ditch into which he has been thrown by a band of thugs. To leave him, still dazed and suffering, by the road-side, to go his way alone, and as best he may, to fall, perhaps into the hands of other thieves and thugs, would be a course which no decent Samaritan would advocate."[107]

For much of the nineteenth century, the Americans had ordered a narrative of proximity into the premise of a claim for a special relationship with Cuba. In 1898 the proposition of nearness served as the principal rationale for war and further provided the dominant discursive arc along which to carry the meaning of proximity to its logical conclusion. The congressional debate over intervention in Cuba took place almost entirely within shared—and indeed consensual—metaphorical domains in which the figurative depiction of proximity served both to inform the rationale for war and confirm the logic of intervention. The United States had "barbarism on our very shores," Georgia sena-

"LET ME LOOSE!"

"Let Me Loose!" From *Philadelphia Inquirer*, April 4, 1898.

. . . .

tor Alexander Clay decried, a "barbarity [that] continues to this day and within four hours' steaming of our shores."[108] Indiana senator Charles Fairbanks alluded to "the proximity of the Island of Cuba" and "the horrors of Spanish rule at our very doors," invoking a slightly different analogy to underscore the nearness of the island: "The murders and atrocities in Cuba have been committed as near to our shores as Philadelphia is to New York."[109] Cuba "lies at our very doors, within a few hours sail from our ports," Nebraska senator

John Thurston insisted, circumstances that required the United States to act. Added Thurston, "There is no nation, there is no place on the face of the earth with which we have such immediate, such direct, such important commercial and other relations as with and in the Island of Cuba."[110] "Cuba is right at our door," Delaware senator George Gray agreed, a condition "that colors and qualifies the duty we owe and the attitude we occupy toward her. If she were on the other side of the ocean, moored off the coast of Africa or Portugal, while our interest might be excited and our feelings stirred, our duty might be different. But there she is where God placed her. There, during all these three years, we have waited while the drama of blood has been enacted under our eyes. . . . We can endure it no longer."[111]

Representatives from southern states especially invoked the proximity of Cuba as reason for war. Alabama senator John Tyler Morgan bemoaned Cuban suffering at "our own borders" and alluded to the "conscience and . . . the convictions of my constituents . . . who are near neighbors to Cuba."[112] Voters in Florida—"nearest the scene of action"—declared Senator Samuel Pasco, supported Cuba, "almost within sight of our peninsula," and insisted that "the Cubans are near neighbors to the people of Florida."[113]

President William McKinley's war message to Congress in April 1898 repeatedly invoked proximity as rationale for intervention in Cuba. McKinley referred to three years of strife that had "raged in the neighboring island of Cuba," a war "at our very door," "at our threshold ravaged by fire and sword," a "conflict waged for years in an island so near us." Indeed, the president summoned the most forceful justification for intervention in the form of a familiar imagery: "It is specially our duty, for [Cuba] is right at our door."[114] The final Joint Resolution of Congress of April 1898 authorized war as a means to end "abhorrent conditions . . . so near our own borders."[115]

★ ★ ★

Across the United States—in town halls and among civic organizations, in poems and popular songs, from the church pulpit to the theater stage—the need to discharge an obligation to a neighbor seized the popular imagination. Margaret Alden's poem "Cuba" alluded to the "cries of our brothers" and asked, "What is their crime, these neighbors of ours? / What have they done that they suffer and die?"[116] In "The Sword Unsheathed" poet S. T. Cocker vowed to "strike the blow that breaks our neighbor's chains."[117] "Shall we see a neighbor perish and withhold the helping hand?" asked J. T. Trowbridge in the poem "Cuba," and E. S. Tway vowed in "As We Go Marching On" that "We will not allow our neighbors / To be scourged with such a pest."[118] In the song "In Our Country Forever" lyricists Frank Stanton and Stanley Clague wrote,

"There's a call from o'er the ocean, there's a call from o'er the sea / From our neighbors who are suffering in their struggle to be free."[119] A petition from "prominent women" in Atlanta in early 1898 bemoaned the fate of the island neighbor. "Does it not seem heartless, yea cowardly, not to offer a strong arm of defense to a suffering, starving, helpless neighbor?" asked one woman. Another insisted that "Cuba is our near and charming neighbor. . . . It is very disagreeable to have a cruel and horrible state of things right at one of our doors, or right in the street in front of our house, and I think the police power of civilization ought to stop it!"[120]

The American theater developed into another site for the enactment of public support for *Cuba Libre*. As early as October 1895, the play *Ambition*, by Henry Guy Carleton, dealing with congressional intrigue for the recognition of Cuban independence, opened at the Fifth Avenue Theater in New York. The J. N. Morris play *The Last Stroke*, set in the fields of insurgent Cuba, opened in St. Paul, Minnesota, in February 1896 and was subsequently produced in New York and Philadelphia. *Cuba Free*, a four-act drama by playwright James Arthur McKnight, premiered in March 1896 at the Academy of Music in New York, with opening night receipts donated to the Cuban cause. Manhattan Beach summer stock theater in 1896 included Ralph Paine's sympathetic play, *Cuba*. The play *Cuba's Vow*, by J. J. McCloskey, premiered in the Star Theater in New York in February 1897. Playwrights Lillian Lewis, Albert Paine, and Lawrence Marston collaborated in the writing of *For Liberty and Love*, a sympathetic account of the Cuban insurrection, which was presented in October 1897 at the Grand Opera House in New York. In Cambridge, Massachusetts, a local theater ensemble staged in early 1898 the play *Boscabello*, dealing with a party of Boston travelers in Cuba who witnessed the cruelty of Spanish pacification efforts.

It is difficult indeed to measure the effects of song or poetry or theater and their impact on shaping public attitudes. Occasionally, however, insight can be obtained from the most unexpected sources. An unnamed *New York Times* theater critic was in the audience on opening night of *The Last Stroke* in 1896 and bore witness to the public mood. "Cuban patriots and liberty-loving Americans cheered for Cuba Libre at the Star Theater last night during the performance for the first time in this city of 'The Last Stroke,'" wrote the critic, "a melodrama founded on the events in the war for independence now being waged in the island dependency of Spain. . . . The house was draped with American and Cuban flags [and] American sympathy for the struggling Cubans gave vent in a mighty shout when the American Consul of the play said: 'No. We don't want diplomacy! Where would America have been if we had had diplomacy instead of Bunker Hill?'" The critic continued:

There is enough of real human interest in 'The Last Stroke' to give it a long lease of life, even if there were not the added interest of a vivid portrayal of the situation in Cuba to-day. When a little Cuban flag was tossed on the stage by a pretty girl at the close of the second act, a gray-haired gentleman in the second row jumped up and proposed three cheers for Cuba. They were given with a will, and twice three more, the audience rising. The applause was kept up until the author of the play, Mr. Morris, was disclosed by the curtain to bow his thanks.[121]

★ ★ ★

Cuba passed into popular realms of the familiar by way of multiple metaphorical representations. Any distinction between the intended meaning and the received message must be considered minimal. The depictive efficacy of metaphor is itself a product of a specific time, formed under specific circumstances, addressing specific needs. That is, metaphors as cultural artifacts rely precisely on the ready accessibility of meaning, widely shared and commonly comprehended. They must resonate with their time and place. "Thinking cannot trade in metaphors directly," cognitive psychologist Steven Pinker is correct to suggest. "It must use a more basic currency that captures the abstract concepts shared by the metaphor and its topic."[122]

That metaphor served as the principal mode by which power holders and opinion makers engaged Cuba raises complex issues having to do with the constituency whose attention was the object of metaphorical purport. The evidence is anecdotal yet persuasive and does indeed demonstrate that metaphors were received as they were intended: the images transacted as political representation appeared to have captured the popular imagination. From the pulpit to the stage, in the lyric of popular music and on the pages of pulp fiction, Americans from all walks of life arrived at their knowledge of Cuba and Cubans principally by way of metaphor.

By 1898, these images had taken hold of the American imagination as a circumstance of reality. Metaphor had more than adequately prepared Americans for intervention in Cuba as a matter of righteous purpose and moral duty. The images served as the vernacular staple of the print media across the country, as the metaphor of neighbor provided the principal discursive device by which Americans persuaded themselves of the need for war. Editorial cartoons offered pictorial representations of proximity and further reinforced the notion of Cuba as neighbor. The island was depicted as sufficiently near to enable the visual representation of Cuba as fully within sight of the United States. This was metaphor as medium of a narrative bearing a moral. If the

JUSTIFICATION ENOUGH!

"Justification Enough!" From *Philadelphia Inquirer*, March 20, 1898.
. . . .

plight of Cuba was not actually visible, it certainly could be "seen" in the form of a pictorial representation.

Metaphorical representation of national interests was conveyed within a framework of self-evident and self-explanatory modes of conduct. Spanish misgovernment in Cuba, the Americans complained, had developed into a chronic nuisance to the United States. In this instance, the idea of proximity conferred on the United States a moral duty of another kind: to intervene to obtain abatement of a disturbance in the neighborhood. As early as 1854, in the Ostend Manifesto, the Americans had fashioned a usable course of action predicated on the metaphor of neighbor drawn to its logical conclusion, and with far-reaching implications for events in 1898. The degree to which "Cuba in the possession of Spain seriously endanger[s] our internal peace and the existence of our cherished Union," the manifesto stipulated, presented the United States with only one choice: "By every law human and Divine, we shall be justified in wresting [Cuba] from Spain if we possess the power; and this, upon the very same principle that would justify an individual in tearing down the burning house of his neighbor, if there were no other means of preventing the flames from destroying his own home."[123]

The metaphor of neighbor invited the presumption of moral entitlement, to take appropriate action to end the disturbance caused by the presence of Spain. Alabama senator John Tyler Morgan insisted outright upon "our national right to be rid of such a neighbor as the Spanish government in Cuba."[124] Texas senator Roger Mills agreed, insisting "that the people of the United States had rights in Cuba," and thereupon he evoked a series of metaphors of portentous implications: "The man who owns a tract of land adjoining mine owns it from the center of the earth to the center of the sky. So the books all tell us. Yet if he builds a powder house upon his land I have a right to have it abated. If that land is so situated that an enemy can seize it at any time and imperil my life and the lives of my wife and children, I have a right in every foot of that land for the preservation of a higher right than his right to the title and possession of his land."[125] The "unusual kindness and even forbearance" with which the American people had accepted the presence of Spain in the New World, proclaimed the *Washington Evening Star*, could be sustained no longer. Moreover, "Spain has been for a good many years a very trying and undesirable neighbor. [She] has made herself so obnoxious . . . that the interests of the United States require that she surrender her sovereignty there. She has become a nuisance at our very door and we have resolved to abate it."[126] Spanish misrule in Cuba, New York representative Townsend Scudder protested, "was like having an open cesspool opposite one's front door. The thing had to be abated."[127] General James Wilson similarly justified the "right to intervene" to secure "the establishment of a quiet and orderly neighborhood,"[128] and William Jennings Bryan supported intervention on the grounds that "any man had the right to prevent the erection of a slaughter house in his own yard."[129] The *New York Times* used a similar set of metaphors: "This Nation . . . has the same objection to war in Cuba that a householder would have to incendiarism in the house next door. If its neighbors will not refrain from menacing its peace and safety it will be amply justified by 'Nature's first law' in expelling them from the premises they so ill-use."[130]

The proposition of neighbor inspired derivative narratives, principally as analogy in the form of argument. The issue of Cuba as a matter explicitly of national interest warranting war all but fully disappeared from the public dis-

"Behold! I Stand at the Door and Knock!" From *Chicago Tribune*, April 2, 1898.

. . . .

course, subsumed irretrievably in metaphorical representations propounding selfless obligation, a duty to perform in behalf of a neighbor in distress. The Americans were thus able to transact national interests as discharge of national virtue, whereby U.S. motives were represented not as a matter of self-interest but, rather, as selfless sacrifice: to rescue the Cubans. The metaphor enabled the Americans to advance self-interest in the guise of moral conduct, by way of appeal to the propriety of neighbor caring for neighbor. This was a metaphor normatively determined and culturally driven, and once deployed it became a means with which to mediate reality and assumed a logic of its own.

By 1898 the Americans had concluded that they could no longer evade their obligations. "At our very doors the most atrocious crimes in the name of Spain have been committed," decried the *Philadelphia Inquirer*. "Have we no duty to perform before God? . . . We will not shirk our duty."[131] The *Minneapolis Journal* drew the metaphorical argument to its logical conclusion: "The old-time claim, that the father of a child, the owner of a horse or the parent nation of a colony had the right to abuse and oppress because of its relationship and was justified in resenting any interference is not longer allowed by intelligent peoples. The obligation to perform this duty increases with nearness to the scene of suffering and when the scene is directly before the eye, the duty to interfere is imperative."[132] Attorney Thomas Shearman summoned another set of images to make international law relevant to intervention in Cuba:

> Suppose the father of several half-grown boys living next door to you, should, with ever so much justice, seek to repress an insurrection on their part, by physical force, but with no result except to prolong, for several days and nights, a doubtful fight, accompanied by screams, oath, and destruction of property within the house, such as would not suffer your family to sleep, you would have a right to call a police officer, who would, in his turn, have both the right and duty of suppressing the disturbance, without regard to the merits of the quarrel. If the revolt of the sons were ever so unjustifiable, yet, if the father could not subdue it without creating a nuisance to all his neighbors, he must take the chances of being turned out of doors by his rebellious sons.[133]

New imagery was layered on old. The claim that Cuba was "within sight" continued to provide a frame of reference to "do something" about conditions on the island. It was the "state of things [that] exists at our doors," Richard Olney protested, and the conflict "raging almost in sight of our shores" that compelled the United States to concern itself with conditions in Cuba.[134] "I do not want the great American Republic to stand idly by and indifferent," protested Alabama senator John Tyler Morgan, "whilst these scenes . . . are being enacted under our eyes."[135] "Before our very eyes, at our very doors" was also the refrain used by California representative Marion de Vries to describe conditions in Cuba, and he repeated, "atrocities perpetrated by the Spanish in Cuba, committed before our very eyes, in sight of the American shores and flag."[136]

Americans eventually imagined Cuba by way of all the senses. They could turn neither a blind eye nor a deaf ear to conditions in Cuba. "Our ears and eyes have been witnesses for nearly three years of this most horrible condition," Utah representative William King pronounced in 1898.[137] To the claim of expanded vision was added the affirmation of enhanced hearing. "As a free people we can listen to their cries and heed them," exhorted Colorado senator Edward Wolcott. "If we fail to listen to the voice of the suffering or the cry of the downtrodden . . . we will be untrue to those principles of liberty, humanity, and Christianity upon which this country is founded."[138] "We are going to war with Spain," Wisconsin senator John Coit Spooner explained in April 1898, "because we can not tolerate any longer Spanish rule in this neighboring island; we are going to war with Spain because we can not any longer listen to the cries, which come floating over the sea upon every breeze from Cuba."[139] The *Washington Evening Star* urged intervention by insisting that "those people are

"Eight out of Every Ten Concentrados Are Doomed. . . ."
From *Judge*, January 22, 1898.

. . . .

under the harrow right at the door of the United States. Their cries and appeals are distinctly heard in every section of this country. And if those cries are permitted to go longer unheeded . . . the attitude of this government will be one of reproach before the bar of civilization."[140] "It was impossible," pronounced the Reverend Lyman Abbott of the Plymouth Church of Brooklyn, "for a great, strong, wealthy nation like America to stand by and see such inhumanity carried on in a neighboring island, so near to us that the cries of the unhappy were almost heard within our borders."[141]

Soon, too, Americans claimed to have discerned the scent of insurrection from Cuba. "We are fighting because we could no longer brook [Spanish] rule over any part of our glorious Western Hemisphere," historian H. E. Von Holst wrote to explain the intervention. "We proclaimed it our duty to put an end to it for ever as an intolerable stench in our nostrils and an outrage upon civilization and humanity."[142]

It was but a short and perhaps inevitable step that Americans also imagined to have "heard" Cubans ask for U.S. intervention—that is, Americans purporting to represent Cuban voices by way of the verse of their poems and the lyric of their music, thereupon ascribing to their own aesthetic production the representation of the Cuban reality. The use of the Cuban voice in the form of appeals for U.S. intervention was invented by the Americans so they could say what they themselves wanted to hear and validate what they themselves wanted to do. "Fair Cuba, we have heard thy cries, / Have seen thy pain and anguish," affirmed the lyric of "Free Cuba."[143] In John Keynton's song "Cuba Shall Be Free!" the lyric proclaimed, "A voice comes o'er the waters to proud Columbia's land / It brings a cry of pleading unto our Nation grand."[144] The lyric of "The Army Sails for Cuba Shortly" was explicit:

> We hear upon the Southern wind
> A helpless, suffering people's cry
> Borne across the Gulf Stream's rushing wave,
> "Bring to us succor, or else we die."[145]

J. R. Martin's appeal in "A Call from Cuba" represented the Cubans pleading with the Americans: "Rouse! Sons of Columbia, hear the cry of despair," and concluded, "They're our neighbors in Cuba; oh, hear their sad cry: / 'Save us, sons of Columbia, or haste, ere we die.'"[146] In "The Wreck of the Battleship Maine" the composers proclaimed, "She strives for liberty / She looks to us, and calls for aid."[147] Years later correspondent David Barry would remember war as a response to "the Cuban people . . . crying loudly to be rescued from the oppression of Spain."[148] Americans could not remain indifferent to the cries they imagined themselves to hear from their suffering neighbors.

IS HELP IN SIGHT AT LAST?

"Is Help in Sight at Last?" From *New York Journal*, April 3, 1898.

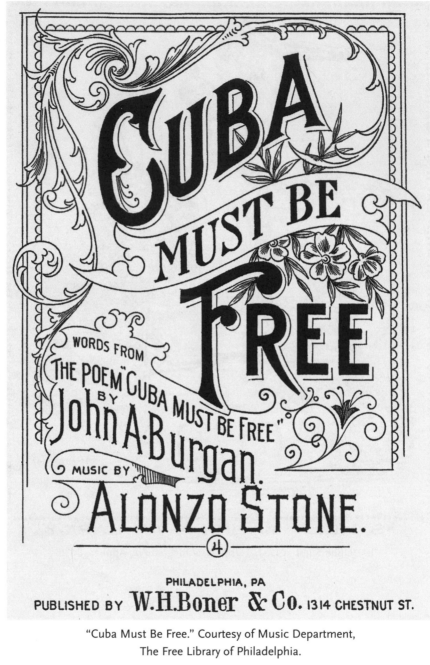

"Cuba Must Be Free." Courtesy of Music Department,
The Free Library of Philadelphia.

"Cuba Free!" Courtesy of Music Department, The Free Library of Philadelphia.

★ ★ ★

Americans assigned multiple metaphorical forms to Cuba throughout the nineteenth century, changing as circumstances changed. What remained constant, however, from which meaning was inferred and course of action implied, and indeed what gave enduring purpose to metaphorical representation, was the proposition of Cuba as "indispensable to the continuance and integrity of the Union itself." The island was depicted variously as Haiti, that is, as a site of potential disorder; as a neighbor to be controlled or to whom assistance was owed; in the form of Gibraltar as strategic fortress; or as ripe fruit ready for harvest. Each metaphor implied a different moral by which the Americans advanced their claim to Cuba. By the late 1890s, as the Cuban insurrection spread, Armenia had developed into another usable metaphor. Between 1894 and 1896, accounts of an estimated 200,000 Armenians having perished at the hands of Ottoman Turks provided a frame of reference to compare reports of Spanish pacification efforts in Cuba. "It is Armenia all over-again," lamented philosopher William James in 1898.[149]

The metaphor of Cuba as Armenia propounded an inescapable moral. "We have right here an Armenia at our own doors," Florida senator Wilkinson Call decried. "Here we stand motionless, a great and powerful country not six hours away from these scenes of useless bloodshed and destruction." Senator Call pointed to the "slaughter in Armenia" to characterize Cuba—"beneath our very eyes and within our reach"—and added, "Here is a war with terrible characteristics flagrant at our very doors. . . . I think we can not escape the responsibility which is so near to us."[150] Spain was "the Turk of the West," proclaimed Virginia senator John Daniel, "who has his hand on the Cuban throat, and who is starving there the women and children of our neighboring state."[151] The "atrocities of remote Armenia evoked the indignation of the civilized world," insisted the *Cleveland Plain Dealer*. "But dreadful as were the Turkish barbarities . . . they fell short . . . Spanish savagery in Cuba. [And] this close to our doors, some of it within a less distance than from Cleveland to Columbus."[152]

The proposition that proximity implied responsibility had found a new metaphorical depiction. New York representative William Sulzer proclaimed outright, "Cuba is our Armenia," and added, "Cuba lies at our very door and is a natural part of our geographical domain. The world will hold us responsible for the cruel, heartless, bloody outrages perpetrated there [by] Spain."[153] War to end Spanish barbarism was a matter of duty, Massachusetts representative Samuel Barrows exhorted, noting, "Spain is the Turkey of the New World and Cuba is our Armenia, and the people of this country have determined

TURK—"SHAKE. YOU'VE BROKEN THE RECORD."

"Armenian Massacres/Cuban Butcheries." Caption: "Turk—'Shake. You've broken the record.'" From *Leslie's Weekly*, April 21, 1898.

. . . .

that slaughter and oppression and massacre and starvation shall cease in that island."[154]

But the metaphor of Cuba as Armenia carried a clear moral. By 1898 the Americans had become inextricably implicated in a metaphor of their own making. Political leaders and opinion makers in the United States had earlier criticized European governments for their failure to intervene to end the bloodshed in Armenia. The logic of the use of the metaphor of Cuba as Armenia must be understood as depictive surrogate: the denunciation of European inaction in Armenia to prompt the Americans into action in Cuba. "Didn't we grate against Turkey for the Armenian outrages?" thundered the Reverend

W. C. Steele. "Didn't we find fault with the powers of Europe? . . . If the Armenians should have been protected, and we found fault because they were not, surely those who are our neighbors, those who are appealing to us for help, those whom we feel we have tried by our sympathy to sustain, should have our aid in a just cause."[155] The *Philadelphia Inquirer* drew the moral explicitly:

> During the continuation of the atrocities of the Turks upon the Armenians this country showed a warm heart for the victims. . . . But we took no action; we left action to the powers of Europe, and they afraid of each other, permitted the atrocities to go on. But here, within less than one hundred miles of our own shores, the result of the butcher [General Valeriano] Weyler claims many more thousands of victims than Armenia has shown. It is time to wipe out this horrible blot upon the history of civilization of this century. . . . The American people cannot close their eyes to the scenes witness[ed] almost within a cannon's shot of the United States.[156]

Proximity mattered. Cubans "are so much nearer to us," the *New York Times* decried, and their "afflictions sharply disturb our tranquility." To the point: "The slaughter of the Armenians never disturbed our peace or threatened to disturb it. They were far away."[157] If Armenia had been as "close to our shores as Cuba is," philosopher Felix Adler, founder of the Society for Ethical Culture, asked rhetorically, "who can question for a moment that the American people would have intervened and should have been justified in intervening?" And to the point: "The circumstance of propinquity makes a great difference."[158] "Not long ago," lamented the *New York Tribune*, "the heart of the American people was profoundly moved by the woes of the Armenians." Continued the *Tribune*, "The woes of the Cuban people are far greater than ever were those of the Armenians. For every one who perished in Armenia five have perished in Cuba. For every one in distress in Armenia five are in distress in Cuba. . . . The history of the world scarcely contains a more horrible chapter. And all this is not, as was Armenia, thousands of miles away, but almost within sight of our own shores."[159]

The metaphor of Cuba as Armenia summoned the Americans to action for precisely the same reasons they had exhorted the Europeans to act. "The concert of Europe was not an effective concert," the *New York Times* lamented, and as a result of internal jealousies failed "to purge Europe of the disgrace of Turkish misrule. It was not an excuse that the citizen of a civilized nation could make without some shame." This was "exactly the position in which we find ourselves with respect to Cuba. The whole power and the whole responsibility is ours." The *Times* added, "The civilized world would have a right to cry shame upon us if we permitted the barbarities of Spanish rule in Cuba to continue."[160] For more than "three years a terrible tragedy has been enacted almost within sight of our shores," the *Minneapolis Journal* reminded its readers in early 1898. To the point: "Americans have damned Great Britain and Russia for not interfering to stay the red hands of the Turkish butchers in Armenia, and yet a worse [condition] than Armenia piteously pleads to us almost at our own shores. This great nation cannot avoid its duty."[161]

The Americans could hardly do less than what they demanded of the Europeans. Indeed, the representation of Cuba as Armenia provided an opportunity for the United States to demonstrate its moral superiority over Europe. "We are attempting to do for Cuba what the moral sense of our people demanded that the great powers of Europe should do for Armenia, and which we censured them for not doing," proclaimed Bishop O. W. Whitaker of the Protestant Episcopal Church.[162] Journalist Talcott Williams agreed and later exulted, "We drew the sword for Cuba when Europe stood with sheathed sword before worse and more brutal deeds in Armenia. We acted; Europe did not." He continued, "Our hearts burned within us as we saw Christian Europe turning back from clear duty for selfish reasons and a sense of the risks that might come [with] war, as if history knew any risk greater than unredressed injustice and duty disregarded. . . . The general decision grew and deepened that this land would have no unavenged Armenia at its doors and would not share the blood-guiltiness of Europe, which knew its duty to humanity and did it not. . . . The duties undone in Armenia were discharged in Cuba."[163]

★ ★ ★

If the image of Armenia provoked condemnation, the accounts of civilian deaths produced indignation. No aspect of conditions in Cuba aroused greater denunciation of Spain in the United States than the reports of Spanish mistreatment of children and, especially, of women. Americans were particularly disposed to heap opprobrium on Spanish authorities for their failure to discharge their responsibility to protect the weak and vulnerable, and in the process added the dimension of gender to the metaphorical constructs of Cuba.

The canons of manhood were deeply inscribed within the duty to protect women and children, and to default on the obligation to protect the weak—as a matter of gender and age—was to flout the very norms by which the prerogatives of patriarchy were ratified. In other words, Spain had forfeited the right to rule.

The failure of Spain to uphold proper manly conduct merged with the obligations of the United States as neighbor. Delaware senator George Gray alluded to "the propinquity of Cuba" as cause sufficient for war in 1898, insisting that "we can not forever keep our place and say we are not our brother's

DOOMED TO DEATH.

"Doomed to Death."
From *New York World*,
December 25, 1897.

. . . .

keeper. God himself will hold us to responsibility if we continue to plead thus." Gray denounced the "violated womanhood and childhood and motherhood . . . perpetrated right at our own doors" and thereupon proceeded to raise the metaphor of neighbor to the level of moral imperative:

> I liken the action which is proposed to be taken in this country . . . to that of a man in a civilized community who is a law-abiding citizen, who has next door to him a villainous and cruel neighbor who every day chokes his wife and starves and maltreats his children, and because he is a law-abiding citizen he bears it and bears it and bears it for days and weeks until at last he can bear it no longer, and, law or no law, he enters the residence of his neighbor, takes him by the throat, and says, "Take your hand off of that woman and let these children go;" and all his neighbors applaud. That is what we propose to do.[164]

The metaphor of Cuba as neighbor in dire circumstances had aroused powerful emotions in the United States and, indeed, was an image that dominated the debate leading to war. That neighbors were depicted principally as women and children, moreover, implied a condition of defenselessness that could not but arouse popular indignation further. "If you see your neighbor in his garden beating out his daughter's brains with a club and breaking the bone of his little son," the *New York Times* argued by metaphor, "it depends solely on you whether you intervene or not." The *Times* continued, "If you can stand the spectacle, why, you go on reading . . . , only occasionally looking out the window of your comfortable chamber to see how the fellow is getting along, and how the children stand it. Other men are so constituted that they cannot endure such sights. They want to jump over the fence and rescue the daughter and the little son and throttle the inhuman father and lug him off to jail. . . . Nations that have gone to the length of intervention to stop bloodshed have commonly been applauded by historians."[165]

New metaphors of Cuba as neighbor and women/children seized the popular imagination. "One may not enter his neighbor's garden without consent," proclaimed the *Cleveland Plain Dealer*, "but if he saw a child being ill treated by a tramp, he would throw ceremony to the wind and rush to the rescue of the child without asking permissions."[166] "The oppressed Cubans and their starving women and children are knocking at our doors," decried former president Benjamin Harrison. "Their cries penetrate our slumbers. . . . We have as a nation toward Cuba the same high commission which every brave-hearted man has to strike down the ruffian who in his presence beats a woman or a child and will not desist. For what, if not for this, does God make a man or a nation strong?"[167]

"PEACE — BUT QUIT THAT."

"Peace—But Quit That." From *New York World*, March 9, 1898.

. . . .

Almost daily accounts of women abused, lurid stories of women assaulted and ravished by the Spanish soldiery, were received in the United States with mounting indignation. Newspaper editorials gave particular attention to the plight of noncombatants. "Hollow-eyed mothers, with nursing babies in their arms," decried the *Baltimore Morning Herald*, "sit in the shadow of doorways and helplessly watch the death-struggles of their darlings, hunger having dried up in the maternal breast the fountains of nourishment. Children, unable to comprehend anything except the craving of the stomach, cry appealingly for bread."[168] The *New York World* protested the "injustice, rapine, the murder of helpless women and children," all occurring "in an island lying at our doors,"

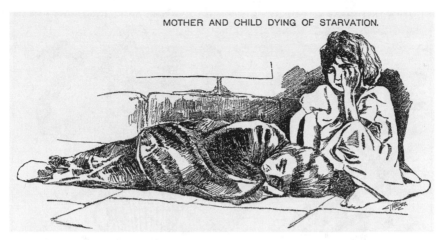

"Mother and Child Dying of Starvation." From *New York World*, December 5, 1897.

. . . .

a condition that "an enlightened nation which has assumed the guardianship of human liberty in this hemisphere ought [not] to permit."[169]

Writers and poets also denounced Spanish pacification methods. Spaniards "made war on women," Trumbull White charged, and were given to the "persecution of the weaker sex."[170] "What have they done that their women are so ravished?" asked poet Margaret Alden in her verse. "Their innocent children torn from their arms / And butchered like sheep? Why is this torture lavished on Cuba?"[171] The Cuban soldiers had "been barbarously robbed of their mothers, wives, sisters and offspring," reported poet-novelist Julian Hawthorne—Nathaniel's son—from Havana. He continued, "[They] are dying with accompaniments of misery and suffering almost inconceivable, wholly indescribable. They fall dead in the streets; they die before your eyes, as you stand in the wretched pens where they are huddled together. They die with an agony of body which is equalled only by the hopeless anguish and forlornness of their minds. . . . They die unpitied and uncared for."[172]

The halls of Congress echoed with thundering denunciation of Spanish conduct. Illinois senator William Mason decried the "killing [of] the Cuban women and children . . . and selling [of] the daughters of the insurgents to the lustful sensuality of the Spanish army," and he spoke of "hearing the voices of children and women in our ears, innocent girls ravished and murdered by the Spanish soldiery," all "within 90 miles of our shore."[173] For Utah senator Frank Cannon, Spanish governor general Valeriano Weyler was "the ravisher of women . . . and the crucifer of children," while Kansas representative

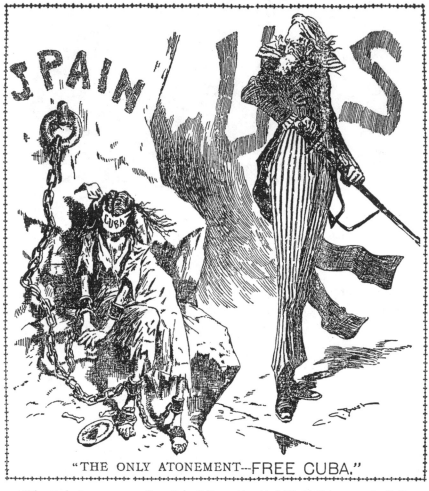

"THE ONLY ATONEMENT---FREE CUBA."

"The Only Atonement—Free Cuba." From *New York World*, February 28, 1898.

. . . .

William Vincent berated the "brutal butcher Weyler for purposefully starv[ing] thousands of . . . innocent women and children to death."[174] "Dogs fatten on the flesh of unburied mothers and babes," California representative Marion de Vries alleged, "to be in turn eaten by the starving who chance to survive a day."[175] From the floor of the Senate, McKinley's future secretary of state John Sherman held sway with graphic accounts of the Spanish capture of Cuban towns and the internment of women, "to be saved for orgies later on." Sherman described Weyler presiding over wholesale abuse of Cuban women: "[General Valeriano Weyler] signaled to his officers to bring forward the girls.

They were pretty, dainty senoritas, in the first flush and blush of womanhood, and Weyler's smile grew more sardonic as they were marched before him. Then and there . . . he had his soldiers strip the youngest women of every article of clothing, and for half an hour force them to dance upon the green turf with all the troops looking on."[176]

Accounts of Spanish abuse of women were joined in a larger narrative in which the island itself underwent anthropomorphic transformation. A new metaphor of Cuba emerged, one that imagined Cuba as woman and depicted the island as victim, mostly the victim of the misdeeds of Spanish men but sometimes also represented as victim of the misconduct of Cuban men. Cuba assumed various representations of a helpless woman, subjected to insult and indignity, victim of violence and violation, often drawn—literally and figuratively—in plaintive pose beseeching the Americans for rescue and redemption.

The moral of the metaphor of Cuba as woman was not difficult to divine. "There are those who say that the affairs of Cuba are not the affairs of the United States," argued Nebraska senator John Thurston, "[those] who insist that we can stand idly by and see the island devastated and depopulated." Thurston continued: "I can sit in my comfortable parlor, with my loved ones gathered about me, and through my plate glass window see a fiend outraging a helpless woman nearby, and I can legally say, 'This is no affair of mine—it is not happening on my premises;' and I can turn away. . . . But if I do I am a coward and a cur unfit to live and, God knows, unfit to die. And yet I cannot . . . save the woman without the exercise of force. We cannot intervene and save Cuba without the exercise of force, and force means war."[177]

Pictorial depictions of Cuba as woman filled daily newspapers and weekly magazines across the country, as editorial cartoons and caricatures, and provided visual corroboration of a metaphor of portentous reach. The image of the island as a woman mistreated by her Spanish oppressors fixed in the political vernacular and popular imagination the image of Cuba as damsel in distress. The metaphor was loaded with moral and meaning, of course, informed by social conventions that never need have been articulated in order to have been acted upon. The pictorial representation of Cuba as woman strengthened—visually and viscerally—notions of chivalric duty from which to infer gender-scripted obligations and culturally derived codes of conduct to act upon. Meaning was understood intuitively; action was required prescriptively. The need to rescue women in distress—in this instance in Cuba in 1898—may well be one of the first occasions on which the Americans employed the defense of women as pretext for armed intervention abroad. "The trope of rescuing women and children," commented historian Emily Rosenberg on pat-

"The Cuban Melodrama." Caption: "The Noble Hero (to the Heavy Villain) — 'Stand back, there, gol darn ye! — If you force this thing to a fifth act, remember that's where I git in *my* work!'" From *Puck*, June 3, 1896.

. . . .

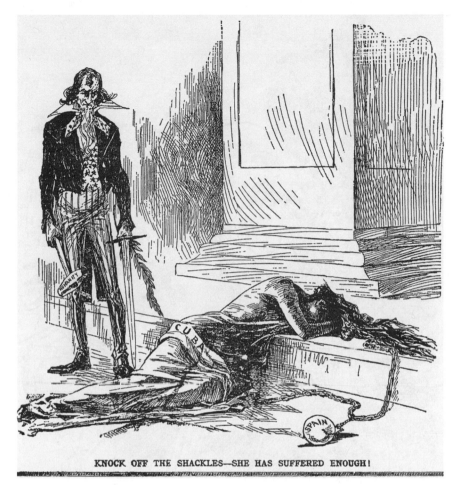

KNOCK OFF THE SHACKLES—SHE HAS SUFFERED ENOUGH!

"Knock Off the Shackles—She Has Suffered Enough!"
From *Philadelphia Inquirer*, March 27, 1898.

. . . .

terns of U.S. intervention, "may be viewed as emerging from a social imaginary dominated by a masculinized national state that casts itself in a paternal role, saving those who are abused by rival men and nations." Rosenberg was correct to note that Americans were thus persuaded "to provide protection to women or to a country—emblematically feminized—that rival men are violating."[178]

★ ★ ★

These were ways that Americans summoned themselves to war in 1898, aroused to uphold those culturally determined codes by which they took mea-

"Hands Off!" From *Chicago Tribune*, April 19, 1898.

. . . .

UNCLE SAM—I'll take care of this lady now.

"Uncle Sam—I'll Take Care of This Lady Now." From
Baltimore Morning Herald, March 12, 1898.

. . . .

sure of their own self-worth. Spanish abuse of women and children trans-
gressed codes of common decency, displaying behavior that a righteous
people could not permit to continue without themselves becoming implicated in shame. But most of all, men—self-styled real men—power brokers
and opinion makers as they were, could not stand idly by and bear witness
to the violation of those norms upon which manhood defended the prerogative of patriarchy. "If your neighbor across the street pens up his children in
a stockade to starve them to death," the *New York World* asked rhetorically,
"varying his diabolism by slashing and shooting women and old men in his
door-yard, is it 'behaving like a man' to shut your door and turn your back?"[179]

"Halt!" From *Chicago Tribune*, May 1, 1898.

. . . .

Some years later, historian Arthur Dunn remembered the drift to war in 1898 in specific gender terms. "The stories about what was taking place in Cuba," Dunn recalled, "were told in a manner to inflame American manhood."[180]

The representation of Cuba as a woman abused and Spain as male abuser provided the context for the celebrated case involving the arrest and rescue of Evangelina Cossío Cisneros in 1897. That the rescue was very much a staged affair matters less than its capacity to reveal the gender intricacies with which the war in Cuba had insinuated itself into the North American imagination, among both men and women. To the unsuspecting public, the story of Evangelina was the stuff of a real-life plot, as moral and melodrama, in the process of which the metaphor worked its effect without a trace of ever having been present. The eighteen-year-old daughter of a Cuban insurgent leader, Evangelina Cossío Cisneros was charged with sedition and incarcerated in 1897 in the notorious Casa de Recojidas prison in Havana, "among depraved Negresses of Havana . . . and the vilest class of abandoned women of Havana," reported the *New York Journal*.[181] Indeed, the imprisonment of Evangelina became a cause célèbre for William Randolph Hearst and was subsequently reported by the *New York Journal* in lurid detail, filled with accounts of threats of ravishment by her Spanish male captors, abuse in prison, and execrable prison conditions.[182]

The plight of Evangelina developed quickly into an American crusade. In a campaign orchestrated principally by Hearst and the *New York Journal*, women across the United States directed letter-writing campaigns to the pope and the Spanish queen regent, sponsored petition drives to Congress, and organized public rallies to demand Evangelina's release from prison. The campaign attracted many of the most prominent women in the United States, including Varina Jefferson Davis, widow of the former Confederate president; Nancy McKinley, the president's mother; Sarah Cecilia Sherman, wife of the secretary of state; Julia Dent Grant, widow of President Ulysses Grant; Letitia Tyler Semper, daughter of President John Tyler; Eugenia Washington, the grandniece of George Washington; and Mary Jane Carlisle, wife of the secretary of the Treasury. Other prominent personalities included Elizabeth Cady Stanton, Clara Barton, and Julia Ward Howe. In late 1897, in a spectacular turn of events, the *New York Journal* reported that it had arranged for the escape of Evangelina to the United States. Upon her arrival in New York, Evangelina was received as the "Cuban Joan of Arc" at a mass rally organized by Hearst and attended by more than 75,000 people.[183] Amy Ephron's 1999 novel of Evangelina, *White Rose/Una Rosa Blanca*, offers a measure of verisimilitude in the rendering of the New York reception:

Thousands had gathered to watch the procession. [She] rode along the New York City streets from the Waldorf-Astoria, down Park Avenue, to Madison Square, behind an honour guard of soldiers, policemen, and white-uniformed naval cadets, all marching in synchronized step to New York's finest marching band. . . . [She was] showered by handfuls of brightly colored confetti and long, thin ribbons of ticker tape by the throngs of people in the streets and the many spectators that crowded the open windows of the buildings on Park Avenue. . . . The crowd cheered so loudly that she was momentarily deafened by it, excited and frightened at the same time. And there shouts of "Evang-e-lina" and "Viva Cuba Libre." The crowd was there for her.[184]

It is difficult to take full measure of the Evangelina Cossío Cisneros affair. Her life was at the center of intense public attention for three months. Her ascent to fame and descent into obscurity were rapid — perhaps a foreshadowing of celebrity culture in the making, a case, too, of victim celebrated as hero/heroine.[185] Certainly her story served the interests of William Randolph Hearst and the circulation of the *New York Journal*. The emphasis on the lurid and the sensational bore the distinctive traits of the "yellow journalism" of the time.[186] That Evangelina so fully captured the popular imagination, however, suggests a cultural phenomenon of far-reaching implications and offers insight into the power of images to arouse public sentiment. "The whole country hung breathless on the fate of Evangelina," Sydney Clark later wrote. "At the breakfast table, at the club, at social gatherings, at church meetings, the traditional cruelty of Spain was played up and focused on its treatment of this girl."[187] Evangelina provided a face and a real-life presence to the allegations of Spanish abuse of Cuban women. And not just any face: she was young, a woman of means, attractive, and white. "Miss Cisneros is," the *New York Journal* pointed out, "according to all who have seen her, the most beautiful girl in the island of Cuba"; she was "delicate, refined, sensitive, unused to hardship, absolutely ignorant of vice" — all of which had "excited the lust" of Spanish officials.[188] Writer George Musgrave was spellbound by Evangelina: "a white face, young, pure, and beautiful; a maiden of perhaps seventeen. . . . She resembled the Madonna of an old master."[189]

The staged rescue of Evangelina from her captors assumed fully the dimensions of a morality play, unfolding as a real-life enactment of a popular narrative, a case of life imitating a metaphor. If one Cuban woman could be rescued from Spanish mistreatment, why not all Cuban women — indeed, why not Cuba imagined as a woman? "The ogre is defrauded. The maiden is rescued," exulted Julian Hawthorne. "Evangelina is not the only woman whom

Evangelina Cossío Cisneros, ca. 1897. From *The Story of Evangelina Cisneros
(Evangelina Betancourt Cossío y Cisneros) Told by Herself* (New York, 1898).

. . . .

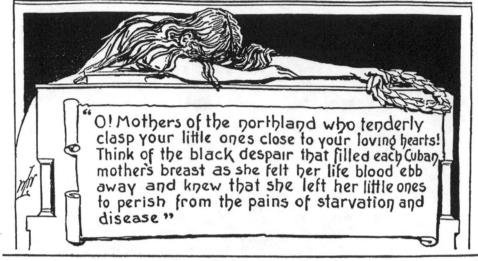

MRS. SENATOR THURSTON'S DYING WORDS TO THE WOMEN OF AMERICA.
[Reprint, by request, from THE TRIBUNE of March 18.]

" O! Mothers of the northland who tenderly clasp your little ones close to your loving hearts! Think of the black despair that filled each Cuban mother's breast as she felt her life blood ebb away and knew that she left her little ones to perish from the pains of starvation and disease "

"Mrs. Senator Thurston's Dying Words to the Women of America."
From *Chicago Tribune*, March 18, 1898.

. . . .

Weyler, with the connivance of the Spanish Government, has outraged. On the contrary, she is the representative of them all. . . . In the person of Evangelina Cisneros, Cuba appeals to us."[190]

The theater of Evangelina Cisneros was followed by the drama of Martha Thurston. The wife of Nebraska senator John Thurston, Martha accompanied her husband on a fact-finding mission to Cuba in March 1898. While in Matanzas, she died of a heart attack. A member of the Daughters of the American Revolution and the National Relief Association for Cuba, Martha Thurston had been active in Cuba-related philanthropy, especially as it had involved the defense of women and children. Upon her arrival in Cuba, she had cabled to several North American women's organizations a series of eyewitness accounts detailing conditions in Cuba. She wrote of abandoned women and orphaned children, of starvation and disease, of death and despair. "Oh! Mothers of the Northland," Thurston pleaded from Havana on March 11, only two days before her death, "who tenderly clasp your little ones close to your loving hearts!" She continued, "Think of the black despair that filled each Cuban mother's breast as she felt her life blood ebb away and knew that she left her little ones to perish from the pains of starvation and disease. I have no words vivid enough to bring before you the poor, shrunken lips, the brown skin on some of them already deprived of life and falling off in great patches, the great sunken eyes, the swollen lips and tongue telling their own tale of woe and misery."[191]

Thurston's association with Cuban relief work—and her death in Cuba— conferred on her something of a martyrdom for the cause of women and children in Cuba. Indeed, her death was attributed to the heartbreak resulting from the despair and destitution that she had witnessed in Cuba. "The shock caused by the unspeakable sufferings of the 'reconcentrados' had killed her," pronounced journalist Andrew Draper.[192] "Mrs. Thurston's dying wish to her husband," reported the *New York Times*, "was that he should lose no time on account of her death to do his utmost to save and free Cuba and its people." The *Woman's Tribune* exhorted its readers to honor Mrs. Thurston's death by pursuing "more earnestly the relief work which had enlisted her sympathies."[193]

★ ★ ★

The power of the metaphor of Cuba as woman lay in its capacity to summon moral indignation. Power brokers and opinion makers, the evidence suggests, almost all of whom were men, detected in allegations of Spanish mistreatment of women a violation of the very responsibility by which men were held accountable and indeed the very obligations upon which the moral claim to patriarchy rested. If manly men in the United States failed to respond and vindicate the honor of American manhood, that, too, would signal a break of the responsibility of patriarchy. The metaphor was packed with culturally prescribed codes of conduct understood intuitively by all and in which men were especially implicated. To represent Cuba as woman was to depict the island as distressed and forsaken, helpless and defenseless; it was to sensationalize the mistreatment of women in Cuba and to summon men to discharge their manly duty and uphold responsibilities inscribed in norms of manhood. "At heart," historian W. E. Woodward would later write with pride of the war with Spain, "we are a nation of Sir Galahads."[194]

On occasion men in power could be also goaded by women to fulfill their manly duties. "There can be no compromise short of absolute liberty [for Cuba]," insisted Mrs. Gordon of Atlanta. "To my woman's thinking it seems that the United States should realize this, and that its manhood, so to speak, should so act that this carnival of blood at its own door should cease!"[195] Marie Madison, editor of the women's monthly *American Home Magazine*, excoriated American political leadership for failure to act in Cuba: "Shame, shame that [President Grover Cleveland] has allowed the wholesale butchery of women and children at his very door."[196] The *Woman's Tribune* was categorical: "Immediate and earnest effort is necessary, not only to relieve the present suffering in the island, but to show that all our national talk and sympathy

ANOTHER OLD WOMAN TRIES TO SWEEP BACK THE SEA.

"Another Old Woman Tries to Sweep Back the Sea."
From *New York Journal*, March 30, 1898.

. . . .

with Cuba was not a sham."[197] Ellen Henrotin, president of the Federation of Women's Clubs, proclaimed that "humanity demands that we cry a halt and force a cessation of these barbarous conditions."[198] Conditions in Cuba, lamented *Woman's Exponent*, were deplorable, "and naturally one would think that this country should send help."[199] With the passage of the congressional war resolution in April 1898, the *Woman's Tribune* was exultant: "The United States, having undertaken in the interests of humanity and civilization to protect its weaker neighbor, is waging a more holy war than even if it were in self-defense. . . . The United States is the weapon in the hand of destiny to limit the power of a nation to continue the bloody atrocities which have always marked its career."[200] That President McKinley appeared to have delayed taking decisive action had in fact raised questions about his manhood. "For this he has been vilified," commented the *Brooklyn Eagle*. "For this he has been told that he has been recreant and nerveless and of meager manhood. For this he has been taunted and reviled."[201] In March 1898, the *New York Journal* published an

"U.S.: 'Don't cry, little girl. Uncle Sam is going to take you home with him.
After that I'll tend to you, young man.'" From *Indianapolis News*,
reprinted in *Chicago Tribune*, April 2, 1898.

. . . .

editorial cartoon depicting President McKinley dressed as an elderly woman
attempting to sweep back the incoming tide of public opinion.

It was indeed as a matter of manly duty that vast numbers of Americans
determined to rescue Cuba from her abusive male captors. Historian Kristin
Hoganson has written persuasively about the fin de siècle gender angst in the
United States, as North American men were beset with deepening concern
about their manhood. The depiction of Spanish men as "savage rapists who
lacked the moral sensibilities and self-restraint of civilized men," Hoganson

suggested, thus invited American men "to assume the role of the heroic rescuer to the Cuban damsel. . . . A failure to intervene . . . would reveal a lack of chivalry in American men."[202]

These concerns did much to define the terms and set the tone of the national debate during the late 1890s. The representation of the conflict in Cuba entered those discursive realms in which the very manhood of North American men was placed in question. To doubt "the natural promptings of humanity and feelings of indignation coursing through the masses of the people," warned one letter writer to the *New York Times*, would have been "to doubt the manhood of the Nation."[203] The *New York World* appealed to metaphor. "If a policeman or any able-bodied citizen should see a ruffian attempting to murder a woman," asked the *World*, "ought he to refrain from interfering on the ground that he might get hurt or that it was none of his affair? A pusillanimous cad who spends his time lying about his neighbors and sneering at 'abstractions' like duty and honor and courage would no doubt run away to his club as quickly as possible. A *man* would interfere."[204] Ohio representative John Lentz called for war against Spain "in the name of the American manhood," while Delaware senator George Gray vowed to "rally the manhood of America" to end the bloodshed in Cuba.[205] "The pitiful cries of the helpless, starving women and children of Cuba can be borne no longer," General P. S. Michie exhorted. "Our helping hand must be stayed no longer. Our patience is exhausted and our very manhood cries out against us as we stand with full granaries and overflowing hearts, ready to act. . . . Let us end the reign of terror, rapine, murder, and treachery that has so long prevailed at our very doors."[206] The Reverend Howard Duffield of the First Presbyterian Church affirmed outright in March 1898 that at stake were no longer political matters but that, rather, "the questions at issue were questions of manhood."[207]

The metaphor of manhood implied masculinity and virility and a relationship between bodily strength and physical prowess, on one hand, and military conquest, on the other. Amy Kaplan has noted the increasing references during the late 1890s to the "body as metaphor for international aggression" and the "biological metaphor justifying territorial expansion . . . [comparing] national growth to an organic body, which must continue to grow or die."[208] Nationhood and manhood were joined by way of metaphor.

But there was another meaning to the metaphors of Cuba as a woman abused and Cuban women as mistreated. If Spanish manhood had forfeited its rightful authority to govern, Cuban manhood had also failed to demonstrate its moral claim to rule. That there was a need at all to deliver Cuba from Spanish misrule and rescue Cuban women from Spanish misconduct, that is, that American men were called upon—or more correctly, called upon themselves—to do what Cuban men were said to be unable to do, could not but raise questions about the fitness of Cuban males to discharge the responsibilities associated with manhood. Cuban men unable to protect women, including and especially as it involved the protection of Cuba itself (imagined as woman)—deemed "indispensable to the continuance and integrity of the Union itself"—implied forfeiture of the privilege of male, including those prerogatives associated with power, self-governance, and independence. The claim of North American men to power in defense of Cuban women was thus understood to supersede the claim of Cuban men to power, precisely because Cubans had failed to protect their women. "The Cuban," commented writer Howard Grose, "is lacking chiefly in the qualities that are conspicuous in American men—virility, initiative, will-power, tenacity, reverence for women, and conscience." Cuban men had "yet to be taught to value and respect the opposite sex at its true worth," Grose concluded, "and this will take a new generation." In the meantime, it would be the task of the Americans to introduce reforms so that "the regeneration of woman be secured up to a plane where her highest faculties of heart, brain, and hand may be fully and freely developed."[209]

That Cubans had failed in the course of thirty years to obtain their own independence, moreover, also raised doubts about their manhood. Writing during the Ten Years War, *New York Herald* correspondent James O'Kelly insisted that "the climate and an indolent mode of life" had "combined to make the Cuban of the city effeminate."[210] Writer James Steele later dwelled at length on the relationship between the failure to end Spanish rule during the Ten Years War and Cuban manhood. He characterized the Cuban man as "the born dandy" who wore jewelry "like a woman, and like a woman's." The face of the Cuban man was "weak . . . and molded in its effeminate features by the things he thinks about." The Cuban man was "weak and vacillating" and "flaccid without fibre"; he was "wanting in appreciation of manliness for its own sake." Concluded Steele, "Many a year will elapse before the Cuban will make a successful effort for liberty, if ever."[211] *Boston Globe* editor Maturin Ballou questioned Cuban manliness at length. "In the consciousness of strength is strength," Ballou wrote in 1888, "but the Creole republicans have never yet evinced the necessary degree of true manhood to . . . command the respect of other nationalities." He continued:

It appears incredible that an intelligent people, within so short a distance of our Southern coast, constantly visited by the citizens of a free republic, and

"Give Me Liberty or Give Me Death." From *Cartoons of the War of 1898 with Spain* (Chicago, 1898).

. . . .

having the example of successful revolt set them by the men of the same race, both in the North and the South, weighed down by oppression almost without parallel, should never have aimed an effectual blow at their oppressors. It would seem that the softness of the unrivaled climate of those skies, beneath which it is luxury only to exist, has unnerved this people, and that the effeminate spirit of the original inhabitants had descended in retribution to the posterity of their conquerors.[212]

"To the faults of the [native Cuban] men of the parent race," argued the *Philadelphia Manufacturer* in 1889, "they add effeminacy and a distaste for exertion which amounts really to disease." And more:

> They are helpless, idle, of defective morals, and unfitted by nature and experience for discharging the obligations of citizenship in a great and free republic. Their lack of manly force and self-respect is demonstrated by the supineness with which they have so long submitted to Spanish oppression, and even their attempts at rebellion have been so pitifully ineffective that they have risen little above the dignity of farce. To clothe such men with the responsibilities of directing [self-]government . . . would be to summon them to the performance of functions for which they have not the smallest capacity.[213]

Not a few—like Congregationalist minister Washington Gladden—drew the obvious inference: "A people incapable of freeing itself is incapable of governing itself."[214]

The metaphor of Cuba as woman abused, together with accounts of Cuban women as defenseless and helpless, provided the Americans with more than adequate reason to preempt the Cuban claim to rule. "We might be obliged to stay there," mused Wisconsin senator John Spooner on the eve of war, "in the discharge of a duty imposed by humanity and civilization, which could not be ignored, until peace was restored and life and womanhood safe." Spooner warned: "If our armies should occupy Cuba, if the Spaniards should be expelled, as the Spanish must and will be expelled from Cuba, and [General Máximo] Gomez should not be able to restrain those [Cubans] who follow his standard—for in them, remember, is the hot blood of the Spanish people . . . —if he should find himself unable to protect the women of that island from lust . . . it would be the duty, as it would be the right of the Government of the United States, to lay a repressive hand upon his forces and to preserve peace."[215]

Cuba would still appear periodically in pictorial depictions as damsel in distress after 1898. Henceforth, however, the villain was no longer the Spaniards but, rather, the Cubans themselves. But it was more complex still. Pictorial representations not only conveyed image; they also assigned voice. Cuba thus imagined—usually as woman—was fashioned as supplicant appealing to the Americans for intercession in behalf of her well-being. In the months and years that followed 1898, pictorial representations of Cuba as woman defended by the United States against mistreatment by Cuban men filled U.S. publications. The Americans thus endowed their representation of Cuba as woman with a voice, disposed to make utterances by which North American self-interests were represented as fulfillment of Cuban wishes. That is, the

"If you leave me to myself it will mean trouble. With your help I can have Peace and Prosperity. Do not desert me!" From *Puck*, November 1, 1899.

. . . .

Americans entitled themselves to pursue national interests in the guise of meeting Cuban desires as imagined by American needs.

★ ★ ★

Metaphorical depictions possessed powerful emotional content. They summoned passion to purpose and conferred propriety on power. The depictive efficacy of the metaphor lay in its capacity to evoke a normative model as means of cognitive transport, to imagine the real in the form of an ideal and thereupon act as if it were a matter of fact. These were images inscribed with meaning inferred from cultural canons, always in the form of an argument. The metaphor worked because meaning was derived from a moral order in which all were implicated, which meant, too, that it is reasonable to presume that all were susceptible to the motive of the moral. It worked mostly also because it had an uncanny ability to reflect back to the Americans their claims to moral authenticity; that is, it was easy to believe because it was faith that informed its use in the first place.

Americans who lived through the final years of the nineteenth century

"Save Me from My Friends!" Caption: "Taking Cuba from Spain was easy.
Preserving it from overzealous Cuban patriots is another matter."
From *Puck*, September 7, 1898.

. . . .

would thereafter arrange the narrative order of the circumstances of the war
in conformity with the dominant imagery of their time. A war of national interests was consecrated as a project of selfless purport, all properly within the
dominant metaphorical constructs of the late nineteenth century. Americans
looked to their political leaders for some confirmation of what they believed,
and especially for reassurance that they were right to believe it. The use of
metaphor blurred the distinction between moral intent and political purpose.
The Americans effectively politicized the language; more precisely, they fashioned a vernacular perfectly suited to the moral imperative with which they
embarked on empire. The idiom of empire privileged metaphor as a dominant
mode of representation. The United States had no motive other than "a desire
to discharge a duty to mankind," William Howard Taft insisted in 1907, an
achievement that "ought to fill every American with pride." The United States
had acted to "end an international scandal at the doors of this country . . .
in accordance with the unselfish desire of the American people to help their
oppressed neighbors."[216] "The revolt in Cuba," Theodore Roosevelt recalled

"Good Government vs. Revolution: An Easy Choice." From *Puck*, April 17, 1901.

. . . .

years later, "had dragged its weary length until conditions in the island had become so dreadful as to be a standing disgrace to us for permitting them to exist." He added, "Cuba was at our very doors. It was a dreadful thing for us to sit supinely and watch her death agony. It was our duty . . . to stop the devastation and destruction."[217] No one less than naval strategist Captain Alfred T. Mahan alluded to the "moral obligation" of "a powerful neighboring State," something akin to "the moral consciousness of a mighty people" faced with "an afflicted community as that of Cuba at their doors" and the fact "that the duty of stopping the evil rests upon them."[218] The United States, Massachusetts senator Henry Cabot Lodge later explained, was obligated to end Spanish misgovernment "in its own neighborhood" and "at our very doors."[219] Writer Andrew Draper insisted that the war would not have "been made if Spain's atrocities had not been perpetrated upon a weak people at our very doors," and added: "A self-respecting people could not permit these things in its presence, any more than a man of honor can see a ruffian strike a woman without interposing."[220]

Metaphorical representations of duty—to aid a neighbor in need and rescue

IMPROVING ALREADY.

Dr. McKinley: "What you need is a rest."

"Improving Already." Caption: "Dr. McKinley: 'What you need is a rest.'"
From *Baltimore Morning Herald*, March 20, 1898.

. . . .

a damsel in distress—developed into the principal narrative through which
the Americans persuaded themselves of righteous motive and noble meaning
for their purpose in Cuba. The national discourse expanded into a belief system, the way that the telling of the past developed into historical knowledge,
at once as vindication of self-esteem and validation of power. This necessarily
must be understood as a process through which Americans confirmed among
themselves the need to be true to self-representation and the self-proclaimed

sources of their own righteousness. This is not to impute cynicism to the sentiments that motivated North American intervention in Cuba. On the contrary, there is, in fact, little basis to dispute the authenticity of popular sentiment. It is difficult to imagine that anyone who reads the poems or examines the lyrics of the songs or studies the texts of church sermons, for example, could doubt the sincerity of public support for the Cuban cause.

That the American people supported the Cuban cause did not mean that their government did, or that the government would not later seek to persuade the American people that independence for Cuba was not feasible—for the best interests of the Cubans, of course. Rather, the point here is to underscore the ease with which national interest was transacted as national ideals, and vice versa. "We should be unworthy of our own heritage of freedom," intoned the *New York World* on the eve of war, "did we fail longer to stretch out our strong arm to succor and to save the Cuban patriots, whose motto now is that proclaimed by Patrick Henry, of Virginia, in 1776: 'Give us liberty or give us death!'"[221] Writer Arthur Pillsbury used a different imagery but with similar effect. "Conceived in the womb of duty," was Pillsbury's way to describe the North American purpose in Cuba, and he added: "The duty at hand was to put an end to a condition no longer tolerable, and the nation's duty became the national policy. It avowed this policy with honesty, and had no other; for there was at hand no other duty to determine another policy."[222] Duty was also on the mind of Nevada senator Francis Newlands, in this instance "toward civilization and humanity and human liberty, and this duty is best discharged by prompt and vigorous action with reference to this struggling country at our very doors."[223] Writing at the end of the North American military occupation of Cuba in 1902, essayist John Kendrick Bangs alluded to "the feeling among Americans . . . that a neighbor was being ill-treated by a harsh master" and to the "frightful condition of affairs which existed at our very doors."[224] The war was to "stop the oppression of a neighboring people whose cry we could almost hear," President William McKinley insisted on one occasion; the United States "preferred [war] rather than witness at its very door the suffering of an oppressed people." And on another occasion the president claimed: "[We could not] blind ourselves to the conditions so near our shores, and turn a deaf ear to our suffering neighbors." It was a theme to which McKinley returned frequently: "The war with Spain was undertaken, not that the United States should increase its territory, but that oppression at our very doors should be stopped." "We went [to war] only that we might relieve the Cuban people of an oppression under which they had been suffering—our neighbors, close to us, almost on our very borders." "We went to war for civilization and humanity, to relieve our oppressed neighbors in Cuba."[225]

In the years that followed, the production of historical knowledge drew freely upon the stock of nineteenth-century metaphorical constructs as the principal explanatory devices of 1898. Metaphor developed into a staple of American historiography. The metaphorical representations used to justify intervention in Cuba as a proposition of proximity subsequently passed into the dominant historical narratives, shaping a scholarship that could not but validate the normative logic from which the very premise of the North American imperial project was conceived. Writing his *History of the American People* in 1902, Woodrow Wilson characterized Americans as troubled "at the sight" of developments "in a populous island lying at their very doors . . . to which [they] were closely bound by . . . all intercourse of neighbors."[226] Historian E. Benjamin Andrews insisted that the American people could not "be indifferent to a neighboring people struggling to be free."[227] War was undertaken, wrote James Callahan, "to remove medievalism from our front doors." The United States, insisted biographers Alexander McClure and Charles Morris, "could no longer close her ears to the wails of the starving people who lay perishing, as may be said, on her very doorsteps."[228] In their survey history of the United States, James Wilford Garner and Henry Cabot Lodge explained the war as a result of the "people of the United States [who] could not remain indifferent to this wholesale murder within sight of their shores."[229] Historian Hollis Barber insisted "that such treatment would [not] go unnoticed by Cuba's next-door neighbor."[230] Historian Archibald Coolidge explained the war as the result of the American people being "tired of a commotion at their very door,"[231] and biographer Leon Burr Richardson wrote in 1940 of the condition of Cubans "at our very door" as cause for war.[232] W. E. Woodward explained the coming of the war in similar terms: "Naturally enough, the people of the United States were greatly interested in these doings, as anyone would be in case of a pistol battle going on in the house of a next-door neighbor."[233] Military intervention "in a neighboring country," historian Richard Leopold wrote in 1962, was undertaken "to abate an indisputable nuisance."[234] War was a matter of Cuba "lying so close to [U.S.] shores," explained historian Foster Rhea Dulles in 1965, adding, "Geography if nothing else linked Cuba and the United States so closely that whatever affected [Cuba] was always of immediate concern to the American people."[235]

The United States thus arrived, as the Americans were wont to affirm metaphorically, onto the world stage in 1898 principally by way of depictive constructs. Metaphors having to do with Cuba enabled Americans to articulate a point of view, a politics with which subsequently to represent their presence and purpose abroad. The intervention in Cuba, a deed that the Americans then and thereafter inscribed with righteous affect, served to fix in the national imagination a novel use of power among a people who were becoming self-consciously aware of their power, becoming even more conscious of the need to expand the scope of national interests. The Americans would thereafter stake their claim to world leadership on the basis of moral superiority, the use of power not for territorial aggrandizement or commercial advantage, but for the service of humanity, just like they had done in Cuba. The intervention in Cuba pointed the way by which the United States could advance self-interests in the guise of selfless intent. This was power deployed in the defense of freedom and liberty, in the service of rescue and redemption. The shedding of American blood in Cuba was for "more than driving Spaniards from the Western Hemisphere," proclaimed Indiana senator Albert Beveridge in 1906. "It meant liberty." Cuba showed the way to the United States, Beveridge indicated, and henceforth the duty of the United States was revealed. "Liberty—that is the method of human progress," Beveridge insisted. "It is toward liberty that all mankind is struggling. And the Nation which, under God, is leading the world to liberty is this American Republic."[236]

These developments would have long-lasting implications. So profoundly dense were the metaphorical representations with which the Americans subsequently claimed to exercise power over Cuba that it became all but impossible for them to imagine their purpose in terms other than those they had invented in the nineteenth century. These terms were the sources from which the Americans fashioned the meaning of their relationship with Cuba.

3

Metaphor as Paradigm

People in power get to impose their metaphors. —George Lakoff and Mark Johnson, Metaphors We Live By (1980)

"When I use a word," Humpty Dumpty said, in rather a scornful tone, "it means just what I choose it to mean—neither more nor less."

"The question is," said Alice, "whether you can make words mean so many different things."

"The question is," said Humpty Dumpty, "which is to be master—that's all." —Lewis Carroll, Through the Looking Glass (1872)

What the powerful say can often be "right" because it is said by the powerful. But this cannot be the sole basis for their claim to be right. There may be occasions when the powerful are in fact right, and they need to distinguish between the two kinds of claim, based on knowledge or power. Similarly, the less powerful may wish to conceal the grounds of their assent, separating the superior reason of their masters from their superior power. —Gunther Kress and Robert Hodge, Language as Ideology (1979)

We are guardians, self-appointed, to the Cuban people. Our honorable duty to our wards demands that we faithfully care for their estate until they are of age and discretion to take care of it themselves. —New York Times (January 3, 1899)

The Cubans need big brothers and sisters in the people of the United States to enlighten them in the principles of democracy and freedom, and to help them straighten up after centuries of grovelling under severe Spanish slave masters. —Havana Post (December 10, 1916)

[Cubans'] soul seems to partake of the spirit of carousal. . . . For they are children, not of the lives of men, but of moments: not of the races mingled in their blood—races burdened with noble memory, but of the passion which rejects burdens, which rejects memory. . . . These Cubans, then, are unreal as a dream precisely because they are children of the senses. What is so unreal as the senses? —New Republic (June 23, 1926)

The Americans went to war in 1898 in a state of joyful exuberance, a people imbued with a sense of noble purpose, mobilized for a self-proclaimed mission of rescue and redemption of a downtrodden neighbor.[1] The war with Spain was a popular war, a war declared amidst great excitement and enthusiasm, proclaimed just and justifiable, waged to end conditions that spoke directly to the conscience of the nation, simultaneously a calling and a crusade for a righteous cause, worthy of the support of a righteous people.

Powerful sentiments indeed, and no doubt served to summon popular will for war. No doubt, too, these attitudes contributed to the passage of the Teller Amendment to the Joint Resolution in April 1898, a sentimental but nonetheless solemn pledge whereby Congress disclaimed in advance "any disposition or intention to exercise sovereignty, jurisdiction, or control over said island" and vowed "to leave the government and control of the island to its people."[2]

There is no reason to doubt the authenticity of public sentiment. On the contrary, the evidence does indeed suggest that popular sympathy for *Cuba Libre* was as deeply felt as it was widely held. In small-town newspapers and large urban dailies alike, from trade union meeting halls to college campuses, among women's social organizations and men's fraternal associations, from church pulpits to sports clubs, and in poems, songs, and letters to the editor, Americans registered heartfelt support for the Cuban cause. Who could doubt the earnest fervor of Mark Twain: "I have never enjoyed a war . . . as I am enjoying this one. For this is the worthiest one that was ever fought, so far as my knowledge goes. It is a worthy thing to fight for one's freedom; it is another sight finer to fight for another man's. And I think this is the first time it has been done."[3] Who could question the heartfelt sincerity of a young Carl Sandburg: "I read about the . . . people of Cuba who wanted independence and a republic. I read about Gómez, García, the Maceos, with their scrabbling little armies fighting against Weyler. They became heroes to me. I tried to figure a way to get down there and join one of those armies. I was going along with millions of other Americans who were about ready for a war to throw the Spanish government out of Cuba and let the people of Cuba have their republic. If a war did come and men were called to fight it, I knew what I would do."[4]

That these were the sentiments of North American power holders and policy makers, however, is less certain. It is, of course, possible to imagine that the men who planned and prosecuted the war may have shared the sympathies of the aroused citizenry. But they also had other objectives in mind. They imagined themselves as acting in fulfillment of a century-old policy, as if a matter of a trust which they were bound to honor and which, in the end, they understood themselves obliged to discharge in the national interest. Years

"Now, Little Man, I'll See What I Can Do for You."
Depiction of the passage of the Joint Resolution of Congress
for war. From *New York Journal*, April 20, 1898.

. . . .

ago historian Charles Chapman observed that the "executive branch of the government" acted out of "a very substantial concern over the island." However, Chapman added, "Americans in general, including their representatives in Congress, had little knowledge of the importance of Cuba to the United States."[5]

The men in the McKinley administration were lucid in their understanding of the objectives of the war. The passage of the Teller Amendment had rankled the McKinley administration and its supporters in Congress as an egregious disregard of the national interest. "Seventy-five years of our diplomacy on this subject," McKinley confidant and former Republican vice-presidential candidate Whitelaw Reid protested, "had pointed steadily to one thing—the absolute necessity of controlling Cuba for our own defense." The "self-denying" Teller Amendment was "a grave mistake," Reid seethed in private correspondence in 1900, something "possible only in a moment of national hysteria, and as little likely to be kept to the letter as was Mr. Gladstone's pledge, twenty-years ago, to leave Egypt."[6] General James Wilson agreed and described the Teller Amendment as "a very bad piece of legislation" and "an unnecessary and serious mistake." Wilson urged a "different course" through which to acquire Cuba, "some other way to take care of her and safeguard our interests in respect to her."[7] Indiana senator Albert Beveridge dismissed the idea of Cuban independence as preposterous, insisting that the Teller Amendment had been enacted "in a moment of impulse but mistaken generosity and it will not be kept." To pledge "a destiny to Cuba separate to our own was a false and foolish doctrine," Beveridge asserted outright. A "separate government over Cuba, uncontrolled by the American government, should never have been promised." Beveridge was categorical. "Cuba independent!" he scoffed in 1900. "Impossible!" And he correctly foresaw what would happen next: "I predict that at the very next session of Congress we shall pass some kind of law giving this Republic control of Cuba's destiny. If we do not we fail in our duty."[8]

In fact, the cause of *Cuba Libre* had few champions in the White House. On the contrary, the prospects of sovereign nationhood for Cuba aroused as much misgiving in the late 1890s as it had in the early 1820s. No credible evidence exists to suggest that the McKinley administration prosecuted the war against Spain for the cause that had summoned Americans to arms. On the contrary, President McKinley used his April 1898 message to Congress to make the purpose of war clear: "The forcible intervention of the United States as a neutral to stop the war" as a matter of "hostile constraint upon both parties to the contest."[9] There was no mention of support for Cuban independence, no reference to the establishment of Cuban sovereignty. Notwithstanding popular belief at the time—and later—U.S. military forces arrived to Cuba neither as allies of the Cuban army nor as agents of Cuban independence. They arrived to advance national interests of the United States.

The distinction between popular sentiment and political purpose must be drawn sharply. It is not at all certain that the McKinley administration embarked upon war with a policy planned and prepared. But the lack of policy did not mean the absence of purpose: war was the means to purpose. The Americans improvised their way toward empire, some trial and error, some fits and starts, but all in all advancing purposefully toward strategic objectives with antecedents fixed early in the nineteenth century. The role of metaphor in this process was central.

★ ★ ★

As the Americans surveyed what victory in war had wrought them, they arrived at an understanding of 1898 as the consummation of history. Certainly with regard to Cuba, 1898 was a moment of denouement: destiny foretold and expectations fulfilled, an outcome long in the making, possessed of providential purpose and realized as an act of national completion.

These were momentous developments. "The acquisition of Cuba by the United States," exulted former secretary of state Richard Olney in 1900—and Olney used the word "acquisition" purposefully—"was neither unnatural nor surprising, but something sure to occur, if not in the year 1898, [then] before many years." Congress was obliged, Olney demanded, to make "Cuba in point of law what she already is in point of fact, namely, United States territory." The Teller Amendment notwithstanding—"ill-advised and futile at the time of its passage," commented Olney—"no such [congressional] resolution can refute the logic of the undisputed facts or should be allowed to impede the natural march of events."[10]

The "natural march of events" would indeed not be impeded. The Americans understood intuitively that the prophetic imperative had come to pass. With possession of Cuba, to paraphrase the Ostend Manifesto, the North American Union could enjoy repose.

★ ★ ★

On January 1, 1899, the American flag was raised over the island, and power was transferred from Spanish colonial administration to North American military occupation. At long last Cuba was in the possession of the United States. No one doubted that possession—in one form or other—was intended to be permanent.

The Americans claimed authority over Cuba as conquerors, exercised by way of a military occupation, and proclaimed themselves to be bearers of progress and defenders of law and order to whom Cubans were expected to submit. So fully had the Americans invested their mission in Cuba with agency of civilization and advocacy of progress that they could not but conclude that opposition to their presence represented a threat to civilization and progress, unable to conceive that opponents could act from honorable motives. This conviction, so essential a part of the self-confidence and moral certainty with which the Americans presumed the right to rule, implied the need to develop usable categories with which to malign the motives and discredit the aspirations of all who opposed North American authority. The American presence acquired a contrapuntal symmetry: on one hand, the Americans as white, representing civilization and proponents of progress and, on the other, their foes, represented as Cubans of color, agents of anarchy, and purveyors of disorder. The *Washington Post* characterized opponents to U.S. authority as "a handful of professional agitators, whom in all probability, we shall have to hang or exile if we want to set up civilized institutions in Cuba."[11]

But it was also true that new cognitive categories were necessary to enact the North American purpose, and these developed by way of a remarkable change of representation: from depiction of Cubans as heroic freedom fighters, as downtrodden neighbors worthy of American sympathy and support, used to justify the necessity of armed intervention in 1898, to depiction of Cubans as a racialized rabble, disposed to pillage and plunder, given to wanton destruction and willful mayhem, used to justify the necessity of military occupation in 1899. "We are dealing here in Cuba with a relatively uninstructed population," pronounced General William Ludlow, "whose sensibilities are easily aroused but who lack judgment, who are wholly unaccustomed to manage their own affairs, and who readily resort to violence when excited and thwarted."[12] Military physician Wilford Nelson warned that "Cuba Libre of the blacks would be a veritable hell upon earth, a blot upon Christian civilization," and enjoined, "Cuba the fair and fertile, to take her place in the family of nations, must have law, order, and peace guaranteed by the United States. Cuba to be a creditable part of the earth must be ruled by a firm hand."[13] The *New York Times* concurred. "If we are to save Cuba," warned the *Times*, "we must hold it. If we leave it to the Cubans, we give it over to a reign of terror—to the machete and the torch, to insurrection and assassination. . . . It would be a tragedy, a crime, to deliver the island into their hands."[14]

The apocalyptic purport of the metaphor of Haiti gained renewed currency. General Leonard Wood shared his concerns with an interviewer, and alluding to the dire consequences of premature sovereignty warned "that the establishment of another Haitian Republic in the West Indies would be a serious mistake."[15] To allow self-government in Cuba, Ludlow warned, would "swamp the better class," with a predictable outcome: "We might just as well retire and let it drift into a Haiti No. 2."[16] Cuban independence was unthinkable, insisted General Daniel Sickles: "The agitators in Cuba, who are clamoring for what they call independence, if allowed to have their own way, will make Cuba another Haiti."[17] The *New York Times* warned of "an irresponsible government of half-breeds," adding, "The negroes, too, who, in varying degrees of mixture, constitute nearly one-half of the population are another uncertain element. . . . We cannot afford to have another Haiti."[18]

Ominous prospects indeed, and not at all auspicious auguries for self-government in Cuba. "Self-government!" General William Shafter remarked contemptuously. "Why those people are no more fit for self-government than gunpowder is for hell."[19] Few North American officials disagreed. "The Cubans are utterly irresponsible," Major Alexander Brodie insisted in 1898, "partly savage, and have no idea what good government means." General Samuel B. M. Young agreed, insisting that Cubans were "no more capable of self-government than the savages of Africa."[20]

It was indeed unfortunate that such a desirable place was populated by such an undesirable people. "This is a great country," offered one U.S. army officer, "but I don't like the people."[21] The *Chicago Tribune* was blunt: "Nothing can be expected of half breeds and negroes in Cuba who have a chronic aversion to work."[22] From time to time the Americans would indulge in genocidal fantasies as the solution to the problem of Cubans, what Albert Memmi suggested as the logical conclusion of the imperial imagination: "to imagine the colony without the colonized."[23] "Cuba would be desirable," Nevada senator Francis Newlands commented, "if for a half hour she could be sunk into the sea and then emerge after all her inhabitants had perished."[24] South Dakota senator Richard Pettigrew offered a similar solution. "The island would not be worth anything to us," he mused, "unless it was sunk for twenty-four hours to get rid of its present population."[25] Asked in 1900 if Cuba would be desirable to annex, businessman Cyrus Duvall responded, "Yes, if the island could be first sunk for about half an hour. . . . If every living thing could be removed and the land purified by fire and water, then resettled by Americans, it would be an earthly paradise."[26] The *Chicago Tribune* suggested during the 1906 insurrection in Cuba that the "undisciplined, turbulent, rebellious people" should be "deported to some tropical land where they can live without work." On the other hand, the *Tribune* concluded upon further reflection, perhaps it would be more useful to contemplate the remove of all Cubans from Cuba: "If it were physically possible and not abhorrent to the principles of civilization it would be desirable to submerge the island of Cuba until most of the population had disappeared and then resurrect it. Then the island would be washed clean and

"Rough on Cuba." Caption: "Billy Mason wants to present Cuba with self-government on the Fourth of next July." Depiction of Illinois senator William Mason's advocacy of self-government for Cuba in 1900. From *Minneapolis Journal*, reprinted in *Literary Digest* 20 (May 19, 1900).

. . . .

it would be a decent and attractive place for Americans to settle."[27] President Theodore Roosevelt's displeasure with Cubans during an insurrection in 1906 produced a similar rant. "I am so angry with that infernal little Cuban republic," Roosevelt seethed, "that I would like to wipe its people off the face of the earth."[28]

The logic of the North American argument was entirely circular—and unyielding. The Americans turned the Cuban desire for independence on its head, insisting that the very demand for self-government was proof of incapacity for self-government. That is, Cubans did not even know enough to understand that they lacked preparation for self-government. "The Cuban people, as a whole," General Leonard Wood explained to President McKinley, "realize very fully that they are not ready for self-government and the only people who are howling for it are those whose antecedents and actions demonstrate the impossibility of self-government at present."[29] Cuban opposition to the U.S. military occupation was itself evidence of incapacity for self-government. "If it is true that the Cubans are not satisfied with the way in which they are being governed by their military rulers," essayist John Kendrick Bangs pronounced in 1901, "then they did not know good government when they see it, and are therefore as yet incapable of governing themselves."[30]

These were not altogether new formulations, of course. They had antecedents early in the nineteenth century and indeed possessed representational utility at the time. It was, in effect, to make the case that Cuban incapacity for self-government implied the necessity of American government. But much had changed between the beginning and the end of the nineteenth century, and mostly what had changed was that the Americans had in fact obtained control of Cuba. With the inauguration of the military occupation of the island on January 1, 1899, the United States had assumed fully the role of a colonial power, in possession of territory to administer, a government to operate, a political system to organize, and an economy to manage—all in function of North American interests.

What had changed, in other words, was the need for new metaphorical representations by which to fashion a usable logic for domination. What had changed, too, was the need for new figurative depictions with which to transact the exercise of power as more or less an ordinary or otherwise unremarkable circumstance.

★ ★ ★

The Americans arrived to their knowledge of Cuba by way of narratives with antecedents early in the nineteenth century. It was not disinterested knowledge, to be sure, for it had been shaped principally by cognitive biases that were themselves products of North American interests, which is to suggest that knowledge in this instance functioned mostly as a means to an instrumental purpose. This was knowledge shaped a priori as a matter of national interests.

But it was also true that Americans were given to represent the defense of self-interest as conduct of selfless purport. This was less dissimulation than self-deception, to make a virtue of necessity and thereupon claim virtue as motive of purpose. To proclaim selfless intent as reason for the intervention in 1898 was to confer moral propriety on the North American presence in Cuba. That power holders had a far more realpolitik view of the war did not prevent them from professing altruism as reason to rule. The representation of the intervention in Cuba as beneficent selflessness was enacted through the use of a series of metaphors, variously as intercession in behalf of a mistreated neighbor or the rescue of a damsel in distress: in sum, the appearance of power deployed as a matter of generous disinterest. "The rule of the United States," President McKinley explained the military occupation, "is for the benefit of the inhabitants of Cuba in furtherance and continuation of the humane purpose with which this country interfered to put an end to Spanish oppression and misrule. . . . To this end, the powerful protection of the United States government will be exerted."[31]

The larger meaning was not difficult to divine. So profoundly integral to the sense of well-being and national security had the Americans imagined Cuba—and even more so at the turn of the century with the anticipation of an isthmian canal—that the prospect of Cuba as a fully sovereign nation was inadmissible. A paradigm shift was under way, one that reflected the need to rearrange the political rationale and moral logic by which the Americans presumed to claim authority over the island.

The propriety of power was inscribed in accessible cultural models of hierarchy. The Americans designated Cubans as wards and assigned themselves the role of care providers. The idea of guardian suited North American needs perfectly. The imagery enacted self-interest as beneficent purpose, that is, the exercise of power as the right-minded and righteous discharge of responsibility within generally shared normative assumptions having to do with the duty to do good. "We owe the ward that which every high-minded guardian feels incumbent upon him to do for his ward in every walk in life," pronounced New York representative Sereno Payne in 1903, "and that is to see to it that the ward is started out on the right path."[32] Woodrow Wilson was stern in his injunction against "complete individual liberty or the full-fangled institutions of American self-government . . . for undeveloped peoples," insisting that they be "still in the childhood of their political growth."[33] Wilson was succinct: "The fact is this, that liberty is the privilege of maturity, of self-control, of self-mastery and a thoughtful care for righteous dealings,—that some peoples may have it, therefore, and others may not."[34] Wilson imagined the process of "maturity" as a "long apprenticeship of political childhood" and thereupon provided the moral framework for the prerequisite of self-government: "Self-government is not a mere form of institutions, to be had when desired, if only proper pains be taken. It is a form of character. It follows upon the long discipline which gives a people self-possession, self-mastery, the habit of order and peace and common counsel, and a reverence for law which will not fail when they themselves become the makers of law: the steadiness and self-control of political maturity. And these things cannot be had without long discipline."[35]

The idea of "political childhood" had far-reaching implications. The need for an alternative figurative depiction with which to imagine—and enact—a new relationship found enduring expression in the representation of Cuba/Cubans as child/children. A new metaphor had come into existence.

★ ★ ★

The metaphor of colonized people as children has long served as a discursive staple of colonialism, a time-honored depiction by which European colonial projects since the sixteenth century have almost everywhere sought to render the enactment of domination as a self-explanatory and self-confirming exercise of power.[36] The imagery served to validate power as a matter of binding reciprocity: authority, properly exercised by adults, and obedience, commonly expected of children. To depict colonized people as children was to evoke metaphor as a moral, a way to insinuate normative plausibility into the logic by which power was exercised and experienced. The norms of conduct expected of adulthood and behavior associated with childhood—no less than the conventions that defined the private interaction and public practice between parents and children, including matters of duty and responsibility; issues of care, conduct, and control; and questions of obedience and deference—constituted discursive spaces into which to inscribe the plausibility of colonial hierarchies. Metaphor in this instance worked as a mode of transfer, to export and expand norms derived from familiar social domains into new political realms.

That the image of child as a colonial trope worked at all was itself an attribute of metaphor to transcend the real and literal, to contemplate the implausible as possible. The capacity to "see" adults of another culture as children, that is, to see another people collectively in a condition of infancy, represented a vast leap of imagination into the realm of the preposterous that must itself be

Depiction of Columbia and Cuba during the debate on the Joint Resolution of Congress. From *Washington Evening Star*, April 16, 1898.

. . . .

understood as the capacity of power to fashion a version of reality as a function of its own needs.

Metaphor allowed for a suspension of disbelief as a condition necessary to sustain the moral certainty of power. In this regard philosopher Douglas Berggren was indeed correct to draw attention to the reach of metaphor as "a believed absurdity, believed because the absurdity goes unrecognized."[37] The characterization of a colonized people as children raises questions as to what attributes the subject population was perceived to share in common and by what attributes it was differentiated from the colonizers to enable the identity of the Self as adult and the Other as child. Metaphor provided a means of moral transport to a usable domain of jurisdiction by which to exercise authority as a function of the normative commonplace. It served as source of logic and legitimacy, to be sure, but also as a means of self-confirming justification for the exercise of power.

The representation of the colonizer as adult and the colonized as children developed into the colonial narrative of choice, in part because it privileged the narrator, of course, but mostly because it provided a coherent cognitive framework into which to inscribe the pursuit of self-interest as a matter of self-righteous purpose. The metaphor implicated larger moral dichotomies imagined as contrapuntal facets of the human condition: civilization versus barbarism, the rational against the irrational, order and progress, on one hand, and chaos and backwardness, on the other.[38] Just as human beings were perceived to pass through successive stages of infancy, childhood, and adolescence to reach adulthood, so, too, all the families of humankind were imagined as having evolved through stages of barbarism and various phases of savagery to arrive at civilization. Knowledge, reason, and discipline, on one hand, were products of adulthood; ignorance, improvidence, and backwardness, on the other, were associated with childhood.

In this scheme of things, some cultures had evolved more than others, that is, they were "older" — in other words, more experienced in matters of political arts, more mature in economic organization, and wiser in social organization. The moral duty of a people of progress — indeed the very definition of a people of progress — was responsibility to the mass of humanity that remained in conditions understood variously as backward and uncivilized. Historian F. S. Marvin alluded to the obligations of "Western races to the world" — "distinguished from all the rest by higher achievements in knowledge and collective power" — as the "work of trustees," by which he meant "to see that their wards . . . are preserved sound in life and limb, but, above all, they have the duty of developing their human powers to the utmost."[39]

The passage from childhood to adulthood as stages associated with the human life cycle suggested a model rich with metaphorical possibilities. Simply put, some cultures had registered greater moral progress and material advances than others, which was to suggest that cultures identified as primitive were developmentally similar to children. "Barbarism is to civilization what childhood is to maturity," pronounced historian Francis Parkman in 1851.[40] In his treatise *Primitive Culture* (1871), anthropologist Edward Tylor alluded to "the often-repeated comparison of savages to children as fairly to their moral as to their intellectual conditions." John Locke proclaimed that "children, idiots, savages, and the grossly illiterate" were all the same: "Their notions are few and narrow."[41] Indeed, these were precisely the arguments used by attorney George Fitzhugh to defend the necessity of slavery in the United States:

> To protect the weak, we must first enslave them, and this slavery must be either political and legal, or social; the latter, including the condition of wives, apprentices, inmates of poor houses, idiots, lunatics, children, sailors, soldiers, and domestic slaves. Those latter classes cannot be governed, and also protected by mere law, and require masters of some kind, whose will and discretion shall stand as a law to them, who shall be entitled to their labor, and bound to provide for them. . . . The despotic power of the master, the husband, and the father is no engine of tyranny, but usually and naturally a tie of affection, and a means of support and protection.[42]

All through the second half of the nineteenth century, notions of progress, evolution, and race combined to inform the larger logic of imperialism. The publication of Charles Darwin's *The Origin of Species* (1859) suggested a theory of biological progression from which to elaborate theories of historical progress.[43] Barbarism and civilization represented different moral and material circumstances, to be sure, but they were also designated as different temporal conditions, often separated by vast distances of time. In *Considerations on Representative Government* (1861), John Stuart Mill drew attention to the "different stages of civilization" through which all nations passed. Many nations, insisted Mill, "in order to advance in civilization, have some lesson to learn, some habit not yet acquired." The "more backward populations" were to be "held in direct subjection by the more advanced," Mill suggested, noting, "This mode of government is as legitimate as any other, if it is the one which in the existing state of civilization of the subject people, most facilitates their transition to a higher stage of improvement."[44]

The idea of progressive stages of human development provided a usable explanation for the varieties of the human condition. It served, too, as the intellectual rationale with which more powerful people claimed the moral authority to exercise domination over backward populations, as a matter of duty having to do generally with the advancement of civilization. The biology of Charles Darwin readily lent itself to the sociology of Herbert Spencer as the tenets of evolution and natural selection insinuated themselves into the larger discourse of culture and colonialism. Anthropologist Edward Tylor alluded in 1871 to "stages of development or evolution, each the outcome of previous history" as a way to compare the "barbarous hordes with civilized nations." Tylor argued that "the educated world of Europe and America practically settles a standard by simply placing its own nations at one end of the social series and savage tribes at the other, arranging the rest of mankind between these limits according as they correspond more closely to savage or to cultured life."[45] In *The Future of Science* (1891), French philosopher Ernest Renan was well in line with mainstream thinking when he insisted that "the phenomena of infancy present to us the phenomena of primitive man." The circumstances of "the everlasting infancy of those non-perfectible races" offered a reminder of "what happened at the outset of man's existence." Advanced peoples "must not forget," Renan warned, "that the immense majority of humanity is still at school, and that to let them out too soon would be to encourage them in idleness." The populations of "infants and savages" required a stern hand, Renan warned, adding, "Are these beasts to be let loose upon men? . . . No, they must be made men of, they must be given their part in the delights of the ideals, they must be elevated, ennobled, made worthy of liberty. . . . Until then, violent actions are necessary, and although to be condemned in the analytical appreciation of facts, they are, in effect, legitimate. The future will absolve them, as we absolve the great Revolution, while deploring its culpable acts and stigmatizing those who provoked them."[46]

For many it was less about culture than about race. "The races of mankind," anthropologist George Richardson mused in 1900, "evidently follow the lines of development noted by Charles Darwin among the lower animals and the plants. Race types appear to be varieties of human beings, divergent in their tendencies." Americans were exhorted "'to take up the white man's burden,'" Richardson paraphrased Kipling, "which is defined as subjugating and dominating weaker people temporarily if not permanently for the purpose of benefitting them . . . by teaching civilization and good government."[47] Sociologist Benjamin Kidd provided perhaps the most comprehensive and coherent rendering of colonialism as a function of the natural evolutionary stages of race. "In dealing with the natural inhabitants of the tropics," Kidd observed in *The Control of the Tropics* (1898), "we are dealing with peoples who represent the same stage in the history of development of the race that the child does in the history of the development of the individual. The tropics will not, therefore, be developed by the natives themselves." People of the tropics were "often separated from [the white man] by thousands of years of development. . . . If he has any right there at all, he is there in the name of civilization; if our civilization has any right there at all, it is because it represents higher ideals of humanity, a higher type of social order." In the tropics, Kidd continued, "we are in the midst of habits and institutions from which our civilization is separated by a long interval of development, where progress upwards must be a long, slow process. . . . It is on the principle that the development of the tropical region occupied must be held to be the fulfillment of a trust undertaken in the name of civilization."[48]

The Americans embraced the proposition of colonialism as duty to civilization with enthusiasm. The enactment of self-interest as a matter of selfless intent, such as the Americans imagined the 1898 intervention in Cuba, found a generally receptive public precisely because it spoke to those attributes that Americans celebrated most about themselves. How could a righteous people not assume responsibility to advance civilization? This was their destiny. Indiana senator Albert Beveridge propounded unabashedly the logic of imperialism as a matter of national duty. The time had arrived, Beveridge insisted at the turn of the century, for the United States to assume its rightful place as disseminator of civilization as a matter of "duty to the world as one of its civilizing powers." Colonialism—what Beveridge characterized as "administration of government"—was

> nature's method for the spread of civilization. Through all history administering peoples have appeared. Always these people have been the most advanced people of their time. These advanced peoples have extended their customs and their culture by the administration of government to less developed peoples. Thus, in the process of the centuries, these backward people have evolved those qualities of mind and character and that mode of living called civilization. . . . In this, as in nearly everything else, the experience of nations duplicates the experience of individual men. . . . The child is instructed and guided; little by little he evolves independent powers; then achieves his manhood and performs his life-work, which work is measured precisely by his vigor, his courage and his moral ideals.[49]

★ ★ ★

The metaphor of Cubans as children insinuated itself deeply into realms of the North American imagination: in popular venues and in political circles, by way of official communication and in private correspondence, through mass media and specialized publications, in text and pictorial representations. The image gained currency as early as the 1890s as one of the representations the Americans used to persuade themselves of the propriety of intervention in Cuba. "Spain is not the 'mother country of Cuba,'" the Senate Committee on Foreign Relations pronounced in 1896, "even in the sense of having supplied that island with a large part of the ancestors of her present population. She is a cruel stepmother, whose introduction into the Cuban family has been the immediate cause of the robbery of the stepchildren of their inheritance."[50] Utah representative William King proclaimed the United States the "self-appointed guardian of Cuba" and thereupon expanded upon his metaphors: "If a strong man is constantly and cruelly wounding his child, and a person is so situated as to be the enforced witness of the crime, human law, receiving moral sanction, approves the effort to arrest the parent's misconduct." The United States had the moral responsibility, King insisted, "to release this innocent, struggling child from the grasp of the inhuman, debased and barbarous parent."[51] Massachusetts representative Samuel Barrows developed an elaborate allegory around the metaphor:

> Under ordinary circumstances it would be an act of trespass to interfere in any man's domestic affairs. The right of parents to discipline and educate their children is recognized. But when paternalism passes into brutality and children are neglected or abused, then the State intervenes and takes the child from the parent that its life and freedom may be protected. When, likewise, a parent State in its treatment of a filial colony overpasses the bounds of paternal authority and becomes cruel and brutal, sapping the life of its child . . . then some sheriff of international law, armed, if need be, may step in and say: "You have forfeited your right to this child."[52]

The Joint Resolution of Congress in April 1898 was imagined as rescue of a child. "Our interest in Cuba," pronounced the *New York World* on the eve of the war, "is as unselfish and as altruistic as that which rescues an overworked horse from a cruel driver or which checks and punishes cruelty to children."[53] The *New York Journal* agreed: "If a policeman should see a young street ruffian of twelve gouging out the eyes of a child of three he would expect to do something about it."[54] Philosopher Felix Adler evoked similar imagery. "We must intervene," Adler insisted, "no matter how onerous the burden we assume by so doing. A child one day, upon whom a brutal father had drawn a knife, appealed to a bystander asking for protection. Would the bystander have been justified in refusing to intervene because he risked the child was likely to become a charge to him for years? This, in my opinion, is the case of Cuba and the United States."[55]

The metaphor of Cuba/Cubans as child/children subsequently served as the moral logic by which to render the proposition of Cuban sovereignty as untenable. Moreover, it would make plausible the claim that North American authority over Cuba was proper and practical, not only—and not even principally—as a matter of U.S. interests but, rather, for the good of the Cuban people themselves. The defense of national interest thus assumed the form of sacrifice and purity of purpose, of righteous motive and noble intent, all in behalf of Cuban well-being. Indeed, it was through the perception of an act of selflessness in behalf of Cubans that the Americans persuaded themselves of the moral necessity to disregard the Teller Amendment. "To construe [the Teller Amendment] as requiring us to abandon the Cuban people to their fate," pronounced Albert Beveridge, "is to do them irreparable wrong."[56]

No longer did the Americans repudiate outright the principle or even the prospects—at some distant time in the future—of Cuban self-government. In fact, the ideal of self-government was celebrated as a lofty aspiration to which all evolving peoples should properly strive. The problem with the Cubans, rather, had to do with the lack of preparation and the absence of experience. For centuries, the Americans insisted, the island had been a backwater New World colony of a backward Old World monarchy. Cubans were a people victimized by history and who, through no fault of their own, had been relegated to the margins of civilization: a society that had registered pitifully few advances in public administration and even fewer achievements in civic virtues, a people without training, without discipline. "The natural child of Spanish tyranny," warned the *Chicago Tribune* in 1899, "is a sort of banditti government, consisting of a cruel personal domination, smothered unrest, [and] open revolt. . . . The result is a nation with little science, less progress, no invention, and uninterrupted backwardness and widespread poverty."[57]

Cubans were thus characterized less as incapacitated by intrinsic defects as hampered by acquired imperfections. They were a weak people, to be sure, ill-prepared to assume immediately the responsibility for self-government. Nor had they advanced as far or as fast as people in other countries. They were not necessarily incorrigible or hopelessly irredeemable, but it would take time—perhaps a great deal of time—before they reached sufficient political maturity to manage their own affairs. This was evolution as politics: the improvement of the race as uplift, the advance of civilization as progress.

Cubans were not to be vilified; they were victims. They were not to be belittled, but befriended. They were to be comforted and consoled, to be taken pity upon and taken under the protective custody of the United States, to be encouraged to self-improvement and self-reliance as a way to help them achieve their aspirations of self-government. "Our indefinite feeling is one of pity for people who are not as we are and things which are not like ours," observed artist Frederic Remington during a visit to Havana in 1899. He added, "Too much cannot be expected at once of a people who have always lived under Spanish misrule and abuse.... It is an old country, time worn, decayed, and debauched by thieving officials and fire and sword. The people are negroes or breeds, and they were sired by Spaniards who have never had social virtues since they were overrun by the Moors. The Cubans have known no civic rectitude; they have had no example of honest, plain-dealing, public men; they are, in the aggregate, the most ignorant people on earth."[58]

"As we think of all these [deficiencies]," missionary Howard Grose counseled, "we shall judge charitably and speak softly, and trust that under a new political, educational, social, and religious order there will evolve a new Cuban."[59] Admiral William Sampson, a member of the U.S. Evacuation Commission, insisted that the Cubans had no idea of self-government, "and it will take a long time to teach them." He added, "It must be remembered that they know of no other form of government except that adopted by the Spanish. The mass of the people have absolutely no conception of voting or what self-government means."[60]

Cubans needed new men and new mentalities for the new century. The new man, Secretary of War William Howard Taft exhorted an audience at the University of Havana, was required to be realistic, practical, and pragmatic. "Your ideals are too high," Taft chided the Cubans. "An idea that is so high that it is beyond reach of the real is not very useful." Taft made his point: "What you need here among the Cubans is a desire to make money, to found great enterprises, and to carry on the prosperity of this beautiful island, and the young Cubans ought, most of them, to begin in business.... The right of property and the motive for accumulation, next to the right of liberty, is the basis of all modern, successful civilization, and until you have a community of political influence and control which is affected by the conserving influences of property and property ownership, successful popular government is impossible."[61]

★   ★   ★

To represent Cubans as children was to deploy metaphor as discursive strategy of domination. It propounded the notion of a relationship in which the United States had the duty to protect and nurture Cuba. The Americans would thus dedicate themselves to the task of uplift: to instilling new values and inculcating new habits, to fostering new methods and teaching new ways.

In the new order of things, new ideas would be inculcated and new principles imparted. The people of Cuba, writer Arthur Pillsbury exhorted, "need to have stretched forth helpfully toward them the guiding as well as protecting hand of a strong and humane government, [so] that order and law and enterprise may be established." He added that "nearness of Cuba demands her elevation," explaining that "Cuba must be reconstructed. Ignorant and superstitious, ground to the earth by three hundred years of repression and oppression, the people of Cuba must be instructed in self-government, in industry, in the value of order and the inviolability of law. To leave them wholly to themselves would be to leave them to self-destruction through internecine warfare."[62]

The metaphor frequently used to depict preparation for self-government was to conjure up the idea of a journey, one in which the Americans would guide the way. "The mass of the people are ignorant," Leonard Wood explained, "largely as a result of Spanish rule. . . . As yet they are not fit for self-government, but they are on the road to it. The road, it is true, is a long one, and there is plenty of hard work to be done by the Cubans before they can be regarded as fit for self-government. I am trying to teach them this, and they respond very willingly."[63]

The Americans determined the entire generation of adult Cubans to be incapable of self-government—that is, the generation of Cubans that led the liberation project were deemed incapable of political leadership. They were already politically formed and far too susceptible to the baneful ways of Spanish practices. "The present generation will, in my judgment," insisted General William Ludlow, "have to pass away before the Cubans can form a stable government."[64] Military Governor John Brooke agreed. "These people," Brooke observed in 1899, "cannot *now*, or I believe in the immediate future, be entrusted with their own government; and neither do I believe that, under the present conditions on this Island, a substantial government can be established here by these people."[65] *Washington Evening Star* correspondent Thomas Noyes reported in 1901 what he had learned from occupation authorities: "It would seem that the present generation in Cuba is unfitted for entire self-government. The next generation, trained in a different school and provided with different ideals of government, could very likely meet the necessary obligations of government with success. . . . The people need a strong hand over them."[66] Correspondent Franklin Matthews appealed to a vaguely familiar metaphor to make the point: "The twig was bent for future growth. Whether the grown tree shall bear the fruit of national independence or of colonial dependence . . . depends largely upon the development and conditions of the future. The twig certainly was trained to stand erect and to grow straight and true by the American army officials."[67]

★ ★ ★

The metaphor of Cubans as children signaled a paradigm shift, one that propounded a politics derived from a cultural system in which domination was transacted within a beneficent moral order. That children were denied agency, autonomy, and authority mattered little because such denial was imagined to be for their own good. Parents' conduct was validated in the knowledge of well-intentioned motives. "We should," urged writer Albert Robinson, "regard them with charity"—counsel with a moral: "That these people, entirely without experience or training in self-government, should make mistakes was quite as inevitable as it is that a child, in learning to walk will tumble down and bump its little nose."[68] "[Cubans] are better controlled by sterness and fairness than leniency," Captain Walter Barker advised, and added, "I pity this people. . . . They are incapacitated for self-government. Reared under a corrupt Government, untrained, with minds of no greater scope than children, how could they be expected to conduct successfully a Government of their own?"[69] Barker, who served in Cuba during the military occupation, insisted that "to fully understand their deficiencies and vices, of which the average American is ignorant, it is necessary to live among them." He continued,

> They are not only dishonest but weak minded; this, of course, is due to the lack of training, for Spain did not allow them to *think* for themselves. . . . They [are] improvident and wholly lacking in executive ability. . . . They are indolent [and] innately dishonest with a low standard of morals. Their chief virtue is that they are not of a turbulent nature, and can (when understood) be made as tractable as a child, controlled as a child with kindness but firmness. Thus it is that I hold the present generation will not prove equal to self-government. I know this people, and sympathize with the poor deluded creatures, and I also know that a guardianship over them must exist for at least a few years to come.[70]

Once Cubans were rendered as children, the proposition that they lacked the experience for self-government assumed plausibility. Indeed, the metaphor of Cubans as children made the denial of self-government a matter of incontrovertible common sense, and more: it presented the Americans with the moral obligation to prepare them for adulthood. "These people," Massachusetts senator George Hoar pronounced in 1902, "are given to us as children, to lead them out of their childhood into manhood."[71] The transition from the old to the new would take time, in the course of which the bad habits and the old ways inherited from Spain, the afflictions that had so incapacitated other Latin American peoples, would be replaced by a new spirit and a new way of doing things. "I find them docile, willing, and careful," wrote Major George Barbour in 1899. "Under our supervision, and with firm and honest care for the future, the people of Cuba may become a useful race and a credit to the world; but to attempt to set them afloat as a nation, during this generation, would be a great mistake. We must wait until the children of to-day are old enough to think for themselves and absorb American ideas."[72] Just as children could hardly be expected to prepare themselves unaided for adulthood, Cubans could not be expected to prepare themselves unassisted for nationhood. The *Brooklyn Eagle* was succinct and to the point: "You might as well talk of the liberty of a baby or the manhood of a 10 year old boy."[73] Colonel Paul Beck arrived at a similar conclusion by way of a different metaphor. "The Cuban people are not yet fitted for self-government," Beck offered metaphorically, "and by giving them self-government we are shirking the 'white man's burden' and are committing a political act which is equivalent to permitting a child to carry a deadly weapon."[74]

The metaphor was not, of course, used solely to impute dependency as a condition of childhood. More importantly, it expanded into those cognitive realms in which the representation of childhood also served to prescribe appropriate modes of conduct corresponding to adulthood. Political purpose was modeled on social practice. This was to render colonial rule into apprehensible form, that is, to imply an equivalence between political behavior (colonialism) and culturally determined conduct (parenthood). The image of Cubans as children, a metaphor summoned by and in the service of political purpose, was situated within a familiar moral order that entailed the need for prescriptive adult behavior. It invoked commonplace experience from familiar social domains as a means to invite self-evident inference to be applied to new circumstances for which alternative images were either unavailable or unusable.[75] To resort to metaphor in this instance was to deploy a priori a shared normative experience as a way to invite the desired inference, without the need to make intent explicit. This was to use a known condition as a frame of reference with which to render an unknown circumstance familiar: to impose on something new an understanding that was at once objectively accessible and subjectively plausible to enable a conduct that was seemingly reasonable. Resemblance was made to represent reality, what essayist Cynthia Ozick suggested of the power of the metaphor relying "on what has been experienced" and a means by which to "transform the strange into the familiar."[76]

The representation of the United States as adult authority in discharge of duty over a distant and different people was a matter of internal dialogue: Americans speaking to each other, in pursuit of some higher purpose to explain and therefore justify to themselves the exercise of power over Cuba in the most positive form. Public acquiescence to imperialism could most readily be obtained as a matter of disinterested discharge of benevolent purpose.

The Americans evoked the metaphor and thereupon assumed the obligations that its logic imposed upon them. These were, in the end, constructs of power, contained and concealed as proper discharge of everyday value-laden obligations. The metaphor created expectations as premise of its formation. Nothing really much to think about, in fact; the moral was self-explanatory, and responsibility was self-evident. It so fully insinuated itself into the transaction of power as to make domination appear normal and natural. This was a version of reality ratified by the very social determinants that produced it. Metaphor in this instance enacted the moral certainties through which the culture represented itself, to be sure, but at the same time produced the normative model through which power reproduced itself. The relationship between the two was inseparable.

That preparation for self-government implied the exercise of North American power over another people—that is, government without the consent of the governed—was in this instance a matter of no consequence, for authority resided presumptively with the adult. "The rule of liberty that all just government derives its authority from the consent of the governed," explained Albert Beveridge, "applies only to those who are capable of self-government." And to the point: "We govern our children without their consent."[77]

Inscribed into the metaphor was both model of the norm and mode of engagement as culturally scripted practice, thereupon inferred intuitively and acted upon prescriptively. Responsible behavior required adult protection of children from the dangers of the world at large, to be sure, but just as often protection from the follies of their own making. The relationship once drawn and rendered plausible served to justify—and indeed it more than justified; it required—the exercise of adult authority, always for the child's own good. This was to proclaim beneficent intent as justification for the exercise of power, to protect Cubans from themselves, to save, in the end, Cubans from the consequences of their own mistakes. Senator Albert Beveridge professed concern for "the welfare of the Cuban people" and identified the Cubans as their own worst enemy. They were threatened by an "enemy and at their weakest point," Beveridge warned. "That point was within and that enemy themselves. . . . Is it not our duty to see that they are not destroyed by themselves?"[78] "We maintain our rule over them," affirmed Andrew Draper in 1899, "only as a duty and for their good. . . . The sincere purpose [is] to promote their good."[79] The *Chicago Tribune* pronounced two years later, "We are obliged to protect Cuba from itself."[80] "We must remember," counseled writer John Kendrick Bangs in 1901, "that we are in Cuba as Trustees for a helpless people." He added,

It is our business to nurse the ward which the chance of war has committed to our care; to see that she is protected not only from her enemies but from herself, and if at times it becomes necessary to be harsh, and by disciplinary acts to compel tears where indulgence would bring smiles, we must choose the harder rather than the easier task. . . . Cuba is an undeveloped child rescued by one of the High Courts of Humanity from a wicked and scheming Trustee who was despoiling her of her riches, sapping her vitality, and stunting her growth. The child has suffered, and is not yet strong enough physically or intellectually to stand alone.[81]

To accept the premise of the metaphor was to be implicated in its logic. It was unthinkable, of course, to leave children unattended and uncared for, and once the imagination expanded to envisage Cubans as children, the need to discharge duty was as self-explanatory as it was self-evident. Without adult supervision the Cubans would fall victim to their own immaturity and inexperience. "It is our mission here," commented Major John Logan as early as 1899, "to establish good government and to instruct the people in the qualifications of good citizenship. . . . I have found in my contact with the Cubans that as a rule they are honest, faithful, patient and long-suffering . . . that they have to be guided and instructed like children."[82] Writer Herbert Pelham Williams agreed: "We must base our dealings with the Cubans on the understanding that they are as yet but children." And "like children," Williams added, "almost anything can be made of them. We have before us the task and responsibility of training them up in the way they should go. . . . Their extreme teachableness, and their quickness to adopt new habits of mind and action . . . render it not impossible that the children of another generation may be fit for citizenship."[83] And like children, Cubans did not appreciate the meaning of freedom. They lacked the capacity to distinguish between liberty and license and would inevitably seize the occasion of self-government as an opportunity for self-aggrandizement. For Cubans, "political liberty simply meant individual license," commented writer C. H. Forbes-Lindsay.[84] "In many respects they are like children," Connecticut senator Orville Platt insisted. "They are passionately devoted to the sentiment of liberty, freedom and independence, but as yet have little real idea of the responsibilities, duties and practical results of republican government."[85]

The model of the metaphor invited the obvious inference. Cubans had to be schooled in the arts of self-government and taught the discipline of representative democracy. The Cuban lacked "the faculty of submitting to the will of the majority," observed correspondent George Kennan, and when "he cannot have exactly the position he wants . . . he acts the spoiled child who 'won't play.'"[86] Colonel Robert L. Bullard, who served in Cuba first during the 1899–1902 occupation and again in the 1906–9 intervention, characterized Cubans as "emotional and over-excitable" and attributed the weakness of Cuban character to child-rearing practices:

> [It] is the fault of the Cuban's raising and training his children from birth to manhood to know not discipline—to know not what it is to restrain one's desires, control one's self. . . . It is the lack of this training that makes the difference between a child and a man, not in body, but in character. . . . It is because of the lack of that which the Cuban is not taught, that, with the body of a man, he appears so much in the character of a child. This accounts for the Cuban emotionality and impracticability. . . . It keeps them children. It makes it necessary for a neighbor to take them in hand, control, direct and manage their government and public polity. It makes the Cuban a Cuban.[87]

The metaphor performed a vital role by inscribing inference of a cultural norm—that is, a value system—into political purpose. The image derived cognitive coherence as a function of social practice, through customs and conventions associated with parenting, a relationship by which the culturally determined assumptions of adult authority were assembled into the prerogative of power. The protocols of parenthood implied a duty to discharge and a responsibility to fulfill. It was out of the knowledge of life as lived, as time-honored modes of learned behavior, that the conventions of domination and dependency entered domains of the commonplace and common sense. What the metaphor of Cuba/Cubans as child/children succeeded in concealing was the fundamental imbalance of power that was inscribed in the propriety of normative relationships, specifically, the ways that the workings of power relations were embedded in the given normality of everyday life as lived. As a culturally conditioned construct, the metaphor implied custom-bound and duty-driven responsibilities. Everyone understood the rules.

The condition of childhood—Cuban—implied immaturity, inexperience, and innocence, with a sense of vulnerability and propensity to mischief. The status of adult—North American—implied a moral obligation to nurture children, to educate, to guide, and when necessary, to discipline, often over their very protests, with the self-assurance that the exercise of adult authority was in the best interest of Cubans. Woodrow Wilson alluded to "our new subjects," in 1902, depicting them as children, "foolish, impulsive, headstrong, unreasonable," and drew the obvious inference:

"Encouraging the Child." Caption: "That's right, my boy! Go ahead! But remember, I'll always keep a father's eye on you!" From *Puck*, February 27, 1901.

. . . .

Liberty is not itself government. In the wrong hands—in hands unpracticed, undisciplined—it is incompatible with government. Discipline must precede it,—if necessary, the discipline of being under masters. . . . They can have liberty no cheaper than we got it. They must first take the discipline of law, must first love order and instinctively yield to it. . . . We are old in this learning and must be their tutors. We must govern as those who learn; and they must obey as those who are in tutelage. They are children and we are men in these deep matters of government and justice.[88]

"You Can't Play in My Back Yard." Depiction of Cuban opposition to the
Platt Amendment. From *Chicago Tribune*, April 14, 1901.

. . . .

"President McKinley: 'I wonder where that woman is who asked me to hold this child for her for a few minutes.'" Depiction of Cuban opposition to the Platt Amendment. From *Minneapolis Journal*, reprinted in *Literary Digest* 22 (February 23, 1901).

. . . .

The metaphor of Cubans as children drew upon the dense web of reciprocities commonly understood to regulate the parent-child relationship as model for governance: the parent to supervise, the child to submit; the parent to discipline, the child to obey; the parent to teach, the child to learn, all a seemingly self-explanatory and self-confirming logic with which to validate the exercise of power less as a matter of prerogative than as discharge of moral obligation, always in the guise of a beneficent parental supervision. The relationship im-

UNCLE SAM : "It looks to me like a foolish piece of business."

"Uncle Sam: 'It looks to me like a foolish piece of business.'" Representation of Cuban self-government without the Platt Amendment. From *St. Paul Pioneer Press*, reprinted in Literary *Digest*, 22 (February 16, 1901).

. . . .

"The Cuban Situation." Depiction of the rationale for the Platt Amendment on Cuba. From *Minneapolis Journal*, April 9, 1901.

. . . .

plied duty of adult guidance, including the firm hand of discipline to be exercised—and justifiably exercised—in order to obtain the child's acquiescence to the superior wisdom of adult authority. It was always in the best interest of the child, to enable the child to grow up with proper values, to be righteous and virtuous pursuant to the standards offered by the adult model. The parent-child metaphor implied reciprocal obligations. The Americans as guardians implied sacrifice and selflessness. The Cubans as children were expected to reciprocate North American largesse with a mixture of obedience and acquiescence, to be heedful and compliant and always properly appreciative and grateful.

Parental authority was institutionalized in the form of the Platt Amendment, initially imposed as an appendix to the Cuban constitution of 1901 and later formally ratified in the form of the permanent treaty of 1903. The new

THE SPRING MEDICINE AND THE SUGAR.

Dr. McKinley — There's always a way to get along with these youngsters, if you know how.

"The Spring Medicine and the Sugar." Caption: "Dr. McKinley—
'There's always a way to get along with these youngsters, if you know how.'"
Depiction of methods by which to secure Cuban ratification of the
Platt Amendment. From *Minneapolis Journal*, April 29, 1901.

. . . .

A PRECAUTIONARY AMENDMENT.

Yes, sonny, you may have the fire works for your celebration; but I must insist on your wearing this extinguisher.

"A Precautionary Amendment." Caption: "Yes, sonny, you may have the fire works for your celebration; but I must insist on your wearing this extinguisher." Depiction of the rationale for imposing the Platt Amendment. From *Minneapolis Journal*, April 22, 1901.

. . . .

"Now, then, open your mouths and shut your eyes,
And you'll all get something that will make you wise."

"Now, then, open your mouths and shut your eyes, And you'll all get something that will make you wise." Depiction of the visit of the five-member Cuban delegation of the Constituent Assembly to discuss the terms of the Platt Amendment with the McKinley administration. From *New York World*, April 25, 1901.

. . . .

Cuban republic was to be shorn of all essential properties of sovereignty prior to its establishment. The Cubans were denied authority to enter into "any treaty or other compact with any foreign power or powers" and denied, too, the authority to contract a public debt beyond their normal ability to repay. The new Cuban government was, further, required to cede to the United States territory adequate for the establishment of what eventually developed into a permanent U.S. naval base in Guantánamo Bay. Lastly, Cubans were required to concede to the U.S. government "the right to intervene" for the "maintenance of a government adequate for the protection of life, property and individual liberty."[89] The Platt Amendment, the Americans insisted, was for the good of the Cubans.

CUBA MAKES A DISCOVERY.

"Why, this isn't a collar, after all; it's a life-preserver."

"Cuba Makes a Discovery." Caption: "Why, this isn't a collar, after all;
it's a life-preserver." Depiction of the North American case for the
Platt Amendment. From *Minneapolis Journal*, May 22, 1901.

. . . .

"Down at Last." Depiction of Cuban acceptance of the Platt Amendment.
From *New York World*, June 14, 1901.

. . . .

★ ★ ★

The representation of power relationships as a matter of conventional wisdom further obtained popular currency by way of pictorial depiction in the form of caricatures and cartoons, a means by which the premise and propriety of the exercise of power over Cubans were propounded as normal and commonplace. The visual representation of Cuba/Cubans as child/children established itself as a recurring presence in newspapers and magazines, there to act as a source of information but most of all as a mode of visual affirmation of both the moral logic and common sense of North American power. It is thus possible to contemplate the ways that caricature contributed to the creation of new forms of knowledge derived from and mediated by hierarchies of race, gender, and power. It suggests, too, one more way by which Americans came to know the Cubans. To ponder the larger impact of these images is, of course, necessarily to meditate on inference and induction, neither of which readily lends itself to historical analysis. But it is also true that image fixed in the popular imagination a habit of thought; an image conveyed an idea and a moral possessed of self-evident propriety. "Caricature has claims to truth as do other forms of art which attempt to represent and reflect reality," observed historian Lawrence Streicher. "Caricature *interprets* nations, figures and events and helps to supplement the news presentation with statements of 'meaning'"—what historian Thomas Milton Kemnitz suggests as a source of "insights into the popular attitudes that underlay public opinion."[90] Writing specifically about political cartoons and 1898, Virginia Bouvier commented on the power of the pictorial image to "create, reinforce, and mirror an attitudinal subtext which . . . may contribute to mythic understandings."[91]

What made the turn-of-the-century metaphor of Cubans as children in editorial caricature particularly noteworthy was the expanded reach of the daily press and weekly periodicals as a popular medium of political representation. It was precisely among the newspapers and magazines that aspired to mass circulation that the pictorial representation of the metaphor reached a public on a scale previously unimaginable.[92] The post–Civil War years in the United States were a time of rising literacy rates and accelerating urbanization; of an expanding newspaper readership, from 10 percent to 26 percent of the total adult population; of increasing numbers of newspapers, from 600 to 2,400; and of a widening circulation of newspapers, from 2.6 million to 15 million. This was also a time when visual images expanded into textual spaces, in newspapers and magazines, when print technology had developed an increased capacity to accommodate pictorial representation.[93] "The mass media," historians Joanne Shattock and Michael Wolff have correctly observed, "are the inescapable ideological and subliminal environment of the modern world. The press, in all its manifestations, became during the Victorian period the context within which people lived and worked and thought, and from which they derived their (in most cases new) sense of the outside world."[94]

The representation of Cubans as children in caricatures and cartoons expanded deeply into domains of public awareness and could not but have contributed to a national consensus around the need to do the right thing for Cubans. Linguists Gunther Kress and Theo van Leeuwen write perceptively of images that "want something from the viewer," specifically in those instances where "the viewer is asked imaginarily to enter a relation of social affinity with the represented participants(s)."[95] It is not difficult to understand how caricatures and cartoons helped to shape a climate of opinion that endorsed political purpose, represented as duty to look after and take care of Cubans, and

"Uncle Sam: 'Be Patient.'" From *Washington Evening Star*, July 23, 1898.

. . . .

indeed contributed to the intellectual environment in which political leaders and policy makers themselves were formed and functioned.

At least as important as the meaning of the metaphor was the mode of communication through which the moral was disseminated. The image of Cubans as children as a pictorial representation circulated widely across the United States, often as dependent children in need of care, at other times as unruly children in need of discipline. In the newspapers and magazines of large cities and small towns alike, in New York, Chicago, Philadelphia, Minneapolis, Cleveland, Charleston, Toledo, and Columbus, Cubans entered the popular imagination as children—innocent infants, mischievous toddlers, and ill-mannered adolescents—over whom the Americans were perforce obliged to

"He Won't Be Happy Till He Gets It." Representing U.S. allegations that Cuban demands for independence were motivated by Cuban desires to plunder the national treasury. From *Chicago Inter-Ocean*, reprinted in *Literary Digest* 22 (April 27, 1901).

. . . .

assume responsibility. The prominence of the imagery within the internal dialogues and national conversations must be considered as having contributed to the enduring terms by which the Americans obtained a sense of moral certainty in their domination of Cuba.

The pictorial image provided visual form to the discourse, and vice versa, of course; but it is necessary also to underscore that together they served as sources of knowledge in dialectical relationship to one another, as picture and text combined to confer on the proposition of hegemony an incontrovertible logic. Each implicated and reinforced the other in constant interplay, provid-

"Uncle Sam to Porto Rico: 'And to think that bad boy came near to being your brother!'" Depiction of election irregularities in Cuba. From *Chicago Inter-Ocean* (1905), reprinted in John J. Johnson, ed., *Latin America in Caricature* (Austin, 1980).

. . . .

ing entree into thresholds of the popular imagination and validating political purpose.[96] It never need have been stated explicitly, of course, for it was always understood implicitly that the future of Cuba simply could not be entrusted to children. "They were childlike, simple and bland," recalled one observer, "but plainly incapable of self-government. . . . Altogether the Cubans were amusing children. . . . But it was plain that a free and independent Cuba would be a very dangerous experiment."[97]

There is no need to impute mischievous intent or malice of forethought to

"Freedom Is Not Far Off!" Depiction of the possible ending of the
U.S. military occupation. From *Detroit News* (1907), reprinted in
John J. Johnson, ed., *Latin America in Caricature* (Austin, 1980).

. . . .

the North American use of the metaphor of Cuba/Cubans as child/children.
On the contrary, it would be unduly facile to ascribe willful contrivance to the
use of metaphor as a mode of knowledge. In fact, it is far more subtle, and
therefore far more insidious. The assumptions by which the Americans arrived
at the notion of themselves as "adults" and Cubans as "children" raise complicated matters having to do with the ways that culture enacted moral hierarchies as a matter of self-interest, but most of all the means by which cultural
models shaped the exercise of power in the pursuit of self-interest in the form
of self-righteous purpose. This was national interest articulated as cultural
practice, at once as source and sustenance of the proposition of self-interest
as a normative condition.

Motive mattered, of course, for to be persuaded of good intentions was to
possess the moral certainty so essential to the logic of the colonial domination.
It was not simply, then, that the view of the Other as child situated the observed
inside a value hierarchy of the observer. Rather, the designation of the metaphor of child served as the rationale with which to exercise domination and

"Can She Go It Alone?" Depiction of preparations for Cuban independence during the second intervention. From *Toledo Blade* (1907), reprinted in John J. Johnson, ed., *Latin America in Caricature* (Austin, 1980).

. . . .

exact submission within a self-confirming paradigm. The very paradigmatic logic of the relationship obtained validation from those normative realms of child-rearing practices, from established convention and time-honored practices based on culturally determined notions of common sense. This was a duty thrust upon the United States by virtue of its post-1898 responsibilities in the world. "We had found the baby on our door-step," affirmed Pennsylvania representative J. Hampton Moore, "and the spirit of fatherhood required that we should put it asleep at night and provide for its maintenance."[98] This was metaphor with custodial implication deeply invested in parental authority.

"If General Wood Is Unpopular with Cuba, We Can Guess the Reason." From *Minneapolis Tribune* (1901), reprinted in *Literary Digest* 22 (March 30, 1901).

. . . .

William Howard Taft spoke of "our parental relation [to Cuba] and our continuing duty to help her and to be patient with faults that may be expected in her," adding, "Cuba is our foster child. As she errs in the childhood and youth of her national life we must bear with her and aid her."[99]

The metaphor of child situated Cubans in readily recognizable cultural hierarchies, within those social arrangements that elicited something of second-nature impulses. It suggested a compelling and indeed an incontrovertible way to make the need for the exercise of North American authority both obvi-

"The Baby's Uncle: 'Why, This Is Not Such a Bad Child after All.'"
Depiction of the end of political disorders in Cuba upon the U.S. intervention
in 1906. From *Baltimore News* (1906), reprinted in John J. Johnson, ed.,
Latin America in Caricature (Austin, 1980).

. . . .

ous and obligatory. The power of the metaphor lay in its capacity to represent
power as a matter of normative common sense, to impose an obvious logic
on the otherwise complex enactment of national interests. This was imperialism enacted as an etiquette: power was represented as caregiving authority
and exercised as responsibility. The power of the metaphor as a commonplace
construct, to be sure, resided in its capacity to enable self-deception. At least
as important, however, it possessed the capacity to raise self-deception to the

"About Ready to Walk." Caption: "Say, Maggie, let's see if she can
go it alone." From *Cleveland Leader* (1908), reprinted in John J. Johnson, ed.,
Latin America in Caricature (Austin, 1980).

. . . .

level of self-righteous purpose, and once power was imagined at the service of
self-righteousness, it would be exercised ruthlessly as a matter of moral rectitude.

★ ★ ★

The metaphors were modeled on familiar norms of authority, as a function of age differential, as a matter of gender binaries, or as a facet of racial
attributes—that is, as children, as women, and as blacks. As an adult female,
Cuba was usually depicted as white; as a female child, Cuba was often represented as black. The exercise of power was almost always depicted as an adult
male undertaking. This was age as a social category, not an unremarkable designation, to be sure, but one that implied a usable framework to enact duties,
rights, and privileges. The representation of the United States as male, almost
invariably in the form of Uncle Sam, summoned to rescue Cuba, depicted as a
helpless child or a damsel in distress, conformed to gender-determined norms
of duty associated with manhood.

VOL. 36 NO. 921   JUNE 10 1899   PRICE 10 CENTS

OUTING NUMBER

Judge

THE FILIPINO'S FIRST BATH.
McKinley—"Oh, you dirty boy!"

"The Filipino's First Bath." Caption: "McKinley—'Oh, you dirty boy!'"
From *Judge*, June 10, 1899.

. . . .

"The Real Conquest of Cuba." From *Life*, February 2, 1899.

. . . .

But the metaphor in pictorial representation often turned established gender roles on their head. Cognitive psychologist Steven Pinker has suggested that "the metaphors of our language imply that the nurturing parent should be a mother, beginning with 'nurture' itself."[100] This may indeed be correct in many domains, but not in the realm of power. The frequency with which men were portrayed discharging the nurture functions traditionally associated with women at the dawn of the overseas empire must be seen as nothing less than astonishing, an indication that on the matter of the representation of power — that is, the imagery of colonial relationships — the realm of metaphorical construct was almost entirely a man's world, even if it obliged men to discharge traditional female roles. The United States was depicted as male but cast in roles ordinarily and otherwise associated with women: as caregiver; as supervisor of children at play, of the feeding and bathing of children, and of putting children to sleep; and as elementary school teacher. One caricature near the end of the second U.S. intervention (1906–9) depicted the infant Cuba in a carriage pushed by Provisional Governor Charles Magoon dressed as a woman preparing Cuba for self-government. In another, General Leonard Wood was shown as bathing the child Cuba. Most typically, it was the United States as Uncle Sam given to the discharge of traditional female roles. It should be noted, moreover, that a female representation of the United States was readily available in the person of Columbia. In fact, the depiction of the United States in the form of Columbia was not common.[101]

The metaphorical image of Cubans as children quickly acquired a logic of

"Governor Wood Begins His Duties." From *Minneapolis Tribune* (1900),
reprinted in *Literary Digest* 20 (June 6, 1900).

. . . .

its own. Everyday articles and artifacts, and commonplace settings and circumstances, assumed symbolic value as method of metaphor and mode of
analogy. The caricatures traded on a number of recurring motifs. The nursery
served as representation of training site for self-government. A high chair, a
stroller, or a playpen, among other items, conveyed moral and meaning in
seemingly unremarkable and familiar ways. Bathing children was depicted as
an act of cleansing and, hence, passage into a condition of civilization. Indeed,
the matter of cleanliness was imagined not only—and not even principally—as
an issue of public health but as passage into a new cultural system, specifically
a sign of discipline and sensibility of civilization, a salient marker of North

ARBOR DAY IN CUBA.

Cuba—You trimmed the limbs back pretty close, didn't you Uncle?

Uncle Sam— Yes; got to do it in transplanting, you know, my boy.

"Arbor Day in Cuba." Caption: "Cuba—'You trimmed the limbs back pretty close, didn't you Uncle?' Uncle Sam—'Yes; got to do it in transplanting, you know, my boy.'" On the occasion of the visit of the five-member Cuban delegation of the Constituent Assembly to discuss the terms of the Platt Amendment with the McKinley administration. From *Minneapolis Journal*, April 26, 1901.

. . . .

"Politics of the Sugar Crop." Caption: "Uncle Sam: 'If I give it back to you this year I'm afraid you'll neglect your work. I'll let you have it later.'" Depiction of the first year of the second U.S. military occupation. From *Minneapolis Tribune*, reprinted in *Literary Digest* 34 (April 27, 1907).

. . . .

American imperial administration. Correspondent George Kennan recoiled in disgust in 1899 at the sight of "the average Cuban," deemed to be "careless and untidy in his personal habits and unclean in his environment." Kennan added, "The Cuban people . . . disregard and ignore the most elementary principles of sanitary science."[102] Cubans "did not want to be clean and healthy," pronounced New York representative Townsend Scudder. "They opposed the American innovations in this respect as so many assaults upon their traditional privileges and personal freedom. They preferred the old way of doing things. They liked smells; they had a fondness for dirt."[103] The advances of civilization

A TRIAL SPIN.

"A Trial Spin." Depiction of Cuban self-government upon passage of the Platt Amendment. From *Chicago Tribune*, June 16, 1901.

. . . .

"The Beginner." Caption: "Uncle Sam: 'Now look out old man,
this is where I let go.'" Depiction of preparations to end the U.S. military
occupation. From *Minneapolis Journal*, March 26, 1902.

. . . .

and progress were registered most notably in cleanliness. "The principle of
cleanliness is being inculcated in them," wrote essayist John Kendrick Bangs
in 1901. "In two short years of military occupation in Cuba . . . , cleanliness has
been brought out of filth."[104] To cleanse was to civilize. A cartoon published in
June 1899 depicted President William McKinley bathing the infant Philippines
in the pool of civilization, with the toddlers Cuba and Puerto Rico donning a
new change of attire fashioned from an American flag.

Association with commonplace products and familiar practices could allow

HE CAN'T MISS IT.

"He Can't Miss It." From *Minneapolis Journal*, March 29, 1901.

. . . .

political purport to pass undetected. The transplanting of a tree on Arbor Day 1901—the "Liberty Tree from the United States Nursery"—depicts pruned branches to signify limitations on Cuban sovereignty as a matter of horticultural wisdom. The bicycle similarly developed into a self-explanatory metaphor, endowed with multiple meanings with which to suggest purpose and convey performance. This was the bicycle as a late-nineteenth-century cultural phenomenon, loaded with social meaning transferred easily enough into political domains. The bicycle had come to symbolize freedom and liberty, self-possession and self-control. For women and children especially, riding

"Teaching Cuba to Ride." From *Minneapolis Journal*, July 25, 1899.

. . . .

bicycles had come to represent a skill associated with autonomy and mobility, what social historian Robert Smith suggested to be the means with which "to reach for even more freedom."[105]

The bicycle thus developed into a metaphor within a metaphor, two complementary and mutually reinforcing figurative references, mostly to the Cuban as a child but occasionally Cuba as woman, learning to ride a bicycle—and later learning to drive an automobile—as learning the skills of self-government. This was a representation of an accomplishment immediately recognizable to

"Self-Government—American Model." From *Philadelphia Inquirer*, June 2, 1901.

. . . .

all: to ride the bicycle unassisted as analogy to the mastery of skills by which a child—or woman—acquired sufficient discipline for mastery of self.

Only slightly less common was the depiction of Cuban self-government as a matter of a boat departing the security of land, often into squalls of uncertainty. In most instances, it was Uncle Sam who presided over the launching, establishing a reassuring presence, and the moral of U.S. rescue was inscribed into the subtext.

"After the First Mile." Depiction of the first year of the Cuban republic.
From *Cleveland Leader* (1903), reprinted in John J. Johnson, ed.,
Latin America in Caricature (Austin, 1980).

. . . .

CASTING OFF.
Little Cuba Will Paddle His Own Canoe.

"Casting Off." Caption: "Little Cuba will paddle his own canoe." Depiction of the end of the U.S. military occupation. From *Minneapolis Journal*, May 20, 1902.

. . . .

The metaphor of child further set in relief the image of the island as classroom, the Cubans as students, and the Americans as their teachers. Indeed, education—both figuratively and literally—was at the core of the metaphor as paradigm. The classroom was imagined as the site for the transmission of new cultural knowledge and the transformation of political values. Indeed, perhaps the most widely disseminated turn-of-the-century image depicted a classroom setting, typically with Uncle Sam as teacher, often with switch in hand, with Cuba as pupil, often in class with other newly acquired territories

GOD SPEED THE NEW REPUBLIC—UNCLE SAM'S PROMISE IS TO-DAY FULFILLED.

"God Speed. The New Republic—Uncle Sam's Promise Is
To-Day Fulfilled." Depiction of the end of the U.S. military occupation.
From *New York Daily Tribune*, May 20, 1902.

. . . .

represented as classmates, receiving proper lessons on civics and civilization. "Cuba has had more than three years of schooling for the part she has to play," exulted the *Washington Post* at the end of the military occupation in 1902. "She will enter the arena as the alumnus of the greatest academy on earth—not as a fourth-class trembler, shrinking at the bully's frown. How effective the tuition has been; with what wisdom the faculty have chosen their material. . . . Our authorities have done their best."[106]

The metaphor enabled Americans—parents—to persuade themselves that Cubans—children—were obliged to defer to adults as a function of the human life cycle. Just as parental wisdom and adult experience could not yield to protests from the child in need of discipline, the Americans could not permit Cubans to challenge U.S. authority. That Cubans protested North American control was equated with tantrums of misbehaved children that required disciplinary action by the parents. The Cuban demand for self-determination, or alternately, Cuban protest of American military intervention, was duly dis-

Uncle Sam: "Remember I'm still runnin' the life saving station."

"Uncle Sam: 'Remember I'm Still Runnin' the Life Saving Station.'" Depiction of the end of the U.S. military occupation. From *Cleveland Plain Dealer*, May 22, 1902.

. . . .

missed, or disregarded, characterized as the complaints of children bemoaning the exercise of parental authority. Experience gave meaning to representation.

The Cuban rebellion against the U.S.-installed government of President Tomás Estrada Palma in 1906 drew universal condemnation in the United States. It was the unruly childlike behavior of Cubans that obliged the United States, in function of its parental responsibility—the Platt Amendment—to intervene and impose discipline upon the quarreling children by suspending self-governance and imposing an American provisional government. President Theodore Roosevelt could hardly contain his indignation. "They have been behaving like exceedingly bad children," he fumed, "with the powers and passions of full grown men, and both sides have acted so badly that at any moment they may simply force us to land troops."[107]

"School Begins." Caption: "Uncle Sam (to his new class in Civilization):
'Now, children, you've got to learn these lessons whether you want to or not!
But just take a look at the class ahead of you, and remember that in a little while,
you will feel glad to be here as they are.'" From *Puck*, January 25, 1899.

. . . .

Almost everyone agreed, and almost in exactly the same terms. President
Roosevelt, the *Washington Post* commented, had "warned the Cubans in
fatherly fashion that they must cease their family quarrel . . . or he will be compelled to apply the rod to them."[108] "Our wayward child" was how the *Chicago
Tribune* characterized Cuba in 1906 and outlined North American responsibilities with reference to the Platt Amendment:

When the United States reserved the right to intervene in the affairs of Cuba
whenever necessary to preserve public order and insure the protection of
life and property it announced itself as standing in loco parentis to the infant republic. That is where we stand now. We are the parent; Cuba is the
child; and the child is about due for a good spanking. It would be a mistake
to spare the rod and spoil the child. If we are going to be the guardian of
that heterogenous and mixed population we must begin to exercise our
rights and exert our authority.[109]

"Uncle Sam's Kindergarten for the Propagation of Liberty." From "Scrapbook of Cartoons, Clippings, etc., Related to the Spanish-America War of 1898," unpublished manuscript, 1898–99, Davis Library, University of North Carolina, Chapel Hill.

. . . .

"Our Cuban neighbors are in truth very much like children," bemoaned the *New York Times* in 1906. "They are above the age of spanking, yet they manifestly stand in need of correction." The *Times* insisted that Cubans had behaved "a good deal like children" and that "leading strings were needed for their [own] good." The insurrection had revealed that Cubans were "not yet mature. They are politically under age, with the disabilities and incapacities pertaining to the minority state." The cessation of hostilities in Cuba upon the arrival of North American mediators in 1906, the *Times* suggested, was like "the sudden silence that falls upon the nursery when the quick ears of embattled childhood detect the heavy parental footstep on the stair."[110] This was Cuba "as a troublesome child," lamented Pennsylvania representative J. Hampton Moore a year later, "which wanted us to feed it and yet let it have its own way, for whose preservation and maintenance we had spent so much in treasure and in blood."

UNCLE SAM'S NEW CLASS IN THE ART OF SELF-GOVERNMENT.

"Uncle Sam's New Class in the Art of Self-Government."
From *Harper's Weekly*, August 27, 1898.

. . . .

"I Wonder if That's the 'Big Stick' I Hear So Much About?" Depiction of the outset of the second U.S. intervention in 1906. From *Washington Star*, October 3, 1906.

. . . .

Moore wrote of "our discontented ward" that had required the United States to intervene to save "the foundling [that] had fallen out with itself."[111] *Outlook* magazine mixed metaphors to make a similar argument:

> In general, in any civilized community each family is left to administer its own affairs. One household does not interfere with the government of another household merely because the children are unjustly disciplined, the wife harshly treated, and the money which should be used for the home is spent in drink. But if there is an end of family government, if the lives of the wife and children are threatened by an irate and drunken master of the house, or if the grown-up children themselves fall to fighting one another with pistols and bowie-knives and the weak-willed parents are unable to control them, the law steps in and takes control. And if this lawless family is living in a border community or a colonial time, when as yet there is no law

CRYING FOR ANNEXATION
Dame Cuba—I think. uncle, he's crying to come to you.

"Crying for Annexation." Caption: "Dame Cuba—'I think, uncle, he's crying to come to you.'" Depiction of the outbreak of armed revolt in 1906. From *Minneapolis Journal*, August 22, 1906.

. . . .

"WAITING."

"Waiting." Depiction of the armed revolt in 1906.
From *Chicago Tribune*, September 26, 1906.

. . . .

Jackie on the spot.

"Jackie on the Spot." Depiction of second intervention.
From *Washington Evening Star*, September 16, 1906.

. . . .

TOO SMALL FOR U. S.

The Policeman—Yes, he's on my beat all right, but he'll have to grow some before it would seem right to use the stick.

"Too Small for U.S." Caption: "The Policeman—'Yes, he's on my beat all right, but he'll have to grow some before it would seem right to use the stick.'"
From *Minneapolis Journal*, September 12, 1906.

. . . .

SECRETARY TAFT IN HIS RESCUE ACT.

"Secretary Taft in His Rescue Act." Depiction of Secretary of War
William Howard Taft's efforts to mediate an end to the insurrection of 1906.
From *Washington Post*, September 30, 1906.

. . . .

framed and organized for such a case, the neighbors step in and intervene
for the protection of life and the preservation of order. They have not only a
right, but a duty so to do.[112]

At the end of the second intervention, on the scheduled day of the U.S.
evacuation, the *New York Times* published a poem by Ella Fanning titled "Her
Coming Out," which proclaimed that Cuba was prepared to resume self-
government:

The big stick in Cuba.

"The Big Stick in Cuba." Depiction of Secretary of War William Howard
Taft's efforts to mediate an end to the insurrection of 1906.
From *Cleveland Plain Dealer*, September 17, 1906.

. . . .

Perky, pert, impatient maid
    Dons her first long skirts to-day,
Does her hair up, child no more;
    Through with youthful pranks and play.

Now cuts loose from leading strings,
    Competent to go alone.
Relatives amused, amazed—
    "Bless us! How the girl has grown!"

Dame Columbia, proud, looks on,
    Half in fondness, half regret;
Hopes that future may be well—
    Proffers aid and counsel yet.

Mere adopted child, of course,
    Yet her own, in love and deed:

"Better Leave Him in a While Longer." Depiction of one year of U.S. occupation. From *Des Moines Register and Leader*, reprinted in *Literary Digest* 34 (April 27, 1907).

. . . .

Pats her cheek and says, "Farewell,
    Little Cuba, and godspeed!"[113]

Another insurrection in Cuba in 1912, and another U.S. armed intervention, drew the same responses. This was Cubans acting again as children, disruptive and unruly, and in need of parental disciplinary action.

The North American notion of adult authority also assigned metaphorical representation to age differentials to depict Cuba as younger sibling. "We stand to Cuba as an elder brother," pronounced Nebraska senator William Allen as justification for war in 1898.[114] W. R. Morgan of the Division of Latin American affairs explained in 1927 that U.S. responsibility in Cuba was "to exert physical or moral pressure either under the Platt Amendment or under a

"Cheese it; here comes the cop!"

"Cheese It; Here Comes the Cop!" Depiction of preparations for U.S. armed intervention. From *Cleveland Plain Dealer*, September 19, 1906.

. . . .

sort of big brother understanding in the hope of helping [Cubans] solve their difficulties."[115] C. H. Forbes-Lindsay also invoked the sibling imagery. "At first sight, you will like the Cuban," Forbes-Lindsay wrote, "and you may continue to do so after you have learned to know him for a weak-minded brother, without any stable qualities in his composition. He has a subtle attractiveness which you will find it difficult to analyze. Perhaps it is his natural *bonhomie* and the genuine affectionateness that draws you, and the undercurrent of *naïve* child-ishness that blinds you to his faults."[116] Metaphor also often depicted Cuba as a younger sister. "Now we, in America, owe a clear duty to our 'Little Sister' Cuba," proclaimed Havana resident Jacob Goldstein in 1921, "whom we saved from the spoiler and to whom we gave her freedom at a time when she was, perhaps, not quite ready for it."[117] This was the image used by General John Pershing in 1925: "We have watched our small sister's wonderful growth with a very keen and sincere solicitude."[118]

★ ★ ★

The metaphor of children served multiple discursive functions and devel-oped into one of the principal modes by which Americans subsequently de-

"Uncle Sam: 'And to Think I Just Bought It For Him Brand New Seven Years Ago.'" Depiction of preparations for U.S. armed intervention. From *Toledo Blade* (1906), reprinted in *Literary Digest* 33 (October 6, 1906).

. . . .

fined their relationship with Cubans. The debate in the United States in 1902 over tariff relief for Cuban imports was conducted by way of conflicting metaphorical meanings in relationship to parental responsibility to children. "We have resting upon us the obligation of a mother to a daughter," pronounced Massachusetts representative Samuel McCall.[119] Michigan senator Julius Burrows opposed reciprocity and protested, "We rushed in there [to Cuba] and drove away the man who was beating his wife, but we did not agree to support the children." To which Senator Orville Platt responded, "No man is bound to adopt a child, as we have adopted Cuba; but having adopted a child, he is bound to provide for it."[120] "To say we owe [Cuba] nothing," exhorted the

"First Aid to the Suffering." Depiction of preparations for U.S. armed intervention. From *Brooklyn Citizen* (1906), reprinted in *Literary Digest* 33 (September 29, 1906).

. . . .

Brooklyn Eagle, "is to deny the duty of a parent to support his child."[121] Louisiana representative Samuel Robertson opposed tariff relief, insisting that the United States had fully discharged its responsibilities to Cuba at the end of the military occupation: "That we have brought her forth in her swaddling clothes is true. That we have put her on her feet and she can walk is true. Shall we continue to nurse her at the breast until she is full grown?"[122] Newspaper editor Carl Schurz made the anti-imperialist argument using the same metaphor: "If we have rescued those unfortunate daughters of Spain, the colonies, from the tyranny of their cruel father, I deny that we are therefore in honor bound to marry any of the girls, or to therefore take them all into our household, where they may disturb and demoralize our whole family."[123]

The metaphor of Cuba/Cubans as child/children insinuated itself into popu-

"Can He Walk without the Support?" Depiction of preparations for the
end of the U.S. occupation. From *Chicago Inter-Ocean* (1908), reprinted in
Literary Digest 36 (February 8, 1908).

. . . .

lar sensibilities and established itself as one of the salient reference points
from which the Americans assembled their knowledge of Cuba. The metaphor
acquired commonplace currency and was produced and reproduced by almost
all who presumed to write authoritatively about Cuba. Most immediately, it
developed into a discursive staple of North American travel books. Motoring
through Cuba in 1909, Ralph Estep described Cubans as "guileless, frank, generous, meek, dirty, willing and altogether submissive and obedient. In other
words, they are children."[124] Travel writer Frank Carpenter introduced Cuba
to American tourists by way of a brief history lesson: "With the downfall of

"Cuban Republic: 'I Reckon I'll Have to Get Out and Walk.'" Depiction of the end of the U.S. occupation. From *Seattle Post-Intelligence* (1909), reprinted in *Literary Digest* 38 (February 6, 1909).

. . . .

Spanish rule, the infant Cuba was taken in hand by Uncle Sam and started on the road to self-government and peace."[125] Basil Woon used similar imagery in his tourist guidebook: "[In 1902] the Americans kept their word, hauled down the Stars and Stripes from Morro Castle, and sailed away, leaving the infant Republic of Cuba to struggle in its swaddling clothes for better or for worse." He continued the metaphor:

> The infant, growing gradually from long clothes into short jeans, from jeans into breeches, and from breeches into trousers, proved an unruly child, as was natural considering its stormy conception. Twice the Americans were forced to return to Cuba, restore order, and depart. Children

"Semi-Sovereign Republic of Cuba." Caption: "Cuba: 'Golly, I've gone an' did it again!'" From *Cleveland Plain Dealer* (1912), reprinted in John J. Johnson, ed., *Latin America in Caricature* (Austin, 1980).

. . . .

of the sun grow to maturity earlier than others, which is perhaps why they retain through their manhood certain traits of childhood and adolescence. They love life, gaiety, laughter. They are quick to anger, easily carried away by faulty eloquence. They are prone to worship their chiefs one moment and then, like a child with his school-teacher, throw stones at their idol.[126]

"They have had no more control of their making than a child has of its," C. H. Forbes-Lindsay wrote in his travel guide to Cuba. "They have always been treated as irresponsible and incapable beings. They have never had fair scope for initiative, nor a free field for endeavor. . . . Under the circumstances is it to be wondered at that the Cuban is deficient in backbone; that he is vacillating and morally wobbly. . . . That his somewhat effeminate . . . features bear a stamp of weakness?" Forbes-Lindsay was emphatic: "What the Cuban seems to need more than anything else is to develop virility. . . . Meanwhile, it is

"Please Be Good!" From *St. Louis Post Despatch*,
reprinted in *Literary Digest* 44 (June 8, 1912).

. . . .

"Uncle Sam: 'I'll Give You One Teaspoonful. More of It Might Make You Sick.'" From *Columbus (Ohio) Dispatch* (1902), reprinted in John J. Johnson, ed., *Latin America in Caricature* (Austin, 1980).

. . . .

always to be remembered that he was freed from his swaddling clothes but yesterday. He never before had a fair chance to grow, to stretch his limbs, to think and act for himself."[127] Visiting Cuba in the mid-1940s, writer Erna Fergusson, otherwise a sensitive observer of the Cuban condition, succumbed to temptation of facile explanation by way of metaphor. "Cuba has always been a problem child," pronounced Fergusson. "Cuba feels that the problems have been hers and that their existence is due entirely to her dominant parent—first

"You Must Give Her a Living Chance Too, Uncle." From *New York World*,
reprinted in *Literary Digest* 24 (May 31, 1902).

. . . .

Spain, and now the United States, which, while hardly a parent might be described as the interfering or intervening uncle."[128]

The historical scholarship served as another means by which to propound
the colonial trope as a usable explanation of the Cuban-U.S. relationship.
The Cuban past was often rendered comprehensible in precisely the terms
by which the exercise of power over the island was justified in the first place.
President William McKinley, wrote biographer Margaret Leech, had believed
that the United States was obliged to adopt a "protective attitude toward the
infant at its doorstep."[129] Efforts at revolutionary change in Cuba were not
to be taken seriously, Hudson Strode scoffed, for they were often "no more
than a proud boy's play."[130] Historian Howard Hill wrote warmly about Presi-

FIRST STEPS

"First Steps." Depiction of inauguration of the Cuban republic.
From *Minneapolis Journal*, May 17, 1902.

. . . .

dent Theodore Roosevelt's policy approach to Cuba: "He assumed toward the island republic an attitude which on the whole resembled that of a father who takes pride in the achievement of his child, but who does not hesitate, if need arises, to admonish and discipline his offspring."[131] Historian Robert Ferrell was only slightly less condescending: "In general, it might be said, the Platt Amendment was not an uncalled-for infringement of Cuban sovereignty, for the islanders badly needed tutelage and preparation for self-government. It certainly was not a heavy burden on Cuban life, even if Latin patriots sought to describe it as such."[132]

The Americans represented hegemony not as a matter of self-interest but

"The First Steps Alone." Depiction of inauguration of the Cuban republic.
From *Puck*, May 21, 1902.

· · · · · · ·

as a commitment of selfless duty; they sought not domination but deliverance. North American conduct sought validation by way of those interior realms of motives and good intentions, through the enactment of ideals of selflessness and sacrifice, and through discharge of a higher morality in behalf of the well-being of others. But motives were never the issue—means were. The United States was not, of course, the first—or the only—country to invoke *mission civilatrice* as the rationale of empire. But it was singular in the degree to which it so thoroughly obscured the distinction between selfless purpose and self-interest. It was only a matter of time that a difference in degree made for a difference in kind.

4

On Gratitude as Moral Currency of Empire

The American is generously and honestly endowed with the desire to relieve suffering and to extend to others what he considers the blessings of his way of life. Believing that his country is history's chosen child, he deems it not merely a right but a duty to give the best part of his heritage to the less fortunate. Some men fight for their country's boundaries or to add a province to their nation's domains. The American is more easily moved to liberate the provinces of the heart and mind. He is seldom repaid in gratitude, rarest of all human currencies. . . . These feelings, so deeply and honestly part of the nation's history and thought, have been the greatest single force in American foreign policy. Cuba in 1898 was a classic example of their operation.
—H. Wayne Morgan, America's Road to Empire: The War with Spain and Overseas Expansion *(1965)*

I expect nothing from the Americans. We should entrust everything to our own efforts. It is better to rise or fall without help than to contract debts of gratitude with such a powerful neighbor.—General Antonio Maceo to Federico Pérez Carbó *(July 14, 1896)*

For the sake of Cuba's best interests, it is to be hoped that she will win her independence without receiving from any quarter, and especially from the United States, any such favors as might hereafter put her in a position of tutelage or in any wise hamper her freedom of action. . . . Undue influence on the part of powerful neighbors is sure to be . . . an impediment.—John Fiske, introduction to Grover Flint, Marching with Gómez *(1898)*

Have we had [recompense] in the continuing gratitude of the people whom we have aided? . . . He who would measure his altruism by the good will and sincere thankfulness of those whom he aids will not persist in good works. . . . The character of the benefits we have conferred on these Spanish-speaking peoples is such as necessarily to imply our sense of greater capacity for self-government and our belief that we represent a higher civilization. This in itself soon rankles in the bosom of the native and dries up the flower of gratitude. It is natural that it should be so. We cannot help it. It is inseparable from the task we undertake. Our reward must be in the pleasure of pushing civilization and in increasing the opportunity for progress to those less fortunate than ourselves in their environment, and not in their gratitude.
—William Howard Taft, "Some Recent Instances of National Altruism: The Efforts of the United States to Aid the Peoples of Cuba, Porto Rico, and the Philippines" *(1907)*

Gratitude is a burden, and every burden is made to be shaken off.
—Denis Diderot, Rameau's Nephew *(1956)*

The Americans imagined their purpose in 1898 as a moral undertaking, a resort to arms in the form of a summons to deliver an oppressed New World people from the clutches of an Old World monarchy that could not but ennoble all who responded. Cubans were depicted as long-suffering neighbors, seemingly overmatched and outmaneuvered, confronting insurmountable obstacles in the attainment of unreachable goals. Almost everyone seemed to celebrate the call to arms as a project of beneficent intent, explicitly as a mission of rescue and redemption.[1]

The Cuban cause was declared righteous, and because it was, the American intervention was deemed rightful. But it is also true that the Americans indulged moral mandate as reason for war because they could; that is, this was a war that the Americans could choose to wage because it was one they were certain they could win. Spain was weak and war-weary. No one doubted the outcome.[2] Simply put, the discharge of moral purpose was facilitated by the advantage of military superiority.

The war was about the Cubans, of course. But it was also about the Americans, and about the capacity of self-representation to disguise self-interest—even, indeed, especially—from itself. "The Cuban question has become the American question," proclaimed the *Washington Evening Star* in February 1898.[3] It was perhaps inevitable that the Americans would be implicated in figurative constructs of their own making. The plight of a people imagined as neighbors could not but arouse moral indignation, precisely because it appeared to make a mockery of the very values the Americans claimed to be at their national essence. Many shared the opinion of political scientist Amos Hershey, who welcomed the declaration of war as a stand against "oppressive tyranny and criminal exploitation perpetrated in the broad daylight of nineteenth-century civilization at the very doors of a nation which prides itself upon its love of liberty and hatred of oppression. . . . We stand convicted in the eyes of the civilized world and of posterity, whether we intervene at this late day or not, of negligence in permitting one of the greatest crimes of the nineteenth century to be perpetrated at our Southern Gate." In exhorting intervention, Hershey pronounced, "We cannot atone for past negligence and weakness, but we may in part, at least, redeem our character as a nation in the eyes of the world, and recover our own sense of national self-respect by prompt and vigorous action."[4]

Failure to act in Cuba would have exposed the Americans as a people of piety without purpose, without the political courage of their moral convictions, without the will to discharge their duty to humanity. They appeared to have been overtaken by the myths of their own making. To do nothing, protested Louisiana senator Donelson Caffery, was to default on "a duty, a high

Christian, civilized duty."[5] The *New York Tribune* provided a stirring celebration of the American purpose: "The greatness of this Nation and its favorable situation place upon it duties which it cannot avoid without showing itself unworthy of its high estate."[6]

Certainly the Americans had a duty to the Cubans, but they had an equally compelling duty to be true to themselves, to act in discharge of the principles from which self-esteem and self-respect were derived. "An end must be put to the reign of starvation and death," the *Washington Post* demanded; "that is our duty—our duty to . . . humanity and to our own character as a people. . . . The people of this country look to their government for such action as will put the nation right in its own conscience."[7] The *New York World* insisted that "we would be unworthy of our own heritage of freedom did we fail to stretch out our strong arm to succor and to save the Cuban patriots."[8] The issue was no longer about Spain, or even about Cuba, insisted the *Philadelphia Inquirer*; it was about "national prestige and national honor." The paper added metaphorically, "This nation has put its hand to the plow and it cannot now turn back."[9] The *Washington Evening Star* was categorical: "Our self-respect is at stake. We must maintain that at all hazards." Furthermore, "we have reached the point now where we must redeem our promises to ourselves or stand the humiliating consequences. Our greatest duty is to ourselves."[10] The necessity to do something in Cuba was an obligation of righteous purpose, a matter of fulfilling duty inscribed in the national character. It was what Americans did because they were American.

To pronounce selfless intent, of course, did not preclude the pursuit of self-interest. Popular sentiment and political purpose engaged one another in dialectical interaction, each serving to validate the other, thereupon passing into the collective memory as the meaning by which the war was understood at the time and remembered later. The proposition of a war imagined in behalf of *Cuba Libre*, waged and won by the United States, emerged as the principal narrative framework in which the representation of 1898 developed into historical knowledge. It is not clear, in fact, how—or even if—popular sentiment, that is "public opinion," shaped North American policy decisions in 1898, either as a factor influencing the purpose of the war or as a condition shaping the meaning of the peace. What is certain, however, is that the conventional wisdom about 1898, from participant observers and professional commentators at the time—and historians later—accorded popular sympathy for *Cuba Libre* privileged explanatory function as reason for war.[11] This proposition developed into the mainstay of a historiography that obtained a consensus of remarkable endurance, one that was itself less a commentary on the historical than a continuity of the sublime narrative of 1898, told and retold as a source of American moral authenticity.

★ ★ ★

It was the victory to which the Americans first laid claim and from which they proceeded to propound moral authority over Cuba. This was the "Spanish-American War," a sixty-day war whose very name denied the presence and dismissed the participation of Cubans as relevant to the outcome. Silences revealed assumptions. The representation of a Spanish-American war suggested in more than symbolic terms a war without antecedents, a war fought between only two parties. Spain had been defeated and expelled through the resolve and resources of the United States, the story was told and took hold, as a result of the efforts of the Americans, through their sacrifices, at the expense of their lives, and through the expenditure of their treasure. The Cubans had contributed nothing.[12]

The Americans understood themselves to have mobilized in behalf of *Cuba Libre* and to have succeeded where the Cubans had failed; from this they could easily enough infer that a war had been waged and won for the purpose proclaimed. The narrative assumed a logic of its own, incontrovertible precisely because it inferred national purpose from popular sentiment: a war waged, exactly as vast numbers of Americans had demanded, for Cuban independence. "Cuba was not able to expel Spain," Indiana senator Albert Beveridge proclaimed an enduring North American truth; he added, "The United States ejected Spanish government from that island. In doing this, the United States expended many scores of millions of dollars. Our soldiers gladly gave their lives."[13] Few Americans at the time—or thereafter—disagreed with Illinois representative T. J. Selby's judgment: "American arms accomplished in a few weeks what Cuba had failed to do in a century and what Cuba never could have done in a century to come."[14]

★ ★ ★

The American soldiers arrived in Cuba certain of their role as benefactors, self-consciously on a mission of liberation, only to discover that the presumed beneficiaries of their exertions had ideas of their own. Cubans were suspicious of North American motives.[15] Weary of three years of war, wary of the North American presence, the Cubans conveyed little of the gratitude their would-be deliverers believed appropriate. "You would expect them to be filled with gratitude towards us who are about to redress their wrongs," remarked one correspondent. "But that is not so."[16] The American officers received "a very cool reception," Trumbull White wrote at the war's end, adding, "The Cubans were very bitter in their expressions. They had only sneers for our soldiers. They made no concealment of the fact that they looked upon them as a species of international thieves, who had come to steal before their open eyes the fruits of their victory. . . . The Cuban considered himself a cruelly wronged man."[17]

That Cubans were not forthcoming with gratitude rankled the Americans. Novelist Stephen Crane, serving as the *New York World* correspondent in Cuba, bore witness to the results. "One must not suppose that there was any cheering enthusiasm at the landing of our army here," Crane cabled from Cuba. On the contrary, the Cubans looked at the Americans "stolidly, almost indifferently." American officers and men, Crane wrote, "have the most lively contempt for the Cubans. They despise them. . . . [The American soldier] thinks of himself often as a disinterested benefactor, and he would like the Cubans to play up to the ideal now and then. His attitude is mighty human. He does not really want to be thanked, and yet the total absence of anything like gratitude makes him furious."[18]

The American reaction was at times visceral. Perhaps nothing so enraged the bearers of good intentions more than suspicion of their motives. "The Cubans themselves were not worth one gill of the good American blood spilled for their benefit" was the shrill denunciation by the *New York Evening Post*. "They are obviously a wretched mongrel lot, . . . ungrateful to the last degree for the condescension of the United States in coming to their relief."[19] Captain H. L. Street characterized Cubans as "the most ungrateful set I have ever come across," and General Samuel B. M. Young agreed: "The insurgents are a lot of degenerates, absolutely devoid of honor or gratitude."[20] General Otis O. Howard, formerly the director of the Freedmen's Bureau, invoked a familiar frame of reference. Howard attributed the deepening "prejudice against the Cubans" principally to "a feeling that these patriots have not properly appreciated the sacrifices of life and health that have been made to give them a free country"—circumstances similar, Howard recalled, to the "dislike of black men in 1863 in our own country because so many of them did not seem to understand, or be grateful for, what had been done for them."[21]

★ ★ ★

The role of gratitude has long been recognized as a central factor in the moral calculus of power. Immanuel Kant wrote at length on gratitude as a "moral duty," insisting that "gratitude consists in *honoring* a person because of a kindness he has done us. The feeling connected with this recognition is respect for the benefactor (who puts one under obligations)." Kant understood gratitude as an obligatory display attesting to "indebtedness . . . for a past kindness," necessitated "by moral law, i.e., duty." Conversely, ingratitude was characterized as "one of the most detestable vices" and "the essence of vileness and wickedness."[22] Sociologist Edward Westermarck insisted that "to requite a benefit, or to be grateful to him who bestows it, is probably everywhere . . . regarded as a duty," while Benedetto Croce explained gratitude as a "duty devolving upon an individual to repay with benefit the benefit received from another individual." Gratitude was "intertwined with an aspect of our moral relations," philosopher Fred Berger argued, principally "as a response to the benevolence of others." Berger added, "Expressions of gratitude are demonstrations of a complex of beliefs, feelings, and attitudes. By showing gratitude for the benevolence of others, we express our beliefs that they acted with our interests in mind and that we benefitted; we show that we are glad for the benefit and the others' concern—we appreciate what was done." The bonds are indissoluble, Berger suggests, noting that "some form of reciprocation is requisite."[23] The instrumental value of gratitude as a means of social control was suggested by psychologists Jack Brehm and Ann Himelick Cole, who concluded that "a favor tends to put pressure on the favored person to return the favor. The pressure to return the favor is a threat to the freedom of the favored person in his relations with the favorer."[24] Philosopher Claudia Card reflected on the ethics of gratitude with particular attention to parties who were "distinctly unequal in power" and observed, "Historically, the powerful and the privileged have imposed *their* guardianship upon the powerless and have felt the latter should be grateful for their 'care.'"[25] Power "actually consists, not in the return of a gift, but in the consciousness that it cannot be returned," sociologist Georg Simmel understood, "that there is something which places the receiver into a certain permanent position with respect to the giver, and makes him dimly envisage the inner infinity of a relation that can neither be exhausted nor realized by any finite return gift or other activity." Simmel referred to the obligations implicit in the "reciprocity of service and return service, even when they are not guaranteed by external coercion."[26]

The historical literature on New World slavery has similarly understood the instrumental function of compassion as a means of social control. Historian David Barry Gaspar examined the power of reciprocal ties in the slave system of Antigua, specifically the ways in which "that elusive but perhaps universal phenomenon of paternalism helped mold desirable slave behavior." He noted, "Paternalistic slaveowners endeavored to convince their slaves that, in return for humane treatment, they owed gratitude, which was most suitably expressed in loyalty and submission."[27] In the compelling account of daily life on the James Henry Hammond plantation in South Carolina, historian Drew Gilpin Faust documented the variety of strategies of domination, including "positive inducement [that] evolved into an elaborate system designed to win the slaves' allegiances." Concluded Faust, "Hammond had supplemented his use of rewards with rituals and symbols designed to persuade the slaves to accept their master's definition of their own inferiority and dependence and simultaneously to acknowledge the merciful beneficence of his absolute rule. . . . Gradually he sought to establish a system of domination in which he could extract willing obedience from compliant slaves, a system in which he could regard himself as benevolent father rather than cruel autocrat."[28] Historian Eugene Genovese commented extensively about "the doctrine of reciprocal duties," inherent in which were "dangerously deceptive ideas of 'gratitude,' 'loyalty,' and 'family'" that transformed "every act of impudence and insubordination—every act of unsanctioned self-assertion—into an act of treason and disloyalty, for by repudiating the principle of submission it struck at the heart of the master's moral self-justification." Observed Genovese,

> But just what is gratitude? Why did slaveholders dwell on it so? . . . In society much turns on giving and receiving equivalences, but where equivalence is out of the question, gratitude enters as a substitute. People are expected to be grateful not so much for the object received as for the experience of the giver himself. Between equals gratitude becomes a mediating force, which binds men into an organic relationship. But paternalism rested precisely on inequality. The masters desperately needed the gratitude of their slaves in order to define themselves as moral human beings.[29]

These strategies loomed large in systems of colonial domination. Colonizers obtained validation as self-appointed agents of progress and civilization, as a matter of disinterested beneficence, to which conquered peoples were proclaimed beneficiary and for which they were expected to display proper appreciation, most appropriately by way of submission, to their colonial benefactors. Octave Mannoni wrote at length about Europeans in Madagascar and the "bonds of dependence" forged by gratitude, which "cannot be demanded, even though in a way it is obligatory." Frantz Fanon early discerned the power calculus inscribed in French claims of medical progress in Algeria: "This is what we have done for the people of this country; this country owes us everything; were it not for us, there would be no country." He noted that "the colonization, having been built on military conquest and the police system, sought a justification for its existence and the legitimization of its persistence in its works." Of course, spurning the blessings of civilization introduced by the colonizer, Albert Memmi understood, exposed subject people to the charge of "notorious ingratitude," with far-reaching implications: "The colonizer's acts of charity are wasted, the improvements the colonizer has made are not appreciated. . . . [A] portrait of wretchedness has been indelibly engraved."[30]

★ ★ ★

The power of the representation of a Spanish-American war as an undertaking of rescue and redemption of Cuba, for which the Americans sacrificed life and treasure, resided in its capacity to implicate Cubans unwittingly in a complex set of binding reciprocities wholly of North American origins. The Americans professed their purpose to be liberation, proclaimed themselves liberators, and pronounced the Cubans as liberated. Certainly Spain had been defeated and expelled in 1898, from which the Americans inferred easily enough that the mission of liberation had been accomplished.

Intention of purpose shaped perception of outcome. The Americans understood themselves to have achieved what they said they set out to do, thereby fixing the enduring representation of 1898. They appropriated full credit for the defeat of Spain and shared none with the Cubans. The knowledge by which the Americans arrived to their understanding of 1898 served to privilege the meaning of their presence. Cubans were transformed from active to passive, from subjects to objects, from agents of their own liberation to recipients of North American largesse. Authority in Cuba hence was not to be shared with Cubans as a liberated people but, rather, was to be exercised over them as a conquered people. "The foundation of our authority in Cuba," proclaimed President William McKinley in December 1898, "is the law of belligerent right over conquered territory."[31] Secretary of War Elihu Root was succinct: "We acquired title to Cuba by conquest."[32]

The Cubans had a different view. The source of the problem in this instance is not difficult to divine. The Americans judged their actions by their motives; the Cubans judged North American motives by their actions. The part played by Cubans in defeat of Spain passed largely unrecognized and unacknowledged. The Cubans defended their claim to independence as an achievement rightfully obtained through their own efforts. During three years of relentless war, Cuban forces had destroyed railroad lines, bridges, and roads and paralyzed telegraph communications, making it all but impossible for the Spanish army to move across the island and between provinces. Cubans recalled that they had inflicted countless thousands of casualties upon Spanish forces and encircled Spanish army units into beleaguered defensive concentrations in the cities, there to suffer further the debilitating effects of disease, illness, and hunger, circumstances that in no small fashion contributed to the ease with which the United States subsequently completed the defeat of Spain in 1898.

The Cubans had brought the Spanish army ever closer to the brink of defeat and more than adequately contributed to the vastly weakened condition in which Spain labored to mobilize for war with the United States. The role played by the Cuban army in joint operations with North American armed forces, moreover, was decisive. Cubans served as scouts, guides, and interpreters, and they provided vital intelligence and information. Cubans secured the beaches and facilitated the uncontested landing of U.S. troops. Indeed, at no point did the Americans encounter Spanish resistance upon landing. One reason the U.S. army command selected southeastern Cuba as a disembarkation site was the fact that Cubans exercised control over the entire countryside, thereby guaranteeing U.S. forces a safe landing. In the days and weeks that followed, Cuban army units deployed across southeastern Cuba to contain and check the movement of Spanish military forces. At Daiquirí and Siboney; in the engagements at Las Guásimas, El Caney, and San Juan; and during the siege of Santiago de Cuba, the Cubans had contributed in decisive fashion to the final defeat of Spain.[33]

Cubans acknowledged with appreciation American assistance, but they were also impatient to bid their allies farewell and get on with the project of nationhood for which so many had sacrificed for so long. "We thank the United States for the assistance it has given us," General José Mayía Rodríguez affirmed in October 1898, "but the time has now arrived when Cubans should be placed in the highest offices and should be prepared to take over the island on the departure of the Spanish."[34] General Máximo Gómez brooded in late 1898 and confided to an aide, alluding to the conditions upon which Cuban gratitude were contingent:

> What is going to be done about independence? The Americans, it seems, are not thinking about it. . . . Even if finally they give it to us, it will be as a gift, while we have gained it. And more than gained it with continuous efforts during more than half a century. The Americans have had an easy campaign because we have exhausted Spanish soldiers and resources. I am obligated to be grateful to the Americans, but only when they fulfill their promises, and if they fulfill them with decency and without aggravation to the Cubans.[35]

Many Cubans agreed with General Enrique Collazo, that to express gratitude to the Americans did not diminish the importance of the role of the Cubans in their own liberation. "The appreciation demonstrated by the Americans to the French ought to serve as the model with which the Cubans should demonstrate to the American people," insisted Collazo. "We are free and independent as the result of the Liberation Army of Cuba and the assistance given by the American government."[36]

The proposition of a war waged and won by the United States alone portended nothing less than a premise for domination. For the Americans to have acknowledged the Cuban contribution to the defeat of Spain could not but have challenged the terms by which they had assigned meaning to their mission and value to their victory. Cubans' claim of a role in their own liberation implied agency and was inadmissible precisely because, drawn to its obvious conclusion, it would have negated the logic by which the Americans presumed to rule postwar Cuba.

These were the fixed certainties by which the Americans arrived at their understanding of 1898. There was never a moment of doubt, never the thought of another possibility; indeed, such certainty played no small part in the implacable righteousness with which the Americans extended their authority over the island. The proposition that the United States—alone—had ended Spanish colonial rule had far-reaching implications and served as the basis upon which the Americans subsequently claimed authority to mediate the terms of Cuban sovereignty. The United States, Elihu Root insisted, had assumed "a moral obligation arising from her destruction of Spanish sovereignty in Cuba . . . for the establishment of a stable and adequate government in Cuba."[37] Connecticut senator Orville Platt was categorical. "When we undertook to put an end to bad government in Cuba," he insisted, "we became responsible for the establishment and the maintenance as well, of a government there. . . . The United States, if true to its history and its character, must train up its child in the way it should go, so that when old it will not depart from it." Platt said at another point, "Our work was only half done when Cuba was liberated from its oppressor. A nation which undertakes to put an end to bad government in a neighboring country must also see that just and good government follows."[38]

The representation of 1898 assumed the function of a legitimizing narrative. The remembered past developed into a means to control the future. So much was derived from the proposition that the United States—alone and unaided—had liberated Cuba. It provided moral plausibility to the claim of political entitlement, by which the Americans presumed thereafter to control Cuban affairs, to exercise power as a matter of fact, and to expect obedience as a matter of course. Americans felt entitled to hold certain attitudes, to make special demands, and to expect complete acquiescence.

This was a matter of power, of course, but it was especially about the way that power insinuated itself in the form of the moral logic within a system of domination. It was not sufficient—or even desirable—to exercise power over Cuba by way of coercion, real or implied, but, rather, through voluntary compliance: acquiescence to authority rendered as the natural order of things. This was the moral inducement to obtain submission, the way that power secured the behavior desired voluntarily, without recourse to force. That the relationship was in part derived from understood if unstated ethical reciprocities suggests a paradigmatic structure to hegemony and indeed sets in relief the moral determinants of power. Sociologist Georg Simmel was prescient to note that "to return the benefit we are obliged ethically; we operate under a coercion which, though neither social nor legal but moral, is still coercion."[39] Essential to this notion was the perception of a deed undertaken entirely out of selfless motive. The efficacy of the obligation of reciprocity, philosopher A. John Simmons was correct to note, required that "the benefactor must not have provided the benefit for reason of self-interest."[40]

The narrative discharged two related functions: on one hand, an internal discourse by which the Americans celebrated their own virtues and, on the other, an external one that implicated the Cubans in a debt to the United States. The Cubans of their own volition, out of a sense of gratitude, perhaps even cheerfully but certainly voluntarily, would thus be disposed to repay the sacrifices made by their benefactors by offering to accommodate North American interests upon demand. Surely Cubans could not be indifferent to American needs, the *New York Tribune* insisted, after "such cost of blood and treasure and at such risk of greater cost, and having . . . rescued Cuba from ruin and placing it upon the road to good government and good neighborship."[41] Tennessee representative Henry Gibson exhorted "the people of Cuba . . . to hasten to inquire of the United States what return they could make to us for what we have done and would scorn the very appearance of withholding anything which a nation prompted by the motives which animated us in our warfare in their behalf might ask."[42] Cuba was morally obliged "to voluntarily and gracefully show their gratitude to us," proclaimed Florida representative Robert Davis. "I believe that the true and real Cuban is grateful to us."[43]

Certainly the United States could have imposed its will on Cuba by other means: by way of force, for example. And indeed on occasion it did. But the virtue of moral suasion as a way to obtain Cuban acquiescence to North American interests was that it reduced the obtrusiveness of American power even as it ratified the Americans' perceptions that they had acted with selfless purpose. The Americans needed Cuban gratitude to validate the premise of their own self-esteem. It was a matter, in the end, as writer Marrion Wilcox commented in 1902, of getting the Cubans to be "as fond of us as we have the right to expect."[44]

★ ★ ★

In the United States the narrative of 1898 expanded fully into an exaltation of self-esteem and a celebration of self-satisfaction. The North American representation of 1898 was remembered as a matter of motives, more of popular intentions than political outcomes. This was a process by which Americans arrived at a sense of who they believed themselves to be, a way to transact the terms of self-identity as a discursive strategy of self-interest. To demand Cuban gratitude for service rendered was itself an inflection of power, a form of moral coercion as a means of political control. It advanced U.S. interests through Cuban compliance rather than North American coercion, an outcome that both met the North American purpose and validated the premise upon which it was based. Cuba owed its independence from Spain, the Americans insisted, to the sacrifices made by the United States, at great cost of life and blood and the expenditure of vast treasure. A war had been won by the Americans for—not with—the Cubans, for which the Americans felt themselves properly entitled to exact from the beneficiaries of their generosity something in return. The moral credibility of power was at least as important as the coercive capacity of power. To seek to parlay gratitude as a means through which to exact compliance, in the end, was to thwart the capacity to develop agency. The Cubans' pretension to sovereignty was not credible precisely because independence had not been won by them; it had been achieved by the Americans. The demand for the discharge of gratitude in this instance implied an obligation that was both self-implicating and self-deprecating. It was, as philosopher Fred Berger reflected on the implications of gratitude, "to use the fact of one's past aid in order to control another life . . . to deny him the independence befitting a moral agent."[45]

The North American claim of selfless purpose in 1898 served as a means of moral leverage to parlay gratitude in a source of moral entitlement writ large. No other single narrative element was as important to the moral premise of U.S. hegemony, or recited as often, as the insistence by the Americans to have liberated Cuba from Spain and to have established the Cuban republic—and always with the reminder to the Cubans—at great cost of life and treasure. Correspondent Stephen Bonsal wrote of "the thousands of men who died and the millions of money that were spent in the liberation of Cuba" and concluded, "We saved the Cubans from extermination, cleaned them up, and put them on their feet at considerable expense in men and money to ourselves."[46] Pennsylvania representative J. Hampton Moore insisted that "we drew upon our blood and treasure to liberate the Cubans," adding, "Cuba was given her liberty through the intervention of the United States, and with our help raised her own flag as a Republic."[47] "We spent hundreds of millions of dollars," proclaimed Minnesota representative Frank Eddy, "and drenched [Cuban] soil with our best and bravest blood to give her independence. . . . Cuba owes us a moral and financial debt."[48] "We expended in the Cuban war upwards of $300,000,000," Secretary of War William Howard Taft intoned, "and we never have invited from Cuba the return of a single cent." Taft continued, "We offered up in deaths and wounds and disease in that war the lives of 148 officers and over 4,100 enlisted men. We paid $20,000,000 to Spain under the treaty of peace."[49]

To accept the premise of the North American narrative was to be hopelessly implicated in its practice. And it was the premise to which the Americans were given to propounding, unabashedly, at times as a matter of hubris, at other times as presumption of privilege. The message was unequivocal and the moral was unambiguous: the Americans—not the Cubans—had liberated the island. "Cuba . . . owes to us her birth," President Theodore Roosevelt proclaimed in 1902; Cuba's "whole future, . . . very life, must depend on our attitude toward her."[50] He reiterated the sentiment one year later: "We gave [Cuba] liberty. We are knit to her by the memories of the blood and courage of our soldiers who fought for her in war; by the memories of the wisdom and integrity of our administrators . . . who started her so well on the difficult path of self-government."[51]

This was a narrative to which almost all Americans readily subscribed. It was a way that a people could feel good about themselves for the good they believed they had done for others, and they were not shy about proclaiming it. The Americans had succeeded where the Cubans had failed, the *Cleveland Plain Dealer* pronounced at the end of the occupation; they had "achieved for the Cuban people what they had for many year unsuccessfully endeavored to gain for themselves."[52] The *St. Louis Globe Democrat* used the occasion of the third anniversary of the Cuban republic to reaffirm the conventional wisdom that "it was the Americans who emancipated the Cubans"; the paper added, "The insurrection which began in 1895 was on the point of collapse when the United States intervened in 1898. . . . Every sane Cuban of to-day understands this. It was the United States, and not Gomez and his followers, who expelled Spain and gave freedom to the Cubans."[53] The *Brooklyn Eagle* was explicit: "Freedom was presented to Cuba, not won by Cuba, and has been accepted not wholly with gratitude or with grace by Cuba herself."[54]

The demand for Cuban gratitude called for more than an acknowledgment of debt. It implied, too, acts of appreciation, that is, deeds by which to demonstrate gratitude, a performance of gratitude as a means to reciprocate North American sacrifices. Indeed, only through the former could the Americans bind the Cubans to the latter. Gratitude obliged the Cubans to recompense the Americans for their sacrifice, if not in kind then certainly in service.

Gratitude as a matter of normative reciprocities expanded into a discursive strategy by which to exact Cuban acquiescence to North American interests as a condition of nationhood, that is, gratitude as a source of leverage by which to parlay a sense of debt into a demeanor of deference. Central to the representation of 1898 as an American war waged and won against Spain for Cuban liberation was the proposition that the Cubans, the beneficiaries, had incurred a debt to the Americans, the benefactors, for which the Cubans were to be thereafter permanently obliged to compensate the United States.

That Cubans would dispute the benefits attending the North American presence, that they wished to be rid of their benefactors who had sacrificed so much to liberate them, inflamed and infuriated the Americans. When the newspapers *Las Dos Repúblicas* and *La Verdad* in Puerto Príncipe demanded an end to the U.S. military occupation, the local North American military commander could hardly contain his ire. "The two newspapers . . . are against American intervention," bristled Colonel L. H. Carpenter. "They go as far in this direction as to appear to be oblivious that they owe anything to the Americans." Correspondent Francis Nichols reached a similar conclusion. "Many of them sincerely believe that the war would have ended just as quickly without the slightest aid from the Americans," Nichols scoffed, and added, "It has always seemed to me that this national conceit is at the root of the national ingratitude. . . . Cubans are, as a rule, one of the most ungrateful peoples on earth. . . . Everyone who knows the Cuban people knows that down in the bottom of their hearts there is no real gratitude, only a hope that Americans will soon receive enough thanks to leave them forever."[55]

The Cuban desire for independence—aspiration to sovereignty, in short—thereafter continued to arouse the ire of the Americans. It implied agency, of course. But it was more complicated: it was in fact received as a repudiation of the beneficence the Americans believed themselves to have extended to the Cubans. To reject the tender of generosity was to provoke a fit of animosity. "It is an old and time-worn saying that ingratitude is the basest of crimes," David Copeland wrote to the editor of the *Washington Post*. "After our country, out of pure sympathy, has spent millions upon millions of treasure and sacrificed many of her noble sons upon the altar of humanity to rescue the Gem of the Antilles from Spanish greed and oppression, we are now called upon to give up all and retire from the field of action so that a hungry horde may reap what we have sown. . . . The amazing impudence to demand immediate independence is unparalleled in all history. . . . We are dealing with base men, devoid of magnanimity."[56] "The Cubans have not generally been accredited with being a very grateful and generous people," lamented the *San Antonio Express* in 1900, "nor with having shown very high appreciation of the efforts of the American people in their behalf." Continued the editorial,

> When matters had finally reached such a point that nothing short of armed intervention would save the Cubans from the prospective extermination at the hands of the Spaniards the . . . American armies landed on the soil of

the Faithful Isle to aid in driving the Spaniards off and to give liberty and peace to the inhabitants. . . . From the day the American troops landed in Cuba until the Stars and Stripes floated over every part of the island it was a Spanish-American war for the deliverance of Cuba. The Cubans really took no further part in the struggle. . . . The Cubans had done little more than help to consume the American rations, yet they were immediately ambitious to assume the reins of government and bid the Yankees good-bye. They have been more or less restless ever since, chafing under the restraint it was necessary to impose to save the Cubans from themselves. It cost the United States many millions of dollars and many precious lives to do what she has done . . . , but the Cubans care nothing for that.[57]

The sacrifice of life and treasure made in behalf of Cuba, the Americans argued, surely entitled them to Cuban solicitude to arrangements desired by the United States. This was the narrative of 1898 put to instrumental use, a way to transact moral righteousness into political coercion. That the Cubans initially spurned the Platt Amendment rankled the Americans and produced a torrent of denunciations against the Cubans for their ingratitude and thinly veiled threats to take appropriate action. The *Philadelphia Inquirer* complained that Cubans who refused to ratify the Platt Amendment — provisions designed solely "to safeguard the independence of the Republic of Cuba" and "to which Cubans can have [no] reasonable occasion to object" — were "military adventurers" and "scheming politicians" who represented "the most ignorant and radical classes of the Cuban population."[58] New York representative Townsend Scudder was indignant. "The constitution recently adopted for the island by a convention of Cubans," Scudder protested, "makes no mention of the obligation due from the islanders to the United States for their emancipation from Spain's rule." "Spending millions of dollars in money and sacrificing many lives," he insisted, entitled the United States "to make demands upon the island much more severe than any we will make, and still the Cubans would have no cause to complain." Cuba "must be grateful to the United States," Scudder insisted, and added,

We are entitled to exercise a protectorate. . . . We should have conceded to us the right to intervene in order that no harm come to her and that a stable government may be maintained. We also should have the privilege of establishing naval stations. . . . All these things Cuba ought to be more than willing to grant, but it seems that [Cubans] have very little gratitude. . . . In view of the cost of Cuba's freedom to this country in treasure and in blood, gratitude should impel her to lean upon America as her best friend and protector.

Concluded Scudder, "It is not pleasant to have to urge upon one whom you have greatly benefitted the duty of manifesting a reasonable gratitude for such benefits, but it would be well were Cuba to show a bit more appreciation of what this Government has done for her. . . . They have a sacred duty to perform toward us, just as we have toward them. A bit of gratitude and friendly feeling on the part of the people whom we brought out of bondage would be a pleasant thing to contemplate just now."[59] Senator Orville Platt did not conceal his impatience with Cuban opposition to the amendment that bore his name. He denounced Cuban "false pride," expressing dismay that there was "no recognition of the United States, no expression of gratitude or friendliness."[60] Cuba was to be "bound to us," Platt demanded, "by the sentiment of gratitude," and he added, "Cuba committed her future to us when in the depth of her misery, she accepted our intervention."[61] Cubans were admonished to demonstrate proper appreciation for the sacrifices made in their behalf. "If the people of Cuba are wise and prudent," Tennessee representative Henry Gibson counseled, "they would be glad to have our Government exercise a sort of mild guardianship for a short time; and the fact that so many of their leaders seem devoid of all gratitude to the United States for the many millions of dollars we have spent in their behalf makes me suspicious of what Cuba's fate may be when wholly committed to their hands." Gibson denounced the Cubans for failure to demonstrate proper gratitude for American generosity. "We found her people dying of starvation in prison pens," he recounted the familiar story, "or slaughtered by a merciless foreign soldiery; and we have driven out these soldiers, opened the prison doors and made every Cuban free, and fed them generously from our own table." He continued,

> We found the Cubans deprived of all voice in their own government, and we have turned their oppressors out of power. . . . We found Cuba desolated by fire and sword from one end of the island to the other, and we have brought peace and law and order. . . . In a word . . . we found Cuba a hell, and we are fast converting it into a paradise. . . . And shall we have no right to guard this island and see to it that disorder shall not take the place of order, and see to it that the island, by unwise treaties, be not given over to our enemies?[62]

The power of the North American narrative lay in its capacity to sustain a politics of self-righteous certainty, wherein Cubans were characterized as bereft of proper appreciation of all the sacrifices made in their behalf—Cubans as a wretched lot, unappreciative of past favors and unworthy of future ones. It was thus the Americans who would claim to be the injured party, disappointed and deceived and hence morally entitled to take whatever action they deemed appropriate to exact proper appreciation of the sacrifices they had made. The Americans warned that for the Cubans to fail to demonstrate their gratitude to the United States—that is, their unwillingness to act in a manner befitting a grateful people—had dire consequences. "If the American people get the impression that Cuba is ungrateful and unreasonable," Elihu Root alluded to the Teller Amendment, "they will not be quite so altruistic and sentimental the next time they have to deal with Cuban affairs as they were in April, 1898." Two months later Root was categorical. "There is only one possible way for them to bring about the termination of the military government," Root admonished. "If they continue to exhibit ingratitude and entire lack of appreciation of the expenditure of blood and treasure of the United States to secure their freedom from Spain, the public sentiment of this country will be more unfavorable to them."[63]

The Cubans acquiesced and, in June 1901, ratified the Platt Amendment. The pressure to demonstrate gratitude to the United States was decisive to the outcome. The weekly *La Tribuna* defended the adoption of the Platt Amendment as a "duty of our people to assist the nation which helped to rescue us."[64] "The brusque and precipitous manner in which the Platt resolution was imposed," future president Tomás Estrada Palma brooded, "has injured my dignity as a Cuban and has caused me profound resentment." But in view of the fact that the United States was "a decisive factor in the achievement of our independence and in the creation of the Republic," Estrada Palma conceded, it was necessary to acquiesce to North American demands as a way to "give full expression to our gratitude."[65]

★　★　★

The military occupation came to an end on May 20, 1902, whereupon the Americans congratulated themselves—then and thereafter—for a pledge nobly made and honorably kept. The conceit was unabashed. This was the stuff of self-admiration, the way that a point of view passed as a matter of fact, told and retold to a people disposed to believe the best about themselves and the worst of everyone who doubted their motives and distrusted their purpose. They congratulated themselves for a mission accomplished and a purpose achieved. "The deed is done," exulted the *New York Tribune*. "The promise the United States made is fulfilled. . . . Free Cuba is an accomplished fact."[66] Georgia senator Augustus Bacon was rhapsodic: "We have a right to the greatest pride and self-congratulation upon our disinterested and noble work in Cuba. Through all the ages it must redound to our honor and glory."[67] The United States, Indiana senator Albert Beveridge proclaimed, "found Cuba a festering place of disease, found it the home of a . . . childish people who knew not

the supreme art of orderly government. . . . We left it purified and cleansed."
Said Beveridge at another point: "No such cleansing, uplifting, civilizing work
was ever done by any people for another as the American people did for the
Cubans."[68] President Theodore Roosevelt was euphoric. Speaking at Carnegie
Hall in New York before the General Assembly of the Presbyterian Church on
the evening of May 20, he extolled "the spirit of character and decency and the
spirit of National righteousness" that culminated in "starting a free republic
on its course" and "setting a new nation free," adding, "I think that the citizens of this republic have a right to feel proud that we have kept our pledges
to the letter."[69] One month later, the president was still in a celebratory mood.
"Our soldiers fought to give [Cuba] freedom," Roosevelt related to Congress,
"and for three years our representatives, civil and military, have toiled unceas-
ingly . . . to teach her how to use aright her new freedom. Never in history has
any alien country been thus administered with such high integrity of purpose,
such wide judgment, and such single-minded devotion to the country's interests."[70]

The Americans congratulated themselves for their accomplishments during the three years of military occupation, including public works projects,
public health programs, and public school reforms—which they expected the
Cubans to acknowledge with gratitude. "What did we do?" Massachusetts
senator George Hoar asked rhetorically, and answered: "We not only lifted
from Cuba the dark and heavy weight of Spanish misrule, but we threw around
that island our great, strong arm, and while in the path of peace and the methods of orderly administration the people of that island were enabled to form
their own government, and to-day Cuba stands out among the nations of this
earth." Indiana senator Charles Fairbanks was unabashedly exultant:

> In the history of this country and of civilized government there has never
> been an event of such splendid significance as that which was witnessed
> in that island yesterday. A solemn national pledge has been redeemed. A
> Republic has been erected under the authority of the United States, and
> the possession of the island has been surrendered to that Republic under
> happy auspices. . . . Where there was monarchical power and tyranny four
> years ago a Republic has arisen and starts peacefully upon her career with
> the congratulations of the nations of the earth. The freedom of Cuba is
> accomplished—accomplished through the valor of American arms and the
> wisdom of American statesmanship.[71]

Self-congratulation begot self-admiration. "We began with them in the
abject extremity of want and desperate disease," pronounced Alabama senator John Tyler Morgan, "and we have raised them and raised them and raised

THE DEBUTANTE.

"The Debutante." Depiction of inauguration of the Cuban republic.
From *Washington Evening Star*, May 20, 1902.

. . . .

ACCEPTED !
All's well that ends well.

"Accepted!" Caption: "All's well that ends well." Depiction of Cuban acceptance of the Platt Amendment. From *New York Daily Tribune*, June 15, 1901.

. . . .

them by our charity, by our benevolence . . . , by our laws, by our moral and legal influence."[72] "The Americans withdraw with clear consciences from the task of governing [Cubans]," the *Chicago Tribune* proclaimed on May 20. "The Americans have been faithful to [their] pledges. . . . Americans have reason to take great pride in their administration of Cuban affairs."[73] The *Washington Evening Star* could hardly contain its sense of accomplishment: "How well we have acquitted ourselves of our task the island itself plainly testifies. . . . We shall be able to show not only a clean bill of health as trustee, but the cleanest in history. For where else is recorded an act fashioned so generously or unselfishly as that which in its first feature marked our intervention in Cuba's behalf, and in its last feature marks our turning over to the Cubans the control of their own affairs?"[74]

Historians followed suit and indeed played no small part in ratifying the moral logic by which the Americans presumed to claim authority over Cuba. Connecticut senator Orville Platt was prescient when he predicted in 1901 that "the future historians will give full credit to the unselfish and wise conduct of the United States."[75] Historian Randolph Greenfield Adams pointed with pride to "one of the most creditable pages in American foreign policy when the United States kept its promise to make Cuba a free and independent nation," and James Ford Rhodes asserted flatly that the "pledge contained in the Teller amendment was faithfully kept." Journalist, historian, and, later, Michigan senator Arthur Vandenberg asserted flatly that the Teller Amendment was "faithfully observed," whereupon he proclaimed the "war as one of the loftiest purposed acts in the history of civilization . . . [and one that] compliments the altruism of a nation . . . which is prepared to serve human-kind in it own way and on its own initiative with a purity of dedication unmatched in any other government on earth."[76] Historians John Holladay Latané and David Wainhouse were unabashedly celebratory: "Never has a pledge made by a nation under such circumstances been more faithfully carried out."[77] Having discharged its duty in Cuba, Mabel Casner and Ralph Henry Gabriel pronounced, "according to its promise, the United States withdrew the American soldiers and made Cuba independent."[78] Foster Rea Dulles interpreted "the withdrawal of the bulk of American occupation forces in 1902" as evidence that "the United States had fulfilled the pledge made on taking up arms against Spain."[79] Historian Archibald Cary Coolidge was categorical: "The treatment [Cuba] has received since she was made free will remain something to be proud of."[80]

Those who understood what actually had transpired knew better. The Platt Amendment had eviscerated the Cuban republic of all the essential properties of sovereignty, conceding self-rule but denying self-determination. The promise of the Teller Amendment—disclaiming "any disposition or intention to exercise sovereignty, jurisdiction, or control over said island" and vowing "to leave the government and control of the island to its people"—was honored in the breach, just as Senator Albert Beveridge predicted it would be. Certainly Leonard Wood understood. "There is, of course, little or no independence left in Cuba under the Platt Amendment," he acknowledged privately to President Roosevelt in 1901. "It is quite apparent that she is absolutely in our hands."[81] The Cubans also understood what had transpired: they had been denied independence and deprived of sovereignty. "The Republic will surely come," a disconsolate General Máximo Gómez wrote to a friend, "but not with the absolute independence we had dreamed about." And on the matter of gratitude, the newspaper *Patria* was unequivocal:

If there is no independence and sovereignty, why should Cubans have to show themselves to be grateful to the United States? For having deceived them? For having replaced Spain as master? . . . What service has [the United States] rendered to Cubans that warrants appreciation? Is it not as clear as daylight that they intervened for their own benefit? And in this instance, should it not be the United States which should be grateful to poor and trusting Cuba for having providing the circumstances for its self-aggrandizement?[82]

★   ★   ★

The North American narrative of 1898 was layered with meaning and moral. This was knowledge arranged as a way to confirm power and disarm the power of others. But mostly it was knowledge arranged around the need for legitimacy: to fashion a morally persuasive premise with which to exercise power as a politically acceptable practice. To propound discharge of a debt of gratitude as moral obligation was at once a means to exact Cuban submission and a source of U.S. entitlement. "Cuba is bound [to the United States]," insisted the *Atlanta Constitution*, "by indestructible ties of gratitude." The *St. Louis Globe-Democrat* drew the logical inference: "The feeling of gratitude which [Cuba] should have for the United States demands that Cuba should hold a different attitude toward this country than it does toward the rest of the world."[83]

The proposition that Cuban independence was the product of North American efforts provided something of a self-confirming rationale with which to lay claim to authority over the new republic. The Americans fashioned a particular version of Cuban sovereignty, one in which the defense of U.S. interests served as the principal organizing logic of Cuban nationhood. "Although technically a foreign country," Elihu Root would acknowledge years later, "practically and morally . . . we have required [Cuba] to become a part of our political and military system, and to form part of our lines of exterior defense."[84]

The belief that Cuba's destiny was an extension of North American needs did indeed inform the ways that the Americans understood the purpose for the very existence of the Cuban republic. "Having sacrificed thousands of lives and millions of treasure to free Cuba from Spanish dominion," affirmed Indiana representative William Zenor in 1902, "[Cuba's] future destiny must ever be inseparably associated with that of ours."[85] President William McKinley was categorical: "The destinies of Cuba are in some rightful form and manner irrevocably linked with our own."[86]

A complex drama was being played out throughout the early decades of the twentieth century. The exercise of power derived moral certainty from representations first fashioned from the metaphors of 1898, a way to remind Cubans of what had been done for them as a means to intimate what was expected of them. Perceptions formulated in 1898 as knowledge of an experience—a matter of perspective and point of view, soon to pass into memory, and finally to develop into historical knowledge—gathered narrative momentum and assumed the form of a sentiment, ever so much more difficult to contest. It passed as received wisdom from which the rationale of North American power seemed as self-evident as it was self-explanatory.

The degree to which the Americans criticized Cubans for insufficient display of gratitude must be understood as a mode of political coercion and a means of moral extortion designed to obtain Cuban acquiescence to U.S. interests. At times the narratives of Cuba/Cubans as child/children and gratitude converged and reinforced one another. The instrumental efficacy of the paradigm of parenthood relied on more than presumption of adult authority over children. It also obtained moral resonance from sensibilities of appreciation, from the premise that one did indeed owe some measure of gratitude to parents for the selflessness of their dedication to child-rearing, a debt of course that could never be adequately repaid but was always to be acknowledged with appreciation. Deference to parental wishes was one way to demonstrate gratitude. The North American insistence that Cubans grant tariff concessions to U.S. imports, for example, was deemed a small price to pay for the great sacrifices made by the United State in behalf of Cuban independence. Illinois representative T. J. Selby chided the Cubans—"with sullen faces, like pouting children"—for their reluctance to accommodate U.S. trade interests. "We have sacrificed our best blood and treasure unstinted for Cuba," Selby taunted. "Is she now indifferent to these sacrifices of ours made in her behalf? . . . Let them rather bow the knee in gratitude and thank their Creator that we were so near to them and they so near to us, that we took up their cause against Spain and fought and won battles for Cuba which Cuba's people never could have fought and won."[87] Many, like General James Wilson, took umbrage that Cuban lawmakers had failed to favor U.S. products. "For all our loss of life, and the tremendous expense which our Government has incurred in expelling Spain from the island," Wilson decried, "it would be no more than fair that the Cubans should enter into an agreement with us by which they should give free entrance to our natural and manufactured products . . . and at the same time establish tariff identical with our own against all European countries."[88] When the new Tomás Estrada Palma government contemplated negotiating a trade treaty with England in 1902, U.S. minister Herbert Squiers bristled with indignation. "I cannot believe that the Cuban Government seriously considers England as a market," he complained to Washington. "That they will make every possible use of the possibility to secure better terms from the United States is probably nearer the truth. The United States can in no wise count on the gratitude of the Cubans in securing the signing of final ratification of this proposed Convention. The Cuban Government is prepared to make the best possible bargain, regardless of what they may owe the United States."[89] Squiers reported learning from Fermín Goicochea, a member of the board of directors of the Planters Association, that sugar producers sought expanded trade relations with Europe. "Mr. Goicochea belongs to a class of Cubans who are willing to sell their souls for the benefit of their pockets," Squiers reported; "they have no love or respect for our flag or any other. . . . They are devoid of gratitude, devoid of any feeling other [than] mercenary."[90] General Tasker Bliss was incredulous. "It would be an extraordinary spectacle," he commented, "if Cuba, geographically a part of our own country and exercising the powers of an independent nation solely as the result of the expenditure of our blood and our capital, should conclude a treaty of friendship and commerce with England and not with us."[91]

This was all about power, of course, but exercised always in the form of moral mandate. In the face of such vast power differentials a punitive U.S. response as a result of pique was not inconsequential. Senator Antonio Sánchez Bustamante understood the consequences of an unpaid debt of gratitude and was, accordingly, persuaded to vote against the trade agreement with England. "Unhappy will it be for us," Sánchez Bustamante warned, "if public opinion in the United States shall come to believe that this people, which has received only favors from the noble and heroic republic of North America, looks upon the United States only with jealousy and suspicion."[92]

Such pronouncements were consequences of the meaning that the Americans had assigned to 1898 and indeed must be viewed as central to the construction of reciprocities by which Cubans were susceptible—or more correctly, made to feel susceptible—to the whim and will of the United States. Cuban conduct seemed always to be measured in reference to 1898, deemed appropriate and adequate—or not—as discharge of the debt owed to the United States.[93] This was a point of view possessed of instrumental purpose, used to obtain Cuban acquiescence to North American needs, which almost always implied subordination of Cuban interests to U.S. demands.

That the Americans were persuaded they had acquitted themselves honorably conferred a powerful sense of moral entitlement to political purpose. A Cuban gesture perceived contrary to North American interests often elicited outbursts of indignation. The American-owned *Havana Post* denounced Cuban aspirations to sovereignty as "the most remarkable exhibition of affrontiveness and ingratitude that the leaders of a race saved from destruction and annihilation have ever shown towards its rescuer."[94] Cuban criticism of the U.S. policy often provoked visceral reactions. "It is forgotten that the United

States finally sent her troops and men to war to battle in Cuba's cause," the *Havana Post* protested, "at an expense of hundreds of millions of dollars and thousands of lives of young men who took up arms through no other motive than for sympathy with suffering Cuba." Continued the *Post*,

> It is forgotten that but for the timely intervention of the United States many of these very ones who now condemn and criticize that people and govern-ment most severely might have been made to stand before the cruel dead line and receive bullets in their backs from Spanish Mausers. All this seems to have been wiped from the pages of the histories read by some of these agitators and political intriguers, and Cuba is placed in the false position of being an ingrate and turning upon the very hand that saved her from destruction.[95]

Cuban criticism of U.S. intervention in Latin America was denounced as a grievous betrayal. When *El Heraldo de Cuba* criticized U.S. policy in Mexico in 1916, the *Havana Post* could hardly contain its ire:

> One would think that after the Americans set Cuba free and guaranteed her sovereignty . . . that there would never be heard anything but kindly phrases for the great and good friend of the North, but such is not the case, for it is a startling fact that practically . . . all [newspapers] are in active sympathy with Mexico in the present controversy between that country and the United States. . . . Has Mexico spent millions for Cuban independence for which she has never rendered a bill as the United States? Did Mexico, when the Cuban reconcentrados were starving by the thousands, send mil-lions worth of food-stuffs here and in every town and village distribute free American army rations to the needy ones as the United States did? . . . Has Mexico guaranteed to the world that the sovereignty of Cuba shall never be impaired, as the United States has? No? Then why this sympathy with Mexico when the United States has borne patiently hundreds and hundreds of insults, has seen its citizens robbed and murdered in Mexico time after time, and finally has even had its own territories invaded by armed Mexi-cans?[96]

When *La Noche* criticized the North American intervention in the Domini-can Republic, the *Havana Post* excoriated Cubans for their misplaced sympa-thies. "What is the purpose of *La Noche* in making such allegations against the American government?" Did *La Noche* wish to arouse "against the United States the hatred of all Latin Americans, especially of the Cubans," against the nation that in 1898 had "sent Americans to bleed in Cuba's cause."[97]

★ ★ ★

The past remembered and recorded as history passed directly into the re-vered narratives of the nation. Perhaps no group had so invested themselves in the proposition of the war of 1898 as a noble mission as the Spanish war veterans themselves. They played a vital role in perpetuating the memory of 1898 as sublime sacrifice. They remembered having volunteered to fight in be-half of a righteous cause out of righteous motives. The authenticity of personal memory can hardly be disputed, of course. Vast numbers of men did indeed volunteer for military service in Cuba out of generous sentiments. But it is also true that noble purpose became implicated in the service of political needs. What was remembered and what was forgotten often depended on those ru-minations with which personal histories were assembled—understandable predilections, of course. People are given to believe in the virtue of their own motives, always with solace in remembrance. But as these life histories and individual memories aggregated into a collective narrative, they evolved, too, into something of a master myth by which national history was informed to characterize the American purpose. Personal motives served as political expla-nation.

Memory was consecrated through the official commemorative acts of vet-erans' organizations and scores of affiliated associations across the United States. In the decades that followed, the Society of the Army of Santiago de Cuba, the Rough Riders' Association, the United Spanish War Veterans Asso-ciation, the American Veterans of Foreign Service (reorganized in 1914 as Vet-erans of Foreign Wars), the Daughters of Liberty, the Daughters of America, the Women's Auxiliary of the United Spanish War Veterans, and, later, the Sons of Spanish-American War Veterans and the Daughters of '98, as well as scores of state and local veterans' organizations, assembled annually to commemo-rate 1898 and celebrate the American liberation of Cuba.

The commemoration of beneficent purpose and selfless sacrifice in 1898 was registered most solemnly in the monuments, statues, and markers dedi-cated across the United States to honor service in the war. Monuments served as premise of intent and proof of reception of meanings assigned to 1898. Celebrated with annual ceremony and commemorated with solemnity, monu-ments ratified the very conventional wisdom from which they were conceived. For vast numbers of Americans, the statues and monuments of 1898 not only memorialized the service of soldiers; they also corroborated the meaning of the war as an undertaking of beneficent purpose. In large cities and small towns, in Dayton, Austin, Chicago, St. Louis, San Francisco, Milwaukee, Seattle, Columbia (South Carolina), and Garder (Massachusetts), among many others, monuments paid tribute to the selfless sacrifice made in 1898. Some monuments, like those in Savannah, Emporia, Hartford, Los Angeles, and Lawrence (Kansas), honored the service of state regiments. The inscription of the Volunteer Monument in Seattle read, "In tribute to the volunteer services of Spanish-American War Veterans Who Liberated the Oppressed Peoples of Cuba, Puerto Rico, and the Philippine Islands." Others commemorated hometown soldiers killed in the war. The Bagley Memorial in Raleigh, North Carolina, honored Ensign Worth Bagley, the first U.S. officer killed in the war. The Spanish-American War monument at St. Paul's School in Concord, New Hampshire, honored the 120 alumni who served in the war. In 1902, the Spanish-American War National Memorial was dedicated at Arlington National Cemetery, and for years thereafter it served as the site for annual February 15 *Maine* commemorations.

The sinking of the battleship *Maine* became emblematic of the American sacrifice in 1898 and indeed was early conflated with the war itself. The lives lost on the battleship in February 1898 were also remembered as lives offered for the liberation of Cuba. "And Cuba free!" exulted Admiral John Chidwick in Havana upon the raising of the *Maine* in 1912. "Heaven-blessed Cuba! How is it possible that you in your honest gratitude will ever cease to remember these men and their companions, martyred in your cause? How can you ever forget the country which espoused your cause, the blood of whose sons mingled with your own on your hillsides and fields of battle?"[98] On the occasion of the dedication of a second national *Maine* monument at Columbus Circle in New York in 1913, Governor William Haines of Maine affirmed "that every American felt justly proud of the part we took, and the aid we gave, to get a greater freedom and wider opportunity for the people of Cuba."[99] The inscription on the New York monument read, "To the Freemen Who Died in the War with Spain that Others Might be Free."

The message and meaning were always the same. "We rejoice that we have kept the faith and that [Cuba's] confidence in our sincerity of purpose has been confirmed," proclaimed the United Spanish War Veterans Association commander John Garrity in 1928. "The history of relations of Cuba and the United States affords the world stout testimony of the unselfishness of America's international conduct."[100] Almost twenty years later, association commander Ralph Crain assured the assembled veterans that Cuba was "most grateful to all of you veterans for having given her independence in 1898. That was one of the proudest pages in the history of the United States, the first time in the history of the world that any country ever gave liberty and independence to any captured territory, something we ought to be proud of."[101]

Volunteer Monument, Seattle, Washington. Photo by Lars Schoultz.

. . . .

★ ★ ★

A point of view had passed into memory, remembered as truth, learned as history, and thereupon considered a source of moral entitlement to power. It would be unduly facile to suggest that this was a remembered past contrived as a matter of convenience and malice aforethought, inspired by motive and informed with intent. In fact, it is more complicated. It had to do with the capacity of power to arrange meaning—past and present—in service of interests, as a matter of commonplace practice by which a people inform themselves about themselves. This was a formulation of history that was useful to power brokers—then and thereafter—a past that ratified a self-satisfied sense of themselves. It served as the frame of reference to make sense of the world, but most importantly it provided the knowledge with which the Americans invoked moral purpose as they pursued national interest. Belief in righteous conduct in 1898 was a matter of self-esteem, of course, but it was also a means of self-interest. It created the moral context in which domination was enacted, which means, too, that it was all the more difficult to challenge, for it obtained validation from the very normative system from which it originated. To dispute the meaning of 1898 was to doubt the very goodness of the Americans. Vast numbers of Americans did indeed believe that they—alone and unaided—had liberated Cuba from Spain, that they had honorably fulfilled their pledge of independence, for which surely the Cubans would be grateful. It set up a norm of moral reciprocity in which the Americans could reasonably expect—and unreasonably demand—Cuban demonstration of gratitude.

The meaning of 1898 insinuated itself into the popular imagination as a matter of received wisdom. What passed for history, or perhaps more precisely phrased, what constituted knowledge of the past, in this instance so much a matter of memory, was not without consequences. There was a politics to this memory, of course, not necessarily conceived with mischief in mind but certainly imagined as a matter of moral certitude that was so very much at the source of the American imperial project. The "Spanish-American War" developed into an enduring embodiment of North American righteousness in an otherwise sordid world of realpolitik. This was a war, as the Americans understood it, of selfless purpose. That Cubans failed to appreciate fully the sacrifices made in their behalf said more about the deficiency of their character than the generosity of American conduct and would not in any case relieve Cubans of their obligations. There was something of a moral stridency to the way that the Americans held Cubans to their presumptive debt to the United States. Essayist John Kendrick Bangs was stern in his injunction to Cuba: "If Cuba in the remotest hour of the remotest century to come forgets this service and the names of these men who have rendered it, then will she be guilty of an ingratitude which is inconceivable, and to be likened only to that of the serpent, who, warmed by the fire of his benefactor, turned and stung the hand that brought him back to life."[102]

The Americans were certain of their history. A consensus about 1898 developed immediately after the war and passed into realms of the unquestioned commonplace. The diffusion of that knowledge informed the ways the Americans conducted themselves, affected the ways they engaged Cubans, and shaped the ways they fashioned a foreign policy. Knowledge was indeed power, and especially in the service of power. Through much of the twentieth century, North American political leaders and policy makers acted within a shared certainty of the meaning of 1898. "All Americans," proclaimed President Woodrow Wilson in 1916, "look back with deep pride and gratification at the part their government was able to play in giving Cuba an independent place among the nations under a stable form of government."[103] In 1948, on the occasion of the fiftieth anniversary of the war with Spain, President Harry Truman pointed to the Teller Amendment as "the foundation upon which our relations with the Cuban Republic are based," a commitment—he emphasized without a hint of irony—that "expressed our determination that once the Cuban people were liberated, they, and they alone, should govern the Island of Cuba." Added Truman: "Few nations of differing languages and cultures have drawn so closely together during the last 50 years, freely and without duress, as have Cuba and the United States." On the same occasion, the *Washington Post* was unabashedly celebratory: "It was just 50 years ago . . . that Cuba with American help attained her independence . . . and respect, and the two countries have perhaps a closer bond than most because of the circumstances of Cuba's deliverance."[104] Years later, during a meeting of the National Security Council, Admiral Arleigh Burke indicated that the United States was paying Cuba $2,000 annually for leasing rights to the Guantánamo Naval Station. Surprised by the "fantastically low price for this piece of real estate," Under-Secretary of the Treasury Fred Scribner asked if the United States was "providing anything else of value in return for base rights," to which Burke responded, "Of course we provided Cuba with its freedom."[105]

The Americans came to understand their relationship with Cuba by way of knowledge that was both self-serving and self-confirming. The narrative of 1898 served as a source of moral validation for the propriety of North American power. The Americans expected gratitude to bind Cuba to the United States forever, with the Cubans to be eternally grateful to the United States for their very national existence. They would be loyal; they would be faithful. Destinies were proclaimed joined in 1898, indissolubly and in perpetuity, a relationship consecrated by the sacrifice of American life and blood and treasure and eternal

Cuban gratitude. "If [Cuba's] government lasts a thousand years," pronounced West Virginia senator Stephen Elkins in 1902, "it cannot discharge its obligations to us. . . . We expelled Spain, established her independence, withdrew our army, and paid every dollar of her indebtedness, and her independence did not cost her $5. . . . Cuba is under lasting obligation to the United States."[106] To have sacrificed so much for Cuba, New York representative William Sulzer predicted, was to "have earned the everlasting gratitude, the respect, and the affection of every Cuban now and for all time to come."[107]

This was a master narrative that endured deep into the twentieth century. Ambassador Earl E. T. Smith characterized the bond as a "special relationship," one that historian Lynn-Darrell Bender later described as a "sentimental relationship" and writer Irving Pflaum called "our intimate relations with Cuba."[108] "Because the relationship was so close between Cuba and the United States, we having obtained their independence for them," reflected Ambassador Arthur Gardner, "it made [us] feel that the bond between us was stronger than anybody else."[109] Ambassador Smith frequently alluded to 1898 as the foundation of "special" Cuba–United States ties. "The close relationship between our two countries goes back many years," Smith wrote in 1962. "The United States and Cuba fought side by side in the Spanish-American War of 1898."[110] As late as 1996, Cuba desk officer Kenneth Skoug could write that "most Americans viewed Cuba with sympathy," that they "welcomed its fight for independence," and that "U.S. intervention in 1898 secured Cuban independence."[111]

★ ★ ★

The narrative of 1898 expanded into the most readily accessible sources of American knowledge of Cuba. It served as a point of view in Hollywood films, most notably in the silent film version of *Message to Garcia* in 1916 and the "talkie" version in 1936, as well as in *The Rough Riders* (1927), *End of the Trail* (1936), *Yellow Jack* (1938), and *Santiago* (1956). It was the subtext of what many Americans were reading in their fiction, in such novels as John Fox Jr.'s *Crittenden: A Kentucky Story of Love and War* (1900); Lawrence Perry's *Holton of the Navy: A Story of the Freeing of Cuba* (1913); Joseph Hergesheimer's *The Bright Shawl* (1922); Gordon Hall Gerould's *Filibuster* (1924); MacKinlay Kantor's *Cuba Libre* (1940); Elswyth Thane's *Ever After* (1945); Walter Adolphe Roberts's *Single Star: A Novel of Cuba in the 90s* (1949); Henry Castor's *Year of the Spaniard: A Novel of 1898* (1950); and James H. Street's *Mingo Dabney* (1950), among others.

Travel books and tourist guides routinely offered the larger meaning of 1898 as "background" information for North American visitors. In addition to information about appropriate attire, fashionable hotels, popular restau-

rants, and exotic nightclubs, American tourists also learned that Cuban independence and indeed the very existence of the Cuban republic were achieved
through the sacrifice of the United States. "Not until the United States came to
the aid of these people were they released from their bondage," Marian George
wrote in her guidebook, adding that before the U.S. military occupation, Cuba
"had no government; there were no schools outside of a few of the largest
towns, the country was full of beggars, the towns were unclean, and . . . there
were swarms of hungry, homeless, destitute people everywhere. There were no
proper hospitals or charities, no money in the public treasuries."[112] The Cuban
"has neither the force nor the executive ability to carry out his designs," travel
writer C. H. Forbes-Lindsay wrote in 1911. "For a full century he has conspired
to throw off the galling yoke of Spain, and he would never have done it but
for the intervention of the United States." Henry Phillips characterized the
Cuban as "the problem stepchild of the United States," and he added, "While
Cuba owes her very existence as a nation to the United States, her gratitude
and friendliness have been of a most doubtful character. . . . No other nation,
perhaps, have we aided so constructively, and been rewarded with so much
distrust and lack of confidence."[113] Olive Gibson informed tourists that "Uncle
Sam rescued [Cuba] at the very moment at which Butcher Weyler's successors
were carrying out his boasted determination to put the Cuban people under
the sod." Henry Wack offered a succinct judgment in 1931: "But for the liberation of our Cuban neighbors by the U.S. . . . Havana would still be the dump it
was in the last century." Hyatt Verrill wrote in the same year of the "competent,
enthusiastic, trained, honest and zealous men" of the U.S. military occupation
under whom "an almost inconceivable amount of reconstruction, sanitation,
reformation and improvement was carried out," adding, "Everything possible
was done to place Cuba and Havana in perfect condition before turning the
island over to the Cubans." Continued Verrill, "Since then its history has been
largely made up of mismanagement, graft, political intrigues, sporadic re-
volts, plots, mad financial speculations, unwonted prosperity and riches, and
periods of depression. . . . Perhaps worst of all is the ingratitude of the people
whom we helped to freedom, for whom we did everything possible to assure
their future. It was a thankless task."[114]

It was perhaps not surprising, hence, that North American tourists often
visited Cuba with a powerful sense of entitlement and expectation of Cuban
gratitude. Writer Caspar Whitney wrote perceptively as early as 1910 of "the
tourist expectation that the native should prostrate himself before every visitor from the U.S.A. because Uncle Sam brought him the hope of freedom."[115]
The trouble with most American tourists in Cuba, observed the *Havana Post*
in 1916, was "that they think because they are Americans, the Cubans should

take off their hats when they pass by or get down on their knees and weep tears of gratitude at every opportunity."[116] Tourist A. T. Spivey from Illinois was delighted with the "hearty welcome" extended by Cubans during his visit in 1921 and could only conclude, "The Cuban people have demonstrated most impressively their appreciation of which the United States government has done for them in securing their independence."[117] Daniel Hart, the mayor of Wilkes-Barre, was unabashedly euphoric after a ten-day vacation in Cuba in 1924:

> I am more than proud that America played its part in giving to Cuba and her people the freedom long prayed for. . . . It remained for an American, General Leonard Wood, to take this American child by the hand and lead her into the paths of progress, of beauty which she is today. Cuba loves America and Americans. There isn't anything they will not do for our country. . . . [From El Morro] I took off my hat and thanked God I am an American for the good she has done for the suffering peoples of other lands. Cuba is our child. I wish her to be the lovable child she is.[118]

★ ★ ★

The North American narrative of 1898 also and inevitably implicated Cubans in its premise. It expanded most visibly into the interior life of the early republic in the form of statues, monuments, and historic markers. Monuments served to inscribe into the realms of Cuban public spaces the account of how the Americans had sacrificed life and treasure to liberate Cuba. Across the island, monuments commemorated the North American campaign in Cuba—the battlefields, the military victories, the war dead—and in the process deepened North American discursive control of the meaning of the war. In 1901, the U.S. government purchased a 200-acre tract on the site of the San Juan battlefield and subsequently constructed the San Juan Hill battle monument to commemorate the victory of the Rough Riders. Three years later, the First Landing Monument was erected at Daiquirí. In 1906, a battle monument at El Caney, with a roster tablet, commemorated the role of Captain Allyn Capron's Artillery Battery E in the July 1898 battle. In 1908 a bronze plaque was dedicated in Siboney to commemorate the tenth anniversary of the U.S. landing. The site of a great ceiba tree in Santiago de Cuba, under whose expansive branches representatives of Spain and the United States negotiated the terms for the surrender of Santiago de Cuba, was made into a small public park. An open bronze book was placed at the base of the ceiba—henceforth designated as the "Peace Tree"—on which was inscribed the names of the American servicemen who lost their lives in military operations. In 1924, a monument to Theodore Roosevelt was dedicated at a new "Roosevelt Park" in Santiago de

Cuba, in recognition, the local U.S. consul reported, of the "valiant service in the capture of Santiago from the Spanish forces in July 1898" and "symbolizing the creation of the Cuban nation by the people of the United States."[119] In the same year, a memorial to the Eighth Massachusetts Regiment was dedicated in Matanzas. In 1925, the Veterans Association of the Seventy-First Regiment New York Volunteers dedicated an eight-foot bronze figure of a U.S. soldier in honor of the volunteers who perished in the campaign of Santiago de Cuba. One year later, on Memorial Day, the newly organized Havana Post No. 1 of the American Legion, made up principally of American veterans of the Spanish war residing in Havana, dedicated a mausoleum in Colón cemetery to inter the deceased ex-soldiers. In 1942, a plaque commemorating the delivery by Lieutenant Andrew Rowan of President McKinley's message to General Calixto García was dedicated in Bayamo. "Appearances indicate a genuine appreciation," traveler Philip Marden concluded in 1921. "Monuments commemorating the salutary deeds of the Americans under General Wood adorn the Prado."[120]

The most commanding monument was dedicated in Havana in 1925 to the battleship *Maine* by the government of President Alfredo Zayas. On it was inscribed simply, "To the Victims of the *Maine*, / The People of Cuba." "The kindly sentiments of gratitude shown by the people of Cuba in erecting this exceptionally beautiful monument," proclaimed General John Pershing, himself a veteran of the war and head of the U.S. delegation on the occasion of the dedication ceremonies, "will be warmly appreciated by the American people as a new evidence of friendship and good will." Pershing extolled the "very intimate relationship" between Cuba and the United States, adding, "By our association with her on the battlefield we helped secure the independence she now enjoys."[121] The *Maine* monument, the *Havana Post* commented at the time, represented "one more link to the cordial and friendly relations existing between Cuba and the United States and in granite and marble perpetuates the gratitude of the Cuban people for America's generous aid in her struggle for freedom."[122] One year later, in February 1926, a bronze tablet bearing the names of the sailors who perished on the *Maine* was added to the base of the monument. The ceremony provided one more occasion to celebrate the American liberation of Cuba. "Out of a war was Cuba born," navy captain W. T. Cluverius recounted to a Cuban audience, "and because my country was responsible for the advent of this smiling child into the family of nations; at the hour of your birth the United States became a world power with domain and duty in every sea."[123]

In October 1926, a hurricane toppled the upper portion of the *Maine* monument. The monument was subsequently reconstructed and rededicated in

Maine Monument, Havana, Cuba. Rear view of the original *Maine* monument, constructed in what was then called the *Maine* Plaza in Havana. From author's collection.

. . . .

February 1928 in a newly renovated *Maine* Plaza, to which was added the busts of William McKinley, Theodore Roosevelt, and Leonard Wood. On July 4, 1943, President Fulgencio Batista added to the *Maine* Plaza a bust of Lieutenant Andrew Rowan.[124]

Every year throughout the first half of the twentieth century, February 15 was celebrated in Cuba as *Maine* Day. Every year it was the same. Every year it was about how the Americans had liberated Cuba. This was the performance dimension of the American narrative of 1898, something akin to a discourse on display. The *Maine* monument served as site of commemorative ceremonies, at which soldiers and sailors from both countries joined together to march in an annual parade. Annual rites and rituals involved the official participation of the American Legion, the Spanish War Veterans, and the Veterans of Foreign Wars, as well as a host of state and local veterans' organizations from the United States. In what must be viewed as an elaborately staged commemorative reenactment of the North American liberation of the island, U.S. army veterans paraded annually in Havana, with the expectation of appreciation of the gathered Cuban public. Reported the *New York Times* in 1929:

Maine Monument annual celebration, 1947. Courtesy United Press International.

. . . .

Cuban armed forces marched side by side with 120 United States Marines in an impressive parade in observance of the thirty-first anniversary of the sinking of the United States battleship *Maine*. The national banners of Cuba and the United States were lowered to half staff as the three-mile procession filed past the reviewing stand. . . . As the strain of 'Nearer My God to Thee' rose from the Cuban Headquarters Division band, nine Cuban Army planes, circling 2,500 feet above the crowd, cut their motors and swooped silently down to shower the memorial monument with flowers.[125]

On *Maine* Day 1930, an estimated 50,000 Cubans and Americans turned out to observe and participate in what was described as "one of the largest and most resplendent parades ever seen in this city of parades and fiestas."[126] "Grateful Cubans," commented the *National Geographic* in 1947, "erected this monument . . . in memory of the officers and men who were lost."[127]

That *Maine* Day in Havana was commemorated at the height of the tourist season raised the event to the level of an annual tourist event. Almost upon its completion, the *Maine* monument itself became a tourist "point of interest."[128] American tourists in Cuba joined annually in the public commemoration of the U.S. liberation of the island, an experience that could not but further enhance a sense of entitlement to their presence in Cuba. The *Maine* monument, stated one Havana tourist guide, "a place of pilgrimage to our American visitors . . . , was erected as a testimonial of Cuba's gratitude to the great American Nation."[129] *Maine* Day, Consuelo Hermer and Marjorie May wrote in their 1941 travel book on Cuba, commemorated "the anniversary of the sinking of the battleship *Maine*, the prime reason for our subsequent entrance into the Spanish-American War. . . . Dignitaries everywhere hold forth at great length about the close ties that bind the two Republics."[130]

★ ★ ★

At a critical point of their national formation, Cubans seemed to have been dislodged as subjects of their own history and displaced as agents of nationhood. The North American representation of 1898 could not but have weakened Cuban claims to sovereignty and self-determination. It was intended to. The power of the North American discourse lay in its capacity to implicate Cubans in a moral hierarchy derived from U.S. needs and inevitably to deny the Cubans presence and participation in their own history.

That the American narrative of 1898 was not intended explicitly as a means of hegemony does not make it any less central a factor to an understanding of the workings of systems of domination, and especially the ways that the exercise of power acquired logic and legitimacy. The memory of national formation as a matter of the past remembered and learned, as well as a matter of myth and reality, must be considered indispensable to the sustenance of nationhood. Cubans were denied the moral authority to advance the primacy of national interests as an attribute of national sovereignty, obliged instead to accommodate North American needs as the principal function of their independence. "The Cuban republic," pronounced the *Washington Evening Star* outright in 1909, "means . . . deference to the United States in all matters."[131]

The Cubans could only ponder what went awry in 1898. Successive popular mobilizations for independence all through the nineteenth century appeared to have dissolved into nothing, producing an anticlimax at the very point of national origins and troubling ambiguities on the meaning of nationality. The subordination of Cuban sovereignty to North American authority implicated the very moral basis of the republic as the source of Cuban frustration and in the process contributed to a deepening awareness of the instrumental function of the past.

The question of 1898 insinuated itself deeply into Cuban sensibilities, which meant, too, that it developed into a subject of an unsettled national introspection. Many Cubans understood 1898 as a usurpation, a point of preemption at which they were displaced as actors and transformed into audience. Cubans had been left to contemplate what had transpired in 1898, what had become of the liberation project for which generations of men and women had struggled and sacrificed. The events of 1898 developed into something of a Cuban preoccupation: a brooding sense that history seemed to have halted in 1898, lost in another people's history, and that Cubans' past was largely a function of a history that happened elsewhere.

The sense of 1898 as a wrong to redress took hold early in the twentieth century. During the 1920s and 1930s, a new generation of Cubans was coming of age. This generation—the first generation of the republic—with no personal memories of 1898, was not compromised in the reciprocities into which their parents had been drawn. The meaning of 1898 was debated anew, and a new Cuban counternarrative emerged. "Independence was the result of a century of enormous [Cuban] sacrifices," writer Eduardo Abril Amores reflected in 1922, "but we do not conceive of independence as thus achieved and properly earned. . . . We have neither faith nor confidence in ourselves. We attribute independence, conquered by the edge of our *machetes*, to the government of the United States."[132] Harvard-educated essayist Jorge Mañach, always a judicious observer of the Cuban condition, reflected in 1933 on the larger meanings and lasting consequences of 1898:

> The Cuban effort for political self-determination resulted thus in semi-subjection, tarnishing the joy and pride of liberation. . . . Despite the most generous intention on the part of the United States, Cuban illusions were still to be humiliated further. . . . When finally the Cubans were granted permission to write their constitution, the sovereignty of the new state was compromised by the Platt Amendment, which imposed on Cuba a permanent treaty, by which the United States was conceded the right of intervening in Cuba in certain specified emergencies. Cuba was irremediably a protectorate. . . . The paternal and perspicacious prudence of the American Congress resulted in crushing the Cuban sentiment of self-determination.[133]

Cubans were increasingly engaged in a reflective contemplation of the past, simultaneously as source of self-definition and means of self-determination, with a deepening awareness of the larger implications of 1898. The angst over 1898 often found expression in popular fiction. In the novel *La danza de los millones* (1923), writer Rafael A. Cisneros speaks through his protagonist: "In Cuba the Americans helped us to become free, which is the same as if they had loaned us one hundred *pesos* when we were hungry, and in return we will be paying them back for the rest of our lives. Don't you see, they seized Guantánamo Bay and their troops have not yet left Santiago. And the sugar mills? Ah! They are virtually all American, as are the mines, commerce, the banks, and all the money. And they say that they don't want the land!" Pedro José Cohucelo's protagonist in *Apostado de amor* (1925) denounces the United States "as a usurper of a victory that was ours. . . . First through the military intervention of the Island and then through the odious Platt Amendment, [the United States] proclaimed that it was not Cuba which, through the efforts of its sons and blood spilled by its martyrs and heroes, had obtained the independence and sovereignty sought for half a century." In Ofelia Rodríguez Acosta's novel *Sonata interrumpida* (1943) the narrator laments that "we owe everything to the Americans. . . . We owe them our independence and . . . we will always owe them . . . our famous sovereignty." To this the protagonist responds: "Owe them! What do we owe them? The Platt Amendment to our Constitution, without which its forced acceptance there would never have been a transfer of power to the Cubans in 1902? Mortgaged forever by our eternal gratitude."[134]

The past developed into something of a *terra irredenta*, certainly as an issue of historiographical disputation, but more importantly as a matter central to making good on the very credibility of pretensions to sovereign nationhood. This was historical knowledge as the means for Cubans to extricate themselves from a version of the past not of their making and from which the very logic of their subservience had been fashioned. This meant most of all the need for Cubans to reestablish their presence into their past and restore agency to their presence.

Some of this process was begun through contestation of the privileged sites of North American monuments on the island. In 1927, municipal authorities in Santiago de Cuba added a second bronze book under the Peace Tree; this one recorded the names of Cuban soldiers who perished in the Santiago campaign. "The fact that . . . no Cuban heroes were recorded," acknowledged the U.S. consul in Santiago de Cuba, "has long been irritating to the Cuban officials and people."[135] The addition of the second bronze book, affirmed the *Diario de Cuba*, "will proclaim that Cuba did not receive its independence as a gift. It will no longer be said that Cubans did not fight in San Juan."[136] One year later, a statue dedicated "To the Glory of the Victorious Liberator" ("*A la Gloria del Mambí Victorioso*") was erected within sight of the bronze statue commemorating North American volunteers. In 1942, in response to a resolution passed by the Second National Congress of History, a bronze plaque was dedicated in San Juan Park with the inscription in Spanish and English: "In 1898 the victory was won through the decisive support given to the U.S. army by the Cuban Army of Liberation under the command of Lieutenant General Calixto García. Therefore this war must not be called the Spanish-American War but the Spanish-Cuban-American War." Two years later the Cuban national congress enacted legislation officially changing the name from the "Spanish-American War" to the "Spanish-Cuban-American War."[137]

ALA MEMORIA

DE LOS OFICIALES, CLASES Y SOLDADOS
DEL EJERCITO LIBERTADOR CUBANO, QUE
OFRENDARON GLORIOSAMENTE SU VIDA A LA
PATRIA, EN LOS COMBATES QUE CULMINARON
EN LA TOMA DE ESTA LOMA DE SAN JUAN.
BRILLANTE HECHO DE ARMAS, DONDE LA
SANGRE DEL BRAVO Y ABNEGADO INSURGENTE
CUBANO Y LA DEL GENEROSO Y NOBLE SOLDA-
DO NORTEAMERICANO, SELLARON EN UN PACTO
DE HONOR LA LIBERTAD Y CONFRATERNIDAD
DE DOS PUEBLOS.

JULIO 1898 - SEPTIEMBRE 1927.

IN MEMORY

OF THE OFFICERS, NON-COMMISSIONED OF-
FICERS AND PRIVATES OF THE CUBAN ARMY OF
LIBERATION, WHO GLORIOUSLY GAVE THEIR
LIVES FOR THEIR COUNTRY, IN THE BATTLES
WHICH CULMINATED IN THE CAPTURE OF THIS
HILL OF SAN JUAN. BRILLIANT EXPLOIT, IN
WHICH THE BLOOD OF THE BRAVE AND TRUE
CUBAN INSURGENT AND THAT OF THE GENER-
OUS AND NOBLE AMERICAN SOLDIER, SEALED
A COVENANT OF LIBERTY AND FRATERNITY
BETWEEN TWO NATIONS.

JULY 1898 - SEPTEMBER 1927.

Bronze plaque at base of statue at San Juan Park, dedicated to the memory
of the officers and men of the Cuban Army of Liberation who perished
in the battle of San Juan Hill. Photo by Deborah M. Weissman.

. . . .

Statue dedicated in 1927 at San Juan Park to the memory of the officers
and men of the Cuban Army of Liberation who perished in the battle
of San Juan Hill. Photo by Deborah M. Weissman.

. . . .

Bronze plaque laid at San Juan Hill Park, pursuant to the resolution of the Second National Congress of History (1942), affirming the new name of the war as the "Spanish-Cuban-American War." Photo by Deborah M. Weissman.

. . . .

The meaning of 1898 also developed into a politically charged issue. In early 1949, in response to mounting political pressure, the government of President Carlos Prío Socarrás suspended Cuban participation in the annual *Maine* commemoration ceremonies. Prío subsequently suspended Cuban sponsorship of official ceremonies commemorating the *Maine*. Historian Duvon Corbitt, at the time a resident of Havana, explained to Secretary of State Dean Acheson the circumstances surrounding the Cuban decision: "During the fifteen years of residence in Cuba, I saw Cuban soldiers file by the [*Maine*] monument on the Malecon, but not always joyfully. And in recent years certain groups have used the occasion to stir up anti-American sentiment. This has been increasingly true of the 'revisionists' who are publicizing the thesis that the Cubans had already won the war with Spain and the United States entered only in time to share in the victory."[138]

Corbitt's allusion to "revisionists" referred to shifting historiographical currents in Cuba. A new self-conscious historicism was in the making, itself a facet of a new self-confident nationalism, one in which the Cuban presence in the narrative of liberation acquired relevance to the formation of the nation. The Cuban claim to sovereign nationhood was perforce obliged to challenge North American representations of 1898, upon which the presumptions of U.S. moral certainty and political authority were based. "The first duty of every Cuban who truly wishes to free Cuba of today's ills," insisted historian Herminio Portell Vilá in 1949, "is to believe in the epic history of Cuba and in the heroes, martyrs, and patriots who forged that history and who belong with dignity to the international lineage of the great liberators of nations."[139]

The new historiography challenged North American representations directly. The proposition of Cuba "owing" its independence to the United States was refuted by historian Emilio Roig de Leuchsenring in *Cuba no debe su independencia a los Estados Unidos* (1950). Roig rejected the proposition that Cubans owed anything to the United States, insisting instead that Spain was on the verge of defeat prior to the North American intervention and that independence, in the end, had been obtained largely by Cuban efforts. The small monograph gave definitive form to the principal tenets of revisionist historiography: "Cuba does not owe its independence to the United States of North America, but to the efforts of its own people, through their firm and indomitable will to end the injustices, abuses, discrimination, and exploitation suffered under the despotic colonial regime."[140] The moral was unambiguous. Cuba was not indebted to the United States for its independence. On the contrary, Cubans had achieved their own independence, which meant, too, that Cubans possessed the moral authority and the political right to exercise self-determination, without outside encumbrance or foreign hindrance; they were free to advance the primacy of national interests as the central function of national sovereignty.

By midcentury, the Americans had developed some appreciation of Cuban disquiet. In 1948, on the occasion of the fiftieth anniversary of the *Maine*, Ambassador R. Henry Norweb sought to bring Cuban concerns to the attention of the Department of State. "There are many in this country," Norweb alerted Washington, "who feel that the important part played by Cubans in bringing about their liberation from Spanish rule has not been adequately recognized, particularly in the United States. . . . We should bear in mind that there are many Cubans . . . who are sensitive about what they feel has been our failure to give proper recognition to Cuba's contribution over Spain . . . [and] who feel that we have tried to monopolize the credit for ousting Spain from this Island."[141] Among the "number of sources of friction" a Department of State secret memorandum identified three years later was that "Cubans resent any tendency on our part to minimize their own contribution in gaining their independence. They still criticize us for having reserved and used the right to intervene in their domestic affairs under the Platt Amendment despite the fact that it was repealed in 1934."[142]

A national consensus developed in Cuba around the notion that something had gone awry in 1898. Unsettled memories haunted the national narrative on the Cuban relationship with the United States and often appeared in unexpected forms under unforeseen circumstances. The 1956 release in Cuba of the Warner Brothers film *Santiago* purporting to depict how the United States had liberated Cuba provoked indignation across the island. "It is grievous that the Americans intervened in our war of independence at the final moments and imposed upon us the Platt Amendment," bristled essayist Agustín Tamargo. He continued:

> The American insults to our sovereignty did not begin with this Warner Brothers film. They go back much further. In the American public school text books, for example, that Cuba was engaged in a struggle for its liberty one hundred years before the explosion of the battleship "Maine" in our harbor is not at all acknowledged. On the contrary, it is said that we obtained independence solely as a result of the *yanqui* intervention, as a result of the declaration of war against Spain. That war, which has always been the war of independence of Cuba, is called the "Spanish-American War." Its veterans are veterans of the "Spanish-American War." Nowhere does the name of Cuba appear, as if it were fought in some barren rocky hillside, where one day the soldiers of the *yanqui* democracy clashed accidentally with the soldiers of the Spanish monarchy. It is one more way to deprive a

people of the most worthy possession that a people can have, and that is its presence in History.[143]

The two versions of 1898 as remembered and recorded in the United States and Cuba were difficult to reconcile. Indeed, Americans and Cubans dwelled in different realms of experience: between motive and conduct, between intention and outcome, and between the past as learned and the past as remembered. What Americans celebrated as deeds of selflessness the Cubans denounced as acts of self-interest. The Americans expected gratitude; the Cubans harbored grievances. The Americans remembered 1898 as something done for Cubans; the Cubans remembered 1898 as something done to them. The Americans referred to the Teller Amendment as proof of beneficent intent; the Cubans pointed to the Platt Amendment as evidence of the self-serving purpose. The Americans had arrived in the name of Cuban independence, as allies, the Cubans believed at the time—certainly that was the purport of the Teller Amendment—but they remained as conquerors. Worse still, many Cubans could not escape the sense that they themselves had served as unwitting accomplices to their own disappointment. The U.S. intervention in 1898, the military occupation, the Platt Amendment, successive military interventions (1906–9, 1912, 1917)—all in all, a disillusioning denouement to decades of heroic mobilizations for sovereign nationhood. There was a sense of something having gone profoundly wrong in the way things ended.

The appeal was made to history as a means of redemption, having to do with the very credibility of the Cuban claim to national sovereignty and with direct implications for self-determination and self-definition. The matter of 1898 acquired new relevance during the revolutionary struggles of the 1950s. Fully sixty years later, the 1958 "Manifesto-Program of the 26 July Movement," led by Fidel Castro, alluded to the events of 1898 as a function of a political vision, one clearly calculated to resonate among those Cubans for whom the outcome of 1898 was remembered as a wrong to redress. The "Manifesto-Program" recalled the "high cost paid for liberty" with the lives of martyrs and acts of heroism. But at the "symbolic moment in which the war ended, Cuba was excluded from the accord in which its political status was settled." Continued the "Manifesto-Program":

The deed established an unfortunate precedent. The final outcome appeared determined by the intervention of the United States rather than the bloody sacrifices of the Cubans. The island thus appeared liberated from the political yoke of Spain thanks only to the "powerful neighbor." The antecedents and consequences of that episode can perhaps be explained within the logic of the facts, but the result was that from that moment forward the former colony was burdened by a situation equivalent to a protectorate, and by an ironic and costly "debt of gratitude" that would over time serve to cloak countless injustices and arbitrary acts.[144]

The triumph of the Cuban revolution in 1959 provided the occasion in which contested representations of 1898 moved to center stage as a facet of the deepening dispute between Cuba and the United States. What had happened sixty years earlier—history, in a word—now mattered, but in new ways, with a new urgency, and with far-reaching implications. The Cuban narrative of 1898 served to set in relief the relationship between historical circumstances and actual conditions: the past shaped by the purposes of the present. This was the Cubans coming to terms with the past, as a means of redress and remedy, all in the form of a deepening preoccupation. Again and again, all through 1959, the new Cuban political leadership remembered and recounted the events of 1898 as an injustice inflicted upon Cuba, the point at which the United States had usurped the Cuban claims to sovereignty and negated the Cuban exercise of self-determination. Nationalism as a legitimizing factor of the revolution— that is, in the Cuban case, nationalism as an affirmation of independence, self-determination, and sovereign nationhood—purchased in part its moral credibility and political vitality from a different reading of the very sources from which the Americans had validated their power sixty years earlier. History had overtaken the past.

Remembrance of 1898 signified the intention to rectify history and reclaim the past. Connections were drawn early and often. Representation of 1898 served again as a source of moral sustenance, except this time it was employed in a Cuban master narrative that had as much to do with political mobilization in 1959 as it did with historical events of 1898. The Cuban narrative in 1959 conferred on the project of revolution a claim of continuity out of which to affirm the historicity of the revolutionary project. It served as a call, an invitation to enter and participate in a historical process as continuity and culmination. "The Republic was not free in [1898]," Fidel Castro recalled as early as January 4, 1959—he had not yet even arrived in Havana—"and the dream of the liberators (*mambises*) was frustrated at the last minute." Castro insisted "that those men who had fought for thirty years and not seen their dreams realized" would have rejoiced in 1959 at the achievement of the "revolution that they had dreamed of, the *patria* that they had imagined."[145] A month later Fidel Castro proclaimed outright that "the *mambises* initiated the war for independence that we have completed on January 1, 1959."[146] Raúl Castro made the point explicitly: "Now, with this Revolution, with this civil war that ended on

January 1, we have done nothing less than to finish the War of Independence begun nearly one hundred years ago by our *mambises*. On January 1 of this year we completed our War of Independence. We inaugurated the Republic on that date."[147] Writer Armando J. Flórez Ibarra drew the connections succinctly: "Analyzing the historical reach of the triumphant revolutionary movement, it appears to us as if the revolutionary armies of 1895 . . . have reached power, finally, free of all mediating influences. We are witness to the vindication of the triumph that the United States, through its armed intervention in 1898, cheated us of. . . . We have finally liberated ourselves from the complex of a protectorate."[148]

Fidel Castro carried Cuban grievances about 1898 to the United Nations. "Spain's power had wasted away in our country," he explained to the General Assembly in September 1960. "Spain had neither men nor money left to continue the war in Cuba. Spain was routed. . . . The Cubans who had fought for our independence, those Cubans who at that time were laying down their lives, trusted completely the Joint Resolution of the United States Congress. . . . That illusion ended in a cruel disappointment." Castro invoked a familiar metaphor to make his point: "Apparently the apple was ripe and the United States Government held out its hand."[149] When a month later Ambassador Philip Bonsal reminded Cuban president Osvaldo Dorticós of "the sacrifice of American lives jointly with those of Cuban patriots in the achievement of Cuban independence,"[150] the Cuban Ministry of Foreign Relations reacted with a blistering response:

> No Cuban can deny the noble support and disinterested contribution of the North American people to the cause of Cuban liberation. However, there is an enormous distance between this explicit acknowledgment and admission that Cuba obtained its independence as the result of the favor of a third party, as is often heard and read in North American speeches and writings. The Cuban people conquered their freedom and their right to self-government at the cost of enormous sacrifices and innumerable heroic deeds; and it is to this stubborn determination and fighting spirit that Cuba owes . . . the level of political, social, and cultural development which it has achieved.[151]

Meanings of 1898 reached deeply into a place of unsettled memories, of dormant sensibilities, and served as a powerful source of moral grievance and, hence, a potent catalyst of political mobilization. What happened in Cuba after 1959 offers insight into the way that the sway of hegemony can abruptly and unexpectedly dissolve when the discursive premise of its existence is challenged. The new Cuban leadership repudiated the North American representation of 1898 as outright deception. "They forced us to live in an illicit concubinage with a lie," Fidel Castro thundered in March 1959. "It is preferable to bring down that world than to live within a lie."[152]

The Cuban narrative was utterly incomprehensible to most Americans. The realization that the Cubans were propounding a different view of the past as the basis to establish a different context for understanding the present was bewildering. From Santiago de Cuba, the U.S. consul Park F. Wollam reported "an increase in anti-American feeling" and referred specifically to 1898: "United States intervention in the war of 1898, failure to include Cuban representatives in surrender and peace negotiations and the political control of the country until 1902 are now recalled without balance or perspective." Added Wollam: "One would think that the Platt Amendment was still in effect."[153] In Washington bafflement appeared as common as it was highly placed. "What do you suppose, sir, is eating [Fidel Castro]?" President Dwight Eisenhower was asked during a press conference in October 1959. The president was at a loss:

> I have no idea of discussing possible motivation of a man, what he is really doing, and certainly I am not qualified to go into such abstruse and difficult subjects as that. I do feel this: here is a country that you would believe, on the basis of our history, would be one of our real friends. The whole history—first of our intervention in 1898, our making and helping set up Cuban independence . . . and the very close relationships that have existed most of the time with them—would seem to make it a puzzling matter to figure out just exactly why the Cubans and the Cuban Government would be so unhappy. . . . I don't know exactly what the difficulty is.[154]

"The President confessed he was stumped," observed the *New York Times*, and added: "The State Department is equally stumped."[155] Almost one year later, President Eisenhower was asked again about deteriorating relations with Cuba, and he responded, "Cuba has been one of our finest friends. We were the ones that conducted the war that set them free. And when they got in trouble, we had an occupation, back about 1908 [1906–9], and again we set them on their feet, and set them free. And we have had a long history of friendly relationships, and we have tried to keep our hands out of their internal affairs."[156]

The Americans appeared to have no idea what the Cubans were referring to. Historian Frank Friedel was more than slightly irked at the Cuban challenge to the established North American historiographical truths, and on the occasion of his review of Ernest May's *Imperial Democracy: The Emergence of America as a Great Power* in 1961 he responded: "Today, when Fidel Castro and his claque are screaming epithets at the United States and charging that the Spanish-American War was fought only for imperialistic reasons, it is heartening to be reminded of the fundamentally humanitarian motives that took Americans into the war." The "history of this island since its liberation from Spain," smarted *New York Times* correspondent Ruby Hart Phillips, "does not record many examples of Cuban gratitude for contributions made by the United States in lives, blood and dollars."[157]

The Americans took umbrage at the Cuban challenge to their established truths of 1898. What was particularly galling to the Americans was that the Cubans were impugning their motives, specifically, that intervention in 1898 was undertaken less to assist Cuba than to advance the interests of the United States. They reacted to the Cuban version of 1898 with indignation. That the Cubans, whom the Americans believed themselves to have sacrificed life and treasure to liberate, would turn against the United States was incomprehensible and attributed to persons who knew no better or were engaged in mischief or were influenced by wicked men with malicious intent, in this instance most likely communists.[158] Newspaper editorials entered into the *Congressional Record* in early 1960 all struck a similar tone. "Castro has rejected friendship with the country that liberated Cuba in 1898," decried the *Charleston News and Courier*, and the *Bangor Daily News* asked, "What is Castro doing to us, the country that liberated Cuba in 1898?" The *Roanoke World-News* recalled 1898 as a "war for Cuba's freedom" and added, "True to the principle that it did not covet territory, the United States gave full freedom to the Cuban people within 2 years — as soon as they could be prepared for it."[159]

A sense of betrayal settled over the Americans, as they recalled anew how at the expense of their lives and the expenditure of their treasure Cuba was liberated; for this they believed themselves deserving of treatment better than they were receiving from the Castro government. Illinois representative Barratt O'Hara, himself a veteran of the Spanish war, lamented that political developments in "the beautiful island so close to our shores and historically embedded in our affection" jeopardized "the friendship that has existed in all the years past."[160] Michigan representative William S. Broomfield gave a pained account of 1898 and indeed even conceded, if belatedly, that "Americans and Cubans fought side by side in [1898]." He continued: "Neither the Cubans nor the Americans were fighting for personal glory, for new territories, for plunder or new possessions. We were fighting for freedom. We Americans were not fighting for our own freedom. We had already achieved this goal. We were fighting for the right of the Cubans to shake off the oppressive yoke of colonialism, to decide their own destinies, to chart their own course in domestic and world affairs."[161] With the "long background of historic relations with

Cuba," South Carolina representative Mendel Rivers asked, "will . . . we forget our obligations toward the Cuban people whom we helped to liberate?" Rivers denounced "the bearded pipsqueak of the Antilles" who "seized American property in a country that was conceived by America, delivered by America, nurtured by America, educated by America and made a self-governing nation by America." Cuban ingratitude justified American retaliation. Warned Rivers: "When ingratitude on the part of a nation reaches the point that it has in Cuba, it is time for American wrath to display itself in no uncertain terms."[162] California representative H. Allen Smith demanded to know Fidel Castro's political leanings: "Does he lean toward democratic ideals—the ideals which gave his country freedom, the ideals which brought Americans as liberators to his shores in 1898, the ideals which made America and Cuba friendly neighbors?"[163]

Remembrance of North American sacrifice in behalf of Cuban liberation provided the discursive leverage with which to seek to reaffirm the propriety of North American moral authority over Cuba and at the same time refute what was emerging as a powerfully empowering narrative inside Cuba. South Dakota senator Karl Mundt expressed dismay and disbelief over developments in Cuba. His thoughts turned to 1898: "We who in living memory rescued the island from medieval bondage; we who have given order, vitality, technical wisdom and wealth are now being damned for our civilizing and cooperative virtues!" Mundt called upon Fidel Castro to show "respect for the memory of the American fighting men who died on San Juan Hill, in Cuban jungles, in the war to give independence to his country."[164] North American sacrifice for Cuba was also what Arizona senator Barry Goldwater recalled. The "conditions and attitudes" of 1898, Goldwater exhorted in 1962, "have an important and vital bearing on present-day conditions and actions. . . . We won a great victory and we liberated a people. And it cost us dearly. It cost us thousands of lives and millions of dollars. We paid in sickness, and suffering and sorrow." The military intervention in 1898 to end "cruelty and oppression," Goldwater insisted, gave the United States the moral authority again to "use our military and economic strength in the defense of freedom in Cuba." He added: "Such a course of action is the type the world should expect from a nation whose blood and heartaches bought freedom for Cuba in the first place."[165]

The Americans clung to a stubborn faith in their historical truths as proof of selflessness and as the premise of propriety of power over Cuba. Florida representative James Haley demanded that the United States "use hard economic sanctions . . . to show we will not be clobbered by a tiny nation made free by us, its freedom guaranteed by us in the Monroe Doctrine."[166] Ambassador Spruille Braden used 1898 as a point of reference. "Cuba's independence from Spain would have been impossible without intervention by the United States in Spanish affairs," Braden asserted outright. Braden invoked the Teller Amendment to justify intervention to overthrow the Castro government. The United States had pledged that Cuba would be "free and independent," Braden recalled, adding, "What has happened to that pledge today? It is lost in a mire of mawkish sentimentality about 'non-intervention.' The Soviets' and Castro's outrages are infinitely more cruel and numerous that were those of Weyler . . . that so enraged the American people that they went to war to free Cuba."[167]

Having won freedom for Cuba, the Americans—as bestowers of Cuban freedom—thus claimed the moral authority to act unilaterally to defend that freedom. The logical conclusion of North American claims was that Cubans could not be permitted to squander the freedom that the United States—at such great cost—had obtained for them in 1898. "Our concern for the freedom of our Cuban neighbors goes back more than a century," pronounced Florida representative Dante Fascell. "It is a concern which continues today. The American people can never rest easy while our friends and neighbors remain enslaved."[168] Among the responses to Cuban claims that President Dwight Eisenhower contemplated was to "announce that in 1898 we fought to free Cubans from tyranny—[and] we will not stand by now and allow Communism to destroy this freedom."[169] New York representative Emanuel Celler responded to the trial and execution of *batistianos* in 1959 with equal adamance. "We did not send Gen. Leonard Wood and 'Teddy' Roosevelt," Celler proclaimed, "to rescue Cuba from Spanish oppression in 1898, only to have that unhappy country now plunged into a blood bath."[170]

The meaning of 1898 was contained in its embodiment of virtues by which the Americans had long made sense of their place and purpose in the world, which was self-confirming, of course, but was also, more importantly, at the very source of the American calculus of power. The larger meaning of the Cuban revolution resided in its capacity to challenge American power and the premise of that power no less than the propriety of that power. Years later, historian Richard Welch would examine the sources of the Cuban-U.S. conflict and conclude that among the most important factors of the dispute was the "assumption that Cuba owed its independence to the United States, and was properly dependent on the latter for its diplomatic security and economic prosperity." Thus any Cuban leader, Welch suggested, "who sought to destroy Cuba's historic ties with the United States could not be acting from motives of concern for the Cuban people but must be a power-hungry dictator with regional ambitions."[171]

The Cuban challenge to North American representations of 1898 served as a powerful source of political mobilization. On May 1, 1961, only days after

Inscription on the *Maine* monument in Havana, added in May 1961: "To the victims of the Maine, who were sacrificed to imperialist greed in its fervor to seize control of the island of Cuba." Photo by Fidel Requeijo.

. . . .

the Cuban victory at the Bay of Pigs, a mass rally assembled around the *Maine* monument in Havana to witness approvingly a wrecking crew topple the American eagle from atop the forty-foot pedestal. A new inscription was added to the base of the remaining twin columns of the monument: "To the victims of the Maine, who were sacrificed to imperialist greed in its fervor to seize control of the island of Cuba." In the years that followed, the monuments, plaques, and statues in San Juan Park commemorating the American deeds in 1898 were all but forgotten, left unattended and abandoned, to waste away and deteriorate, often objects of graffiti and vandalism.

★ ★ ★

Through much of the first half of the twentieth century, the Americans sustained a moral claim to power over Cuba based on the proposition that they had succeeded where Cubans had failed, that through the sacrifice of their lives and their treasure they had liberated Cuba from Spain and subsequently—true to the Teller Amendment—had declined "to exercise sovereignty, jurisdiction, or control over said island" and left "the government and control of the island to its people." Certainly North American hegemony was sustained by the obvious inequality of power. The internal logic of the relationship, however, and especially the assumptions by which the propriety of the relationship was validated in both the United States and Cuba were sustained by factors far more complex than a disparity of power. Central to the plausibility of the legitimacy of North American hegemony was the premise of power properly established and rightfully exercised as a function of a vital service rendered. This could not but take the form of a conviction of moral entitlement over Cuba, the basis upon which the Americans could expect—and indeed demand—Cuban accommodation to U.S. needs as appropriate recompense for an outstanding debt. It made not only for the efficacy of domination of the Other but also for the gratification of Self.

In fact, the Americans celebrated a false history, the type of fictional narrative that a people embrace in order to invent a heroic past: in part affirmation of self-esteem, in part projection of self-importance. Almost fifteen years after the war's end, Theodore Roosevelt could continue unflinchingly to insist that the United States had honorably discharged its pledge to Cuban independence. "We made the promise to give Cuba independence," he affirmed in his *Autobiography*, "and we kept that promise."[172] This was also the central dogma of American historiography well into the twentieth century. Like all national myths, this one, too, had some basis in fact. The U.S. intervention most certainly shortened the Cuban war. Vast numbers of Americans did indeed champion Cuban independence. But their elected leaders did not, and the policies they crafted—most notably the Platt Amendment and later the permanent treaty—rendered meaningless all but the most cynical definition of Cuban independence. The narrative of 1898 was a triumph of appearance over reality, more about self-representation than self-interrogation. The meaning of the war was inscribed into the national consciousness as a narrative that privileged popular sentiment over political conduct, intent over outcome, and ideals as motive—not interests. The Americans' capacity for self-deception was exceeded only by their insistence that the Cubans, too, subscribed to the deception—and should be grateful.

In Cuba the meaning of 1898 insinuated itself into those popular domains where politics and passions converged as a matter of shared aspirations, as indeed inevitably it had to, for these were issues that reached deeply into Cuban national sensibilities and implicated the very sources of nationhood and nationality. Given the scope of authority that the Americans claimed from their representation of 1898, it is certainly an arguable proposition that the larger issues of 1898 could not have been resolved by any means other than political ones. This was not simply a historiographical debate. The exercise of self-determination could be attained only as an act of self-knowledge. The challenge to North American hegemony, Cubans understood, was an obligation to revisit 1898 and challenge the very representations by which Cubans had been denied autonomy and agency. To propound self-expression as a gesture of self-determination was to contest and counter the narrative through which North American power was exercised and experienced. One of the decisive if often unrecognized facets of popular mobilizations after 1959 had to do with the repudiation of the representations by which the Americans had depicted Cubans. That was where the Cuban revolution began.

5

Shifting Metaphors, Changing Meanings

Representing Revolution

Every man has an idea, more or less vivid, of lands he has never seen. It is an image stored in some corner of the imagination, adequate and satisfactory for all his personal uses. . . . He has no difficulty in presenting it to himself without so much as an effort. . . . It was painted without design, by a process of which he was not even conscious. —James W. Steele, Cuban Sketches (1881)

Cuba is really our sugar bowl. . . . Cuba [is] the world's cigar box. —National Geographic *(January 1947)*

[Havana] is an all-round pleasure laboratory. —Arts and Decoration *(February 1931)*

Cuba is the natural playground of America. —Havana Post *(March 1, 1916)*

Havana is a cocktail. —Outlook *(February 5, 1930)*

Cuba is the Mecca of tourists. —United Railways of Havana, A Winter of Paradise *(Buffalo, 1913)*

Cuba [is] the Mecca for subversives. —Kenneth N. Skoug Jr., Cuba as a Model and a Challenge *(1984)*

Little Cuba is like the smallest member of a family, who may be disregarded but who is underrated only at one's peril. —Erna Ferguson, Cuba *(1946)*

Cuba mattered because it seemed to bear so directly on the well-being of the United States. That property interests subsequently developed into concerns of comparable importance should not obscure the original preoccupation, in the words of John Quincy Adams, with matters related to "the continuance and integrity of the Union itself," so very much at the source of the North American fixation on Cuba. Not to understand the manner in which Cuba insinuated itself into the calculus of nineteenth-century concerns over national well-being is to overlook the psychological determinants by which the Americans developed consciousness of Cuba.

What mattered most about the island and its people had to do with the ways that the Americans imagined Cuba as a source of their security and a means of their prosperity. This was Cuba as a place inscribed into the American imagination as a means to an end. The Ostend Manifesto in 1854—"the Union can never enjoy repose, nor possess reliable security, as long as Cuba is not embraced within its boundaries"—must be considered as the definitive pronouncement of a deepening North American preoccupation with Cuba. It was not always certain that these concerns were wholly rational, but it is clear that they informed the ways that the Americans arrived at an understanding of the relevance of Cuba to their lives, which is to say that these were the concerns that shaped the meaning with which Cuba settled into the popular imagination. It was perhaps, in the end, difficult to be entirely rational about a place imagined as "indispensable to the continuance and integrity of the Union itself."

That metaphor served as the principal discursive mode by which the Americans arrived at their knowledge of Cuba meant, too, that the island and its people existed largely as representations that often bore no relationship to the place and population that it purported to depict. Cuba as a metaphorical construct developed as a matter of North American needs: imagined as vital to the well-being of the United States and populated with a people who were expected to accommodate North American interests as a condition of their national existence.

These were complex issues, of course, a combination of emotional fixation and pragmatic purpose, with attention to the question of national security as both a psychological condition and a strategic calculation. The conviction in the nineteenth century of Cuba as "indispensable to the continuance and integrity of the Union itself" insinuated itself deeply into North American consciousness and could not but have rendered the need to control Cuba as obvious as it was obligatory. If Cuba seemed to have no proper destiny other than as an extension of American needs, it was because the United States appeared to have no secure future without Cuba.

★ ★ ★

Possession of Cuba was an end unto itself, to be sure, but the end also served as a means to other possibilities, a way to enact the presumption of North American primacy in the Western Hemisphere into a reality. This was to contemplate Cuba as a point of strategic intersection with Latin America, to imagine the island metaphorically as the linchpin of U.S. power in the hemisphere. So much seemed to depend on Cuba; so much more was possible with Cuba. It was about control and command, about power and domination—those early intimations of empire where hyperbole and hubris combined to reveal the self-absorption of a people with aspirations to supremacy. Possession of Cuba filled the North American imagination with prospects of global reach. "Give us Cuba," Georgia senator Robert Toombs exulted in the mid-nineteenth century, "and we shall command all the . . . wants of the human race; we shall control their commerce in everything." With Cuba, Toombs predicted, "we can make first the Gulf of Mexico, and then the Caribbean sea, a *mare clausum*," whereupon the day would not be too distant "when no flag shall float there except by permission of the United States of America."[1] The *Merchants' Magazine* imagined Cuba as "the pivot of a coast trade such as the world never saw."[2] Commerce was also on the mind of *DeBow's Review*, which predicted outright that possession of Cuba promised "control over the commerce and wealth of this new world," adding, "And with that commerce we can control the power of the world. Give us [Cuba], and we can make the public opinion of the world."[3] Missouri senator Trusten Polk envisioned Cuba as a means to "possess and command the Gulf; [to] control the transit routes across the continent, and hold the commercial intercourse between the Atlantic and Pacific in our grasp." The United States, Polk predicted, would then be "in a position to win the mastery over the Caribbean sea, and to subject the productions of its tropical river basins to our uses, and its commerce to our aggrandizement."[4] It was perhaps only a matter of time, and indeed perhaps inevitable, that Americans would persuade themselves that the well-being of the entire world depended on the U.S. possession of Cuba. "The future interests not only of this country," proclaimed Delaware senator James Bayard at midcentury, "but of civilization and of human progress, are deeply involved in the acquisition of Cuba by the United States."[5]

After 1898, Cuba entered the popular imagination as a country of opportunity. Americans by the thousands, many still reeling from the effects of an economic crisis during the early 1890s, emigrated to the island, attracted by the promise of land and prospects for livelihood, but mostly by the possibility of starting life anew.[6] How propitious that Cuba should appear as a "new frontier" at about the time that Frederick Jackson Turner was lamenting the passing of the old one. "Nowhere else in the world are there such chances for success for the man of moderate means . . . as Cuba offers today," pronounced one developer in 1904.[7]

The metaphors followed. "On to Cuba!" was the cry that reverberated immediately after the war, reported the *New York Journal*, adding, "The war-ridden isle is expected to prove to be a veritable Klondike of wealth." Americans celebrated Cuba as "a new country," a "virgin land," a "new California," and "the land of promise."[8] "The island may be called a brand-new country," exulted General Leonard Wood in 1901. "Remarkable in the extreme are the opportunities that exist in Cuba for both homeseekers and investors," was how the *Commercial and Financial World* characterized the island in 1906, adding alluring imagery: "It is simply a poor man's paradise and the rich man's mecca." Writer George Reno depicted eastern Cuba as a "new frontier" and proclaimed, "Oriente [province] is the California of Cuba."[9] "The land of tropical fruits" was how the Cuban Land and Steamship Company advertised Cuba in 1899, boasting, "Such a field of wealth has never before been opened. It may mean a fortune to you. It certainly means happiness, comfort, and competence to those who accept our offer. . . . Why toil and starve, and freeze, when by at once taking advantage of this offer you can reap a golden harvest, and live a life of comparative ease?"[10]

Cuba developed into something of a Rorschach blot: variously a source of anxiety, an object of fantasy, and a place of tropical enchantment, but almost always as a function of American needs. Its multiple figurative representations, often rendered in the possessive form, propounded Cuba as belonging to the United States: "America's finest playground," Cuba as "the playground of the United States," Cuba as "our sugar bowl."[11] Novelist Joseph Hergesheimer could actually claim Havana to be "an authentic part of my inheritance."[12] This was Cuba as a tropical island of easy exotica, imagined as a place of pleasure in which to dwell and delight. It was variously referred to as a "Garden of Paradise," a "Paradise of the earth," a "modern Eden" and a "lost Eden," "a terrestrial paradise," a "Garden of Delight," and a "mañana-land."[13]

★ ★ ★

The Americans ascribed multiple metaphorical forms to Cuba, each inscribed with a different function: at times dissimulation as denial, on other occasions as euphemism to dissemble, but almost always as a means of cognitive manipulation to accommodate North American needs. And because needs changed, so, too, did metaphors.

The late 1910s and 1920s were years of cultural transformation in the United States, of shifting moral boundaries and changing social mores. The years were a time of boundless hedonism and self-indulgence, a time when many Americans gave themselves unabashedly to the pursuit of amusement and entertainment. Cuba emerged as the site of choice for Americans to experiment self-consciously with moral transgression and fulfill forbidden fantasies. It offered easy sex and hard drinking, and drugs and debauchery; it was a place of pleasure for purchase. The metaphors followed.

New metaphorical depictions of Cuba had mostly to do with representations of the island as a site for fun, adventure, and abandon; it was a setting for honeymoons and a playground for vacations. This was Cuba as a brothel, a casino, a cabaret, a good liberty port—a place for flings, sprees, and binges, represented variously as "the playhouse of the Caribbean," "the playland of the Americas," "a veritable fairyland," "a land of enchantment," and "a paradise on earth." It was the "gamblers' haven" and "a paradise for the yachtsman."[14] During the years of Prohibition, North American metaphors depicted Cuba variously as a "paradise of the cocktails," "a famed oasis," "the U.S. saloon," and "a mahogany island surrounded by a brass rail." Havana was "a veritable city of romance," exulted visitor Idaless Westly in 1921.[15] "A winter playground" was how journalist Gary Schumacher described Cuba during his vacation in 1930, even as the island reeled from the effects of the Great Depression.[16] An "American playground"—Ava Gardner fondly recalled the Havana of her honeymoon in 1951—"complete with gambling houses, whorehouses, and brightly lit cafes ... [and] all combined to form a Latin town that aimed to please."[17] And more metaphors: Cuba was "the Riviera of the Caribbean," "the Nice of the Atlantic," "the Monte Carlo of the Western Hemisphere," and "the Las Vegas of the Caribbean." Mariel Bay was depicted as "the Newport of Cuba"; Havana was celebrated as "Paris of the Caribbean," "Paris of the Americas," and "Paris of the Western Hemisphere."[18] Providence and proximity seemed again to have combined to shape the destiny of Cuba as a function of North American needs. "It might be said," pronounced one tourist advertisement, "that nature has purposely placed this Holiday Isle of the Tropics at the door of the great American nation for the pleasure, repose and health of its inhabitants."[19]

The notion of Cuba as site of easy virtue and loose morals, a place of lewd amusement and bawdy delights, was fixed early. Vice developed into the principal virtue of Havana. An "extraordinary city," exulted Graham Greene, "where every vice was permissible and every trade possible." This was Havana represented as a city of sumptuous bordellos and squalid brothels; of sex on the streets, on the screen, and onstage; of pornographic theaters and pornographic bookstores. "One of the last of the world's sinful cities," pronounced the *Saturday Evening Post* in 1953.[20] American tourists in Cuba, novelist Joseph Hergesheimer commented, were "animated by the Cuban air" and "galvanized

ROULETTE

BACCARAT - CRAPS

Complete Floor Show - 2 Orchestras

1st. SHOW 11:00 p.m.
2nd. SHOW 1:15 a.m.

RESTAURANT OPEN EVERY NIGHT

GRAN CASINO NACIONAL
MARIANAO, HAVANA, CUBA

"The Monte Carlo of America." From *Havana Weekly*, February 26–March 4, 1949.

. . . .

by drink and the distance from their responsibilities." Hergesheimer reveled in Havana: "No other city in the world could so perfectly create the illusion of complete irresponsibility."[21] Cuba was a place of escape and escapades—where "conscience takes a holiday," rhapsodized travel writer Sydney Clark.[22] Americans "love to go [to Havana]," one travel writer explained, "where the neighbors won't see them behaving as they would never behave at home."[23] It was the ideal place—the *Havana Post* assured tourists—to satisfy the "appetite for pleasure and indulgence."[24] The island would fill with Americans stalking the streets for sex: sailors and marines who delighted in Cuba as a good liberty port; conventioneers who flocked to Cuba for annual trade shows, business meetings, and conventions; high school and college boys on spring break. U.S. ambassador Arthur Gardner could only observe with mounting incredulity and lamely lament, "The masses of people who come here are bent only on pleasure and think of Cuba except in terms of fun, rum and nightclubs."[25]

The proposition that the United States had liberated Cuba conferred on American tourists a powerful sense of entitlement; they could do whatever they wanted to do because Cuba belonged to them. "We gave Cuba her liberty," proclaimed one U.S. army veteran vacationing in Cuba in 1925, "and now we are going to enjoy it."[26]

Cuba in the first half of the twentieth century dwelled in the American imagination principally as a site of moral license. It was not a country to be taken seriously, hardly thought about before 1959 as anything more than a place of tropical promiscuity, illicit pleasures, and risqué amusements. Metaphorical depiction in this instance worked as innuendo and intimation. This was Cuba in the service of the North American libido: a place to flaunt conventions and fulfill fantasies; to indulge unabashedly in fun and frolic, in play and pleasure, in bars and brothels, at the racetrack and the gambling casinos; to do illegal drugs and have illicit sex. Cuba entered domains of the North American familiar as a place of promiscuity, as site of sexual encounter with the tropical Other. Metaphor provided meaning without the need for explanation: "one of the last of the world's sinful cities," a "fleshpot city," "one of the world's fabled fleshpots," "the brothel of the New World," "the Red Light district of the Caribbean."[27]

The metaphor of Cuba as woman again gained currency, this time not as damsel in distress but as whore available—even eager—to satisfy the North American sexual appetite. "Like a gaily attired Spanish señorita," the *National Geographic* swooned in 1933, "Cuba charms the eye."[28] Cuba was "like a woman in love," travel writers Consuelo Hermer and Marjorie May assured their readers. "Eager to give pleasure, she will be anything you want her to be—exciting or peaceful, gay or quiet, brilliant or tranquil. What is your fancy? She

FIRST AMERICAN: We did a good job when we gave these Cubans their freedom.
SECOND PATRIOT: You said it....*WAITER!*

"First American: 'We did a good job when we gave these Cubans their freedom.' Second Patriot: 'You said it. . . . WAITER!'" Depiction of Americans in Cuba during Prohibition in the United States. From *Havana*, February 1929.

. . . .

is only too anxious to anticipate your desires, to charm you with her beauty."[29] Havana was "temptingly coquettish," commented one travel writer, and decades later journalist Georgie Anne Geyer described prerevolutionary Cuba as "America's most beautiful mistress." These were the years that writer Andrei Codrescu would later characterize as "the heyday of American good living in Cuba, when the whole country was a cheap and bountiful mistress." Writer Thomas Freeman invoked a succession of familiar metaphors to represent the end of diplomatic relations between Cuba and the United States after 1961: "At first a foster child, Cuba was at the last a kept woman. . . . The United States never understood her, nor did she understand the U.S. But perhaps, had the U.S. been a bit more *hombre*, and not been afraid to take the stick to her now and then, she might have hated Uncle Sam just as much, but not have taken another nation's bread and board."[30]

In this order of things, Cuban self-representation was admitted rarely, if at all. Perhaps Cuba possessed an interior history, perhaps not; it really did not matter. What mattered most was the degree to which Cubans accommodated North American needs. This is the point novelist John Sayles made with poignance through his protagonist in *Los Gusanos* (1991). "You Americans will never understand us," Blas de la Peña concludes ruefully, to which the American responds, "We don't really need to, do we?"[31]

★   ★   ★

After 1961, Cuba became a place proscribed. Yet even in its banishment it continued to hold the North American imagination in its thrall. All through the decades of suspended diplomatic relations and economic sanctions, of political isolation and travel bans, the idea of Cuba retained much of its seductive appeal. The Cuba of North American fantasy developed into a ubiquitous marketing device in product development and as a brand name, as advertising strategy, and as retail practice. This was to evoke Cuba—again—as exotic tropical sensuality, unabashedly nostalgic, only this time it was vicarious, an experience to be obtained as a function of consumption. Many hundreds of consumer products reached diverse retail markets bearing the names "Havana" and "Cuba" as brand designations. Designer sunglasses named "Havana" were marketed by Gucci, Costa del Mar, Ralph Lauren, Christian Dior, Armani, and Prada. Cosmetics included "Havana" lipsticks (Designory and Paula Dorf) and "Café Havana" (Sacha); "Havana" facial power (Christian Dior); "Mocha Havana" blush (Lancôme); and "Havana" eyeshadow (Vasanti Cosmetics). Other products included wristwatches named "Havana" (Festina and Tommy Bahama). Hayden-Harnett introduced a "Havana" line of handbags; Magnussen designed a "Havana" furniture line; and Design within Reach introduced a "Havana Sofa." Perfumes and colognes included the perfume "Havana" (Aramis) and "Old Havana" men's cologne (Tommy Bahama).

Manufacturers and retailers understood exactly the forms in which Cuba dwelled in the popular imagination—and proceeded to reinforce them. Products were often accompanied with explicit subtexts as descriptions and advertisement copy. The Blancpain "Havana" wristwatch, the advertisement insisted, was "making being Cuban cool again"; it continued, "Forget about Castro, communism, and poverty because Cuba is about *hot girls*, mojitos, and timepieces."[32] Yves Saint Laurent marketed "Starry Havana" lip gloss with the promise to create "more seductive lips."[33] The "Havana" cologne by Aramis advertised "Havana, the city that produces the ultimate in masculinity, the Cuban cigar. Picture the aroma of tobacco as the smoke envelopes you and serves as a calming influence from the bustling day around you. The fragrance

'Havana' will have affected you similarly as you allow its luxurious spicy notes to swathe you with a masculine sensuality. For the romantic occasion when good is not good enough. When better is expected."[34]

The themes are unambiguous, even if only as innuendo, intimation, and double entendre. The "Havana" candle by Archipelago Botanicals is a "sultry fragrance . . . sure to be the perfect touch to create an exotic atmosphere," to which one customer responded, "'Havana' is the sexiest, most alluring smell."[35] The "Havana Nana" soft drink with its "exotic tropical blend of forbidden fruits is unique, captivating the consumer with lush settings and exotic taste while bridging the gap between inland and island cultures. Havana Nana invites consumers to open a chilled bottle of this enticing beverage, to close their eyes and taste the tropics and, for a refreshing moment, let Havana Nana transport them to an island paradise." "Havana Iced Cappuccino" is "young in nature, adult in taste, cosmopolitan and sensual. A product with flair and sex appeal."[36] Advertising its "Havana" swim briefs, Kiniki claims "Latin lovers will shine in 'Havana,' a style inspired by a sensual musical beat under starry night skies." According to Ujena, "Anything goes in our Havana Bikini!"[37] The "Havana Bamboo Shade" line, "with its rich, warm blending of textures, . . . will evoke images of trade wind destinations and exotic locales. . . . An alternating weave of natural matchstick and bamboo creates a sensual pleasure for the eyes."[38] Target department store advertised its Havana Rattan Futon Frame Collection as "a sultry, tropical touch to a sunny room."[39] Also available are Havana Jack's Café Canefield Palm Sheet Set ("Get away to a tropical destination just by hitting the sheets!") and Havana Jack's Café St. Marcus Comforter Set ("Step into a tropical paradise every time you enter your bedroom with this exotic comforter set!").[40] Or try the "Cuban Black Bean Dip" from the El Paso Chile Company: "Waving palms, a cool island breeze. Visit a forbidden paradise of silky black beans, sweet red pepper and an undercurrent of rich gold rum, resulting in a Cuban sensation that may taste mild, but is definitely hot, hot, hot!"[41]

★ ★ ★

Metaphorical knowledge had consequences. It propounded a parallel social reality, in much the way that Harold Lasswell wrote of "hypothetical patterns of reality."[42] Metaphorical representation served to inform and inevitably mediate the character of the North American engagement with Cubans, both as a matter of people-to-people interaction and government-to-government relations. It shaped perceptions and influenced attitudes, precisely those perspectives by which interpersonal decorum was enacted. Meaning was not always the essential property of metaphor: purpose was. The representation of Cubans as children, for example, could not—to enter the logic of the meta-phor—readily contemplate the possibility of Cuban adulthood without sub-verting the premise of power upon which it was based. To acknowledge adult-hood—that is, parity—was to admit to the very condition that the metaphor was meant to deny in the first place. The metaphor of children, as both prem-ise and proof of the propriety by which the Americans presumed authority over Cuba, persisted through the 1940s and into the 1950s. "The Cuban people are a race still in the making," pronounced Episcopalian minister J. Merle Davis in 1942, "and are in the adolescent period of development."[43] Cuban politi-cal leaders more properly belonged in a "Rogue's Gallery than [on] a roster of responsible public servants," U.S. ambassador R. Henry Norweb commented several years later. "Many of them possess the superficial charm of clever chil-dren, spoiled by nature and geography,—but under the surface they combine the worst characteristics of the unfortunate admixture and interpretation of Spanish and Negro cultures—laziness, cruelty, inconstancy, irresponsibility and inbred dishonesty." Norweb described Cubans as having "a natural ten-dency to flaunt their 'independence' in small ways—much as a puppy might yelp bravely at a mastiff behind a fence."[44] Reacting to Cuban protests over sugar legislation in 1947, Ellis Briggs scoffed peremptorily, "It is time that Cuba grow up."[45] During the 1940s, State Department analysts prepared a series of psychological profiles of Cubans as "background" country notes, the dominant frame of reference of which was the proposition of Cubans as children. Cubans had a "tradition of indiscipline," one analyst commented in 1947, a marked propensity toward "insubordination and indiscipline." Cuban conduct of foreign affairs was "childish" and wholly lacking of "any system of restraints." Another profile in the following year emphasized the Cuban "lack of discipline" and the tendency "to act impulsively."[46]

The metaphor of Cubans as children lost much of its depictive efficacy with the triumph of the revolution in 1959. The premise from which it had derived plausibility no longer bore any relationship to the changing Cuban reality. A new generation of Cubans had arrived to power in 1959, possessed of a new-found sense self-esteem and self-confidence, determined to pursue a des-tiny distinctly Cuban. The revolution had been against political dictatorship and social injustice, certainly, but it was also about aspirations to national sovereignty and self-determination, and especially about Cubans affirming control—control over their resources, control over their lives, control of their future—on their own terms, for their own interests. "I believe that this coun-try has the same rights of other countries to govern itself," Fidel Castro pro-nounced as early as January 13, 1959, "to devise for itself its own destiny." And Castro said days later: "[The Americans] now know that there exists in Cuba a government disposed to defend its interests."[47] Things were different in Cuba, U.S. ambassador Philip Bonsal sensed by April 1959. Cubans viewed Fidel Castro's planned visit later that month to the United States as a "historical precedent," Bonsal observed, with an "attitude of confidence and assured independence," the "first time [that] a Cuban ruler has visited the United States representing a fully sovereign and equal nation, free from any domination or control."[48]

Almost everything changed after the triumph of the Cuban revolution. Events moved quickly: a state of affairs in continuous flux as developments with portentous implications seemed to gather momentum from one day to the next in vertiginous succession. History had speeded up. Change seemed to beget more change as the normal course of events.

But it is also true that some things did not change, and one of the things that did not change was the character of the North American engagement with Cuba. The Americans continued to hold on to old metaphors as the principal mode through which to seek to make sense of developments in Cuba and hence as a means to inform the content of policy and influence the conduct of politics. It was impossible, of course, to discard the stock of existing metaphors without first replacing the paradigms from which they originated. Therein lay the problem: paradigms in the United States were slow to shift at a time of rapid change in Cuba. The revolution had, in fact, rendered old paradigms unusable.

But it was more complicated still. The very proposition of Cuba for Cubans— that is, Cubans no longer disposed to accommodate North American needs— was difficult for the Americans to contemplate. Bonsal did indeed discern that "the people of Cuba were recovering control of their destiny," but without fully appreciating how this process challenged the very premise by which the Americans had presumed the propriety of their power.[49] "I must think in terms of what is good for Cuba, not for the United States," Fidel Castro explained to Illinois representative Barratt O'Hara.[50] That Cubans would assert claim to their destiny in function of their own interests, that they would affirm their interests as distinct and different from those of the United States, was to challenge a paradigm with antecedents early in the nineteenth century. "Until the revolution," Castro proclaimed, "none of us had any say in the future of our country."[51]

Few in the United States seemed to appreciate how the changes taking place in Cuba had nullified the depictive efficacy of old metaphors, from which the premise of policy had previously been derived. So fully were the Americans implicated in the logic of their own metaphors that they failed to discern—

or perhaps they were unable to discern—the revolution as a phenomenon of Cuban empowerment. The presumption of power revealed itself in many ways, of course, but all were cause and effect of the complete certainty with which the Americans believed themselves possessed of the means and endowed with the right to control events in Cuba. "We should decide," Assistant Secretary of State J. C. Hill pronounced with casual confidence in September 1959, "whether or not we wish to have the Cuban revolution succeed."[52]

The Americans continued to invoke the metaphor of Cubans as children as the principal discursive framework with which to make sense of Cuba in 1959. The new Cuban leaders were considered lacking the maturity to understand their best interests, incapable of functioning in the adult world of Cold War politics, and therefore obliged to cleave to the Americans for guidance. "The Cubans look upon us as big brothers," Louisiana senator Allen J. Ellender confided smugly to his diary in December 1958. Two months later Illinois representative Barratt O'Hara affirmed happily that "today our role [with Cuba] is that of the elder sister Republic."[53] Ambassador Bonsal attributed Cuban conduct in 1959 to "extreme sensitivity of Cuba's position as a small brother. This leads frequently to exaggerated reactions intended to assert complete independence and equality."[54]

The Americans did not take Fidel Castro seriously. He was endlessly the object of caricaturists' drawings, variously ridiculed, mocked, and satirized. He fared no better at the hands of opinion makers and power holders. Columnist Drew Pearson scoffed at "how naive Castro is and how much he has to learn about Cuba's relations with the outside world."[55] Tennessee representative Brazilla Reece denounced Castro's "sophomoric nonchalance" and "immaturity";[56] Castro was "immature and irrational," Secretary of State Christian Herter concluded.[57] "When Castro came into power, everybody thought he was going to be a very good boy" was the way labor attaché John Correll later remembered 1959; "He wasn't a good boy at all."[58] New York senator Kenneth Keating characterized Fidel Castro as "Pecks bad boy of international politics"; *New York Times* correspondent Tad Szulc described Fidel Castro in 1959 as an "an over-grown boy," and columnist George Sokolsky dismissed him as "an immature boy."[59] Correspondent Edwin Tetlow characterized Castro as "an irresponsible adolescent," adding, "I do not believe that Fidel Castro ever grew up fully; I have never known him to display that kind of emotional stability we attribute to the mature adult." However, there was another possibility, Tetlow suggested: "Perhaps he was just being Cuban."[60] During a National Security Council meeting in 1959, in anticipation of a visit by a Cuban delegation to Washington, Central Intelligence Agency (CIA) director Allen Dulles insisted to his colleagues that "the new Cuban officials had to be treated more or less like children. They had to be led rather than rebuffed," for "if they were rebuffed, like children, they were capable of doing almost anything."[61]

These were not auspicious portents. In April 1959, Fidel Castro visited the United States; a close Castro aide would later characterize the visit as "the last opportunity the U.S. government had to attract Fidel with a policy of friendship and rapprochement."[62] The Cuban-as-child metaphor appears to have set the tone with which North American officials received the Cuban leader. Vice-President Richard Nixon later recounted with satisfaction the character of his meeting with Castro. "I talked to him like a Dutch uncle," Nixon recalled.[63] Robert Stevenson, at the time the Cuba desk officer, later reported that Nixon "had talked to Dr. Castro just like a father."[64] Secretary of State Christian Herter also made notes of his meeting with Fidel Castro in April 1959 and thereupon forwarded his impressions to President Dwight Eisenhower: "He [is] very much like a child in many ways, quite immature regarding problems of government."[65] Not long after, the *Charleston News and Courier* published an editorial cartoon in which Fidel Castro was depicted as an unruly child in a playpen, with an adage in the form of metaphor as caption exhorting, "Spare the rod and spoil the child."

Nor was Fidel Castro insensible of North American demeanor. He took umbrage at Vice-President Nixon's condescension and later confided to an aide his consternation at having been "reprimanded" by Nixon.[66] Cuban minister of the treasury Rufo López-Fresquet was also present and later recalled, "I was next to the door when they came out of the office of the Capitol in which they had met. Castro was angry. He swore and added, 'This man has spent the whole time scolding me.'"[67] Apparently Nixon was not the only U.S. official to talk down to the Cuban leader. Herbert Matthews recounted in 1960 a conversation with Fidel Castro: "Bitterly resentful of the way he said Ambassador Bonsal had talked to him and treated him from the beginning, he said several times, 'it was so humiliating.' He contrasted this with the respectful, friendly attitude of the Russians."[68]

It was a theme to which Fidel Castro returned often: the metaphor turned upside down as a means of agency. "They deprived the Cuban people of the prerogative to govern themselves," Castro recalled the past; "they deprived the Cuban people of their sovereignty; they treated the Cuban people like little children to whom they said: 'We give you permission to do just this, and if you do more we will punish you.' The Platt Amendment was imposed [and] we either behaved ourselves—behaved ourselves in the manner convenient to the foreign country—or we would lose our sovereignty."[69]

SPARE THE ROD AND SPOIL THE CHILD

"Spare the Rod and Spoil the Child." From *Charleston News and Courier*, January 1, 1960.

. . . .

★ ★ ★

The Americans viewed developments in Cuba with a mixture of incomprehension and incredulity. There was no frame of reference with which to make sense of events: no precedent, no counterpart, no context. The sheer effrontery of the challenge posed by the Cubans was unimaginable. This was Fidel Castro defiant and strident, delivering spellbinding—and at times virulent—denunciations, hours at a time, day after day, stretching into weeks and then into months, an unrelenting condemnation of the United States for nearly sixty years of deeds and misdeeds in Cuba. "Arrogant, insolent and provocative," Ambassador Bonsal wrote at the time; "galling" was how presidential advisor Arthur Schlesinger Jr. remembered Cuban behavior in those early days.[70] Never before—certainly never before in Latin America—had a duly constituted and recognized government mounted so strident an attack on the past policies and practices of the United States. "We have never in our national history," Henry Ramsey of the State Department policy planning staff wrote with dismay and disbelief in early 1960, "experienced anything quite like it in magnitude of anti-US venom."[71]

Without historical depth perception, the Americans were unable to comprehend that the Cubans were addressing a history, not a policy. Indeed, in the early weeks and months it was all about history. Policy came later. Without awareness of that history, the Americans mistook their ignorance for innocence: they had done nothing to provoke the Cubans. The "policy toward Cuba," the Office of National Estimates of the CIA insisted in early 1961, "had been marked by caution and restraint," furthering the claim that the turns of events on the island had not been "a function of US policy and action."[72] And, in fact, to a certain degree, this was not entirely incorrect. But the politics was in the memory. All at once in the early months of 1959, the past and present conflated, and without knowledge of the former an understanding of the latter was impossible.

The incoherence of the American response to the policies and politics of the Cuban revolution in 1959 must also in part be understood as a matter of cognitive dissonance: the inability to order into coherent narrative form a comprehension of developments so profoundly counterintuitive and utterly inconceivable as a Cuban challenge to North American power. There was nothing in the available stock of North American knowledge of Cuba to enable the Americans to comprehend the forces released by the triumph of the revolution: a soaring self-confidence, rising expectations, a heightened anticipation of national fulfillment, but most of all a powerful sense of empowerment. Cubans in 1959 were a people who believed themselves to have recovered their history and reclaimed their historical agency.

It was, in part, the genius of Cuban political leaders, on one hand, and the inability of U.S. political leaders to see beyond the reach of their own metaphors, on the other, that created the space in which the Cuban revolution consolidated itself. Arizona senator Barry Goldwater was entirely correct in describing Americans who "shook their heads in bewilderment" at what was happening in Cuba.[73] That the Cubans would presume to challenge the premise of U.S. power was as implausible; that they would question its propriety was unimaginable. Only months before the triumph of the Cuban revolution, a study of the Caribbean region prepared by Vermont senator George Aiken for the Senate Foreign Relations Committee acknowledged the deepening insurgency in Cuba but could not imagine any outcome that would adversely affect the United States. "Happily for the United States," Aiken predicted with confidence, "if there should be a change in the Government of all Cuba it is difficult to conceive of the possibility that any new regime would be unfriendly to the United States. There is a vast reservoir of good feeling toward the United States in Cuba. The Cubans know and cherish the fact that we assisted them to attain independence."[74] The ability of the Americans to make sense of developments in Cuba could only draw upon what was known, on the knowledge that was at hand and available, which in this instance implied reliance on accumulated metaphorical constructs as framework for comprehension. The problem was that old metaphors were unable to provide usable information to aid understanding of new conditions. "The lack of communication with [Castro]," brooded Henry Ramsey of the State Department policy planning staff in early 1960, "has reduced us to a state of semi-paralysis. . . . I think we fail to realize that Castro does not speak our language and does not want to listen to it."[75] By late 1959, Assistant Secretary of State John Hill reported on the "puzzlement" among senior officials at the Department of Defense who "do not know either that we have a definite policy or what its nature is."[76]

Cuban grievances were received in the United States as a deeply felt affront, for in challenging the premise and disputing the propriety of American power, the Cubans also challenged the master narrative of beneficent purpose so central to the normative determinants from which the Americans derived the moral authority to presume power over Cuba. The use of metaphor had enabled the Americans to pursue national interest in the guise of selfless moral enactment, a way to deploy cultural models as discursive strategies of power. For Cubans to charge that American actions were based on self-interest—and not disinterest—was to challenge North American power at the very point of its moral origins, at the level of motive, and in part explains the visceral force with which the Americans responded to the Cuban revolution. To negate the propriety of authority propounded from the claim of beneficent intent was to challenge the basis of North American self-esteem and self-representation.[77]

The propriety of North American hegemony in Cuba had assumed such utter commonplace normality as to take on the appearance of the natural order of things, hardly noticed at all except as a confirmation that all was right in the world. That Cubans in 1959 called attention to this condition as an anomaly in their lives, as wrong and improper, drew responses of blank incredulity from the Americans: How could they comprehend the Cuban denunciation of a relationship that most Americans—if they thought about it at all—were certain had been entirely ideal and always in the best interest of Cubans?

What happened in Cuba mattered in the United States because Cuba was a place that the Americans had claimed as their own and in which they had invested themselves as a matter of their own well-being and amour propre. The efficacy of metaphors of Cuba had to do with their capacity to inscribe the logic of power into those culturally determined practices from which normality was conceived. This was to exercise power as a matter of moral purpose by which Americans themselves had arrived at self-knowledge, intrinsic to the nature of the people Americans believed themselves to be. So fully had the Americans persuaded themselves of the propriety of their power that Cuban acquiescence to the United States was itself a corroboration of the esteem in which Americans held themselves. Cuba had long served both as a means and an end of U.S. self-representation: Cuba as an American-made artifact, pointed to with pride and proof of the moral purpose with which the United States had projected its presence in the world at large. Cuba was a source of validation of North American self-esteem. Cuba "is the show window of United States policy," pronounced Ambassador Spruille Braden in 1944, "and a powerful influence on our relations with all the American republics."[78] The Cubans were accordingly expected to discharge a supporting role in ratifying the terms of North American self-representation as disinterested liberators and generous benefactors and well-intentioned neighbors. This changed in 1959.

So deeply had Americans invested themselves in the metaphors of Cuba as a means of self-confirmation that the island itself became a reflection of American sense of self. As early as 1898, Whitelaw Reid, publisher of the *New York Tribune*, made the case for North American authority on the basis of moral duty and ethical obligations. "Are we not . . . bound in honor and morals to see to it that the government which replaces Spanish rule is better?" Reid asked rhetorically, and continued: "Are we not morally culpable and disgraced before the civilized world if we leave it as bad, or worse? Can any consideration of mere policy, of our own interests, or our own ease and comfort, free us from that solemn responsibility which we have voluntarily assumed, and for which we have lavishly spilt American and Spanish blood?"[79] Leonard Wood insisted as early as 1899 upon the need "to establish [in Cuba] a government which shall be creditable to the United States."[80] Wood was adamant: "There is no escaping the fact that, even if we do not own the Island, we are responsible for its good conduct." The United States, proclaimed Wood, "must always control the destinies of Cuba."[81] To achieve less was a discredit to the North American moral purpose. Twenty years later, General Enoch Crowder reflected that "if the experiment of Republican Government fails in Cuba it is not so much the prestige of Cuba but rather the prestige of the United States that is discredited and impaired."[82]

★ ★ ★

Thus it was that the Cuban revolution in 1959 wrought havoc on North American terms of self-esteem. Under-Secretary of State George Ball agonized over Cuba. He characterized developments there as having "formed an over-hanging cloud of public shame and obsession [and] seemed an affront to our history."[83] Senator Barry Goldwater denounced in mid-1961 the very existence of the Castro government as "a disgrace and an affront which diminishes the respect with which we are held by the rest of the world in direct ratio to the length of time we permit it to go unchallenged."[84] "Our national honor is vilified," decried Colorado senator Gordon Allott.[85] "An insult to American prestige, a challenge to American dignity" was how South Carolina representative Mendel Rivers depicted the Cuban revolution.[86] His assessment was similar to New York senator Kenneth Keating's denunciation of Cuba as "an affront . . . to the dignity of the United States."[87]

The Americans reacted to developments in Cuba in profoundly emotional and personal ways. Officials and commentators alike bore witness to a deepening dismay in the United States. Ambassador Bonsal later characterized Americans having "experienced a sense of injury, irritation, and alarm."[88] Dean Rusk recalled Cuba years later as having "a devastating psychological impact on the American people."[89] Walter Rostow would recount that Cuba had produced "a visceral reaction in the government."[90] Writer Thomas Freeman alluded to the "psychic damage" caused by the "establishment of a hostile government close to [U.S.] shores,"[91] and Theodore Draper wrote of "the hysterical approach to the Cuban problem."[92] Journalist Daniel James agreed, observing in 1959 that Americans were "filled with an anguish that was almost personal." Unable to move beyond the paradigms at hand, James was baffled at how "a country as close to us as Cuba" would turn against the United States: "Our armed forces helped Cuba free herself from Spanish rule in 1898 and American blood fertilizes Cuban soil. . . . Our tired bodies often found relaxation in the warm sun of tropical Cuba. How could this Caribbean paradise with its delightful people suddenly become an ugly and menacing expression of the cold war?"[93]

The watchword during the early 1960s was "humiliation." The Cubans appeared to have done something to the Americans that had rarely been done before: humiliated them. For this they would not be forgiven. "I cannot allow my country," protested Massachusetts representative Silvio Conte in 1960, "to continue to suffer the constant humiliation and opprobrium heaped upon her in an irresponsible manner."[94] Texas representative Robert Casey wrote of the "American people [having] suffered repeated humiliation, as well as heavy financial loss, by actions of the Communist regime now in power in Cuba."[95] Under-Secretary of State Chester Bowles used a familiar metaphor when he confided to his diary the administration's determination "to punish Castro for the humiliation that he has brought to our door."[96] Presidential advisor Richard Goodwin recalled that President John F. Kennedy was "furious at Castro, who had humiliated his fledgling administration."[97]

★ ★ ★

The Americans succumbed to representations of their own making. They had imagined Cuba entirely as a function of their own needs and insisted upon dealing only with the artifact of their creation. They took their metaphors literally: figments of the imagination as facts of life. There is an insightful passage in the memoirs of George Clarke Musgrave, an American who fought with the Cubans in their war for independence in 1895. Musgrave reflected on the images of Cubans that had been invented by North American correspondents during the war, many of which had created the expectations with which the Americans arrived on the island in 1898. "Some of the very writers," Musgrave observed, "who in Havana had misled the public with faked stories of victorious insurgent armies sweeping the Island, now found material at the expense of the Cubans in the exposé of the phatasmas created by their own imagination."[98] Almost sixty years later, *New York Times* correspondent Herbert Matthews observed that the North American press had romanticized Fidel Castro "as if he were a knight in shining armor who had come to Havana on a white horse and who was going to make democracy, bring social justice but otherwise let things go on as before. . . . In reality, Americans were welcoming a figure who did not exist, expecting what could not and would not happen, and then blaming Fidel Castro for their own blindness and ignorance."[99] Some years ago, historian Hugh Thomas suggested that the disappointment the Americans experienced with Fidel Castro was of their making, "stretching out their hands to embrace a hero whom they had partly created, because of their own ardent demands for heroism."[100]

Cuba had ceased to be comprehensible in the United States. The Americans were baffled. Robert Alexander found developments in Cuba in 1960 "mystifying" and admitted to being "somewhat perplexed."[101] In mid-1960 the *New York Times* pondered how "to explain the inexplicable" and concluded: "What is happening in Cuba is a mystery."[102] The *Saturday Evening Post* similarly observed that developments in Cuba were "a mystery to the outsider."[103] Fidel Castro "is an enigma . . . to the diplomats and journalists who have dealt with him," wrote correspondent Irving Pflaum in 1960.[104] This was also the official view in Washington. Former ambassador Earl E. T. Smith attributed the lapse of judgment to "a general misconception" and "the greatest confusion."[105] Assistant Secretary of State Roy Rubottom came a little closer to the truth in his January 1960 observation that "since his landing in Cuba the Department has tried unsuccessfully to pin a definite label on Castro in order to take stronger action against him."[106] "We do not have any comprehension of the way they feel or to a considerable extent what is happening there," concluded *New York Times* correspondent Herbert Matthews in early 1960.[107] The failure of policy was, in fact, a failure of metaphor.

All at once, the accumulated stock of North American knowledge of Cuba — so deeply inscribed in metaphorical representation — was useless, and there was nothing readily available to take its place. Almost all that was previously known about Cuba was in need of reexamination, which revealed that what was previously known was either insufficient or unusable. The existing cognitive assets with which the Americans had come to know Cuba no longer corresponded to the new reality on the island, and that new reality was all about the inability to contain and control Cuban agency. The Americans continued to depend on old knowledge, even as they sensed uneasily that things were not quite right; they were aware that the depictive efficacy of old metaphors was not exactly relevant to new conditions but were unable to develop alternative forms of usable knowledge. Old metaphors no longer worked.

The Americans were not only unable to make sense of Cuba, but they were also unable to understand why. They persisted in transacting power through the premises of old paradigms but increasingly failed to obtain the desired outcomes; they could not respond to developments beyond the scope of their knowledge without first reordering into some coherent narrative structure a usable representation of reality. For this they needed new metaphors.

North American efforts to arrive at an understanding of developments in Cuba passed through several phases. Old metaphors slowly passed into desuetude. Never again would Fidel Castro be characterized as a child.[108] There had to be another way to "explain the inexplicable." Castro's challenge to the United States surely could not be the doings of a rational person. Perhaps he was confused and had lost his grasp of reality. Perhaps he was insane. Columnist George Sokolsky speculated on Castro's "psychological peculiarities" as early as April 1959, and author Nathaniel Weyl diagnosed the Cuban leader as suffering from "paranoid schizophrenia"; journalist Edwin Stein was convinced that an unhappy childhood formed the "unstable and schizophrenic character of a revolutionary that he became."[109] Correspondent Edwin Tetlow recounted that as a young man Fidel Castro was thrown off a motorcycle and upon recovering after days of unconsciousness he was "never normal again."[110] Director of the Office of Intelligence and Research for the American Republics Carlos Hall concluded that the Cuban leader was a "complete hysteric with a Messianic complex, if not a manic-depressive," while Lloyd Free of the United States Information Service wrote of "Castro's psychotic anti-American campaign." "He is nearly in the lunatic category," wrote constituent J. G. Rusnak to Texas senator Lyndon B. Johnson. By the end of the first year, Ambassador Bonsal had come to characterize Castro as a "highly emotional individual" who suffered "definite mental unbalance at times," adding that a speech delivered by Castro in late 1959 "was not that of [a] sane man." Secretary of State Christian Herter had also come to believe that Castro was "showing signs of increasing mental instability." By early 1960 President Eisenhower had arrived at the conclusion that the Cuban leader was beginning "to look like a madman" — "a man mentally unbalanced," Eisenhower recalled in his memoirs.[111] One year later, the Office of National Estimates of the CIA attributed developments in Cuba to "Castro's psychotic personality" and "disordered mind," adding, "Castro arrived in Havana in a state of elation amounting to mental illness."[112]

By early 1960, the Americans began to develop a conceptual framework with which to make sense of events in Cuba. The announcement of a major trade agreement between Cuba and the Soviet Union in February 1960 confirmed what many in Washington had suspected. A paradigm shift was under way that, when completed, served to open new discursive spaces into which to inscribe a new depiction of Cuba into the popular imagination. A newfound sense of lucidity settled over the North American power holders and opinion makers. Communism would henceforth serve as the principal source for new metaphors.[113] "We have lost the Cuba we knew," observed Herbert Matthews.[114] One month after the Cuban-Soviet trade agreement, President Eisenhower authorized the CIA to prepare for the overthrow of the Cuban government.

★ ★ ★

Only the fullness of time will allow the perspective with which to take full measure of the impact of the Cuban revolution on North American sensibilities.

It will be a task that will absorb the attention of the next generation of scholars of Cuban-U.S. relations. Here it is sufficient only to note that "shock" was the word that the Americans most commonly used to describe their reaction to developments in Cuba after January 1959. "Cuba's move toward communism," Secretary of State Dean Rusk later remembered, "had been a deep shock to the American people." That Cuba "allied itself eagerly and wholeheartedly to the chief threat of the national security of the United States," Kenneth Skoug affirmed, "came as a shock to the American people."[115] News broadcaster Walter Cronkite conveyed a vivid essence of the impact of the revolution in the United States:

> The rise of Fidel Castro in Cuba, his successful revolution against Batista . . . was a terrible shock to the American people. This brought communism practically to our shores. Cuba was a resort land for Americans; we went there by boat from Key West, Florida, a few hours, and it was just a part of America, we kind of considered it part of the United States—of course, it is part of America—we considered it part of the United States practically, just a wonderful little country over there that was of no danger to anybody. . . . The country was a little colony. Suddenly, revolution, and it became communist and allied with the Soviet Union. . . . An ally of the Soviet Union off our shores—it was frightening.[116]

It is, hence, from the perspective of trauma that the impact of the Cuban revolution must be understood. It had at least as much to do with psychology as it did with ideology. Americans had "been stunned and shaken by the course of events in Cuba since Castro took power in 1959," historian David Burks commented in 1964.[117] Thinking about Cuba many years later, former diplomat Wayne Smith reflected that most Americans had "a sense . . . of the right order of things violated. Our former relationship with Cuba was too intimate for us not to take this view." It was a matter of loss of control, Smith suggested: "In the minds of most Americans, Cuba was independent because we allow it to be. Cuba did our bidding and was a fun place to visit for a few days. No longer."[118]

★ ★ ★

The Soviet presence in Cuba seemed to have brought the worst fears of the nineteenth century to pass: an adversary had installed itself "almost within sight" of the United States. Precisely because Cuba had been imagined to have no purpose other than to meet North American needs, the perception of Cuba as a woman who had transferred her affections to the Soviet Union was almost unbearable. When Cuba and the Soviet Union signed a trade agreement in

1960, Colorado senator Gordon Allott described the Soviets as "sugar daddies" and warned that they "may be taking advantage of a naive girl's anxious innocence."[119]

It was through metaphor that Cuban novelist José Soler Puig depicted the inability of the Americans to reconcile themselves to the new order of things: "We are inside them, we live in their throat."[120] The metaphor did indeed seem to convey a sense of the American angst. "For the first time in history," presidential candidate John F. Kennedy warned in 1960, "an enemy stands at the throat of the United States."[121] Years later Grayston Lynch, one of the CIA planners of the Bay of Pigs, defended the 1961 invasion: "They were looking right down our throats."[122]

Once again Cuba had become one of the most important places in the world. "The Cuban problem," brooded Under-Secretary of State Livingston Merchant in 1960, "[is] the most difficult and dangerous in all the history of our relations with Latin America, possibly in all our foreign relations."[123] The Americans were overtaken by apocalyptic forebodings. "Cuba was the key to all of Latin America," warned CIA director John McCone; "if Cuba succeeds, we can expect most of Latin America to fall."[124] The outcome of the Cold War seemed to hang in the balance. "Cuba is both the key to the struggle for Latin America and the present fulcrum of the Cold War itself," the American Security Council insisted.[125]

Old metaphors assumed new meanings. The notion of Cuba as "linchpin," as a means of American strength, was subsequently reconfigured to signify vulnerability. Cuba desk officer Kenneth Skoug warned that Cuba had developed into "the linchpin between Soviet power and a hemisphere which is engaged in a struggle to see if its future lies with liberal democracy or totalitarian communism dressed up as national liberation." Castro had provided "a linchpin between Soviet power and Latin American revolutionaries."[126]

New metaphors were summoned into service. Thomas Freeman warned ominously of "an atom-tipped dagger [pointed] at America's soft-underbelly." U.S. Information Service officer Alexander Klieforth used a similar metaphor: "Cuba is a dagger pointed at the soft underbelly of the United States." The Department of State white paper on Cuba of April 1961 described "the seizure by international communism of a base and bridgehead in the Americas" and the Castro government as "the spearhead of attack on the inter-American system."[127] Nathaniel Weyl wrote of a Soviet "beachhead in the Americas," and presidential advisor Adolf Berle depicted Cuba as "the spearhead of the Soviet and Chinese propaganda." Cuba was again imagined as a "fortress" almost within sight, but this time it was "Russia's American base of aggression close to our shores" and "the first Communist citadel in the New World."[128]

Cold War imagery transformed the old metaphorical meanings of proximity.[129] Proximity now implied peril. This was Cuba "within 90 miles," warned writer Edwin Stein, as "an unsinkable aircraft carrier and missile base."[130] Cuba was "no longer a peaceful tropical island," Assistant Secretary of State Robert Hill despaired in 1960, "but an advanced landing strip of the Soviet Union and Communist China at our very doorsteps."[131] Senator Barry Goldwater denounced the emergence of Cuba as "a showcase for international communism on the southern doorstep of the United States."[132] A "dangerous threat to our peace and security . . . at our very doorsteps," Richard Nixon decried, a "Soviet beachhead," with the Cubans having "given the Soviets squatters' rights in our backyard."[133] Communism had taken hold "right under our very noses," pronounced Deputy Assistant Secretary Robert Hurwitch.[134] Grayston Lynch conveyed his dismay "watching Castro and the Soviets extend the Iron Curtain to our backyard" and that "in one tremendous leap, the Communists had landed on our doorstep."[135] Cuba was an "issue [that] confronts us in our own backyard," Edwin Stein warned.[136]

Metaphorical allusions increasingly depicted Cuba as a health threat: an ailment, an illness, a disease. Some depicted Cuba as an annoyance akin to an irritation. Presidential advisor Paul Nitze characterized Cuba as "a sharp thorn in our flank," while Cuba desk officer Kenneth Skoug referred to "a hostile Cuba on our doorstep" having assumed the "self-appointed role to be a thorn in the side of the United States."[137] Constituent J. G. Rusnak wrote to Lyndon Johnson and likened Cuba to a "tick in our hide," and Arkansas senator William Fulbright insisted that the "Castro regime is a thorn in the flesh; but it is not a dagger in the heart."[138]

As the American sense of vulnerability deepened, so, too, did the urgency of metaphors. This was metaphorical depiction of disease threatening the body of the empire. Cuba was increasingly characterized as a "communist infection in the Western Hemisphere"[139] and "center of infection."[140] Under-Secretary of State George Ball depicted Cuba as a "Communist infection."[141] Adlai Stevenson warned that the "only way to immunize the rest of Latin America to the Cuban virus is to improve its social, political and economic health."[142] The metaphor of virus took hold. Cuba was "a point of infection by the Communist virus for the whole hemisphere," commented the *New York Times*.[143]

The dominant metaphorical representation in subsequent years alluded to the notion of Cuba as a malignancy, usually in the form of cancer. In *Illness as Metaphor* (1988), Susan Sontag correctly observed that the use of cancer as a metaphor suggested "that the event or situation is unqualifiedly and irredeemably wicked. It enormously ups the ante." Cancer as metaphor, wrote Sontag, provided incentive to act; more specifically, it was "an incitement to violence."

The metaphor "in political discourse encourages fatalism and justifies 'severe' measures. . . . It is invariably an encouragement to simplify what is complex and an invitation to self-righteousness, if not to fanaticism."[144] Critic Edwin Black also suggested that cancer as metaphor implied a fatal illness, for which only radical surgical measures were appropriate. "What alternative is there? The patient is dying; is it not time for the ultimate surgery? What is there to lose?"[145]

The metaphor of Cuba as cancer, that is, as a malignancy threatening to spread if not contained and removed, invited obvious inferences.[146] Reader Axel Gravem wrote to the *New York Times* demanding the removal of "the cancer of a communist regime at our doorstep before its metastasis invades Central and South America."[147] Richard Nixon warned of the need "to eradicate this cancer in our own hemisphere" and asked rhetorically, "Can we allow this cancer of Communism to stay there?"[148] Presidential candidate John F. Kennedy offered an ensemble of metaphors in a 1960 campaign speech. "This is a critical situation," warned Kennedy, "to find so dangerous and malignant an enemy on our very doorsteps only eight minutes by jet from Florida. . . . How could the Iron Curtain have advanced to our very front yard?"[149] Barry Goldwater insisted that Cuba was "a cancer spreading poison through the Americas,"[150] and Senator Kenneth Keating demanded that "the cancer of communism must not be allowed to grow."[151] The American Legion called for the removal of the Castro government, "lest the Communist cancer take hold throughout the region."[152] For Paul Nitze, the Soviet Union had "inserted itself in our backyard by stealth and deception in the form of the Castro regime," and he added, "Like a spreading cancer it should, if possible, be excised from the Americas."[153] Senator Gordon Allott insisted, on one occasion, upon the need "to fight this Red cancer which is growing on our underside, 90 miles from our shores" and, on another, to take action against "the Communist infestation which is now well developed 90 miles from our shores."[154] Representative Mendel Rivers was categorical: "I would rather see this Nation go down in defeat in one mighty blow rather than suffer the agonies of Communist cancer, which most assuredly will engulf the Nation if Cuba is allowed to fester as the cell from which this cancerous growth will spread."[155]

True to the prescriptive purport of metaphor, the Americans called for a variety of "medical" responses. In the 1960 campaign candidate Kennedy promised "to quarantine the Cuban revolution." Assistant Secretary of State Roy Rubottom suggested in 1960 that to protect U.S. interests "a scalpel is called for; not a meat axe."[156] Arthur Schlesinger invoked the image of a "surgical strike" to aid the Bay of Pigs invasion.[157] Deputy Assistant Secretary of State

Robert Hurwitch wrote of the need to "surgically excise this cancer from the hemispheric body politic by using military force."[158]

★　★　★

Metaphor had situated Cuba fully into imagined realms of the figurative, where the Americans seemed capable of accommodating representations of Cubans in the most implausible forms. The Americans were rarely rational about Cuba. Perhaps their irrationality could be traced to the beginning, that is, to the moment in the nineteenth century when Cuba entered North American awareness as a place John Quincy Adams characterized as "indispensable to the continuance and integrity of the Union itself." The matter of survival of the nation was not always conducive to rational discourse. The gravity of Cuba, Ambassador Earl E. T. Smith insisted in 1962, was related to the fact "that we are in the midst of a struggle for survival."[159]

The use of metaphor as the principal mode of knowledge of Cuba, a practice that itself must be understood as a means by which the implausible obtained cognitive credibility, precluded the possibility of recognizing Cuban aspiration to self-determination and sovereign nationhood as a legitimate striving. Cuba was imagined to have existed principally to serve U.S. interests, to enable the Americans to meet their needs. This was the function of metaphor: to provide the discursive logic by which to render the island as a means of U.S. fulfillment. The "loss" of Cuba—the neighbor, the child, the damsel, the people rescued by the United States, the republic founded through U.S. sacrifices— was a blow deeply felt, one to which the Americans could not readily reconcile themselves. The issue of U.S. relations with Cuba ceased to be a matter of rational policy calculation and passed into the realm of pathology.[160] Otherwise reasonable and rational political leaders and policy makers appeared to have lost all sense of proportion when it came to the matter of Cuba. "As a nation," observed former secretary of state Cyrus Vance, "we seemed unable to maintain a sense of perspective about Cuba."[161] It was indeed, as Wayne Smith often commented, that Cuba was to the Americans what the full moon was to the werewolf.

The Americans had long fixed a sense of their well-being as a function of a relationship with Cuba. That Cuba no longer served North American interests—indeed, that Cubans appeared to threaten those interests—so deeply aggrieved the Americans as to preclude the possibility of reconciliation in the lifetime of Cuban leaders. By the terms of the Helms-Burton Act of 1996— the law of the land—the United States could deal only with a government in Cuba that "does not include Fidel Castro or Raul Castro."[162] Cuba was to be banished and punished until once again it acquiesced to its historic role in the service of North American interests. The Strategic Studies Institute of the U.S. Army War College admonished the "innate emotional appeal" driving U.S. policy, further cautioning, "To many, Castro is not merely an adversary, but an enemy—an embodiment of evil who must be punished for his defiance of the United States. . . . In this sense, U.S. policy has sought more than a simple solution or containment of Cuba. There is a desire to hurt the enemy that is mirrored in the malevolence that Castro has exhibited towards us. If Fidel suffers from a 'nemesis complex,' so most assuredly do we."[163] In a sense, it ends where it began. The United States, Representative Mendel Rivers pledged in 1960, would not forget its "obligations toward the Cuban people whom we helped to liberate," and added, "[Cuba] is as important to us as any of our own States; she forms part of our hegemony. God, through His divine workings, created our geographical proximity."[164] Cuba's destiny was the possession of the United States. It had been providentially mandated.

6

Through the Prism of Metaphor

Accommodation to Empire

Cuba has long been one of the "cards" of American party politics. For over fifty years one party or another has proposed to help itself by the deliverance of Cuba.
—The Nation *(March 31, 1898)*

We are like flies crawling across the ceiling of the Sistine Chapel: we cannot see what angels and gods lie underneath the threshold of our perceptions. We do not live in reality; we live in our paradigms, our habituated perceptions, our illusions; the illusions we share through culture we call reality, but the true historical reality of our condition is invisible to us. How can you fix up history if you cannot see it? —*William Irwin Thompson,* Evil and World Order *(1976)*

The [senior White House] aide said that guys like me [journalists and analysts] were "in what we call the reality-based community," which he defined as people who "believe that solutions emerge from your judicious study of discernible reality." I nodded and murmured something about enlightenment principles and empiricism. He cut me off. "That's not the way the world really works anymore," he continued. "We're an empire now, and when we act, we create our own reality. And while you're studying that reality—judiciously, as you will—we'll act again, creating other new realities, which you can study too, and that's how things will sort out. We're history's actors . . . and you, all of you, will be left to just study what we do." —*Ron Suskind, "Without a Doubt"* (New York Times Magazine, October 17, 2004)

[Cuba] is so near to us that we can not free ourselves of her destiny if we would. —*Senator Albert J. Beveridge (1906)*

The imperial project expanded rapidly after 1898. As contact with new lands and other peoples increased, so, too, did the need for usable knowledge—usable in the sense of expanding the representational reach of metaphors of self-interest. Metaphor was vital to the moral plausibility of empire, and moral plausibility was necessary to the logic of the American imperial practice. The political content of metaphor lurked under a morality so self-confirming as to make the existence of ulterior purpose virtually impossible to detect. To be sure, and it bears repeating, the Americans were not averse to the use of force and violence to impose their will upon other people in distant lands. They undertook—often—armed intervention and military occupation. Through overt action and covert means they deposed unfriendly governments and imposed friendly ones. They plotted the assassination of foreign leaders and, through the use of political isolation, embargoes, and trade sanctions, repeatedly endeavored to destabilize foreign economies.

But it is also true that these were not the preferred methods of imperial management. The distinction between perceptions of illegitimate and legitimate authority often depended on whether the exercise of power was in the form of sheer coercion or not. Systems of domination worked best when the premise of their purpose was embedded in a moral order that was at once recognizable and plausible to the polities on both sides of the power divide.

The Americans believed that the exercise of power was less a matter of self-interest than an act for the greater good of others, abstractly for humanity, in behalf of those ideals that Americans celebrated most in themselves. They chose to depict their purpose abroad the way they represented their values at home: a realpolitik disguised as moral discharge, self-interest represented as selfless intent. Metaphor facilitated the cognitive leap necessary to conceal the contradictions often produced by the pursuit of national interests in the guise of the practice of national ideals.

★ ★ ★

The former Spanish insular territories in the Caribbean and Pacific seized by the United States after 1898 were most commonly depicted as bereft of adult supervision—orphans, in a word. Spain had been deemed both unfit and ill-equipped to discharge adult authority and hence was properly punished for its dereliction of duty by military defeat and the forfeiture of parental claim. But neither could the orphans be released into an adult world without adequate protection and proper preparation. The Americans had, by their own calculations, assumed moral responsibility for the former Spanish colonies, to care for them and prepare them for adulthood. It was the burden of greatness. "Events had forced upon the country a group of remote insular lands

THE WARMEST BABY IN THE BUNCH.

"The Warmest Baby in the Bunch." From "Scrapbook of Cartoons, Clippings, etc., Related to the Spanish-America War of 1898," unpublished manuscript, 1898–99, Davis Library, University of North Carolina, Chapel Hill.

. . . .

inhabited by wild, dark-skinned races"—this was how James Wilford Garner and Henry Cabot Lodge explained the outcome of 1898. "[Control] was all unpremeditated and intended solely for the welfare of the weak and untutored races whom we had freed from the tyranny of Spain."[1]

The depiction of Cuba, Puerto Rico, and the Philippines, and at times Guam and Hawaii as well, as orphaned children under the custodial care of the United States emerged as one of the principal turn-of-the-century metaphorical renderings of the emerging colonial project.[2] The moral was in the metaphor, summoned as a function of self-proclaimed beneficence, but most of all as an instrumental means to maintain empire, principally because its political character could be readily disguised as moral purpose, an inference decipherable without need to acknowledge intent. There was hardly a hint of self-serving purpose in this arrangement. It was, on the contrary, presented

KEEPS THEM AWAKE NIGHTS.

"Keeps Them Awake Nights." From "Scrapbook of Cartoons, Clippings, etc.,
Related to the Spanish-America War of 1898," unpublished manuscript,
1898–99, Davis Library, University of North Carolina, Chapel Hill.

. . . .

in the guise of selfless discharge of righteous duty, in the service of humanity,
always for the good—if without the consent—of subject peoples.

The dominant pictorial representation of the emerging empire depicted
Uncle Sam as the United States presiding dutifully over his brood of nieces
and nephews, sometimes as a stern taskmaster, at other times as a watch-
ful caretaker, ambiguously in loco parentis to children recently orphaned or
otherwise set adrift in a dangerous world without adequate adult supervision.
This was the Uncle Sam given to the performance of parental duty, committed
to the well-being and the best interests of the wards under his care. Cartoons
and caricatures depicted the islands as children, located variously in orphan-
ages, in nursery settings, but most typically in a classroom environment, with
the United States, sometimes represented by President William McKinley, on
occasion as Columbia, in at least one instance as Liberty, but usually as Uncle
Sam, variously in the role of care provider or guardian or teacher expounding
upon the principles of civilization and the practice of self-government.

★ ★ ★

Metaphorical representation served as the principal mode through which
the Americans proclaimed moral leadership of the world, the way they persuaded themselves that the exercise of power over other people was right and
proper. Empire was something—figuratively and literally—of a terra incognita

"The Cares of a Growing Family." From *New York Bee* (1898), reprinted in
John J. Johnson, ed., *Latin America in Caricature* (Austin, 1980).

. . . .

for vast numbers of Americans. The very proposition of colonial possessions, of the United States controlling lives of distant peoples, seemed for many oddly incompatible with democratic principles, a violation of the proposition of government with the consent of the governed.

The colonial project was not without controversy, and indeed territorial expansion produced a spirited turn-of-the-century national debate. Vast numbers of Americans opposed the acquisition of colonial possessions, fearful that ruling over countless millions of people as subjects and not citizens, in the first instance, violated time-honored principles of democratic government and, eventually, threatened to subvert civil liberties at home. "A democracy cannot . . . long play king over subject populations," warned editor Carl Schurz, "without creating within itself ways of thinking and habits of action most dangerous to its own vitality." For Schurz the issue was very simple: "The vital principle of a democracy is self-government of the people. It cannot rule another people without denying the very reason of its being."[3] William Jennings Bryan opposed colonial expansion and spurned the claim of duty "to conquer and

"The Uncle Sam of the Future." Caption: "And a Little Child Shall Lead Them."
From *Cartoons of the War of 1898 with Spain* (Chicago, 1898).

. . . .

govern, when we find the pretext for doing so, every nation which is weaker than ours or whose civilization is below our standard."[4] Bryan was not susceptible to the emerging metaphorical constructs by which imperialism had seized hold of the American imagination:

> Imperialists are always telling us about our duty, as if they were able to measure it with exactness by metes and bounds, and only intent upon performing it. They prate about their unselfish love for inferior races and their determination to act as the guardians of these "children" entrusted to their care by a discriminating and considerate Providence. It is fortunate for our

"How Some Apprehensive People Picture Uncle Sam after the War."
From *Detroit News* (1898), reprinted in John J. Johnson, ed.,
Latin America in Caricature (Austin, 1980).

. . . .

own people and for the new people with whom we have to deal that this mask of hypocrisy and false pretense is torn away so behind it can be seen the features of greed.[5]

Central to the proposition of the American imperial project was precisely the notion of duty: the necessity to discharge a higher moral obligation mandated by providential design for the greater good of humanity. The war, journalist Talcott Williams exulted with a newfound sense of purpose in 1899, forged a "common conception of moral responsibility" and "a new conception of national duty." More to the point, the war had been fought so "that the American lands to the south of us shall never by our will be left in any inhuman oppression and wrong we can right. We have fought a war to vindicate our duty." This was precisely the point made by Ohio senator Joseph Foraker, but with far more portentous implications. "We were justified . . . in intervening [in Cuba]," he insisted, "and it was our duty, when we did intervene . . . to make it clear to all concerned that our voice must be attended to and our wishes carried out."[6] President William McKinley appealed often to the ideal of duty-bound responsibilities to justify possession of colonial territories after the war. "We must follow duty," McKinley exhorted, and assume "the weight of responsibility which has been so suddenly thrust upon us." McKinley insisted that "conscience and civilization require us to meet our duty bravely," adding that "desertion of duty" was not the American way.[7] It was from this perspective that the Americans found the Filipino resistance to the U.S. occupation inexplicable. "We never dreamed," McKinley reflected, "that the little body of insurgents whom we had just emancipated from oppression—we never for a moment believed that they would turn upon the flag that had sheltered them against Spain. . . . Our flag is there [and] wherever that standard is raised . . . it stands for liberty, civilization, and humanity."[8] This was imperialism as a matter of providential purpose. Proclaimed McKinley,

> The sole purpose to be kept in mind . . . was the welfare and happiness and the rights of the inhabitants of the Philippine Islands. Did we need their consent to perform a great act for humanity? . . . Did we ask their consent to liberate them from Spanish sovereignty? . . . We did not ask these things; we were obeying a higher moral obligation, which rested on us and which did not require anybody's consent. We were doing our duty by them as God gave us the light to see our duty, with the consent of our own consciences and with the approval of civilization. . . . Nor can we now ask their consent. . . . It is not a good time for the liberator to submit important questions concerning liberty and government to the liberated while they are engaged in shooting down their rescuers.[9]

The Americans were the chosen instrument of divine purpose, McKinley insisted: "Our flag is [in the Philippines]; our boys in blue are there. They are not there for conquest; they are not there for dominion. They are there because, in the providence of God who moves mysteriously, that great archipelago has been placed in the hands of the American people."[10]

The appeal to moral purpose, so very central to how Americans represented themselves and ruled others, served at once as motive and means by which to transact self-interests. Americans were a people disposed to acquiesce to the imperial project if it was depicted as a function of the values by which they had arrived at self-representation; they were a righteous people, of generous motive and selfless intent, given to do good in the world.

Throughout the twentieth century and beyond, the Americans projected power and pursued national interests as a matter of national character transacted in the form of moral conduct. Character was destiny, and destiny had conferred on the United States a special duty. All in all, it was a self-confirming process: the normative determinants of self-representations provided the moral logic of self-interest. In propounding a policy of "benevolent global hegemony," William Kristol and Robert Kagan argued in 1996 for the need to "[educate] the citizenry to the responsibilities of global hegemony," that is, to forge the consensus through which to sustain the imperial project. "It is foolish to imagine," they warned, "that the United States can lead the world effectively while the overwhelming majority of the population neither understands nor is involved in any real way, with its international mission." Kristol and Kagan appealed to the proposition that U.S. "moral goals and its fundamental national interests are almost always in harmony" as the way to inspire Americans "to assume cheerfully the new responsibilities that went with increased power and influence."[11]

★ ★ ★

Metaphors passed through phases as a function of shifting national interests. They were summoned into service in response to long-term interests as often as to short-term needs. This is not to suggest that the overarching purpose they served necessarily changed. On the contrary, there is more than adequate evidence to suggest that the self-confirming purpose that sustained the moral logic of imperialism at the end of the nineteenth century continued to inform the exercise of American power into the beginning of the twenty-first century.

The proposition of proximity, for example, provided a malleable concept and indeed served multiple instrumental functions. The idea of neighbor and its attending moral obligations expanded into a rationale of far-reaching range—to all of Latin America, in fact. In pronouncing the "corollary" to the Monroe Doctrine in 1904, President Theodore Roosevelt repeatedly invoked the notion of "neighboring countries" and "our southern neighbors" to make political purpose explicit: "Chronic wrongdoing, or an impotence which results in a general loosening of the ties of civilized society, may . . . ultimately require intervention by some civilized nation."[12] President Franklin D. Roosevelt committed the United States to practice self-restraint in the neighborhood and proceeded to elevate the concept of neighbor fully to the level of a foreign policy. "I would dedicate this Nation to the policy of the good neighbor," Roosevelt announced in his inaugural address in 1933, "the neighbor who resolutely respects himself and, because he does so, respects the rights of others, the neighbor who respects his obligations and respects the sanctity of his agreements in and with a world of neighbors."[13] The new policy was the result of the realization of "the dangers threatening its prestige with its southern neighbors," wrote Samuel Guy Inman in 1937 and thereupon affirmed a commitment to "building an inter-American neighborhood."[14] The entire Western Hemisphere was thus transformed into a "neighborhood" with all Latin American countries rendered as "neighbors" of the United States. In 2005, during a visit to Brazil, President George W. Bush proclaimed that it was "in our interest that our neighborhood be a prosperous neighborhood. It's in our interests that we work with the largest country in the neighborhood."[15]

On the other hand, the political estrangement between Cuba and the United States after 1959 suggests that the concept of "neighbor" had less to do with spatial conditions than it did with political ones. The United States was "motivated by noble impulses," Illinois representative Barratt O'Hara insisted in 1959, and he added,

> We do not seek to run our neighbor's home. When he shows his neighborly spirit in all his acts and in all of his words, as when he keeps his home and his yard in clean condition, and we commend him we have rendered a service and encouragement that cannot be misunderstood. When we scold our neighbor because he does not run his home as we run ours, and we pour out our condemnation because his home is not as neat and tidy as his neighbor's we provoke discord and contribute to the widening and not the narrowing of animosities. So should it be in foreign policy.[16]

The "truculent neighbor" was how *Time* magazine characterized Cuba in 1960, adding that Cubans were "a people the U.S. once thought its good friend."[17] The metaphor of neighbor was rarely employed after 1961; an unrepentant Fidel Castro could not be considered accepted as a neighbor. "We should make it clear what we intend to do if Castro persists in being a bad neighbor," warned Colorado senator Gordon Allott in 1960.[18] There could be "no long-term living with Castro as a neighbor" was the way Arthur Schlesinger Jr. recalled the thinking inside the Kennedy administration.[19] The attitude endured for fifty years. "It has long been the hope of the United States," President George W. Bush imagined a post-Castro Cuba in 2006, "to have a free, independent and democratic Cuba as a close friend and neighbor."[20] One year later, President Bush characterized Cuba as the "one nondemocracy in our neighborhood," and casting an eye toward President Hugo Chávez of Venezuela he added, "In the neighborhood there is a person who is undermining democracy. And therefore we need to be concerned about the loss of democracies in our neighborhood."[21]

★ ★ ★

The proposition of proximity as determinant of North American interests seemed to possess unlimited reach and found expression in a variety of figurative depictions. The multiple metaphorical allusions to "backyard" enabled the Americans to advance far-ranging claims on the basis of proximity. The need to guarantee U.S. security, Wisconsin senator Alexander Wiley explained the removal of the government of Jacobo Arbenz in Guatemala in 1954, was "to make sure we do not overlook our own backyard."[22] The moral the *New York Times* drew from the overthrow of Arbenz was the need for the United States "to shore up the nations in its own backyard."[23] National security advisor Robert McFarlane explained the need in 1983 "to act" against Grenada in response to "the prospect of a second Cuba at our door step."[24] McFarlane similarly explained the Iran-Contra intrigue four years later by insisting that "if we could not muster an effective counter to the Cuban-Sandinista strategy in our own backyard, it was far less likely that we could do so in the years ahead in more distant locations."[25] President Ronald Reagan defended U.S. policy in Central America as necessary to halt "Communist aggression in our own backyard."[26] When Cuba awarded petroleum leasing rights to China and India in 2006, U.S. oil producers clamored for authorization to drill in Florida's coastal waters. "This is the irony of ironies," protested Charles Drevna, vice-president of the National Petrochemical and Refiners Association. "We have chosen to lock up our resources and stand by to be spectators while these two come in and benefit from things right in our own back yard." Idaho senator Larry Craig agreed, if with slightly less elegant imagery: "China should not be left to drill for oil within spitting distance of our shores without competition from U.S. industries."[27] President George W. Bush heralded the CAFTA-DR agreement as evidence that "the world's leading trading nation was committed to a closer partnership with countries in our own backyard, countries which share our values," and concluded, "The United States was built on freedom—and the more of it we have in our backyard, the freer and safer and more prosperous all of the Americas will be."[28] The announcement by the Bush administration of the Andean Regional Initiative in 2001 similarly proclaimed "the Andean countries [to be] in our backyard."[29]

Metaphorical representation of proximity thus enabled the Americans to imagine the United States as a presence, everywhere, sharing contiguous space with the every country in the world. "The whole world had already become a single vicinage," reflected Woodrow Wilson as early as 1900. "Each part had become neighbor to all the rest. No nation could live any longer to itself, the tasks and the duties of neighborhood being what they were." It was thus, Wilson concluded, "the duty of the United States to play a part, and a leading part" in the world.[30] It is, as the narrator's voice in Nadine Gordimer's novel *Get a Life* (2005) reflects, the United States as "the power with a foot on everyone's doorstep."[31]

The use of the adult-child metaphor similarly persisted all through the twentieth and into the twenty-first century and indeed seemed to have expanded to characterize virtually all non-European peoples. Precisely because it purported to render reality through readily accessible normative hierarchies, the metaphor suggested a usable stock of discursive strategies with which to represent political purpose as moral conduct. If the world at large was indeed at the "doorstep" of the United States, then virtually all subject people everywhere could be—as circumstances warranted—children. Latin America seemed to dwell permanently in the North American imagination as a region of perpetual children. Theodore Roosevelt suggested the remedy to what he called Latin American "misconduct" in very specific terms. "If any South American State misbehaves towards any European country," he wrote, "let the European country spank it."[32] Sumner Welles explained the "good neighbor policy" as an American effort to end "the disorders of adolescence which affected many of the Ibero-American republics."[33] Louis Halle of the State Department policy planning staff pondered in 1950 "whether the backward countries of Latin America were to be regarded as responsible adults or as irresponsible children" and responded, "We therefore took it upon ourselves to exercise a paternalistic police power in the Caribbean. Theodore Roosevelt's 'corollary' to the Monroe Doctrine told the Europeans, in effect, that we would be responsible for keeping order among the children in our own yard. . . . These republics had not reached the stage of development at which they could be responsible for their actions."[34] Robert Hurwitch later reflected on his tenure as deputy assistant secretary of state during the early 1970s and recalled the thinking that inspired U.S. policy toward Latin America: "We wanted to encourage in every appropriate way that our friends to the south learn to stand on their own feet—*to become mature*. . . . Slowly, over time, just as with a young adult leaving home for the first time, we felt confident that the initial pain and feeling that 'you don't love me anymore' would eventually be replaced by the gratifying sense of independence, freedom and the respect and dignity one achieved as a mature person."[35]

The infantilization of the Other expanded beyond Latin America. "They are a community of children in their simplicity, honesty, and happy lack of all care," was how explorer Robert Peary characterized Eskimos along the Arctic Circle in 1898. And at another point he said, "In disposition and temperament these people are a race of children, simple, kindly, cheerful, and hospitable."[36] Whitlaw Reid characterized Filipinos as a people who "will enter [as] political infants in the kindergarten of governmental school, and by slow degrees, those infants will be brought up to the stature of manhood, intelligence, and responsibility."[37] General Douglas MacArthur concluded that the Japanese, "in spite of their antiquity measured by time, were in a very tuitionary condition. Measured by the standards of modern civilization, they would be like a boy of twelve as compared with our development of 45 years."[38] Commenting on the needs of East Timor in 2006, National Public Radio reporter Michael Sullivan invoked a familiar colonial trope, with an added mixed metaphor: "New nations are sort of like little children. They need a little help, a little nurturing, they need to be taken care of while they grow, and if they don't get that they run the risk of becoming failed states."[39]

★ ★ ★

By the mid-twentieth century, as the process of decolonization expanded through Africa, Asia, and the Middle East, the plausibility of *mission civilatrice* as the rationale for imperialism could no longer be readily sustained. The logic of the imperial project was subsequently encoded within new depictive constructs, principally as a matter of democracy, human rights, and civil society, always with the promise to enhance the lives of the very peoples who fifty years earlier were deemed to be in need of civilization. The Americans at the turn of the new century proselytized the virtues of democracy with as much moral rectitude as when they had propounded the promise of salvation through civilization in the nineteenth century.

The idiom of empire may have undergone modification—a concession no doubt to the sensibilities of Third World people—but the metaphors of the colonial arrogance of the nineteenth-century metaphors obtained renewed use early in the twenty-first century. *New York Times* columnist Thomas Friedman could write in 2003 that "we just adopted a baby called Baghdad."[40] U.S.

"You're Ready to Take Off the Training Wheels." Depiction of Deputy
Defense Secretary Paul Wolfowitz's comment on Iraq learning to ride a bicycle.
From *Raleigh News and Observer*, May 21, 2004. Courtesy of Dwane Powell
and Mary Ann Veldman/Creators Syndicate.

. . . .

relations with Iran and North Korea often turned on platitudes derived from
unstated metaphors. For the United States to negotiate directly with Iran and
North Korea would "reward bad behavior," a construct alluding to child-rearing
practices and/or classroom conduct.[41] A war of choice in Iraq obtained validation by way of metaphor: the war against terror. Once the metaphor passed
unchallenged, the president could proceed to govern as commander in chief,
civil liberties were subordinated to national security, and national security
justified torture, suspension of habeas corpus, and extralegal wiretaps. It all
began with a metaphor.

The bicycle again reappeared as a metaphor within a metaphor. Testifying
before the Senate Committee on Foreign Relations in 2004, Deputy Defense
Secretary Paul Wolfowitz reached deeply into the metaphorical repertoire of
empire to explain the preparations for elections in occupied Iraq: "I don't
mean this at all condescending, but when you're teaching a youngster to ride
a bicycle, you don't keep your hand on the seat the whole time. At some point,
you have to take it off."[42] Nevada senator Harry Reid used a slightly different

version of the same metaphor to urge an end to the U.S. military occupation of Iraq: "We think it's time the training wheels came off of Iraq."[43] And only days before his resignation in November 2006, Secretary of Defense Donald Rumsfeld proposed "modest withdrawals" of U.S. armed forces from Iraq as a means to start "taking our hand off the bicycle seat."[44] Testifying before the Senate Foreign Relations Committee in February 2007, General Brent Scowcroft likened the U.S. relationship to the future Iraqi government to being "a big brother, offering helpful hands, admonishing here, helping there." Asked by Nebraska senator Chuck Hagel to identify the circumstances appropriate for U.S. military withdrawal, Scowcroft could provide no precise answer and responded, "When you're training your child with training wheels on the bicycle, how do you know when to take the training wheels off?"[45] Lieutenant Colonel Ralph Peters used the same metaphor with a different sequence. "Can the Iraqis themselves step up?" Peters asked, and answered: "We put the training wheels on the bicycle, but they do have to ride it themselves."[46]

★ ★ ★

"There has always been a 'Cuban question' in the United States," observed historian Francis Shepardson in 1906 and predicted, "There probably always will be."[47] And indeed few countries have so preoccupied the Americans as Cuba. This was Cuba alternately as a source of dreams and a cause of nightmares, a place that Americans came to believe was profoundly relevant to their very well-being and in whose fate their destiny was implicated. It insinuated itself simultaneously into North American political consciousness and popular culture, from which the presumption of familiarity served as premise of the relationship.

But it is also true that the Cubans seem always to have disappointed the Americans, something that had very much to do with the metaphors by which the Americans engaged the Cubans. The expectations created by North American metaphors could have been met only if Cubans had fully surrendered themselves to the fulfillment of U.S. needs. Any act of agency to advance the proposition of Cuba for the Cubans—and not for the Americans—was bound to disappoint the Americans. The Cuban *insurrectos* of 1895–98 were found wanting—"the insurgents were a disappointment," correspondent Murat Halstead wrote[48]—something less than the heroic warriors that Americans had celebrated in the lyrics of their music and the verses of their poetry. The collapse of the republic in 1906—the pride of American early imperial workmanship—caused widespread disillusionment in the United States and raised anew questions about the plausibility of Cuban nationhood. It happened again in 1912 and again in 1917. President Ramón Grau San Martín in 1933 caused considerable consternation in the United States, and he was eliminated. The American disappointment was perhaps never greater than after 1959. "Many long-time friends of Cuba in the United States," lamented President Dwight Eisenhower in 1960, "who were heartened by the ideals expressed by the present leaders of Cuba when they assumed control of the Government have been gravely disillusioned by what is coming to be considered a betrayal of these ideals."[49]

The representation of the revolution betrayed developed into the principal North American counternarrative as the breach between Havana and Washington widened. It was an affirmation of remarkable cynical reach, and the Americans would persuade themselves that they actually supported a revolution that the Cubans betrayed. "The Cuban Government has betrayed the revolutionary ideal that had aroused the sympathy of many Americans," lamented the Department of State in 1960.[50] "Castro and his gang," presidential candidate John F. Kennedy decried, "have betrayed the ideals of the Cuban revolution and the hopes of the Cuban people."[51]

In fact, the "revolution betrayed" line was conceived as the moral cover to covert operations. The first step for "covert operations to effect a change in Cuba," explained CIA director Allen Dulles in March 1960, was "to form a moderate opposition group in exile. . . . Its slogan will be to 'restore the revolution' which Castro has betrayed."[52] And indeed, one year later, timed with the proxy invasion that was the Bay of Pigs, the Americans released the Cuban white paper as the rationale to overthrow the Cuban government. The message was focused and direct: the Cuban leaders had betrayed "the authentic and autonomous revolution" to "achieve freedom, democracy, and social justice," aspirations which the United States shared with the Cuban people. The white paper was relentless: "the leaders of the revolutionary regime betrayed their own revolution"; the revolution "[had] been perverted"; "the record of the Castro regime has been a record of the steady and consistent betrayal" of the revolution; Castro "decided to betray the promises of the revolution"; Castro had "betray[ed] his pledges."[53]

The phenomenon of disappointment becomes comprehensible when understood as a way to register disapproval of Cuban agency. Therein lay the premise of power: that Americans would have expectations of Cubans at all was itself a measure of North American entitlement. Historian Van Gosse was correct to note that "the reporters, editors and publishers who wrote or condoned pro-Castro coverage earlier did genuinely feel betrayed by Castro in power." It was, Gosse suggested, "as if North Americans discovered that Fidel really did mean what he said about a great cleansing national revolution. . . . The resulting outrage helps explain why the 26 of July Movement's US partisans, in the press and outside it, so quickly deserted from the fray: they had no understanding of how undeferential Castro would be."[54]

It is from this perspective that a measure of the impact of the Cuban revolution on North American sensibilities can be taken. Certainly it has to do with the Americans unreconciled to the "loss" of a historic client state. Certainly, too, the Cuban alliance with the Soviet Union during the Cold War had shattered the North American sense of security, something for which Castro would never be forgiven. But it is more complex still. That a policy of covert operations, of economic sanctions and trade embargo, of political pressure and diplomatic isolation—all designed to "hasten" the fall of the Cuban government—endured fifty years virtually unchanged as a palpably failed policy was indeed the most powerful evidence of the pathology of Cuba among the Americans. This is not to suggest, of course, that U.S. sanctions have not been without a political constituency, possessed of an agenda and endowed with the capacity to allocate substantial financial resources through which to exercise political influence and affect electoral outcomes. The lobbying success of the Cuban American National Foundation (CANF) was well-known. So, too, was the significance of the Cuban American vote in Florida in national elections. But it is an arguable proposition that the anti-Castro Cuban American lobby was itself a product of the North American pathology, that, in fact, it was an instrument—not an instigator—of policy. The creation of the CANF was the inspiration of the administration of Ronald Reagan. National Security Advisor Richard Allen, recalled Raúl Masvidal, one of the founders of CANF, offered sponsorship "to start an organization that would help popularize the Reagan administration's policies. And so was born the Cuban American National Foundation."[55] To invoke a metaphor: the Cuban American lobby was not the tail that wagged the dog but, rather, the tail wagged by the dog.

The Cuban revolution deeply offended North American sensibilities. Fidel Castro's continuance in power served as a constant reminder of the inability of the United States to will the world in accordance with its own interests, made all the more egregious by the fact that this was a country upon which the United States had routinely imposed its will. It challenged long-cherished notions about national well-being and upset prevailing notions of the rightful order of things. The North American response was exorcism in the guise of policy, an effort to purge Fidel Castro as an evil spirit who tormented North American equanimity for five decades.

The Cuban transgression appears to have its origins at some point in the nineteenth century, when Cubans arrived at the conviction that they, too, had a destiny; that they, too, had a right to self-determination and sovereign nation-

hood; that they, too, had interests to pursue. These were not sentiments invented by Fidel Castro; they formed part of the larger political culture to which
Cuban leaders were heir and in which they themselves had been formed. The
Cuban leadership after 1959 acted to realize long-frustrated aspirations and, at
the same time, hold the Americans to account for nearly sixty years of thwart-
ing Cuban aspirations to sovereign nationhood. In the end, the Americans
contributed to the very outcome they had from outset sought to prevent. "The
grievances we carry within us are old," reflected Fidel Castro in early January
1959.[56] It was indeed a rare historical event that the Americans were held accountable for their past deeds. To a lesser or greater extent, the Cubans succeeded, but at considerable cost. Their success could not pass unpunished.
The proposition of Cuba beyond the control of the United States was inadmissible, if for no other reason than control was as an end unto itself. It was
indeed as George Orwell suggested in *1984*: "The object of power is power."[57]

The Americans acted purposefully throughout the final years of the twentieth century and the early ones of the twenty-first century, determined to
recover power over Cuba as a matter of the natural order of things. Official
preparations for a "post-Castro Cuba" engaged the U.S. government in the
expenditure of many millions of dollars in anticipation of "transition." The
U.S. Agency for International Development subsidized scores of projects in
the United States, including funds for a "Cuba Transition Project" at the University of Miami; preparations for "assistance to a Cuban transition government" project at Rutgers University; preparations for "transitional elections
in Cuba" under the auspices of the International Foundation for Election Systems; funding for the U.S.-Cuba Business Council to prepare for "the eventual
reconstruction of the Cuban economy"; and funds to study the restitution of
nationalized property at Creighton University Law School. All in all, it was an
astonishing presumption of entitlement, among both policy makers and officials distributing the money and the academics and administrators accepting
the money—always no doubt in the best interest of the Cuban people. That the
Americans in the twenty-first century could presume that planning the future
of Cuba without the participation of any of the 11 million people who lived on
the island was an attitude worthy of the arrogance of their predecessors in the
nineteenth century.

Notes

INTRODUCTION

1. *Congressional Globe*, February 21, 1859, 35th Congress, 2nd session, vol. 36, pt. 2, p. 1186.

2. Ronald Steel, *Pax Americana* (New York, 1967), p. 15.

3. Michael H. Hunt, "Ideology," in *Explaining the History of American Foreign Relations*, 2nd ed., ed. Michael J. Hogan and Thomas G. Paterson (Cambridge, 2004), pp. 222, 224.

4. Alexander H. Everett to John Quincy Adams, November 30, 1825, in Alexander H. Everett and Edward Everett, *The Everett Letters on Cuba* (Boston, 1852), p. 6.

5. General Nelson A. Miles, "America's War for Humanity," *Cosmopolitan*, October 1911, pp. 637–50. See also John J. Ingalls, *America's War for Humanity* (New York, 1898). The proposition of war for humanity developed into one of the dominant causal explanations of 1898. President William McKinley proclaimed often, "We have won great triumphs for humanity. We went to war, not because we wanted to, but because humanity demanded it. And having gone to war for humanity's sake, we must accept no settlement that will not take into account the interests of humanity." See William McKinley, "Speech at Springfield, Illinois," October 15, 1898, in *Speeches and Addresses of William McKinley* (New York, 1900), pp. 127–28.

6. William Howard Taft, "Some Recent Instances of National Altruism: The Efforts of the United States to Aid the Peoples of Cuba, Porto Rico, and the Philippines," *National Geographic*, July 1907, pp. 429–30.

7. A. D. Hall, *Cuba: Its Past, Present, and Future* (New York, 1898), pp. 170, 174–75.

8. Archibald Cary Coolidge, *The United States as a World Power* (New York, 1908), pp. 132–33.

9. Norman A. Graebner, *Foundations of American Foreign Policy* (Wilmington, Del., 1985), p. 354.

10. H. C. Taylor, "The Future of Our Navy," *Forum* 27 (March 1899): 4.

11. Albert J. Beveridge, "Institutional Law," March 29, 1900, in *The Meaning of the Times and Other Speeches* (Indianapolis, 1908), pp. 107–8.

12. William McKinley, "Speech at Banquet of the Ohio Society of New York, New York," March 3, 1900, in *Speeches and Addresses*, p. 365.

13. See Sidney Bell, *Righteous Conquest: Woodrow Wilson and the Evolution of the New Diplomacy* (Port Washington, N.Y., 1972), pp. 10–66; August Heckscher, *Woodrow Wilson* (New York, 1991), pp. 128–30.

14. Woodrow Wilson, "A Memorandum: What Ought We Do?," August 1, 1898, in

The Papers of Woodrow Wilson, 69 vols., ed. Arthur S. Link et al. (Princeton, 1966–94), 10:574.

15. Woodrow Wilson, *A History of the American People*, 5 vols. (New York, 1902), 5:274–75.

16. Woodrow Wilson, "The Ideals of America," December 26, 1901, in *Papers of Woodrow Wilson*, 12:215–17. A slightly different version of this speech appeared late in published form as "The Ideals of America," *Atlantic Monthly*, December 1902, pp. 721–27.

17. Arthur H. Vandenberg, *The Trail of a Tradition* (New York, 1926), p. 321.

18. Julius W. Pratt, *America's Colonial Experiment* (New York, 1950), pp. 2–3.

19. H. Wayne Morgan, *America's Road to Empire: The War with Spain and Overseas Expansion* (New York, 1965), p. 113.

20. Paul T. McCartney, *Power and Progress: American National Identity, the War of 1898, and the Rise of American Imperialism* (Baton Rouge, 2006), p. 2. The United States is "a country with a national mission," observed Anatol Lieven in 2004, a purpose that "is absolutely central to the American national identity." See Anatol Lieven, *America Right or Wrong: An Anatomy of American Nationalism* (New York, 2004), p. 33. See also Walter LaFeber, *The New Empire* (Ithaca, 1963), pp. 407–17.

21. *New York Journal*, September 1898, p. 6.

22. "The decisiveness of the victory," pronounced historian Charles Manfred Thompson twenty-five years later, "directed the attention of European power to the military strength of the [United States], . . . gave the people a higher regard for their own fighting ability and made them consider more seriously the probability of future wars." See Charles Manfred Thompson, *History of the United States*, rev. ed. (Chicago, 1922), p. 474.

23. William McKinley, "Address at the Trans-Mississippi Exposition at Omaha, Nebraska," October 12, 1898, in *Speeches and Addresses*, p. 104; "Speech at Decatur, Illinois," October 15, 1898, ibid., p. 126; "Speech at the Citizens' Banquet, Chicago," October 9, 1899, ibid., p. 246.

24. William McKinley, "Speech at Redfield, South Dakota," October 14, 1899, ibid., p. 288.

CHAPTER 1

1. Catarina Cacciari, "Cognitive Psychology of Figurative Thought and Figurative Language," in *International Encyclopedia of the Social and Behavioral Sciences*, 26 vols., ed. Neil J. Smelser and Paul B. Baltes (Amsterdam, 2001), 8:5636; Catarina Cacciari, "Why Do We Speak Metaphorically? Reflections on the Functions of Metaphor in Discourse and Reasoning," in *Figurative Language and Thought*, ed. Albert N. Katz et al. (New York, 1998), p. 138. See also Max Black, *Models and Metaphors* (Ithaca, 1962), pp. 25–47.

2. Earl R. MacCormac, *A Cognitive Theory of Metaphor* (Cambridge, Mass., 1985), p. 149. Allan Collins and Dedre Gentner write in terms of "mental models" that people create "to generate predictions about what should happen in various situations in the real world." See Allan Collins and Dedre Gentner, "How People Construct Mental Models," in *Cultural Models in Language and Thought*, ed. Dorothy Holland and Naomi Quinn (Cambridge, 1987), pp. 243–65.

3. Raymond W. Gibbs Jr., *The Poetics of Mind: Figurative Thought, Language, and Understanding* (Cambridge, 1994), pp. 1, 5.

4. George Lakoff and Mark Johnson, *Metaphors We Live By* (Chicago, 1980), p. 158.

5. Writing of linguistic access to new concepts, Sapir explains, "As soon as the word is at hand, we instinctively feel, with something of a sigh of relief, that the concept is ours for the handling." See Edward Sapir, *Language* (New York, 1949), p. 17.

6. J. Christopher Crocker, "The Social Function of Rhetorical Forms," in *The Social Use of Metaphor: Essays on the Anthropology of Rhetoric*, ed. J. David Sapir and J. Christopher Crocker (Philadelphia, 1977), pp. 32–66.

7. Gunther Kress, *Linguistic Process in Sociocultural Practice* (Oxford, 1989), pp. 71, 72–73.

8. Christopher Tilley, *Metaphor and Material Culture* (Oxford, 1999), p. 9.

9. Mary Douglas, *How Institutions Think* (Syracuse, 1986), p. 100.

10. Gemma Corradi Fiumara, *The Metaphoric Process: Connections between Language and Life* (London, 1995), pp. 131–32; Lakoff and Johnson, *Metaphors We Live By*, p. 236.

11. Wallace Stevens, *The Necessary Angel: Essays on Reality and the Imagination* (New York, 1951), p. 118.

12. For a discussion on metaphors as "verbal and nonverbal artifacts" see Carl R. Hausman, *Metaphor and Art: Interactionism and Reference in the Verbal and Nonverbal Arts* (New York, 1989), pp. 198–201.

13. Robert Hodge and Gunther Kress, *Language as Ideology*, 2nd ed. (London, 1993), p. 14.

14. See Sam Glucksberg, *Understanding Figurative Language: From Metaphors to Idioms* (Oxford, 2001), pp. 14–15.

15. One of the earliest histories of Cuba, written by José Martín Félix de Arrate—*Llave del Nuevo Mundo, antemural de las Indias Occidentales: La Habana descripta*—completed originally in 1761 but not published until 1827, embraced the metaphorical designations as a marker of creole identity. The Cuban coat of arms, adopted in the mid-nineteenth century by separatists, incorporated the image of "Key of the New World" as a golden key placed over the Gulf of Mexico between the Yucatan Peninsula and Florida as the symbol of the position of Cuba between the two Americas.

16. Herbert H. Clark and Catherine R. Marshall, "Definite Reference and Mutual Knowledge," in *Elements of Discourse Understanding*, ed. Aravind K. Joshi, Bonnie L. Webber, and Ivan A. Sag (Cambridge, 1981), p. 36. Writing of language generally—but

having direct implications for metaphor—John Gumperz describes semantic structure as "a social process in which utterances are selected in accordance with socially recognized norms and expectations." Political scientist Seth Thompson comments that opinion makers and power holders use metaphors that are generally "accessible to everyone else" as a means to create "a policy-making community": metaphor as "necessary to link tangible means to intangible ends." See John J. Gumperz, "The Speech Community," in *Language and Social Context*, ed. Pier Paolo Giglioli (Middlesex, 1972), p. 219; Seth Thompson, "Politics without Metaphors Is Like Fish without Water," in *Metaphor: Implications and Applications*, ed. Jeffrey Scott Mio and Albert N. Katz (Mahwah, N.J., 1996), p. 188. See also Jonathan Charteris-Black, *Corpus Approaches to Critical Metaphor Analysis* (New York, 2004), pp. 10–13.

17. C. C. Anderson, "The Psychology of Metaphor," *Journal of Genetic Psychology* 105 (1964): 58.

18. Philosopher Mark Johnson notes that imagination has to do with the "capacity to organize mental representations (especially percepts, images, and image schemata) into meaningful, coherent unities." The process makes for an understanding of "how it is possible for us to 'have a world' that we can make sense of and reason." See Mark Johnson, *The Body in the Mind: The Bodily Basis of Meaning, Imagination, and Reason* (Chicago, 1987), p. 140.

19. For a discussion of the emotive power of metaphor see Earl R. MacCormac, *Metaphor and Myth in Science and Religion* (Durham, 1976), pp. 92–93; MacCormac, *Cognitive Theory of Metaphor*, pp. 29–31, 159–60; Lynn Fainsilber and Andrew Ortony, "Metaphorical Uses of Language in the Expression of Emotions," *Metaphor and Symbolic Activity* 2 (1987): 223–37.

20. See Zoltán Kövecses, *Metaphor in Culture* (Cambridge, 2005), pp. 283–84.

21. Deborah Durham and James W. Fernandez, "Tropical Dominions: The Figurative Struggle over Domains of Belonging and Apartness in Africa," in *Beyond Metaphor: The Theory of Tropes in Anthropology*, ed. James W. Fernandez (Stanford, 1991), p. 196; Ted Cohen, "Metaphor and the Cultivation of Intimacy," *Critical Inquiry* 5 (Autumn 1978): 11. See also Laurel J. End, "Grounds for Metaphor Comprehension," in *Knowledge and Language*, ed. I. Kurcz, G. W. Shugar, and J. H. Danks (Amsterdam, 1986), pp. 327–45.

22. Robert Rogers, *Metaphor: A Psychoanalytic View* (Berkeley, 1978), p. 38.

23. As heard by Charles Warren Currier, "Why Cuba Should Be Independent," *Forum* 30 (October 1900): 142. To which Currier added, "We undertake to govern [Cuba] for its own good" (ibid.).

24. Department of Commerce and Labor, *Commercial Cuba in 1905* (Washington, D.C., 1905), p. 3908.

25. "Speech of Wm. H. Taft, Provisional Governor of Cuba, at the opening Exercise of the National University of Havana," October 19, 1906, in U.S. Congress, House of

Representatives, *Annual Reports of the War Department for the Fiscal Year Ended June 30, 1906*, 59th Congress, 2nd session, Document No. 2, 3 vols. (Washington, D.C., 1906), 1:541. The intervention in 1906, President Theodore Roosevelt explained, was undertaken so that Cubans would "be prosperous and happy." See Theodore Roosevelt to Henry White, September 13, 1906, Theodore Roosevelt Papers, Manuscript Division, Library of Congress, Washington, D.C.

26. "The Platt Amendment," *Statutes at Large of the United States*, XXI (Washington, D.C., 1902), pp. 879–98.

27. Paul B. Lieberman, "Imagination: Looking in the Right Place (and in the Right Way)," in *Imagination and Its Pathologies*, ed. James Phillips and James Morley (Cambridge, Mass., 2003), p. 25.

28. Londa Schiebinger, *Has Feminism Changed Science?* (Cambridge, Mass., 1999), p. 147.

CHAPTER 2

1. John Quincy Adams to Hugh Nelson, April 28, 1823, in U.S. Congress, House of Representatives, *Island of Cuba*, 32nd Congress, 1st session, Executive Document No. 121 (Washington, D.C., 1852), p. 6.

2. Ibid., p. 7.

3. James Buchanan to Romulus M. Saunders, June 17, 1848, in *Diplomatic Correspondence of the United States: Inter-American Affairs*, 12 vols., ed. William R. Manning (Washington, D.C., 1932–39), 11:62; William L. Marcy to Pierre Soulé, November 13, 1854, ibid., 11:197; William L. Marcy to Augustus C. Dodge, May 1, 1855, ibid., 11:210.

4. James Buchanan to John M. Clayton, April 17, 1849, in *The Works of James Buchanan: Comprising His Speeches, State Papers, and Private Correspondence*, ed. John Bassett Moore, 12 vols. (Philadelphia, 1908–11), 8:361.

5. *Congressional Globe*, February 11, 1859, 35th Congress, 2nd session, vol. 36, pt. 1, p. 963.

6. J. D. B. DeBow, "The Late Cuba Expedition," *DeBow's Review* 9 (August 1850): 173.

7. "The Cuban Debate," *United States Democratic Review* 31 (November–December 1852): 444.

8. U.S. Congress, House of Representatives, *The Ostend Conference*, October 18, 1854, 33rd Congress, 2nd session, Executive Document 93 (Washington, D.C., 1855), p. 128. The annexation of Cuba, James Buchanan predicted in 1848, would "relieve [the United States] from the apprehensions which we can never cease to feel for our own safety and the security of our commerce whilst it shall remain in its present condition." Senator J. P. Benjamin made the point explicitly in 1859: "The instincts of the American people have already taught them that we shall ever be insecure against hostile attack until this important geographical and military position is placed under

our protection and control." See James Buchanan to Romulus M. Saunders, June 17, 1848, in U.S. Congress, House of Representatives, *Island of Cuba*, p. 43; "Speech of the Honorable J. P. Benjamin, of Louisiana, on the Acquisition of Cuba," February 11, 1859, in U.S. Congress, Senate, Committee on Foreign Relations, *Recognition of Cuban Independence*, 54th Congress, 2nd session, Senate Report No. 1160 (Washington, D.C., 1896), p. 53.

9. Roger Q. Mills, "Spanish Despotism in Cuba Supported by the United States," in *Story of Spain and Cuba*, ed. Nathan C. Green (Baltimore, 1896), pp. 431–32. "The destinies of Cuba," President William McKinley pronounced after the war with Spain, "are in some rightful form and manner irrevocably linked with our own." See William McKinley, "Annual Message of the President," December 5, 1899, in U.S. Congress, House of Representatives, *Papers Relating to the Foreign Relations of the United States*, 56th Congress, 1st session, Document No. 1 (Washington, D.C., 1901), p. xxix.

10. U.S. Congress, House of Representatives, *Ostend Manifesto*, p. 128.

11. Martin Van Buren to Cornelius P. Van Ness, October 2, 1829, in *Diplomatic Correspondence of the United States Concerning the Independence of the Latin-American Nations*, 3 vols., ed. William R. Manning (New York, 1925–26), 1:306; James Buchanan to Romulus M. Saunders, June 17, 1848, in Manning, *Diplomatic Correspondence of the United States: Inter-American Affairs*, 11:62.

12. *Congressional Globe*, February 15, 1859, 35th Congress, 2nd session, Appendix, pp. 155, 160.

13. U.S. Congress, Senate, Committee on Foreign Relations, *Report*, 35th Congress, 2nd session, Committee Report 351 (Washington, D.C., 1859), p. 1. It was necessary only to "cast one's eye on the map," insisted Edward Everett, "to see . . . how intimate those [relations] of the United States with this island." See Edward Everett to Comte de Sartiges, December 1, 1852, in Alexander H. Everett and Edward Everett, *The Everett Letters on Cuba* (Boston, 1852), p. 3. This was the same language used by the *Democratic Review* in 1859: "From the day we acquired Louisiana, the attention of our ablest statesmen was fixed on Cuba. . . . To cast the eye upon the map was sufficient to predict its destiny." See "Continental Policy of the United States: The Acquisition of Cuba," *Democratic Review* 43 (April 1859): 26.

14. Walt Whitman, "The Gem of the Antilles," January 12, 1858, in Walt Whitman, *I Sit and Look Out: Editorials from the Brooklyn Daily Times*, ed. Emory Holloway and Vernolian Schwarz (New York, 1932), p. 157.

15. Hamilton Fish to Caleb Cushing, November 5, 1875, in U.S. Congress, Senate, *Report of the Committee on Foreign Relations, United States Senate, Relative to Affairs in Cuba*, 55th Congress, 2nd session, Senate Report No. 885 (Washington, D.C., 1898), p. 48; Caleb Cushing to Hamilton Fish, February 14, 1878, ibid., p. 90. See also Hamilton Fish to Caleb Cushing, February 6, 1874, in U.S. Department of State, *Papers Relating to the Foreign Relations of the United States, 1874* (Washington, D.C., 1874), p. 859.

16. *Congressional Globe*, February 10, 1859, 35th Congress, 2nd session, Appendix, p. 148.

17. Hamilton Fish to Daniel E. Sickles, February 6, 1874, in *A Digest of International Law*, 8 vols., ed. John Bassett Moore (Washington, D.C., 1906), 6:79.

18. *Congressional Record*, March 23, 1898, 55th Congress, 2nd session, vol. 31, pt. 1, p. 3131.

19. Alexander H. Everett to John Quincy Adams, November 30, 1825, in Everett and Everett, *Everett Letters on Cuba*, p. 5; Edward Everett to Lord John Russell, September 17, 1853, in Edward Everett, *Correspondence on the Proposed Tripartite Convention Relative to Cuba* (Boston, 1853), p. 61.

20. Albert J. Beveridge, "The Star of Empire," September 25, 1900, in *The Meaning of the Times and Other Speeches* (Indianapolis, 1908), p. 122; Albert J. Beveridge, "Business and Government," September 22, 1906, ibid., pp. 284, 286; *Minneapolis Journal*, September 30, 1906, p. 8.

21. Augustus C. Dodge to Lewis Cass, November 19, 1858, in Manning, *Diplomatic Correspondence of the United States: Inter-American Affairs*, 11:959; Edward Everett to Comte de Sartiges, December 1, 1852, in Everett and Everett, *Everett Letters on Cuba*, p. 9.

22. *Congressional Record*, June 18, 1860, 36th Congress, 1st session, vol. 28, pt. 4, p. 3120.

23. *Congressional Globe*, February 26, 1859, 35th Congress, 2nd session, Appendix, p. 89.

24. *Congressional Record*, February 26, 1857, 34th Congress, 3rd session, Appendix, p. 357.

25. Richard B. Kimball, *Cuba and the Cubans* (New York, 1850), p. 194.

26. U.S. Congress, House of Representatives, *Ostend Manifesto*, p. 128.

27. "The West India Islands," *DeBow's Review* 5 (June 1848): 470.

28. *Congressional Globe*, January 24, 1859, 35th Congress, 2nd session, vol. 36, pt. 1, p. 539.

29. Ramon O. Williams to John Bancroft Davis, February 23, 1882, Despatches from U.S. Consuls in Havana, 1783–1906, General Records of the Department of State, Record Group 59, National Archives, Washington D.C.

30. Maturin M. Ballou, *Due South, or Cuba Past and Present* (Boston, 1888), pp. 312, 316.

31. Isaac N. Ford, *Tropical America* (New York, 1893), p. 287.

32. John Quincy Adams to Hugh Nelson, April 28, 1823, in U.S. Congress, House of Representatives, *Island of Cuba*, p. 7.

33. It appears that the metaphor of "ripe fruit" to explain colonial expansion possesses a proper history. "[A. J. R.] Turgot," wrote English historian John R. Seeley, "compared colonies to fruit which hangs on the tree till it is ripe." Seeley hastened to add,

however, "There is no objection to such an image, provided it is regarded only as an image, and is not converted by sleight of hand into an argument." See John R. Seeley, *The Expansion of England* (Boston, 1883), p. 256.

34. *Congressional Globe*, January 24, 1859, 35th Congress, 2nd session, vol. 36, pt. 1, p. 53.

35. U.S. Congress, Senate, Committee on Foreign Relations, *Report*, p. 10.

36. Parke Godwin, *Political Essays* (New York, 1856), p. 169.

37. *Congressional Globe*, February 15, 1859, 35th Congress, 2nd session, Appendix, p. 160.

38. Ibid., February 17, 1859, vol. 36, pt. 1, p. 1086. Writing in the aftermath of the war with Spain in 1900, former secretary of state Richard Olney pronounced with confidence that "the pear was ripe and ready to fall into our laps." See Richard Olney, "Growth of Our Foreign Policy," *Atlantic Monthly*, March 1900, p. 292.

39. Alexander Jones, "The Invasion of Cuba," *Southern Quarterly Review* 5 (January 1852): 4; James Ford Rhodes, *The McKinley and Roosevelt Administrations, 1897–1909* (New York, 1922), p. 67.

40. *Congressional Globe*, January 24, 1859, 35th Congress, 2nd session, vol. 36, pt. 1, p. 542; ibid., February 26, 1859, Appendix, p. 89.

41. *Congressional Record*, May 17, 1897, 35th Congress, 1st session, vol. 30, pt. 1, pp. 1091–92.

42. U.S. Congress, Senate, Committee on Foreign Relations, *Report*, pp. 1, 9.

43. *Congressional Record*, March 2, 1896, 54th Congress, 1st session, vol. 28, pt. 3, p. 2349.

44. Hamilton Fish to Caleb Cushing, March 1, 1876, in U.S. Congress, Senate, *Report of the Committee on Foreign Relations*, p. 102.

45. David Rieff, *A Bed for the Night* (New York, 2002), p. 129.

46. U.S. Congress, House of Representatives, *Message of the President of the United States to the Two Houses of Congress at the Commencement of the Thirty-Third Congress*, December 6, 1853, 33rd Congress, 1st session, Executive Document (Washington, D.C., 1853), pp. 5–6.

47. James Buchanan to William L. Marcy, November 1, 1853, in *Works of James Buchanan*, 9:85.

48. *Congressional Globe*, February 21, 1859, 35th Congress, 2nd session, Appendix, p. 1191.

49. Ulysses Grant, "Annual Message," December 6, 1871, in U.S. Congress, House of Representatives, *Message of the President of the United States*, 42nd Congress, 2nd session, House Executive Document No. 1 (Washington, D.C., 1871), p. 7; Ulysses Grant, "Annual Message," December 6, 1869, in U.S. Congress, House of Representatives, *Message of the President of the United States* 41st Congress, 2nd session, House Executive Document No. 1, pt. 1 (Washington, D.C., 1869), p. viii.

50. Hamilton Fish to Daniel E. Sickles, February 6, 1874, in Moore, *Digest of International Law*, 6:79; Hamilton Fish to Caleb Cushing, November 5, 1875, in U.S. Congress, House of Representatives, *Correspondence between the United States Government and Spain in Relation to the Island of Cuba*, 44th Congress, 1st session, Executive Document Report No. 90 (Washington, D.C., 1876), pp. 7–10; Hamilton Fish to Mauricio López Roberts, April 13, 1869, in Hamilton Fish to Mauricio López Roberts, April 30, 1869, in U.S. Congress, Senate, *Message of the President of the United States*, 41st Congress, 2nd session, Executive Document No. 7 (Washington, D.C., 1869), p. 74.

51. Hamilton Fish to Daniel E. Sickles, June 29, 1869, in U.S. Congress, House of Representatives, *Struggle for Independence in the Island of Cuba*, 41st Congress, 2nd session, Executive Document 160 (Washington, D.C., 1870), pp. 13, 15.

52. Hamilton Fish to Caleb Cushing, February 6, 1874, in U.S. Department of State, *Papers Relating to the Foreign Relations of the United States, 1874*, p. 861.

53. William L. Marcy to James Buchanan, July 2, 1853, in U.S. Congress, House of Representatives, *The Ostend Conference*, 33rd Congress, 2nd session, Executive Document No. 93 (Washington, D.C., 1855), p. 10.

54. *Congressional Globe*, February 10, 1859, 35th Congress, 2nd session, vol. 36, pt. 1, p. 937.

55. U.S. Congress, House of Representatives, Committee on Foreign Affairs, *Cuba: Report*, 41st Congress, 2nd session, House Report No. 80 (Washington, D.C., 1870), p. 11.

56. John S. Thrasher, *Preliminary Essay on the Purchase of Cuba* (New York, 1859), p. 92; *Congressional Globe*, June 14, 1854, 33rd Congress, 1st session, Appendix, p. 936.

57. James Buchanan to William L. Marcy, November 1, 1853, in *Works of James Buchanan*, 9:84.

58. U.S. Congress, House of Representatives, *Ostend Manifesto*, p. 131.

59. John A. Quitman to Thomas Reed, August 2, 1854, in J. F. H. Claiborne, *Life and Correspondence of John A. Quitman*, 2 vols. (New York, 1860), 2:205–6.

60. Daniel E. Sickles to Hamilton Fish, November 24, 1872, in U.S. Congress, House of Representatives, *Papers Relating to the Foreign Relations of the United States*, 43rd Congress, 1st session, Executive Document 1, 2 vols. (Washington, D.C., 1873), 2:826.

61. Max Black, "Metaphor," in *Aristotelian Society Proceedings* (1954–55): 287–88.

62. "It cannot be denied," Hamilton Fish explained the U.S. position during the Cuban Ten Years War, "that there pervades the whole American people a special desire to see the right of self-government established in every region of the American hemisphere, so that the political destiny of America shall be independent of transatlantic control." See Hamilton Fish to Mauricio López Roberts, April 17, 1869, in Hamilton Fish to Mauricio López Roberts, April 30, 1869, in U.S. Congress, Senate, *Message of the President of the United States*, 41st Congress, 2nd session, Executive Document No. 7, p. 17.

63. John Quincy Adams to Hugh Nelson, April 28, 1823, in U.S. Congress, House of Representatives, *Island of Cuba*, p. 8.

64. Henry Clay to Alexander H. Everett, April 26, 1825, ibid., p. 17.

65. See Lars Schoultz, *Beneath the United States: A History of U.S. Policy toward Latin America* (Cambridge, Mass., 1998), pp. 58–77.

66. Alexander H. Everett to John Quincy Adams, November 30, 1825, in Everett and Everett, *Everett Letters on Cuba*, p. 7.

67. *Congressional Globe*, January 15, 1855, 33rd Congress, 2nd session, vol. 31, Appendix, p. 92.

68. Ibid., February 15, 1859, 35th Congress, 2nd session, Appendix, p. 167.

69. Robert B. Campbell to James Buchanan, May 18, 1848, in Manning, *Diplomatic Correspondence of the United States: Inter-American Affairs*, 11:440.

70. Caleb Cushing to Hamilton Fish, March 31, 1876, in U.S. Congress, Senate, *Report of the Committee on Foreign Relations*, p. 120; Caleb Cushing to Hamilton Fish, August 2, 1875, in U.S. Congress, House of Representatives, *Papers Relating to the Foreign Relations of the United States*, 44th Congress, 1st session, House Executive Document No. 1 (Washington, D.C., 1875), p. 1138.

71. Caleb Cushing to Hamilton Fish, February 21, 1876, in U.S. Congress, Senate, *Message from the President of the United States*, 54th Congress, 1st session, Document No. 213 (Washington, D.C., 1896), p. 99.

72. Edmond Wood, "Can Cubans Govern Cuba?," *Forum* 32 (September 1901): 66–67, 69, 73.

73. *Congressional Globe*, February 17, 1859, 35th Congress, 2nd session, vol. 36, pt. 1, pp. 1080–81.

74. U.S. Congress, Senate, Committee on Foreign Relations, *Report*, p. 10.

75. Edward B. Bryan, "Cuba and the Tripartite Treaty," *Southern Quarterly Review* 9 (January 1854): 13. John Quincy Adams feared the island would "be revolutionized by the negroes." See *The Diary of John Quincy Adams, 1794–1845*, ed. Allan Nevins (New York, 1951), p. 289.

76. See James Buchanan to Romulus M. Saunders, June 17, 1848, in Manning, *Diplomatic Correspondence of the United States: Inter-American Affairs*, 11:54.

77. *Congressional Globe*, June 14, 1854, 33rd Congress, 1st session, Appendix, p. 951.

78. John C. Calhoun, "Speech on the Proposed Occupation of the Yucatan," May 15, 1848, in *The Papers of John C. Calhoun*, ed. Clyde N. Wilson and Shirley Bright Cook (Columbia, S.C., 1959–), 25:410.

79. John M. Clayton to Daniel M. Barringer, August 2, 1849, in Manning, *Diplomatic Correspondence of the United States: Inter-American Affairs*, 11:69–70. "[The United States] government," the U.S. minister in Madrid assured Spanish authorities, "is resolutely determined that the Island of Cuba should never be in the possession of any other

power than that of Spain or the United States." See Daniel M. Barringer to John M. Clayton, June 19, 1850, ibid., 11:506.

80. U.S. Congress, Senate, *Affairs in Cuba*, ser. 4053 (Washington, D.C., 1896), p. 73.

81. *Congressional Record*, March 24, 1896, 54th Congress, 1st session, vol. 28, pt. 4, p. 3121.

82. Richard B. Olney to Enrique Dupuy de Lôme, April 4, 1896, in U.S. Department of State, *Papers Relating to the Foreign Relations of the United States, 1897* (Washington, D.C., 1898), p. 543.

83. Grover Cleveland to Richard B. Olney, July 16, 1896, in *Letters of Grover Cleveland*, ed. Allan Nevins (Boston, 1933), p. 448.

84. William H. Mills, *The Purpose of the Nation in the Present War* (San Francisco, 1898), pp. 25, 36–37.

85. Stewart L. Woodford to William McKinley, March 9, 1898, Despatches from U.S. Consuls to Spain, 1792–1906, General Records of the Department of State, and Stewart L. Woodford to William McKinley, March 17, 18, 1898, Private Correspondence, General Woodford to the President, August 1897 to May 1898, John Bassett Moore Papers, Manuscript Division, Library of Congress, Washington, D.C.

86. Thomas Jefferson had at one point contemplated resorting to war as a means to seize Cuba. John Quincy Adams conveyed Jefferson's thinking in 1822: "We ought, at first possible opportunity, to take Cuba, though at a cost of a war with England; but as we are not now prepared for this . . . our great object must be to gain time" (*Diary of John Quincy Adams*, p. 289).

87. *New York Times*, April 22, 1898, p. 6.

88. John M. Clayton to Daniel M. Barringer, August 2, 1849, in Manning, *Diplomatic Correspondence of the United States: Inter-American Affairs*, 11:69–70.

89. This theme is expanded upon in Louis A. Pérez Jr., *The War of 1898: The United States and Cuba in History and Historiography* (Chapel Hill, 1998), pp. 1–56.

90. Cleveland, "Annual Message," December 7, 1896, in Moore, *Digest of International Law*, 6:125.

91. Hannis Taylor, "A Review of the Cuban Question in Its Economic, Political and Diplomatic Aspects," *North American Review* 165 (November 1897): 61, 62.

92. William R. Day to Enrique Dupuy de Lôme, December 27, 1897, in U.S. Department of State, *Papers Relating to the Foreign Relations of the United States, 1897*, p. 513. Conditions were "unbearable to a Christian nation geographically so close as ours to Cuba," Day insisted at another point. See William R. Day to Stewart L. Woodford, March 26, 1898, in U.S. Department of State, *Papers Relating to the Foreign Relations of the United States, 1898* (Washington, D.C., 1901), p. 704.

93. John Sherman to Enrique Dupuy de Lôme, June 26, 1897, in U.S. Department of State, *Papers Relating to the Foreign Relations of the United States, 1897*, p. 507; John Sherman to Woodford, July 16, 1897, ibid., p. 558.

94. John Sherman to Stewart L. Woodford, July 16, 1897, in U.S. Department of State, *Papers Relating to the Foreign Relations of the United States, 1898*, pp. 559–60.

95. Joseph Benson Foraker, "Our War with Spain: Its Justice and Necessity," *Forum* 25 (June 1898): 385–95.

96. Washington Gladden, "The Issues of the War," *Outlook*, July 16, 1898, pp. 673–74.

97. *New York Times*, March 29, 1898, p. 8; April 22, 1898, p. 6; April 14, 1898, p. 8; April 19, 1898, p. 1.

98. Ibid., March 6, 1898, p. 18; March 8, 1898, p. 6.

99. *New York World*, April 16, 1897, p. 6.

100. *Baltimore Morning Herald*, March 1, 1898, p. 6.

101. *Cleveland Plain Dealer*, March 8, 1898, p. 4.

102. *Congressional Record*, April 15, 1898, 55th Congress, 2nd session, vol. 31, pt. 4, p. 3878.

103. Ibid., May 17, 1897, 55th Congress, 1st session, vol. 30, pt. 1, p. 1101.

104. Ibid., April 13, 1898, 55th Congress, 2nd session, vol. 31, pt. 4, p. 3783.

105. Andrew Draper, *The Rescue of Cuba: An Episode in the Growth of Free Government* (Boston, 1899), p. 7.

106. *Congressional Record*, February 9, 1898, 55th Congress, 2nd session, vol. 31, pt. 2, p. 1584.

107. John Kendrick Bangs, "The Cuban Situation," *Harper's Weekly*, April 13, 1901, p. 382.

108. *Congressional Record*, April 4, 1898, 55th Congress, 2nd session, vol. 31, pt. 4, p. 3497.

109. Ibid., April 14, 1898, p. 3845.

110. Ibid., May 20, 1897, 55th Congress, 1st session, vol. 30, pt. 1, p. 1168.

111. Ibid., April 14, 1898, vol. 31, pt. 4, p. 3841.

112. Ibid., December 15, 1896, 54th Congress, 2nd session, vol. 29, pt. 1, p. 167.

113. Ibid., April 16, 1898, 55th Congress, 2nd session, vol. 31, pt. 4, pp. 3968, 3970.

114. William McKinley, "Special Message," April 11, 1898, in Moore, *Digest of International Law*, 6:211–20.

115. "Joint Resolution," April 20, 1898, House Document 428, 55th Congress, 2nd session (Washington, D.C., 1898), p. 5.

116. Margaret H. Alden, "Cuba," in *Spanish-American War Songs*, ed. Sidney A. Witherbee (Detroit, 1898), pp. 46–47.

117. S. T. Cocker, "The Sword Unsheathed," ibid., p. 239.

118. J. T. Trowbridge, "Cuba," ibid., p. 884; E. S. Tway, "As We Go Marching On," ibid., p. 891.

119. Frank L. Stanton and Stanley Clague, *Our Country Forever* (Boston, 1898), p. 2.

120. *Atlanta Constitution*, February 13, 1898, p. 18.

121. *New York Times*, March 24, 1896, p. 4.

122. Steven Pinker, "Block That Metaphor!," *New Republic* October 9, 2006, p. 25. For useful discussions of intention and reception see Martyn P. Thompson, "Reception Theory and the Interpretation of Historical Meaning," *History and Theory* 32 (1993): 248–72, and D. A. Boswell, "Speakers' Intentions: Constraints on Metaphor Comprehension," *Metaphor and Symbolic Activity* 1 (1983): 153–70.

123. U.S. Congress, House of Representatives, *Ostend Manifesto*, p. 131.

124. John T. Morgan, "What Shall We Do with the Conquered Islands?," *North American Review* 166 (June 1898): 648.

125. *Congressional Record*, March 24, 1896, 54th Congress, 1st session, vol. 28, pt. 4, p. 3119.

126. *Washington Evening Star*, April 8, 1898, p. 6.

127. *Congressional Record*, March 1, 1901, 56th Congress, 2nd session, vol. 34, pt. 4, p. 3370.

128. James H. Wilson, *Our Relations with Cuba* (Wilmington, Del., 1902), p. 12.

129. *New York Times*, April 14, 1898, p. 6.

130. Ibid., April 12, 1898, p. 6. Major J. E. Runcie later explained the cause of war precisely by way of these images: "The United States expelled Spain from Cuba because the island, under Spanish rule, had become an intolerable neighbor. . . . We forcibly abated a nuisance which had long been maintained in our neighborhood." See J. E. Runcie, "American Misgovernment of Cuba," *North American Review* 170 (February 1900): 284.

131. *Philadelphia Inquirer*, April 21, 1898, p. 8.

132. *Minneapolis Journal*, April 5, 1898, p. 4.

133. Thomas G. Shearman, "International Law and the Cuban Question," *Outlook*, April 16, 1898, p. 987.

134. Richard B. Olney to Grover Cleveland, December 7, 1896, in U.S. Department of State, *Papers Relating to the Foreign Relations of the United States, 1896* (Washington, D.C., 1897), p. lxxx; Richard B. Olney to Enrique Dupuy de Lôme, April 4, 1896, in U.S. Department of State, *Papers Relating to the Foreign Relations of the United States, 1897*, p. 543.

135. *Congressional Record*, April 20, 1897, 55th Congress, 1st session, vol. 30, pt. 1, p. 762.

136. Ibid., April 27, 1898, 55th Congress, 2nd session, Appendix, pp. 444–45.

137. Ibid., January 20, 1898, Appendix, p. 245.

138. Ibid., April 15, 1898, vol. 31, pt. 4, p. 3893.

139. Ibid., Appendix, p. 295.

140. *Washington Evening Star*, March 21, 1898, p. 6.

141. *Brooklyn Eagle*, November 24, 1898, p. 7.

142. H. E. Von Holst, *The Annexation of Our Spanish Conquests* (Chicago, 1898), p. 20.

143. Frank L. Brace, "Free Cuba," in Witherbee, *Spanish-American War Songs*, p. 153.

144. John Keynton, "Cuba Shall Be Free!" (n.p., 1896). Copy of sheet music in author's possession.

145. Frank Alaston Davis, "The Army Sails for Cuba Shortly," in Witherbee, *Spanish-American War Songs*, p. 284.

146. J. R. Martin, "A Call from Cuba," ibid., p. 632.

147. Arthur J. Lamb and H. W. Petrie, "The Wreck of the Battleship Maine" (Chicago, 1898).

148. David S. Barry, *Forty Years in Washington* (Boston, 1924), p. 236.

149. William James to Henry James, May 3, 1898, in *The Correspondence of William James*, 12 vols., ed. Ignas K. Skrupskelis and Elizabeth M. Berkeley (Charlottesville, 1992–), 3:33.

150. Wilkinson Call, "The Right of Cubans to Recognition as Belligerents and to Independence," in Green, *Story of Spain and Cuba*, p. 381; *Congressional Record*, February 20, 1896, 54th Congress, 1st session, vol. 28, pt. 2, p. 1972.

151. *Congressional Record*, April 15, 1898, vol. 31, pt. 4, p. 3887.

152. *Cleveland Plain Dealer*, March 19, 1898, p. 4.

153. *Congressional Record*, March 2, 1896, 54th Congress, 1st session, vol. 28, pt. 3, p. 2350.

154. Ibid., April 22, 1898, 55th Congress, 2nd session, Appendix, p. 421.

155. *Brooklyn Eagle*, April 18, 1898, p. 12.

156. *Philadelphia Inquirer*, March 15, 1898, p. 8.

157. *New York Times*, March 28, 1898, p. 6.

158. Ibid., April 11, 1898, p. 4.

159. *New York Tribune*, January 13, 1898, p. 6.

160. *New York Times*, April 15, 1898, p. 6.

161. *Minneapolis Journal*, March 21, 1898, p. 4.

162. *New York Times*, May 11, 1898, p. 1.

163. Talcott Williams, "Cuba and Armenia," *Century*, February 1899, 635.

164. *Congressional Record*, April 14, 1898, pp. 3841–42.

165. *New York Times*, April 3, 1898, p. 18.

166. *Cleveland Plain Dealer*, April 4, 1898, p. 4.

167. *New York Times*, May 4, 1898, p. 7.

168. *Baltimore Morning Herald*, March 19, 1898, p. 8.

169. *New York World*, February 9, 1898, p. 6, and March 7, 1898, p. 6.

170. Trumbull White, *United States in War with Spain and the History of Cuba* (Philadelphia, 1898), p. 294.

171. Margaret H. Alden, "Cuba," in Witherbee, *Spanish-American War Songs*, pp. 46–47.

172. *New York Journal*, February 18, 1898, p. 34.

173. *Congressional Record*, May 18, 1897, 55th Congress, 1st session, vol. 30, pt. 2, pp. 1131, 1135; ibid., March 29, 1898, 55th Congress, 2nd session, vol. 31, pt. 4, p. 3294.

174. Ibid., May 19, 1897, 55th Congress, 1st session, vol. 30, pt. 2, p. 1150; ibid., April 15, 1898, 55th Congress, 2nd session, vol. 31, pt. 8, p. 304.

175. Ibid., April 27, 1898, 55th Congress, 2nd session, Appendix, p. 444.

176. In Green, *Story of Spain and Cuba*, pp. 234, 241.

177. *New York Times*, March 25, 1898, p. 3.

178. Emily S. Rosenberg, "Rescuing Women and Children," in *History and September 11*, ed. Joanne Meyerwitz (Philadelphia, 2003), pp. 83, 85.

179. *New York World*, March 26, 1898, p. 6.

180. Arthur Wallace Dunn, *From Harrison to Harding: A Personal Narrative Covering a Third of a Century, 1881–1921*, 2 vols. (1922; reprint, Port Washington, N.Y., 1971), 1:231.

181. *New York Journal*, August 18, 1897, p. 1.

182. See Joseph E. Wisan, *The Cuban Crisis as Reflected in the New York Press (1895–1898)* (New York, 1934), pp. 324–31.

183. *New York Times*, October 17, 1897, p. 5. For accounts of the case of Evangelina Cossío Cisneros see Karen Roggenkamp, "The Evangelina Cisneros Romance, Medievalist Fiction, and the Journalism That Acts," *Journal of American Culture* 23 (Summer 2000): 25–37; W. A. Swanberg, *Citizen Hearst: A Biography of William Randolph Hearst* (New York, 1961), pp. 116–29.

184. Amy Ephron, *White Rose/Una Rosa Blanca* (New York, 1999), pp. 243–44, 246. Another fictional account of the Evangelina rescue is Omar Torres, *Al partir* (Houston, 1986).

185. In 1898 Evangelina married Carlos Carbonell, a Cuban who had played a part in her rescue. They returned to Cuba, and shortly after the death of Carbonell she remarried, in 1918, to Cuban attorney Miguel Romero, with whom she had two daughters, Liliana and Sady. Evangelina lived modestly the rest of her life in Havana. Upon her death in May 1970, she was buried in Colón Cemetery in Havana with honors corresponding to those of a captain in the Cuban Liberation Army.

186. "The Cisneros rescue is perhaps one of the most notable instances of newspaper aggressiveness in history," pronounced Marcus M. Wilkerson, *Public Opinion and the Spanish-American War: A Study in War Propaganda* (Baton Rouge, 1932), p. 87.

187. Sydney A. Clark, *Cuban Tapestry* (New York, 1936), p. 116.

188. *New York Journal*, August 17, 1897, p. 1, and August 22, 1897, p. 5. Julian Hawthorne gave candid admission to his concerns: "I must admit that one anxiety haunted me from the first: I was afraid that Evangelina would turn out to be less beautiful than had been alleged. In newspaperdom all women are presumed to be beautiful until they have been proved ugly; and it seemed to me that precisely because the ideal had been realized in other respects there would be a break at this point, and that our heroine would outwardly at least fail to come up to the fairy-tale standard. . . . No fairy princess could be more lovely than this fairy-like little Cuban maiden." As late as 1968, in a popular account of the Evangelina episode, Wilbur Cross would affirm that she was "the most beautiful girl on the island of Cuba." See Julian Hawthorne, introduction to *The Story of Evangelina Cisneros (Evangelina Betancourt Cossío y Cisneros) Told by Herself* (New York, 1898), p. 26; Wilbur Cross, "The Perils of Evangelina," *American Heritage* 19 (February 1968): 36.

189. George Clarke Musgrave, *Under Three Flags in Cuba: A Personal Account of the Cuban Insurrection and Spanish-American War* (Boston, 1899), p. 93.

190. Hawthorne, introduction to *Story of Evangelina Cisneros*, pp. 25, 27.

191. "Mrs. Thurston's Plea to American Mothers," *New York Journal*, March 13, 1898, p. 41; Martha Thurston to Editor, March 11, 1898, *Woman's Tribune*, March 19, 1898, p. 23.

192. Draper, *Rescue of Cuba*, p. 47.

193. *New York Times*, March 25, 1898, p. 3; "In Memoriam," *Woman's Tribune*, March 19, 1898, p. 23.

194. W. E. Woodward, *A New American History* (New York, 1938), p. 685.

195. Isma Dooly, "Atlanta's Women Say Put a Stop to Spain's Warfare on the Island of Cuba," *Atlanta Constitution*, February 13, 1898, p. 18.

196. Marie Madison, "The Passing of Maceo," *American Home Magazine*, January 1897, p. 1.

197. *Woman's Tribune*, January 9, 1898, p. 2.

198. Ellen M. Henrotin, "American Women Are Ready to Suffer and Work," *New York Journal*, April 17, 1898, p. 18.

199. *Woman's Exponent*, February 15–March 1, 1898, p. 252.

200. *Woman's Tribune*, May 14, 1898, p. 1. "At last President McKinley has spoken," was how the *Woman's Exponent* reacted to the president's war message. See "The War Cry," *Woman's Exponent*, March 15–April 1, 1898, p. 260.

201. *Brooklyn Eagle*, April 10, 1898, p. 6.

202. Kristin L. Hoganson, *Fighting for American Manhood* (New Haven, 1998), p. 11.

203. *New York Times*, April 10, 1898, p. 18.

204. *New York World*, March 19, 1898, p. 6. Emphasis in original.

205. *Congressional Record*, March 31, 1898, 55th Congress, 2nd session, vol. 31, pt. 4, p. 3444; ibid., April 14, 1898, p. 3843.

206. *Brooklyn Eagle*, April 15, 1898, p. 11.

207. *New York Times*, March 27, 1898, p. 5. President McKinley celebrated success in war as a triumph of American manhood. "[Victory] has brought us great responsibilities," exulted McKinley in 1899, "and it is for us to accept those responsibilities, meet them with manly courage, respond in a manly fashion to manly duty, and do what in the sight of God and man is just and right." See William McKinley, "Speech at Madison, Wisconsin," October 16, 1899, in *Speeches and Addresses of William McKinley* (New York, 1900), p. 318.

208. Amy Kaplan, *The Anarchy of Empire in the Making of U.S. Culture* (Cambridge, Mass., 2002), pp. 95, 99.

209. Howard B. Grose, *Advance in the Antilles: The New Era in Cuba and Porto Rico* (New York, 1910), pp. 70, 76–77.

210. James J. O'Kelly, *The Mambi-Land, or Adventures of a "Herald" Correspondent in Cuba* (Philadelphia, 1874), p. 29.

211. James W. Steele, *Cuba Sketches* (New York, 1881), pp. 33–43.

212. Ballou, *Due South*, p. 99.

213. *Philadelphia Manufacturer*, March 15, 1889, p. 3.

214. Washington Gladden, "The Issues of the War," *Outlook*, July 16, 1898, p. 674.

215. *Congressional Record*, April 15, 1898, 55th Congress, 2nd session, Appendix, pp. 287, 297.

216. William Howard Taft, "Some Recent Instances of National Altruism: The Efforts of the United States to Aid the Peoples of Cuba, Porto Rico, and the Philippines," *National Geographic*, July 1907, pp. 429–30.

217. Theodore Roosevelt, *An Autobiography* (New York, 2004), pp. 463–64.

218. Alfred T. Mahan, "The Peace Conference and the Moral Aspect of the War," *North American Review* 169 (October 1899): 442.

219. Henry Cabot Lodge, *The War with Spain* (New York, 1899), pp. 6, 11.

220. Draper, *Rescue of Cuba*, pp. 168, 173. More than seventy years later, Ambassador Philip Bonsal reflected on 1898 in precisely the same way: "The intervention was due, in my judgment, to the decision of the American people no longer to tolerate at their doorstep a spectacle so repugnant to the humanitarian sentiments and the desire for freedom for all peoples traditional with Americans." See Philip W. Bonsal, *Cuba, Castro, and the United States* (Pittsburgh, 1971), p. 247.

221. *New York World*, April 8, 1898, p. 6.

222. Arthur J. Pillsbury, "The Destiny of Duty," *Overland Monthly*, February 1899, pp. 168–69.

223. Francis G. Newlands, "The Evolution of Liberty," April 4, 1896, in *The Public Papers of Francis G. Newlands*, 2 vols., ed. Arthur B. Darling (Boston, 1932), 1:141.

224. John Kendrick Bangs, *Uncle Sam Trustee* (New York, 1902), pp. 99, 106.

225. William McKinley, "Speech at the Citizens' Banquet in the Auditorium, Chi-

cago," October 19, 1899, p. 134; "Speech at Indianapolis, Indiana," October 21, 1898, p. 145; "Speech at Columbus, Ohio," October 21, 1898, pp. 151–52; "Speech at the Auditorium, Atlanta, Georgia," December 15, 1898, p. 163; "Speech at Mount Horeb, Wisconsin," October 15, 1899, p. 317; "Speech at Madison, Wisconsin," October 15, 1899, p. 319, all in *Speeches and Addresses*.

226. Woodrow Wilson, *A History of the American People*, 5 vols. (New York, 1902), 5:250–51.

227. E. Benjamin Andrews, *History of the United States* (New York, 1929), pp. 192–93.

228. James Morton Callahan, *Cuba and International Relations* (Baltimore, 1899), p. 485; Alexander K. McClure and Charles Morris, *The Authentic Life of William McKinley* (Philadelphia, 1901), p. 229.

229. James Wilford Garner and Henry Cabot Lodge, *The United States*, 2 vols. (New York, 1907), 2:1022.

230. Hollis W. Barber, *Foreign Policies of the United States* (New York, 1953), p. 258.

231. Archibald Cary Coolidge, *The United States as a World Power* (New York, 1908), p. 128.

232. Leon Burr Richardson, *William E. Chandler, Republican* (New York, 1940), p. 571.

233. Woodward, *New American History*, p. 683.

234. Richard W. Leopold, *The Growth of American Foreign Policy* (New York, 1962), p. 175.

235. Foster Rhea Dulles, *Prelude to World Power: American Diplomatic History, 1860–1900* (New York, 1965), p. 163.

236. Beveridge, "Business and Government," pp. 287–88.

CHAPTER 3

1. "No one who lived through them will forget those gay days of 1898," wrote historians Samuel Eliot Morison and Henry Steel Commager. "With what generous ardor the young men rushed to the colors to free Cuba, while the bands crashed out the chords of Sousa's *Stars and Stripes Forever!* And what a comfortable feeling of unity the country obtained at last, when Democrats vied in patriotism with Republicans. . . . It was more close and personal to Americans than World War I; it was their own little show for independence, fair play, and hip-hurray democracy, against all that was tyrannical, treacherous, and fetid in the Old World." See Samuel Eliot Morison and Henry Steel Commager, *The Growth of the American Republic*, 2 vols (1930; rev. ed., New York, 1950), 2:331.

2. The Teller Amendment included Article I—"That the people of the island of Cuba are and of right ought to be free and independent"—and Article IV—"That the United States hereby disclaims any disposition or intention to exercise sovereignty, jurisdic-

tion, or control over said island except for the pacification thereof, and asserts its de
terminations, when that is accomplished, to leave the government and control of the
island to its people." See *Congressional Record*, April 16, 1898, 55th Congress, 2nd session, vol. 31, pt. 4, pp. 3988–89.

3. Mark Twain to Joseph H. Twichell, June 17, 1898, in *Mark Twain's Letters*, ed.
Albert Bigelow Paine, 2 vols. (New York, 1917), 2:663.

4. Carl Sandburg, *Always the Young Strangers* (New York, 1953), pp. 376–77, 403–4.

5. Charles E. Chapman, *A History of the Cuban Republic* (New York, 1927), p. 90.

6. Whitelaw Reid to General James H. Wilson, September 11, 1900, General Correspondence, James H. Wilson Papers, Manuscript Division, Library of Congress, Washington, D.C.

7. James H. Wilson to Theodore Roosevelt, July 5, 1899, Theodore Roosevelt Papers,
Manuscript Division, Library of Congress; James H. Wilson to Elihu Root, November 3,
1899, General Correspondence, Wilson Papers.

8. Albert J. Beveridge, "Cuba and Congress," *North American Review* 62 (July 1901):
540–50; Albert J. Beveridge, "Business and Government," September 22, 1906, in *The
Meaning of the Times and Other Speeches* (Indianapolis, 1908), p. 283; *Minneapolis Journal*, September 30, 1906, p. 8; Albert J. Beveridge, "The Star of Empire," September 25,
1900, in *Meaning of the Times*, p. 124.

9. William McKinley, "Special Message," April 11, 1898, in *A Digest of International
Law*, 8 vols., ed. John Bassett Moore (Washington, D.C., 1906), 6:211–20.

10. Richard Olney, "Growth of Our Foreign Policy," *Atlantic Monthly*, March 1900, pp.
290–91.

11. *Washington Post*, June 9, 1901, p. 18.

12. William Ludlow to Chief of Staff, Division of Cuba, October 4, 1899, File 287874,
Records of the Adjutant General's Office, 1780s–1917, Record Group 94, National Archives, Washington, D.C.

13. *New York Times*, August 24, 1898, p. 4.

14. Ibid., July 29, 1899, p. 4.

15. Ibid., June 24, 1899, p. 1.

16. Ibid., November 7, 1899, p. 7.

17. Ibid., May 5, 1901, p. 12.

18. Ibid., August 1, 1898, p. 6.

19. Ibid., December 19, 1898, p. 2.

20. Ibid., July 22, 1898, p. 2; Young quoted in Walter Millis, *The Martial Spirit: A Study
of Our War with Spain* (Cambridge, Mass., 1931), p. 362.

21. *The State*, January 16, 1899, p. 5.

22. *Chicago Tribune*, September 13, 1906, p. 6.

23. Albert Memmi, *The Colonizer and the Colonized*, trans. Howard Greenfeld (Boston, 1967), p. 66.

24. *Congressional Record*, December 9, 1903, 58th Congress, 2nd session, vol. 38, pt. 1, p. 168.

25. See Arthur Wallace Dunn, *From Harrison to Harding: A Personal Narrative, Covering a Third of a Century, 1888–1921*, 2 vols. (1922; reprint, Port Washington, N.Y., 1971), 1:231–32.

26. *Washington Post*, August 13, 1900, p. 6.

27. *Chicago Tribune*, September 15, 1906, p. 8.

28. Theodore Roosevelt to Henry White, September 13, 1906, Roosevelt Papers.

29. Leonard Wood to William McKinley, February 6, 1900, Special Correspondence, Elihu Root Papers, Manuscript Division, Library of Congress.

30. John Kendrick Bangs, "The Cuban Situation," *Harper's Weekly*, March 9, 1901, p. 249.

31. William McKinley to General John R. Brooke, December 22, 1898, John R. Brooke Papers, Pennsylvania Historical Society, Philadelphia.

32. *Congressional Record*, November 16, 1903, 58th Congress, 1st session, vol. 37, pt. 1, p. 260.

33. Woodrow Wilson, "Democracy and Efficiency," October 1, 1900, in *The Papers of Woodrow Wilson*, 69 vols., ed. Arthur S. Link et al. (Princeton, 1966–94), 12:19.

34. Woodrow Wilson, "The Ideals of America," December 26, 1901, ibid., 12:218.

35. Woodrow Wilson, *Constitutional Government in the United States* (1908; reprint, New Brunswick, 2002), p. 52.

36. For a useful brief overview see William B. Cohen, "The Colonized as Child: British and French Colonial Rule," *African Historical Studies* 3 (1970): 427–31.

37. Douglas Berggren, "The Use and Abuse of Metaphor (I)," *Review of Metaphysics* 16 (December 1962): 244.

38. This imagery found ready usage in Cuba. Thus, U.S. ambassador to Cuba Harry Guggenheim described a relationship existing "between a ward and a trustee." Allan Nevins and Henry Commager wrote that the United States acted as "tutor of backward peoples." See Harry F. Guggenheim, *The United States and Cuba* (New York, 1934), p. 60; Allan Nevins and Henry Steele Commager, *America: The Story of a Free People* (New York, 1942), p. 425.

39. F. S. Marvin, *Western Races and the World* (Oxford, 1922), p. 16.

40. Francis Parkman, *The Conspiracy of Pontiac* (1851; reprint, New York, 1962), pp. 182–83.

41. Edward B. Tylor, *Primitive Culture* (1871; reprint, New York, 1924), p. 31; John Locke, *An Essay Concerning Human Understanding* (London, 1947), p. 14.

42. George Fitzhugh, "Southern Thought," *DeBow's Review* 23 (November 1857): 454, 456.

43. This theme is addressed expertly in Patrick Brantlinger, *Dark Vanishings: Discourse on the Extinction of Primitive Races, 1800–1930* (Ithaca, 2003).

44. John Stuart Mill, *On Liberty and Other Essays*, ed. John Gray (New York, 1998), pp. 212, 260, 453–54.

45. Tylor, *Primitive Culture*, pp. 1, 67, 26.

46. Ernest Renan, *The Future of Science* (Boston, 1891), pp. 153, 335, 375.

47. George A. Richardson, "The Subjugation of Inferior Races," *Overland Monthly*, January 1900, pp. 50, 52.

48. Benjamin Kidd, *The Control of the Tropics* (New York, 1898), pp. 52–56, 76.

49. Albert J. Beveridge, "The Development of a Colonial Policy for the United States," *Annals of the American Academy of Political and Social Science* 30 (July 1907): 3–4.

50. U.S. Congress, Senate, Committee on Foreign Relations, *Recognition of Cuban Independence*, 54th Congress, 2nd session, Senate Report No. 1160 (Washington, D.C., 1896), p. 26.

51. *Congressional Record*, January 20, 1898, 55th Congress, 2nd session, Appendix, pp. 246, 247.

52. Ibid., April 28, 1898, Appendix, p. 420.

53. *New York World*, April 8, 1898, p. 6.

54. *New York Journal*, March 11, 1898, p. 6.

55. *New York Times*, April 11, 1898, p. 4.

56. Beveridge, "Development of a Colonial Policy for the United States," p. 6.

57. *Chicago Tribune*, January 11, 1899, p. 6.

58. Frederic Remington, "Under Which King?," March 10, 1899, in *The Collected Writings of Frederic Remington*, ed. Peggy Samuels and Harold Samuels (New York, 1979), pp. 359, 361.

59. Howard B. Grose, *Advance in the Antilles: The New Era in Cuba and Porto Rico* (New York, 1910), p. 73.

60. *New York Times*, December 24, 1898, p. 9.

61. "Speech of Wm. H. Taft, Provisional Governor of Cuba, at the opening Exercise of the National University of Havana," October 19, 1906, in U.S. Congress, House of Representatives, *Annual Reports of the War Department for the Fiscal Year Ended June 30, 1906*, 59th Congress, 2nd session, Document No. 2, 3 vols. (Washington, D.C., 1906), 1:541–42.

62. Arthur J. Pillsbury, "The Destiny of Duty," *Overland Monthly*, February 1899, pp. 169–70.

63. *Washington Daily Star*, June 20, 1899, p. 11.

64. *New York Evening Post*, November 17, 1899, p. 2.

65. John R. Brooke to Thomas H. Carter, October 29, 1899, Brooke Papers. Emphasis in original.

66. *Washington Evening Star*, March 21, 1901, p. 11.

67. Franklin Matthews, *The New-Born Cuba* (New York, 1899), p. v.

68. Albert G. Robinson, *Cuba Old and New* (New York, 1915), pp. 242–43.

69. Captain Walter B. Barker to Senator John T. Morgan, April 2, 1901, Philip C. Jessup Papers, Manuscript Division, Library of Congress. There were nineteenth-century antecedents to this point of view. "I pity the poor oppressed Cubans," commented writer Richard Kimball in 1850, "and I look with loathing upon the infamous government which has systematically destroyed all moral and social good among them." See Richard B. Kimball, *Cuba and the Cubans* (New York, 1850), p. 144.

70. Captain Walter B. Barker to J. Addison Porter, November 28, 1899, William McKinley Papers, Manuscript Division, Library of Congress. Emphasis in original.

71. *Brooklyn Eagle*, May 22, 1902, p. 19.

72. Quoted in George Kennan, "Cuban Character," *Outlook*, December 23, 1899, p. 1022.

73. *Brooklyn Eagle*, December 5, 1902, p. 18.

74. Paul W. Beck, "Office Memorandum for Information of Successor," April 15, 1920, File 2056-196, Records of the War Department, General and Special Staffs, Record Group 165, National Archives. The metaphor appears to have had enduring resonance. To have ceded independence to Cuba in 1902, lamented writer Thomas Freeman as late as 1963, "was like placing a loaded pistol into the hands of a child." See Thomas Freeman, *The Crisis in Cuba* (Derby, Conn., 1963), p. 35.

75. These themes are expertly addressed in Naomi Quinn, "The Cultural Basis of Metaphor," in *Beyond Metaphor: The Theory of Tropes in Anthropology*, ed. James W. Fernandez (Stanford, 1991), pp. 56–93, and Andrew Ortony, "Some Psycholinguistic Aspects of Metaphor," in *Cognition and Figurative Language*, ed. Richard P. Honeck and Robert R. Hoffman (Hillsdale, N.J., 1980), pp. 69–83. See also Virginia M. Bouvier, "Imperial Humor: U.S. Political Cartoons and the War of 1898," *Colonial Latin American Historical Review* 8 (Winter 1999): 5–41, and "Imagining a Nation: U.S. Political Cartoons and the War of 1898," in *Whose America? The War of 1898 and the Battles to Define the Nation*, ed. Virginia M. Bouvier (Westport, Conn., 2001), pp. 91–122.

76. Cynthia Ozick, "The Moral Necessity of Metaphor," *Harper's Magazine*, May 1986, p. 67.

77. Albert J. Beveridge, "The March of the Flag," September 16, 1898, in *Meaning of the Times*, p. 49.

78. Beveridge, "Cuba and Congress," p. 545.

79. Andrew Draper, *The Rescue of Cuba: An Episode in the Growth of Free Government* (Boston, 1899), p. 184.

80. *Chicago Tribune*, April 16, 1901, p. 12. See also John G. Rockwood, "Rescuing Cuba from the Cubans," *World To-Day*, November 1906, pp. 1190–1203, and Harold J. Howland, "Saving a People from Themselves," *Outlook*, October 27, 1906, pp. 455–64.

81. Bangs, "Cuban Situation," p. 249.

82. Major John A. Logan, Provost Marshall, to Adjutant General, Department of

Santa Clara, February 3, 1899, File 294/11, Records of the Bureau of Insular Affairs, Record Group 350, National Archives.

83. Herbert Pelham Williams, "The Outlook in Cuba," *Atlantic Monthly*, June 1899, p. 827.

84. C. H. Forbes-Lindsay, *Cuba and Her People of To-Day* (Boston, 1911), p. 154.

85. Orville H. Platt, "The Pacification of Cuba," *Independent*, June 27, 1901, p. 1467.

86. Kennan, "Cuban Character," p. 1021.

87. Robert L. Bullard, "How Cubans Are Different from Us," *North American Review* 186 (November 1907): 418, 421.

88. Woodrow Wilson, "The Ideals of America," *Atlantic Monthly*, December 1902, pp. 730–31.

89. *Statutes at Large of the United States*, XXXI (Washington, D.C., 1902), p. 897. The Platt Amendment was abrogated in 1934, with the exception of the naval station clause.

90. Lawrence H. Streicher, "On a Theory of Political Caricature," *Comparative Studies in Society and History* 9 (July 1967): 483; Thomas Milton Kemnitz, "The Cartoon as a Historical Source," *Journal of Interdisciplinary History* 4 (Summer 1973): 93. See also Ray Morris, "Visual Rhetoric in Political Cartoons: A Structuralist Approach," *Metaphor and Symbolic Activity* 8 (1993): 195–210.

91. Bouvier, "Imperial Humor," p. 7.

92. Emily Sorkin, "An Analysis of United States Cartoons of the Spanish-American War and World War I" (M.A. thesis, University of North Carolina, Chapel Hill, 1976), p. 5; Paul P. Somers Jr., *Editorial Cartooning and Caricature* (Westport, Conn., 1998), p. 13.

93. W. A. Coupe, "Observations on a Theory of Political Caricature," *Comparative Studies in Society and History* 11 (January 1969): 79–95.

94. Joanne Shattock and Michael Wolff, introduction to *The Victorian Press: Samplings and Soundings*, ed. Joanne Shattock and Michael Wolff (Toronto, 1982), p. xiv.

95. Gunther Kress and Theo van Leeuwen, *Reading Images: Sociocultural Aspects of Language and Education* (Geelong, Victoria, Australia, 1990), p. 27.

96. See Virgil C. Aldrich, "Visual Metaphor," *Journal of Aesthetic Education* 2 (January 1968): 73–86.

97. *The Spanish-American War: The Events of the War Described by Eyewitnesses* (Chicago, 1899), pp. 15–16.

98. J. Hampton Moore, *With Speaker Cannon Through the Tropics* (Philadelphia, 1907), p. 305.

99. *New York Times*, May 13, 1913, p. 3.

100. Steven Pinker, "Block That Metaphor!," *New Republic*, October 9, 2006, p. 26.

101. Recent scholarship has discerned the presence of gender-determined dispo-

sitions in the use of figurative language. The virtual absence of metonymy in the discursive ordering of power relationships, for example, suggests the degree to which metaphorical depiction of domination depends on cues and codes derived from male roles. "Women are socialized to be more communal," observe psychologists Jeffery Scott Mio and Albert N. Katz, "whereas men are socialized to be more independent. Community resonates more than metonymy's part-to-whole essence, whereas independence resonates more with metaphor's implicit comparison of one thing to another." Literary critic Jane Gallop writes of the "feminine metonymy" and the "masculine metaphor," suggesting that the "privilege of metaphor over metonymy" reflects the male bias of cultural constructs. More specifically, Gallop suggests, women experience greater facility with contiguity of metonymic constructs as a cognitive device, while men respond more readily to metaphorical imagery. "A shadow of femininity haunts the juncture of metonymy and realism," Gallop writes, "that by contiguity, by metonymy, a certain femininity is suggested." See Jeffery Scott Mio and Albert N. Katz, preface to *Metaphor: Implications and Applications*, ed. Jeffery Scott Mio and Albert N. Katz (Mahwah, N.J., 1996), p. xiii; Jane Gallop, *Reading Lacan* (Ithaca, 1985), pp. 114–32. See also Patricia A. Chantrill and Jeffery Scott Mio, "Metonymy in Political Discourse," in Mio and Katz, *Metaphor*, pp. 171–84. Genevieve Lloyd writes of metaphor within a context of the "maleness of reason." See Genevieve Lloyd, "Maleness, Metaphor, and the 'Crisis' of Reason," in *A Mind of One's Own: Feminist Essays on Reason and Objectivity*, ed. Louise M. Antony and Charlotte Witt (Boulder, 1993), pp. 69–83.

102. Kennan, "Cuban Character," pp. 964–65.

103. *Congressional Record*, March 1, 1901, 56th Congress, 2nd session, vol. 34, pt. 4, p. 3371.

104. Bangs, "Cuban Situation," p. 249. One of the first things that one noticed about the Cuban, wrote Lieutenant John Parker in 1898, was "that he is dirty." Parker continued: "He is not merely dirty, he is filthy. He is infested with things that crawl and creep, often visibly, over his half-naked body, and he is accustomed to it that he does not even scratch." See John H. Parker, *History of the Gatling Gun Detachment, Fifth Army Corps, at Santiago, with a Few Unvarnished Truths Concerning that Expedition* (Kansas City, 1898), p. 78.

105. Robert A. Smith, *A Social History of the Bicycle: Its Early Life and Times in America* (New York, 1972), p. 76.

106. *Washington Post*, May 20, 1902, p. 6. See Karen Sánchez-Eppler, "Raising Empires Like Children: Race, Nation and Religious Education," *American Literary History* 8 (Autumn 1996): 399–425.

107. Theodore Roosevelt to Eugene Hale, September 28, 1906, Roosevelt Papers.

108. *Washington Post*, September 17, 1906, p. 6.

109. *Chicago Tribune*, September 19, 1906, p. 8.

110. *New York Times*, September 18, 1906, p. 8; September 21, 1906, p. 8; September 23, 1906, p. 8.

111. Moore, *With Speaker Cannon Through the Tropics*, pp. 305–6.

112. "America's Duty to Cuba," *Outlook*, October 6, 1906, pp. 304–5.

113. Ella A. Fanning, "Her Coming Out," *New York Times*, January 28, 1909, p. 8.

114. *Congressional Record*, March 31, 1898, 55th Congress, 2nd session, vol. 31, pt. 4, p. 3412.

115. W. R. Morgan, "Dr. Fernando Ortiz: Political Situation in Cuba," April 29, 1927, 837.00/2657, General Records of the Department of State, Record Group 59, National Archives. (Hereinafter cited as DS/RG 59.)

116. Forbes-Lindsay, *Cuba and Her People of To-Day*, pp. 88–89.

117. Jacob Goldstein, "Our Little Sister Cuba," August 1921, enclosure in 837.00P 81/13, DS/RG 59.

118. A copy of General Pershing's speech was enclosed in John Pershing to Secretary of State, n.d., John Pershing Papers, Manuscript Division, Library of Congress.

119. *Congressional Record*, April 14, 1903, 58th Congress, 1st session, vol. 37, p. 387.

120. In Grose, *Advance in the Antilles*, p. 40.

121. *Brooklyn Eagle*, August 23, 1902, p. 4.

122. *Congressional Record*, April 14, 1902, 57th Congress, 1st session, Appendix, p. 199.

123. Carl Schurz, "The Issue of Imperialism," January 4, 1899, in *Speeches, Correspondence, and Political Papers of Carl Schurz*, ed. Frederic Bancroft, 6 vols. (New York, 1913), 6:32.

124. Ralph C. Estep, *El Toro: A Motor Car Story of Interior Cuba* (Detroit, 1909), p. 63.

125. Frank G. Carpenter, *Land of the Caribbean* (Garden City, N.Y., 1930), p. 176.

126. Basil Woon, *When It's Cocktail Time in Cuba* (New York, 1928), pp. 278–79.

127. Forbes-Lindsay, *Cuba and Her People of To-Day*, pp. 86, 90.

128. Erna Fergusson, *Cuba* (New York, 1946), p. 136.

129. Margaret Leech, *In the Days of McKinley* (New York, 1959), p. 394.

130. Hudson Strode, *The Pageant of Cuba* (New York, 1934), p. xix.

131. Howard C. Hill, *Roosevelt and the Caribbean* (Chicago, 1927), p. 69.

132. Robert H. Ferrell, *American Diplomacy: A History* (New York, 1959), p. 245.

CHAPTER 4

1. *Harper's Weekly* described the "popular movement in this country" and the "wild frenzy of desire" to free Cuba and added, "The horrible tales . . . have fired the imaginations of our people, and have made them ready to incur the miseries and horrors of war in behalf of a struggling people." Carl Schurz wrote of "a war of liberation, of humanity, undertaken without any selfish motive, . . . a war of disinterested benevo-

lence." See "The War Spirit of the People," *Harper's Weekly*, April 16, 1898, p. 363; Carl Schurz, "Thoughts on American Imperialism," *Century*, September 1898, p. 783.

2. "I do not think," Theodore Roosevelt concluded as early as 1896, "a war with Spain would be serious enough to cause much strain on the country, or much interruption to the revival of prosperity." The *Philadelphia Inquirer* agreed: "The result of such a contest could not be doubtful." The *New York Journal* was almost scornful: "A war between the United States and Spain hardly deserves to be called a war. It is so one-sided that it is disgraceful for us to display apprehension about its effects, financial or other." General William Palmer wrote of seizing "the throat of a poor neighbor one-fourth our size and with but a small fraction of our resources, [without] money, and not much ammunition, and he can't get coal, and his soldiers are frail, undrilled boys." Naval analyst H. C. Taylor characterized the conflict as "a slight scratch of war." See Theodore Roosevelt to Henry Cabot Lodge, December 4, 1896, in *Selections from the Correspondence of Theodore Roosevelt and Henry Cabot Lodge*, 2 vols. (New York, 1925), 1:243; *Philadelphia Inquirer*, March 10, 1898, p. 8; *New York Journal*, February 27, 1898, p. 45; William J. Palmer, "The Argument for Neutrality," *Outlook*, April 23, 1898, p. 1015; H. C. Taylor, "The Future of Our Navy," *Forum* 27 (March 1899): 3.

3. *Washington Evening Star*, February 24, 1898, p. 4.

4. Amos Hershey, "Intervention and the Recognition of Cuban Independence," *Annals of the American Academy of Political and Social Science* 11 (May 1898): 72, 77, 80.

5. *Congressional Record*, April 16, 1898, 55th Congress, 2nd session, vol. 31, pt. 4, p. 3957.

6. *New York Tribune*, April 17, 1898, p. 6.

7. *Washington Post*, March 24, 1898, p. 6.

8. *New York World*, April 8, 1898, p. 6.

9. *Philadelphia Inquirer*, April 14, 1898, p. 8.

10. *Washington Evening Star*, April 11, 1898, p. 6; April 12, 1898, p. 6.

11. See Marcus M. Wilkerson, *Public Opinion and the Spanish-American War: A Study in War Propaganda* (Baton Rouge, 1932); Thomas A. Bailey, *The Man in the Street: The Impact of American Public Opinion on Foreign Policy* (New York, 1948); Gabriel A. Almond, *The American People and Foreign Policy*, 2nd ed. (New York, 1960).

12. War correspondent Herbert Sargent offered a representative view: "While the freedom of Cuba was being decided under their very eyes, they stood by, inefficient, inactive. The rewards were theirs, but the Americans made the sacrifice. By the blood of the Americans the victories were won." See Herbert H. Sargent, *The Campaign of Santiago de Cuba*, 3 vols. (Chicago, 1907), 2:164–66.

13. Albert J. Beveridge, "Cuba and Congress," *North American Review* 157 (April 1901): 541.

14. *Congressional Record*, April 17, 1902, 57th Congress, 1st session, Appendix, p. 204.

15. "I found that the Cubans of the east," Stephen Bonsal wrote at the time, "were under the impression that, with more or less equanimity, the American people had witnessed the devastation of the island by inhuman warfare, and had stood idly by while half a million people were done to death by the inhuman Concentration decrees. I found that they were one and all of the opinion that we simply embarked upon the war . . . not to save what was left of Cuban life in the island, but to avenge the 150 sailors who sank with the Maine." See Stephen Bonsal, *The Fight For Santiago* (New York, 1899), pp. 533–34.

16. Thomas R. Dawley Jr., "With Our Army at Tampa" (unpublished manuscript, 1898, P. K. Yonge Library, University of Florida, Gainesville), p. 146.

17. Trumbull White, *Our New Possessions* (Richmond, Va., 1898), p. 585. "There was little whole-hearted support of the American campaign," historian Charles Chapman wrote several decades later. "This attitude . . . was a source of no little surprise to the invaders, who expected to be received with open arms." See Charles E. Chapman, *A History of the Cuban Republic* (New York, 1927), p. 92.

18. *New York World*, July 14, 1898, p. 3. Crane also conveyed the psychological exaltation derived from receiving gratitude from the Cubans, thereby setting in relief the disappointment—and dismay—when it was withheld. A party of Americans came upon a Cuban detachment, Crane reported: "I suppose we felt rather godlike. We were almost the first Americans they had seen, and they looked at us with eyes of grateful affection. I don't suppose many men have the experience of being looked at with eyes of grateful affection." Stephen Crane, "War Memories," *Anglo-Saxon Review* (December 1899), in *The War Despatches of Stephen Crane*, ed. R. W. Stallman and E. R. Hagemann (New York, 1964), p. 275.

19. *New York Evening Post*, July 21, 1898, p. 2.

20. *Washington Evening Star*, May 2, 1899, p. 3; General Young quoted in Walter Millis, *The Martial Spirit: A Study of Our War with Spain* (Cambridge, Mass., 1931), p. 362.

21. Otis Oliver Howard, "The Conduct of the Cubans in the Late War," *Forum* 26 (October 1898): 155.

22. Immanuel Kant, *The Doctrine of Virtue*, trans. Mary J. Gregor (New York, 1964), pp. 123, 128; Immanuel Kant, *Lectures on Ethics*, ed. Lewis White Beck, trans. Louis Infield (New York, 1963), p. 218. (Emphasis in original.) For a survey of the historical place of gratitude in philosophical treatises see Charles Stewart-Robertson, "The Rhythms of Gratitude: Historical Developments and Philosophical Concerns," *Australasian Journal of Philosophy* 58 (June 1990): 189–205.

23. Edward Westermarck, *The Origin and Development of the Moral Ideas*, 2 vols. (London, 1917), 2:155; Benedetto Croce, *The Conduct of Life*, trans. Arthur Livingston (New York, 1924), p. 85; Fred R. Berger, "Gratitude," *Ethics* 85 (July 1975): 300–302.

24. Jack W. Brehm and Ann Himelick Cole, "Effect of a Favor Which Reduces Freedom," *Journal of Personality and Social Psychology* 3 (1966): 421.

25. Claudia Card, "Gratitude and Obligation," *American Philosophical Quarterly* 25 (April 1988): 115, 124. (Emphasis in original.)

26. Georg Simmel, *The Sociology of Georg Simmel*, ed. Kurt H. Wolf (New York, 1950), pp. 387, 392. Philosopher Terrance McConnell alluded to a "contractual relationship" that binds the beneficiary to the benefactor. See Terrance McConnell, *Gratitude* (Philadelphia, 1993), pp. 19–26. These themes are further elaborated upon in Alvin W. Gouldner, "The Norm of Reciprocity: A Preliminary Statement," *American Sociological Review* 25 (April 1960): 161–78; Martin S. Greenberg and Solomon P. Shapiro, "Indebtedness: An Adverse Aspect of Asking for and Receiving Help," *Sociometry* 34 (1971): 290–301; Abraham Tesser, Robert Gatewood, and Michael Driver, "Some Determinants of Gratitude," *Journal of Personality and Social Psychology* 9 (1968): 233–36.

27. David Barry Gaspar, *Bondmen and Rebels: A Study of Master-Slave Relations in Antigua* (Baltimore, 1985), p. 130.

28. Drew Gilpin Faust, *James Henry Hammond and the Old South: A Design for Mastery* (Baton Rouge, 1982), pp. 89, 101.

29. Eugene D. Genovese, *Roll, Jordan, Roll: The World the Slaves Made* (New York, 1974), pp. 91, 145–46.

30. Octave Mannoni, *Prospero and Caliban: The Psychology of Colonization*, trans. Pamela Powesland (New York, 1964), pp. 44–47; Frantz Fanon, *A Dying Colonialism*, trans. Haakon Chevalier (New York, 1965), p. 122; Albert Memmi, *The Colonizer and the Colonized*, trans. Howard Greenfield (Boston, 1967), p. 82.

31. William McKinley to General John R. Brooke, December 22, 1898, John R. Brooke Papers, Pennsylvania Historical Society, Philadelphia.

32. Philip Jessup, "Interview with Mr. Root," November 19, 1929, Philip Jessup Papers, Manuscript Division, Library of Congress, Washington, D.C.

33. Among the best accounts of the Cuban campaign are "La cooperación militar de los cubanos," *Maceo* 1 (October 20, 1898): 15–28; Enrique Collazo, *Los americanos en Cuba* (Havana, 1905); Cosme de la Torriente, *Calixto García cooperó con las fuerzas armadas de los EE. UU. en 1898, cumpliendo órdenes del gobierno cubano* (Havana, 1952); Aníbal Escalante Beatón, *Calixto García: Su campaña en el 95* (Havana, 1978), pp. 465–672; Herminio Portell Vilá, *Historia de la guerra de Cuba y los Estados Unidos contra España* (Havana, 1949).

34. *New York Journal*, October 27, 1898, p. 14. See also the editorial "Nuestra impaciencia," *Patria*, October 5, 1898, p. 1.

35. Orestes Ferrara y Marino, *Mis relaciones con Máximo Gómez*, 2nd ed. (Havana, 1942), pp. 220–21.

36. Enrique Collazo, "A mis amigos de Oriente," *La Lucha*, June 1, 1902, p. 2.

37. Elihu Root to Leonard Wood, February 14, 1901, Correspondence Between General Leonard Wood and Secretary of War Elihu Root, 1899–1902, Bureau of Insular Af-

fairs, Record Group 350, National Archives, Washington, D.C. (Hereinafter cited as BIA/RG 350.)

38. Orville H. Platt, "Cuba's Claim Upon the United States," *North American Review* 185 (August 1902): 146; Orville H. Platt, "The Solution of the Cuban Problem," *World's Work*, May 1901, p. 730.

39. Simmel, *Sociology of Georg Simmel*, p. 392.

40. A. John Simmons, *Moral Principles and Political Obligations* (Princeton, 1979), p. 172.

41. *New York Tribune*, June 15, 1901, p. 6.

42. *Congressional Record*, March 1, 1901, 56th Congress, 2nd session, vol. 34, pt. 4, p. 3380.

43. Ibid., p. 3343.

44. Marrion Wilcox, "Our Honor and Cuba's Need," *Forum* 32 (January 1902): 624.

45. Berger, "Gratitude," pp. 304–5.

46. Stephen Bonsal, *The American Mediterranean* (New York, 1913), pp. 39, 46.

47. J. Hampton Moore, *With Speaker Cannon Through the Tropics* (Philadelphia, 1907), pp. 300, 405.

48. *Brooklyn Eagle*, August 23, 1902, p. 4.

49. William Howard Taft, "Some Recent Instances of National Altruism: The Efforts of the United States to Aid the Peoples of Cuba, Porto Rico, and the Philippines," *National Geographic*, July 1907, p. 430.

50. Theodore Roosevelt, *Message from the President of the United States, with Reference to Reciprocity with Cuba*, June 13, 1902, U.S. Congress, Senate, 57th Congress, 1st session, Document No. 405 (Washington, D.C., 1902), p. 3.

51. Theodore Roosevelt, *Message of the President of the United States*, November 10, 1903, U.S. Congress, House of Representatives, 58th Congress, 1st session, Document No. 1 (Washington, D.C., 1903), p. 2.

52. *Cleveland Plain Dealer*, May 19, 1902, p. 4.

53. *St. Louis Globe Democrat*, June 4, 1905, p. 4.

54. *Brooklyn Eagle*, May 20, 1902, p. 4.

55. L. H. Carpenter to Adjutant General, Division of Cuba, July 10, 1899, War Department, *Annual Reports of the War Department 1899*, House of Representatives, 56th Congress, 1st session, Ser. 3901 (Washington, D.C., 1899), pp. 316–17; Francis H. Nichols, "Cuban Character," *Outlook*, June 29, 1899, pp. 710–11.

56. *Washington Post*, August 27, 1900, p. 9.

57. *San Antonio Express*, November 30, 1900, p. 6.

58. *Philadelphia Inquirer*, April 8, 1901, p. 8.

59. *Congressional Record*, March 1, 1901, 56th Congress, 2nd session, vol. 34, pt. 4, pp. 3370, 3375, and Appendix, pp. 357–58.

60. Platt, "Solution of the Cuban Problem," p. 731; Louis A. Coolidge, *An Old-Fashioned Senator: Orville H. Platt of Connecticut* (New York, 1910), p. 337.

61. Platt, "Cuba's Claim Upon the United States," p. 146.

62. *Congressional Record*, February 7, 1901, 56th Congress, 2nd session, Appendix, p. 358; ibid., March 1, 1901, vol. 34, pt. 4, pp. 3370, 3375.

63. Elihu Root to Leonard Wood, January 9, 1901, Special Correspondence, Elihu Root Papers, Manuscript Division, Library of Congress; Elihu Root to Leonard Wood, March 2, 1901, File 331-71, BIA/RG 350. The *New York World* lamented the need to have imposed the Platt Amendment upon the Cubans by ultimatum, preferring instead Cuban acquiescence by way of appeal "to the friendliness and gratitude of the Cubans." See *New York World*, April 14, 1901, p. 6.

64. *La Tribuna*, March 26, 1901, p. 1.

65. Tomás Estrada Palma to Gonzalo de Quesada, March 14, 1901, in *Archivo de Gonzalo de Quesada*, 2 vols., ed. Gonzalo de Quesada y Miranda (Havana, 1948–51), 1:151–52.

66. *New York Tribune*, May 21, 1902, p. 8.

67. *Congressional Record*, May 20, 1902, 57th Congress, 1st session, vol. 35, pt. 6, p. 5714.

68. *Minneapolis Journal*, September 30, 1906, p. 8; Albert J. Beveridge, "The Development of a Colonial Policy for the United States," *Annals of the American Academy of Political and Social Science* 30 (July 1907): 8.

69. *New York Times*, May 21, 1902, p. 2.

70. Roosevelt, *Message from the President of the United States*, p. 3.

71. *Congressional Record*, May 20, 1902, 57th Congress, 1st session, vol. 35, pt. 6, pp. 5686, 5719.

72. Ibid., February 26, 1901, 56th Congress, 2nd session, vol. 34, pt. 4, p. 3041.

73. *Chicago Tribune*, May 20, 1902, p. 4.

74. *Washington Evening Star*, May 20, 1902, p. 4.

75. Orville H. Platt, "The Pacification of Cuba," *Independent*, June 27, 1901, p. 1466.

76. Randolph Greenfield Adams, *A History of the Foreign Policy of the United States* (New York, 1933), p. 277; James Ford Rhodes, *The McKinley and Roosevelt Administrations, 1897–1909* (New York, 1922), p. 177; Arthur H. Vandenberg, *The Trail of a Tradition* (New York, 1926), p. 321.

77. John Holladay Latané and David W. Wainhouse, *A History of American Foreign Policy*, 2nd ed. (New York, 1940), p. 511.

78. Mabel B. Casner and Ralph Henry Gabriel, *The Rise of American Democracy* (New York, 1938), p. 531. One hundred years later, biographer Edmund Morris celebrated Theodore Roosevelt for "handing Cuba its independence in May 1902 after a brief period of military government that transformed the island from an abused, insanitary and poverty-stricken Spanish colony to a healthy new nation amply equipped to govern

itself." See Edmund Morris, "Theodore Roosevelt and Expansionism," *Times Literary Supplement*, March 8, 2002, p. 17.

79. Foster Rea Dulles, *The Imperial Years* (New York, 1956), pp. 190–91.

80. Archibald Cary Coolidge, *The United States as a World Power* (New York, 1908), p. 130.

81. Leonard Wood to Theodore Roosevelt, October 28, 1901, Leonard Wood Papers, Manuscript Division, Library of Congress.

82. Máximo Gómez to Sotero Figueroa, May 8, 1901, in *Papeles dominicanos de Máximo Gómez*, ed. Emilio Rodríguez (Ciudad Trujillo, 1954), pp. 396–97; *Patria*, March 19, 1901, p. 2.

83. *Atlanta Constitution*, January 3, 1901, p. 4; *St. Louis Globe-Democrat*, in *Literary Digest* 22 (February 16, 1901): 183.

84. Elihu Root to Andrew Carnegie, March 20, 1920, Jessup Papers.

85. *Congressional Record*, April 18, 1902, 57th Congress, 1st session, Appendix, p. 183.

86. William McKinley, "Annual Message of the President," December 5, 1899, in U.S. Congress, House of Representatives, *Papers Relating to the Foreign Relations of the United States*, 56th Congress, 1st session, Document 1 (Washington, D.C., 1901), p. xxix.

87. *Congressional Record*, April 17, 1902, 57th Congress, 1st session, Appendix, p. 206.

88. James H. Wilson to Joseph Benson Foraker, May 12, 1899, General Correspondence, James H. Wilson Papers, Manuscript Division, Library of Congress.

89. Herbert Squiers to John Hay, October 9, 1902, Despatches of U.S. Ministers to Cuba, 1902–1906, General Records of the Department of State, Record Group 59, National Archives. (Hereinafter cited as DS/RG 59.)

90. Herbert Squiers to John Hay, October 23, 1902, DS/RG 59.

91. U.S. Congress, Senate, *Hearings on Cuban Reciprocity: Statement of General Bliss Before Senator Cullom*, December 19, 1902, 58th Congress, 1st session, Senate Document No. 2 (Washington, D.C., 1903), p. 7.

92. *Havana Daily Telegraph*, May 23, 1905, p. 1.

93. The offers of territory for the establishment of a U.S. naval station, President Theodore Roosevelt proclaimed, were an instance in which Cuba was "loyally observing her obligations to us." Cuban participation in World War I on the side of the allies was represented as a gesture in discharge of the obligations incurred to the United States in 1898. "The United States came to the aid of Cuba in her great struggle for liberty in 1898," pronounced Ambassador Noble Judah in 1929. "Twenty years later Cuba repaid her debt when the United States entered the World War." See Theodore Roosevelt, *Message of the President of the United States Communicated to the Two Houses of Congress*, November 10, 1903, U.S. Congress, House of Representatives, 58th Congress, 1st session, Document No. 1 (Washington, D.C., 1903), p. 2; "Ambassador Judah's

Address at Maine Memorial Exercises," February 15, 1929, 837.413/M28–34, DS/RG 59; Noble Brandon Judah, "Diary of My Stay in Cuba," February 15, 1929, Noble Brandon Judah Papers, Manuscript Division, Library of Congress.

94. *Havana Post*, December 8, 1900, p. 2.

95. Ibid., July 13, 1900, p. 2.

96. Ibid., June 28, 1916, p. 4.

97. Ibid., September 18, 1920, p. 4.

98. *New York Times*, May 17, 1912, p. 1.

99. Ibid., May 13, 1913, p. 3.

100. "Address of Gen. John J. Garrity, Commander in Chief, United Spanish War Veterans," October 8, 1928, in U.S. Congress, House of Representatives, *Proceedings of the Stated Convention of the 30th National Encampment, United Spanish War Veterans*, October 7–11, 1928, 70th Congress, 2nd session, House Document No. 387 (Washington, D.C., 1929), p. 57.

101. U.S. Congress, House of Representatives, *Proceedings of the Stated Convention of the 46th National Encampment, United Spanish War Veterans*, August 13–17, 1944, 78th Congress, 2nd session, House Document No. 685 (Washington, D.C., 1944), p. 150.

102. John Kendrick Bangs, *Uncle Sam Trustee* (New York, 1902), p. 342.

103. Woodrow Wilson to Rafael Conte, May 8, 1916, Series 4, File 97, Woodrow Wilson Papers, Manuscript Division, Library of Congress. Almost all U.S. diplomatic officials who served in Cuba were formed by the same history. "Cuban independence and sovereignty," Ambassador Spruille Braden wrote, "in large part were won and have been and are preserved by the United States." Ambassador Ellis Briggs declared outright that "it was the United States that freed Cuba from Spain in 1898." Ambassador Harry Guggenheim insisted that the "American intervention gave to Cuba its independence," from which he made the obligatory inference, "We then felt a moral responsibility for the new State which we had brought into being." See Spruille Braden, "Memorandum for Policy Committee on Conditions in Cuba and Our Policies in Respect Thereto," August 1, 1944, Spruille Braden Papers, Rare Book and Manuscript Library, Butler Library, Columbia University, New York, N.Y.; Ellis O. Briggs, *Anatomy of Diplomacy: The Origin and Execution of American Foreign Policy* (New York, 1968), p. 186; Harry F. Guggenheim, *The United States and Cuba* (New York, 1934), pp. 45–46, 243.

104. Harry S. Truman, "Address Before a Joint Session of the Congress in Observance of the 50th Anniversary of Cuban Independence," April 19, 1948, in *Public Papers of the Presidents of the United States: Harry S. Truman, 1948* (Washington, D.C., 1964), p. 225; *Washington Post*, April 27, 1948, p. 12.

105. Marion W. Boggs, "Memorandum of Discussion at the 435th Meeting of the National Security Council," February 18, 1960, in U.S. Department of State, *Foreign Relations of the United States: Cuba, 1958–1960* (Washington, D.C., 1991), p. 792. (Hereinafter cited as *FRUS:1958–1960*.)

106. *Congressional Record*, June 30, 1902, 57th Congress, 2nd session, vol. 35, pt. pp. 7641, 7643.

107. Ibid., March 2, 1896, 54th Congress, 1st session, vol. 28, pt. 3, p. 2350.

108. Earl E. T. Smith, *The Fourth Floor: An Account of the Castro Communist Revolution* (New York, 1962), p. 23; Lynn-Darrell Bender, *Cuba vs. United States: The Politics of Hostility*, 2nd ed. (Hato Rey, Puerto Rico, 1981), p. 2; Irving Peter Pflaum, *Tragic Island: How Communism Came to Cuba* (Englewood Cliffs, N.J., 1961), p. x.

109. U.S. Congress, Senate, *Hearings Before the Subcommittee to Investigate the Administration of the International Security Act and Other Internal Security Laws of the Committee of the Judiciary: Communist Threat to the United States Through the Caribbean*, 86th Congress, 2nd session (Washington, D.C., 1960), pt. 9, p. 16.

110. Sumner Welles, *Relations Between the United States and Cuba* (Washington, D.C., 1934), p. 2; Harry S. Truman, "Address Before a Joint Session of the Congress in Observance of the 50th Anniversary of Cuban Independence," April 19, 1948, in *Public Papers of the Presidents of the United States: Harry S. Truman, 1948*, p. 225; *Washington Post*, April 27, 1948, p. 12; Smith, *Fourth Floor*, p. 23.

111. Kenneth N. Skoug Jr., *The United States and Cuba under Reagan and Shultz: A Foreign Service Officer Reports* (Westport, Conn., 1996), p. 1.

112. Marian M. George, *A Little Journey to Cuba and Puerto Rico*, rev. ed. (Chicago, 1930), pp. 7, 79–80.

113. C. H. Forbes-Lindsay, *Cuba and Her People of To-Day* (Boston, 1911), p. 87; Henry Albert Phillips, *White Elephants in the Caribbean* (New York, 1936), p. 129.

114. Olive G. Gibson, *The Isle of a Hundred Harbors* (Boston, 1940), p. 176; Henry W. Wack, "Cuba and West Indies Winter Charm," *Arts and Decoration*, February 1931, p. 53; Hyatt Verrill, *Cuba of Today* (New York, 1931), pp. 157–58.

115. Caspar Whitney, "Cuba Fulfilling Its Promise," *Collier's*, July 2, 1910, p. 20.

116. *Havana Post*, May 3, 1916, p. 4.

117. Ibid., March 29, 1921, p. 1.

118. Ibid., May 18, 1920, p. 10.

119. Francis R. Stewart to Secretary of State, December 16, 1924, 837.413T26/7, DS/RG 59.

120. Philip S. Marden, *Sailing South* (Boston, 1921), p. 34. See also U.S. Congress, Senate, *Dedicatory Ceremonies at Santiago de Cuba*, 59th Congress, 1st session, Document No. 157 (Washington, D.C., 1906), pp. 2–11.

121. A copy of General Pershing's speech was enclosed in John Pershing to Secretary of State, n.d., John Pershing Papers, Manuscript Division, Library of Congress. "The Cuban people," President Alfredo Zayas responded to Pershing's comments, "like all beings inspired by loyal and noble sentiments, must be eternally grateful to the United States." See *La Lucha*, March 9, 1945, p. 4. The most complete accounts of the construction and dedication of the *Maine* monument can be found in Emeterio S. Santovenia,

Libro conmemorativo de la inauguración del Maine en La Habana (Havana, 1928), and Felipa Suárez Ramos, *U.S. Maine en la memoria habanera* (Havana, 1995).

122. *Havana Post*, March 9, 1925, p. 9. "Grateful Cubans erected this monument," Melville Bell Grosvenor commented in *National Geographic* twenty years later. See Melville Bell Grosvenor, "Cuba—American Sugar Bowl," *National Geographic*, January 1947, p. 2. In February 1998, on the occasion of the centennial of the explosion of the *Maine*, the *New York Times* described the memorial as an expression of Cuban "gratitude for the United States role in the struggle for independence." See *New York Times*, February 14, 1998, p. A4.

123. "Address of Capt. W. T. Cluverius, United States Navy, on the Occasion of the Unveiling of the Tablet on the 'Maine' Monument at Habana, Cuba," February 15, 1926, in U.S. Congress, House of Representatives, *Proceedings: 28th National Encampment, United Spanish War Veterans*, August 15–18, 1926, 69th Congress, 2nd session, House Document No. 550 (Washington, D.C., 1927), p. 305.

124. For details on the Rowan bust see Ellis O. Briggs, *Farewell to Foggy Bottom: The Recollections of a Career Diplomat* (New York, 1964), pp. 252–53.

125. *New York Times*, February 16, 1929, p. 3.

126. Ibid., February 16, 1930, p. 31.

127. Grosvenor, "Cuba—American Sugar Bowl," p. 2. The last commemoration of the *Maine* was observed in February 1958, on the occasion of the sixtieth anniversary. Reported the *New York Times* in a brief back-page news item, "Five gray-haired United States veterans stood in solemn tribute to their comrades who fought and fell in the Spanish-American War, launched sixty years ago with the cry 'Remember the *Maine*.'" The American-owned *Havana Post* also took note of the occasion. "Hardly anybody remembered the 'Maine' in Havana yesterday," one staff writer of the *Post* lamented the following day. "Yesterday was a landmark for Cubans and for Americans, yet it passed virtually unnoticed. Up to only ten years ago, the occasion was honored each year with parades, speeches, music—the full panoply with which peoples honor the great events in their histories. Today this is no more. Why?" See *New York Times*, February 16, 1958, p. 30; *Havana Post*, February 16, 1958, p. 1.

128. See Ruby Hart Phillips, "New Regime Planning to Develop Special Resort Areas for the Tourist Trade," *New York Times*, April 13, 1952, p. 3.

129. Cuban Tourist Commission, *Havana Weekly*, February 19, 1938, p. 10.

130. Consuelo Hermer and Marjorie May, *Havana Mañana: A Guide to Cuba and the Cubans* (New York, 1941), p. 94.

131. *Washington Evening Star*, January 29, 1909, p. 5.

132. Eduardo Abril Amores, *Bajo la garra* (Santiago de Cuba, 1922), p. 155.

133. Jorge Mañach, "Revolution in Cuba," *Foreign Affairs* 12 (October 1933): 50–51. See also Jorge Mañach, *Pasado vigente* (Havana, 1939), p. 18.

134. Rafael A. Cisneros, *La danza de los millones* (Hamburg, 1923), p. 316; Pedro José

Cohucelo, *Apostado de amor* (Havana, 1925), p. 300; Ofelia Rodríguez Acosta, *Sonata interrumpida* (Mexico City, 1943), p. 117.

135. Edward I. Nathan to Secretary of State, May 11, 1928, 837.413/31, DS/RG 59.

136. *Diario de Cuba*, May 10, 1928, p. 1. "The pages of the [bronze] book," Colonel José González Valdés, the local provincial commander, explained to the U.S. consul, "will be inscribed with the names of the Cuban soldiers who fell side by side with the American officers and soldiers at the glorious engagement on San Juan Hill, thus saving their names from oblivion in an identical form with that which the United States has adopted for the memory of their heroes in said battle. We wish history to perpetuate equally the names of the North Americans and Cubans who died there." See José González Valdés to Francis R. Stewart, March 18, 1927, 837.413/6, DS/RG 59.

137. The weekly tourist guide *Havana Weekly* in 1938 described the battle sites around Santiago de Cuba "made famous during the Spanish-American War." Ten years later, the same publication described the sites "that perpetuate the principal events of the Spanish-Cuban-American War." See *Havana Weekly*, February 19, 1938, p. 23, and February 26, 1949, p. 23.

138. Duvon C. Corbitt to Dean Acheson, March 8, 1949, 837.415/3-849, DS/RG 59.

139. Portell Vilá, *Historia de la guerra de Cuba y los Estados Unidos contra España*, p. ii.

140. Emilio Roig de Leuchsenring, *Cuba no debe su independencia a los Estados Unidos* (Havana, 1950), p. 153. Roig de Leuchsenring was a prodigious scholar, and virtually the full weight of his scholarship was dedicated to advancing the principal tenets of revisionist historiography. His other works include *Cuba y los Estados Unidos, 1805–1898* (Havana, 1949); *Los Estados Unidos contra Cuba Libre* (Havana, n.d.); *La guerra hispano-cubanoamericana fué ganada por el lugarteniente general del Ejército Libertador* (Havana, 1952); *Por su propio esfuerzo conquistó el pueblo cubano su independencia* (Havana, 1957); *1895 y 1898. Dos guerras cubanas. Ensayo de revaloración* (Havana, 1945). For a general discussion of revisionist historiography in Cuba see Duvon C. Corbitt, "Cuban Revisionist Interpretations of Cuba's Struggle for Independence," *Hispanic American Historical Review* 32 (August 1963): 395–404.

141. R. Henry Norweb to Secretary of State, March 18, 1948, 837.415/3-1848, DS/RG 59.

142. U.S. Department of State, "Policy Statement: Cuba," January 11, 1951, 611.37/1-1151, DS/RG 59.

143. Agustín Tamargo, "Quien injuria a Martí y a Maceo no puede ser amigo de Cuba," *Bohemia*, August 26, 1956, pp. 49–50.

144. "Manifesto-Programa del Movimiento 26 de Julio," *Humanismo* 7 (November–December 1958): 14.

145. *Revolución*, January 5, 1959, p. 4.

146. Ibid., February 25, 1959, p. 4.

147. Ibid., April 8, 1959, p. 8.

148. Armando J. Flórez Ibarra, "La hora del deber americano," ibid., February 2, 1959, p. 2.

149. "Speech by Mr. Castro, Prime Minister of Cuba," United Nations, General Assembly, Fifteenth Session, 872nd Plenary Meeting, September 26, 1969, *Official Records*, p. 118.

150. U.S. Department of State, "U.S. Expresses Concern to Cuba Over State of Relations," *Department of State Bulletin* 41 (November 16, 1959): 715.

151. *Revolución*, November 14, 1959, p. 28. An English translation of the Cuban note appeared as a pamphlet published by the Ministry of Foreign Relations, *Cuba Replies to the U.S.A. Note: In Defense of National Sovereignty* (Havana, 1959).

152. *Revolución*, March 17, 1959, p. 2.

153. Park F. Wollam to Department of State, September 24, 1959, 611.37/9-2459, DS/RG 59. As early as January 19, 1959, Wollam reported that "the feeling about the Platt Amendment is not yet dead." See Park F. Wollam to Edward Little, January 19, 1959, 611.37/1-1959, DS/RG 59.

154. *Public Papers of the Presidents of the United States: Dwight D. Eisenhower, 1959* (Washington, D.C., n.d.), p. 271.

155. *New York Times*, November 8, 1959, p. E7.

156. *Public Papers of the Presidents of the United States: Dwight D. Eisenhower, 1960–61* (Washington, D.C., n.d.), p. 268.

157. *New York Times Book Review*, October 29, 1961, p. 22; Ruby Hart Phillips, *Cuba: Island of Paradox* (New York, 1959), p. 7.

158. "He seems to be incredibly naive about Communism or under Communist discipline," Vice-President Richard Nixon described Fidel Castro after their meeting in April 1959. See "Summary of Conversation," April 24, 1959, in *FRUS:1958–1960*, p. 476.

159. *Congressional Record*, January 25, 1960, 86th Congress, 2nd session, vol. 106, pt. 1, p. 1200; ibid., March 8, 1960, Appendix, p. A2043; ibid., February 17, 1960, Appendix, p. 1329.

160. Ibid., June 30, 1960, vol. 106, pt. 11, p. 15231. Illinois congressman O'Hara was a sixteen-year-old volunteer who served in Cuba during the war with Spain.

161. Ibid., March 10, 1960, vol. 106, pt. 4, p. 5227.

162. Ibid., June 25, 1960, vol. 106, pt. 2, p. 14385; ibid., January 25, 1961, 87th Congress, 1st session, vol. 107, pt. 1, p. 108.

163. Ibid., January 14, 1960, 86th Congress, 2nd session, vol. 106, pt. 1, p. 586.

164. Karl E. Mundt, "How Cuban Freedom Was Really Won: The Documented Facts as Against Castro's Propaganda," *Reader's Digest*, August 1960, pp. 161, 168.

165. Barry Goldwater, "Tragic Situation in Cuba," *Vital Speeches* 27 (May 1, 1961): 422–23; Barry Goldwater, *Why Not Victory?* (New York, 1962), pp. 78, 82, 88.

166. *Congressional Record*, June 30, 1960, 86th Congress, 2nd session, vol. 106, pt. 11, p. 15230.

167. Spruille Braden, *Diplomats and Demagogues: The Memoirs of Spruille Braden* (New Rochelle, N.Y., 1971), p. 429.

168. Dante Fascell, *Fascell on Cuba*, ed. Jaime Suchlicki (Miami, 2001), p. 90.

169. "White House Staff Notes," June 25, 1959, in *FRUS:1958–1960*, p. 552.

170. *Congressional Record*, January 15, 1959, 86th Congress, 2nd session, vol. 105, pt. 1, p. 690.

171. Richard E. Welch Jr., *Response to Revolution: The United States and the Cuban Revolution, 1951–1961* (Chapel Hill, 1985), p. 186.

172. Theodore Roosevelt, *Autobiography* (1913; reprint, New York, 1946), p. 504.

CHAPTER 5

1. *Congressional Globe*, January 24, 1859, 35th Congress, 2nd session, vol. 36, pt. 1, pp. 540, 543.

2. "Cuba: The Key of the Mexican Gulf," *Merchants' Magazine*, November 1849, p. 519.

3. "Destiny of the Slave States," *DeBow's Review* 17 (September 1854): 281.

4. *Congressional Globe*, February 17, 1859, 35th Congress, 2nd session, vol. 36, pt. 1, p. 1084.

5. Ibid., January 24, 1859, pp. 540, 543.

6. For accounts of U.S. emigration to Cuba early in the twentieth century see José Vega Suñol, *Presencia norteamericana en el área nororiental de Cuba: Etnicidad y cultura* (Holguín, 1991); José Vega Suñol, *Norteamericanos en Cuba* (Havana, 2004); Carmen Diana Deere, "Here Come the Yankees! The Rise and Decline of United States Colonies in Cuba, 1898–1930," *Hispanic American Historical Review* 78 (1998): 729–65.

7. *Cuban Bulletin* 2 (February 1904): 12.

8. *New York Journal*, August 16, 1898, p. 2; Pulaski F. Hyatt and John T. Hyatt, *Cuba: Its Resources and Opportunities* (New York, 1898), pp. 115–16; *New York Times*, August 3, 1898, p. 10; "Developing Oriente," *Cuba Magazine*, September 1909, pp. 4–7; George Reno, "Oriente, the California of Cuba," *Cuba Review*, August 1927, pp. 14–20; George Fortune, "'What's Doing' in Cuba for the Younger American," *Cuba Magazine*, February 1912, pp. 336–40; Thomas J. Vivian and Ruel P. Smith, *Everything about Our New Possessions* (New York, 1899), pp. 112–19; C. H. Forbes-Lindsay, "Cuba: The Land of Promise," *World To-Day*, February 1908, pp. 141–50.

9. Edward Marshall, "A Talk with General Wood," *Outlook*, July 20, 1901, p. 670; *Commercial and Financial World*, April 7, 1906, p. 10; Reno, "Oriente," pp. 14–20.

10. See *McClure's Magazine*, April 1899, p. 66.

11. "Portrait of City: Havana, Booming Playground," *Latin American Report* (New Orleans), September 1956, p. 14; Carl F. Norden interview, Association for Diplomatic

Studies and Training, U.S. Foreign Affairs Oral History Collection, 2001, Arlington, Va.; Melville Bell Grosvenor, "Cuba—American Sugar Bowl," *National Geographic*, January 1947, p. 1.

12. Joseph Hergesheimer, *San Cristóbal de La Habana* (London, 1921), p. 8.

13. Charles Rosenberg, *Jenny Lind in America* (New York, 1851), p. 130; Edward N. Tailer Diary, Manuscript Department, New-York Historical Society, New York, N.Y.; Silvia Sunshine, *Petals Plucked from Sunny Climes* (Nashville, 1880), p. 407; F. L. Oswald, "A Lost Eden—Cuba," *Forum* 27 (March 1899): 95–100; John S. Abbott, *South and North* (New York, 1860), p. 52; William Henry Hurlbert, *Gan-Eden; or, Pictures of Cuba* (Boston, 1854), p. vii; J. P. McEvoy, "McEvoy in Mañana-Land," *Reader's Digest*, November 1951, pp. 49–52.

14. *Havana Post*, July 3, 1925, p. 4; Nina Hawkins, "Some Glimpses of Cuba," *Havana Post*, January 6, 1924, p. 8; Olive G. Gibson, *The Isle of a Hundred Harbors* (Boston, 1940), p. 17; *Miami Herald*, January 9, 1958, p. 1; *Havana Post*, February 19, 1930, p. 5.

15. *Havana Post*, December 14, 1930, p. 11; *Fortune*, November 1933, p. 46; Norval Richardson, *My Diplomatic Education* (New York, 1923), p. 32; Idaless Westly, "What I Found in Cuba," *Havana Post*, August 29, 1921, p. 4.

16. *Havana Post*, January 17, 1930, p. 5.

17. Ava Gardner, *My Story* (New York, 1990), p. 161.

18. Ruby Hart Phillips, *Cuba, Island of Paradox* (New York, 1959), p. 283; *Miami Herald*, January 1, 1920, p. 11; *Times of Havana*, January 16, 1958, p. 9; William Seymour Edwards, *On the Mexican Highlands, with a Passing Glimpse of Cuba* (Cincinnati, 1906), p. 265; David Atlee Phillips, *The Night Watch* (New York, 1977), p. 60; *Latin American Report* (New Orleans), September 1956, p. 15; *Times of Havana*, April 4, 1959, p. 9.

19. *Anuario Azucarero, 1942* (Havana, 1943), p. 149.

20. Graham Greene, *Ways of Escape* (New York, 1980), p. 248; Lester Velie, "Suckers in Paradise," *Saturday Evening Post*, March 28, 1953, pp. 32–33.

21. Hergesheimer, *San Cristóbal de La Habana*, pp. 105, 142.

22. Sydney A. Clark, *Cuban Tapestry* (New York, 1936), p. 98.

23. Nina Wilcox Putnam, "To Havana with the Fly by Night Club," *Travel*, February 1947, p. 30.

24. *Havana Post*, November 2, 1918, p. 4.

25. Arthur Gardner to Henry F. Holland, January 13, 1956, Lat File 570295, Confidential U.S. Department of State Central Files, Cuba, Internal Affairs, 1955–1958, General Records of the Department of State, Record Group 59, National Archives, Washington, D.C. (Hereinafter cited as DS/RG 59.)

26. *Havana Post*, September 19, 1925, p. 5.

27. Velie, "Suckers in Paradise," pp. 32–33; "Cuba: A Game of Casino," *Time*, January 20, 1958, p. 32; *Time*, April 21, 1952, p. 38; Ernest Havermann, "Mobsters Move in on Troubled Havana and Split Rich Gambling Profits with Batista," *Life*, March 10, 1958,

p. 34; Hugh Bradley, *Havana: Cinderella's City* (Garden City, N.Y., 1941), p. 415; *Havana Post*, January 19, 1956, p. 2; W. Adolphe Roberts, *Lands of the Inner Sea* (New York, 1948), p. 19.

28. Enrique C. Canova, "Cuba—The Isle of Romance," *National Geographic*, September 1933, p. 345.

29. Consuelo Hermer and Marjorie May, *Havana Mañana: A Guide to Cuba and the Cubans* (New York, 1941), pp. 3–4.

30. "Portrait of a City," p. 15; Georgie Anne Geyer, *Guerrilla Prince* (New York, 1991), p. 46; Andrei Codrescu, "Picking the Flowers of the Revolution," *New York Times Magazine*, February 1, 1998, p. 35; Thomas Freeman, *The Crisis in Cuba* (Derby, Conn., 1963), p. 40.

31. John Sayles, *Los Gusanos* (New York, 1991), p. 420.

32. See <http://www.styleant.com/category/3>. Emphasis in original.

33. See <http://www.nextag.com/Yves-Saint-Laurent>.

34. See <http://www.fragrancex.com/products>.

35. See <http://www.scentsandsprays.com/havana.html>.

36. See <http://www.bevnet.com/reviews/havananana>.

37. See <http://www.kiniki.com> and <http://www.exoticcloset.com>.

38. See <http://www.everythingfurniture.com>.

39. See <http://www.target.com>.

40. See <http://www.kohls.com/products>.

41. See <http://www.elpasochile.com>.

42. Harold D. Lasswell, "The Relation of Ideological Intelligence to Public Policy," *Ethics* 53 (October 1942): 30.

43. J. Merle Davis, *The Cuban Church in a Sugar Economy* (New York, 1942), p. 36.

44. R. Henry Norweb to Secretary of State, January 14, 1946, 837.00/1-446; R. Henry Norweb to Secretary of State, September 12, 1946, 711.37/9-1246, DS/RG 59.

45. Ellis O. Briggs, "Memorandum of a Telephone Conversation," June 25, 1947, 837.61351/6-2547, DS/RG 59.

46. H. Bartelett Wells, "A Study in Cuban-American Relations: Some Causes of Tension and Suggested Approaches," September 8, 1947, 711.37/9-847, DS/RG 59; James N. Cortada, "Component Elements of Cuban Temperament," February 4, 1948, 837.50/2-948, DS/RG 59.

47. Fidel Castro, *Pensamiento de Fidel Castro: Selección temática*, 2 vols. (Havana, 1983), 1:5, 7.

48. Philip Bonsal to Department of State, April 15, 1959, in U.S. Department of State, *Foreign Relations of the United States, 1958–1960* (Washington, D.C., 1991), p. 466. (Hereinafter cited as *FRUS:1958–1960*.)

49. Philip W. Bonsal, "Cuba, Castro and the United States," *Foreign Affairs* 45 (January 1967): 267.

50. As recounted by Representative Barratt O'Hara in the *Congressional Record*, February 18, 1959, 86th Congress, 1st session, vol. 105, pt. 2, p. 2586.

51. "Speech by Mr. Castro, Prime Minister of Cuba," United Nations, General Assembly, Fifteenth Session, 872nd Plenary Meeting, September 26, 1969, *Official Records*, p. 120.

52. "Memorandum of a Conversation, Department of State, Washing, DC," September 18, 1959, in *FRUS:1958–1960*, p. 605. Ambassador Earl E. T. Smith later recalled officials in Washington in 1958 as fully confident "that they would be able to control Castro." See Earl E. T. Smith, *The Fourth Floor: An Account of the Castro Communist Revolution* (New York, 1962), p. 158.

53. "Diary Entry by Senator Allen J. Ellender," December 14, 1958, in *FRUS:1958–1960*, p. 288; *Congressional Record*, February 18, 1959, 86th Congress, 1st session, vol. 105, pt. 2, p. 2585.

54. Philip Bonsal to Secretary of State, November 27, 1959, 611.37/11-2759, DS/RG 59.

55. Drew Pearson, "Castro's Stand on Russia Cited," *Washington Post*, April 17, 1959, p. B-11.

56. *Congressional Record*, February 9, 1959, 86th Congress, 1st session, vol. 105, pt. 2, pp. 2151–52.

57. "Memorandum of a Conversation," June 24, 1959, in *FRUS:1958–1960*, p. 540.

58. See John Correll interview, Association for Diplomatic Studies and Training, U.S. Foreign Affairs Oral History Collection.

59. *Congressional Record*, January 22, 1960, 86th Congress, 2nd session, vol. 106, pt. 1, p. 1100; Tad Szulc, "As Castro Speaks: 'The Wall!' 'The Wall!'" *New York Times Magazine*, December 13, 1959, p. SM 84; George E. Sokolsky, "Fidel Castro," *Washington Post*, April 20, 1959, p. A-13.

60. Edwin Tetlow, *Eye on Cuba* (New York, 1966), pp. 33, 98.

61. S. Everett Gleason, "Memorandum of Discussion at the 396th Meeting of the National Security Council," Washington, D.C., February 12, 1959, in *FRUS:1958–1960*, p. 398. The parallels were striking: exactly sixty years earlier, Major John Logan had also suggested that Cubans had "to be guided and instructed like children." See Major John A. Logan, Provost Marshall, to Adjutant General, Department of Santa Clara, February 3, 1899, File 294/11, Records of the Bureau of Insular Affairs, Record Group 350, National Archives.

62. Teresa Casuso, *Cuba and Castro*, trans. Elmer Grossberg (New York, 1961), p. 208. For a useful overview of Fidel Castro's visit to the United States in April 1959 see Alan McPherson, "The Limits of Populist Diplomacy: Fidel Castro's April 1959 Trip to North America," *Diplomacy and Statecraft* 18 (2007): 237–68.

63. See also Richard M. Nixon, *The Memoirs of Richard Nixon* (New York, 1978), pp. 201–3. For the full text of the Nixon memorandum of his April 1959 meeting with Castro

see Jeffrey J. Safford, "The Nixon-Castro Meeting of 19 April 1959," *Diplomatic History* 4 (Fall 1980): 425–31. Nor was this the only time that the Americans imagined their relationship to Cubans as a matter of avuncular familiarity. Former assistant secretary of state for inter-American affairs Roy Rubottom reminisced years later about the final days of the government of Fulgencio Batista, musing on what could have been done to prevent the rise of Fidel Castro. "I, personally," reflected Rubottom, "might have gone down there earlier in the game and talked a little bit more like a Dutch uncle to Batista to try to get him to see the steps that he had to take if he hoped to survive personally." See "A Transcript of a Recorded Interview with R. Roy Rubottom, Jr.," June 12, 1966, John Foster Dulles Oral History Project, Princeton University Library, Princeton, N.J.

64. Robert A. Stevenson to Philip Bonsal, April 22, 1959, Philip Bonsal Papers, Manuscript Division, Library of Congress, Washington, D.C.

65. Andrew J. Goodpaster, "Memorandum of a Conference Between the President and the Acting Secretary of State," Augusta, Georgia, April 18, 1959, in *FRUS:1958–1960*, p. 475.

66. This information was conveyed to the Department of State. See William A. Wieland, "Memorandum by the Director of the Office of Mexican and Caribbean Affairs," April 21, 1959, in *FRUS:1958–1960*, p. 477.

67. Rufo López-Fresquet, *My 14 Months with Castro* (Cleveland, 1966), p. 169. Castro also indicated to an unnamed Latin America journalist after the meeting that Nixon had "reprimanded" him. Ambassador Philip Bonsal later acknowledged that "Castro's reaction to this interview was unfavorable." See William A. Wieland, "Memorandum by the Director of the Office of Mexican and Caribbean Affairs," p. 477; Philip W. Bonsal, *Cuba, Castro, and the United States* (Pittsburgh, 1971), p. 64.

68. Herbert L. Matthews, "Memorandum," August 17, 1960, Herbert L. Matthews Papers, Rare Book and Manuscript Library, Butler Library, Columbia University, New York, N.Y.

69. Castro, *Pensamiento de Fidel Castro*, 1:5. Some years later, Fidel Castro commented to Frank Mankiewicz, "No country fights for decades for its independence to have a Platt Amendment imposed upon them." See Frank Mankiewicz and Kirby Jones, *With Fidel: A Portrait of Castro and Cuba* (New York, 1975), p. 112.

70. Philip W. Bonsal to Department of State, January 19, 1960, in *FRUS:1958–1960*, p. 747; Arthur M. Schlesinger Jr., *Robert Kennedy and His Times* (Boston, 1978), p. 468.

71. Henry C. Ramsey to Gerard C. Smith, February 18, 1960, in *FRUS:1958–1960*, p. 794.

72. Sherman Kent, Office of National Estimates, Central Intelligence Agency, "Memorandum for the Director: Why the Cuban Revolution of 1958 Led to Cuba's Alignment with the USSR," February 21, 1961, <http://www.foia.cia.gov/>.

73. Barry Goldwater, *Why Not Victory?* (New York, 1962), p. 70.

74. U.S. Congress, Senate, Committee on Foreign Relations, *Study Mission in the*

Caribbean Area: Report of Senator George D. Aiken to the Committee on Foreign Relations, 85th Congress, 2nd session (Washington, D.C., 1958), pp. 1, 5.

75. Henry C. Ramsey to Gerard C. Smith, February 18, 1960, in *FRUS:1958–1960*, p. 795.

76. John C. Hill Jr., to R. Roy Rubottom Jr., December 10, 1959, in *FRUS:1958–1960*, p. 697.

77. Americans could thus congratulate themselves for their superior moral stance in 1906 for not annexing Cuba and thereupon demand appreciation from the world at large. Former secretary of state John W. Foster insisted that U.S. action served "to show to the world that we are animated by a policy of sincerity and disinterestedness." The *Independent* insisted that "by right and by might, we could have kept the island which the folly of its people had put into our hands. We have made a new record for the nations of international altruism. . . . It gives more glory to the country than the victory over Spain. It strengthens the position of the United States in the family of nations, because it gives us moral character. . . . [It] proves to [Latin American] republics that their elder sister had no selfish designs upon them. Let [them] understand what is the generous spirit of our Government." See John W. Foster, "The Annexation of Cuba," *Independent*, October 25, 1906, p. 966; "One More Chance for Cuba," *Independent*, October 4, 1906, pp. 826–27.

78. Spruille Braden, "Memorandum for Policy Committee on Conditions in Cuba and Our Policies in Respect Thereto," August 1, 1944, Spruille Braden Papers, Rare Book and Manuscript Library, Butler Library, Columbia University.

79. Whitelaw Reid, "The Territory with Which We Are Threatened," *Century*, September 1898, p. 789.

80. Leonard Wood, "The Present Situation in Cuba," *Century*, August 1899, p. 640.

81. Leonard Wood to Theodore Roosevelt, October 28, 1901; Leonard Wood to Elihu Root, October 22, 1901, Leonard Wood Papers, Manuscript Division, Library of Congress.

82. Enoch Crowder to Frank Steinhart, April 16, 1920, Enoch Crowder Papers, Correspondence, File 226, Western Historical Manuscript Collection, University of Missouri, Columbia.

83. George W. Ball, "JFK's Big Moment," *New York Review of Books*, February 13, 1992, p. 16.

84. Barry Goldwater, "Tragic Situation in Cuba," *Vital Speeches* 27 (May 1, 1961): 422–23.

85. *Congressional Record*, February 25, 1960, 86th Congress, 2nd session, vol. 106, pt. 3, p. 3452.

86. Ibid., January 4, 1961, 87th Congress, 1st session, vol. 107, pt. 1, p. 108.

87. Ibid., January 22, 1960, 86th Congress, 2nd session, vol. 106, pt. 1, p. 1100.

88. Bonsal, *Cuba, Castro, and the United States*, p. 196.

89. Dean Rusk, *As I Saw It* (New York, 1990), p. 230.

90. W. W. Rostow, *The Diffusion of Power* (New York, 1972), p. 211.

91. Freeman, *Crisis in Cuba*, p. 102.

92. Theodore Draper, *Castroism: Theory and Practice* (New York, 1965), p. 237. Cuba aroused American emotions on a scale rarely ever seen. Under-Secretary David Newsom made a similar point if in slightly different terms: "Few issues are as emotionally charged in American foreign policy as those relating to Cuba." Wayne Smith agreed: "Emotion is the enemy of pragmatism in Cuban relations. Cuba excites American passions as do few other foreign-policy issues." And Smith at another point said, "Cuba is a peculiarly emotional issue in the United States; clear analysis is at a premium." See David D. Newsom, *The Soviet Brigade in Cuba: A Study in Political Diplomacy* (Bloomington, 1987), p. 10; Wayne S. Smith, *The Closest of Enemies: A Personal and Diplomatic Account of U.S.-Cuban Relations since 1957* (New York, 1987), p. 280; Wayne S. Smith, foreword to *The Cuban Threat*, by Carla Anne Robbins (New York, 1983), p. xii.

93. Daniel James, *Cuba, the First Soviet Satellite in the Americas* (New York, 1961), p. 15. The personal turned political. Deputy director of the Central Intelligence Agency Richard Bissell attributed to the Kennedy administration an "obsession with Cuba" related to the determination "to avenge their personal embarrassment." Former deputy under-secretary of state U. Alexis Johnson later remembered President John F. Kennedy feeling "personally humiliated by a communist Cuba, and toppling Castro became something of an obsession for him." Walt Rostow also wrote of the "obsession with Cuba" that overtook the Kennedy administration. See Richard M. Bissell, *Reflections of a Cold Warrior: From Yalta to the Bay of Pigs* (New Haven, 1996), p. 201; U. Alexis Johnson, *The Right Hand of Power* (Englewood Cliffs, N.J., 1984), pp. 329, 343; Rostow, *Diffusion of Power*, p. 211.

94. *Congressional Record*, June 30, 1960, 86th Congress, 2nd session, vol. 106, part 11, p. 15245.

95. Bob Casey to John F. Kennedy, July 28, 1961, ibid., August 3, 1961, 87th Congress, 1st session, vol. 107, part 24, p. 14554.

96. Chester Bowles, "Notes on the Cuban Crisis," May 1961, Box 392, Folder 154, Chester Bowles Papers, Manuscript and Archives, Yale University Library, New Haven, Conn.

97. Richard N. Goodwin, *Remembering America: A Voice from the Sixties* (Boston, 1988), p. 180.

98. George Clarke Musgrave, *Under Three Flags in Cuba: A Personal Account of the Cuban Insurrection and Spanish-American War* (Boston, 1899), p. 283.

99. Herbert L. Matthews, *The Cuban Story* (New York, 1961), pp. 135–36.

100. Hugh Thomas, *Cuba: The Pursuit of Freedom* (New York, 1971), p. 1208.

101. Robert J. Alexander, "Contradictions of the Castro Regime," *Liberation*, April 1960, pp. 9, 11.

102. *New York Times*, June 25, 1960, p. 26; January 22, 1961, p. SM-8.

103. Harold H. Martin, "Cuba: State of Confusion," *Saturday Evening Post*, March 26, 1960, p. 35.

104. Irving P. Pflaum, "Fidel of Cuba: Portrait of a Controversy," *American Universities Field Staff Reports Service* 5 (August 1960): 18.

105. Smith, *Fourth Floor*, pp. 230, 232.

106. "Memorandum of Discussion at the Department of State–Joint Chiefs of Staff Meeting," January 6, 1960, in *FRUS:1958–1960*, p. 732.

107. Herbert L. Matthews, "Memorandum," March 15, 1960, Matthews Papers. Matthews later reflected on "how slow the United States was to grasp the essence of what was happening." See Matthews, *Cuban Story*, p. 90.

108. By mid-1960, Secretary of the Treasury Robert Anderson conceded that "Castro is an intelligent man." See "Memorandum of a Conference, Department of State," June 27, 1960, in *FRUS:1958–1960*, p. 959.

109. George E. Sokolsky, "Four Areas of Crisis," *Washington Post*, April 6, 1959, p. 13; Nathaniel Weyl, *Red Star over Cuba* (New York, 1960), p. 8; Edwin C. Stein, *Cuba, Castro, and Communism* (New York, 1962), p. 25.

110. Tetlow, *Eye on Cuba*, p. 26. Nathaniel Weyl provided a slightly different version of this story, whereby Fidel Castro was said to have crashed his bicycle purposefully into a wall, after which there was "some reason to suspect" that he suffered brain damage. See Weyl, *Red Star over Cuba*, pp. 44–45.

111. Carlos Hall to Hugh S. Cumming Jr., November 18, 1958, in *FRUS:1958–1960*, p. 672; Lloyd A. Free, "The Cuban Situation," April 13, 1960, ibid., p. 891; J. G. Rusnak to Lyndon B. Johnson, November 18, 1959, 1959 Subject Files, Foreign Relations: Cuba, Lyndon B. Johnson Papers, University of Texas, Austin; Philip Bonsal to the Department of State, November 6, 1959, in *FRUS:1958–1960*, p. 658; Major John S. D. Eisenhower, "Memorandum," October 27, 1959, ibid., p. 645; "Memorandum of a Conference with the President, White House, Washington, D.C.," January 25, 1960, ibid., pp. 763–64; Dwight D. Eisenhower, *Waging Peace, 1956–1961* (Garden City, N.Y., 1965), p. 524.

112. Sherman Kent, Office of National Estimates, Central Intelligence Agency, "Memorandum for the Director: Why the Cuban Revolution of 1958 Led to Cuba's Alignment with the USSR," February 21, 1961, <http://www.foia.cia.gov/>.

113. Psychologist Leon Festinger posited three ways to reduce and/or eliminate cognitive dissonance: (1) "by changing one's own opinion, so that it corresponds more closely with one's knowledge of what others believe"; (2) "to influence those persons who disagree to change their opinion so that it more closely corresponds to one's own"; and (3) "to make the other person, in some manner, not comparable to oneself . . . [whereby] one can attribute different characteristics, experiences, or motives to the other person . . . or even reject him and derogate him." See Leon Festinger, *A Theory of Cognitive Dissonance*, 2nd ed. (Stanford, 1962), p. 182.

114. Matthews, *Cuban Story*, p. 273.

115. Rusk, *As I Saw It*, pp. 210–11; Kenneth N. Skoug Jr., *Cuba's Growing Crisis*, U.S. Department of State, Bureau of Public Affairs, Current Policy No. 976 (Washington, D.C., 1987), p. 4.

116. "Interview with Walter Cronkite," n.d. [ca. 2005] National Security Archives, George Washington University, <http://www.gwu.edu/~nsarchiv/coldwar/interview/episode-10/cronkite1.html>.

117. David D. Burks, *Cuba under Castro* (New York, 1964), p. 3.

118. Smith, *Closest of Enemies*, p. 280.

119. *Congressional Record*, February 25, 1960, 86th Congress, 2nd session, vol. 106, pt. 3, p. 3451.

120. José Soler Puig, *En el año de enero* (Havana, 1963), p. 162.

121. *New York Times*, August 27, 1960, p. 6.

122. Grayston L. Lynch, *Decision for Disaster: Betrayal at the Bay of Pigs* (Washington, D.C., 1998), p. 13.

123. Rusk, *As I Saw It*, pp. 210–11; Skoug, *Cuba's Growing Crisis*, p. 4; "Memorandum of Discussion of 432nd Meeting of the National Security Council, Washington, D.C.," January 14, 1960, in *FRUS:1958–1960*, p. 742. See also Philip W. Bonsal to R. Roy Rubottom Jr., August 6, 1960, Bonsal Papers.

124. John A. McCone, "Memorandum of Meeting with President Kennedy," August 23, 1962, in U.S. Department of State, *Foreign Relations of the United States, 1961–1963* (Washington, D.C., 1997), p. 955.

125. American Security Council, *Peace and Freedom: Guidelines for Cold War Victory* (Chicago, 1964), p. 49.

126. Kenneth N. Skoug Jr., *A Spotlight on Cuba*, October 22, 1986, U.S. Department of State, Bureau of Public Affairs, Current Policy No. 881 (Washington, D.C., 1986), p. 1; Kenneth N. Skoug Jr., *Cuba: "Our Last Adversary,"* May 13, 1988, U.S. Department of State, Bureau of Public Affairs, Current Policy No. 1085 (Washington, D.C., 1988), p. 2.

127. Freeman, *Crisis in Cuba*, p. 141; Alexander A. L. Klieforth interview, Association for Diplomatic Studies and Training, U.S. Foreign Affairs Oral History Collection; U.S. Department of State, Bureau of Public Affairs, *Cuba* (Washington, D.C., 1961), pp. 2, 36.

128. Weyl, *Red Star over Cuba*, p. 33; Adolf A. Berle, "The Communist Invasion of Latin America," *Reporter*, July 7, 1960, p. 23; Jay Mallin, *Fortress Cuba: Russia's American Base* (Chicago, 1965), p. 178; Ellis O. Briggs, *Anatomy of Diplomacy: The Origin and Execution of American Foreign Policy* (New York, 1968), p. 161.

129. For informative accounts of Cold War metaphors see Paul A. Chilton, *Security Metaphors: Cold War Discourse from Containment to Common House* (New York, 1996); Richard B. Gregg, "Embodied Meaning in American Public Discourse during the Cold War," in *Metaphorical World Politics*, ed. Francis A. Beer and Christ'l De Lundtsheer

(East Lansing, 2004), pp. 59–73; Robert L. Vie, "Metaphor and the Rhetorical Invention of Cold War 'Idealists,'" in *Readings in Rhetorical Criticism*, ed. Carl R. Burgchardt (State College, Pa., 1995), pp. 357–64.

130. Stein, *Cuba, Castro, and Communism*, p. 174. The metaphor took hold. Senator Kenneth Keating depicted Cuba "as an aircraft carrier off our shores," an image— "Cuba, 90 miles away from Florida, is an aircraft carrier for the Soviets"—that Timothy Naftali repeated in the Adriana Bosch film *Fidel* (2005). See *Congressional Record*, January 22, 1960, 86th Congress, 2nd session, vol. 106, pt. 1, p. 1100.

131. Robert C. Hill, "Confidential Report and Suggestions on Latin America," enclosure with Robert C. Hill to Robert Kennedy, December 14, 1960, Robert C. Hill Papers, Rauner Special Collections Library, Dartmouth College, Hanover, N.H.

132. Goldwater, *Why Not Victory?*, p. 84.

133. Richard M. Nixon, "Cuba, Castro and John F. Kennedy," *Reader's Digest*, November 1964, pp. 283, 300; *New York Times*, April 21, 1963, pp. 1, 62.

134. Robert A. Hurwitch, *Most of Myself: An Autobiography in the Form of Letters to His Daughters*, 2 vols. (Santo Domingo, Dominican Republic, 1990–92), 2:112.

135. Lynch, *Decision for Disaster*, p. 13.

136. Stein, *Cuba, Castro, and Communism*, pp. 171, 175.

137. Paul H. Nitze, *From Hiroshima to Glasnost: At the Center of Decision. A Memoir* (New York, 1989), p. 182; Skoug, *Cuba's Growing Crisis*, p. 4.

138. J. G. Rusnak to Lyndon B. Johnson, November 18, 1959, 1959 Subject Files, Foreign Relations: Cuba, Johnson Papers; J. William Fulbright to President John F. Kennedy, March 29, 1961, Box 38, Folder 1, J. William Fulbright Papers, Special Collections Division, University of Arkansas Libraries, Fayetteville. Mario Lazo countered the metaphor, saying that Cuba was indeed a "dagger in the heart." See Mario Lazo, *Dagger in the Heart: American Policy Failures in Cuba* (New York, 1968).

139. Weyl, *Red Star over Cuba*, p. 213.

140. American Security Council, *Peace and Freedom*, p. 48.

141. George Ball, "Principles of our Policy toward Cuba," *Department of State Bulletin* 50 (May 11, 1964): 740.

142. Adlai E. Stevenson, "Our Plight in Latin America," 1960, in *The Papers of Adlai E. Stevenson*, 8 vols., ed. Walter Johnson (Boston, 1977), 7:439.

143. *New York Times*, April 23, 1961, p. B3. *New York Times* columnist Anthony Lewis, on the other hand, mocked the U.S. travel ban to Cuba as an effort "to isolate us from the Castro virus." See Anthony Lewis, "Big Brother Says No," *New York Times*, September 17, 1984, p. A19.

144. Susan Sontag, *Illness as Metaphor* (New York, 1988), pp. 82–83, 85.

145. Edwin Black, "The Second Persona," in Burgchardt, *Readings in Rhetorical Criticism*, p. 195. See also Andreas Musolff, "Ideological Functions of Metaphor: The Conceptual Metaphors of *Health* and *Illness* in Public Discourse," in *Cognitive Models in*

Language and Thought, ed. René Dirven, Roslyn Frank, and Martin Pütz (Berlin/New York, 2003), pp. 327–52.

146. As early as February 1958, the U.S. consulate in Santiago de Cuba characterized Fidel Castro as having "grown from an annoying thorn in the side of the Batista Government to a slowly spreading cancerous tumor." See Oscar H. Guerra to Department of State, February 21, 1958, in *FRUS:1958–1960*, p. 33.

147. *New York Times*, May 5, 1961, p. 28.

148. Richard M. Nixon, *Six Crises* (Garden City, N.Y., 1962), p. 352; *New York Times*, November 8, 1962, p. 18.

149. *New York Times*, October 7, 1960, p. 20.

150. Ibid., October 14, 1964, p. 28.

151. *Congressional Record*, January 22, 1960, 86th Congress, 2nd session, vol. 106, pt. 1, p. 1100.

152. *New York Times*, October 21, 1960, p. 5.

153. Nitze, *From Hiroshima to Glasnost*, p. 184.

154. *Congressional Record*, February 25, 1960, 86th Congress, 2nd session, vol. 106, pt. 3, p. 3455; ibid., March 16, 1960, vol. 106, pt. 5, p. 5747.

155. Ibid., January 4, 1961, 87th Congress, 1st session, vol. 107, pt. 1, p. 108. According to former secretary of state Henry Kissinger, Cuba also appears to have induced a medical condition in President Richard Nixon. "Cuba was a neuralgic problem for Nixon," Kissinger recalled years later. See Henry Kissinger, *The White House Years* (New York, 1979), p. 633.

156. "Memorandum of Discussion at the Department of State–Joint Chiefs of Staff Meeting," January 8, 1960, in *FRUS:1958–1960*, pp. 731–32.

157. Arthur M. Schlesinger Jr., *A Thousand Days: John F. Kennedy in the White House* (Boston, 1965), p. 252.

158. Hurwitch, *Most of Myself*, 2:113.

159. Smith, *Fourth Floor*, p. 226.

160. *New York Times* foreign affairs editor Thomas Friedman was entirely correct in suggesting that the U.S. position on Cuba is "not really a policy. It's an *attitude*—a blind hunger for revenge against Mr. Castro." See Thomas L. Friedman, "Give That Man a Cigar," *New York Times*, September 29, 1999, p. 9. Emphasis in original.

161. Cyrus Vance, *Hard Choices* (New York, 1983), p. 358.

162. "Cuban Liberty and Democratic Solidarity (Libertad) Act of 1996," Public Law 104-114, March 12, 1996.

163. Donald E. Schulz, *The United States and Cuba: From a Strategy of Conflict to Constructive Engagement* (Carlisle Barracks, Pa., 1993), p. 18.

164. *Congressional Record*, June 24, 1960, 86th Congress, 2nd session, vol. 106, pt. 11, p. 14385.

CHAPTER 6

1. James Wilford Garner and Henry Cabot Lodge, *The United States*, 2 vols. (New York, 1907), 2:1033–34.

2. For a useful discussion of the metaphors the Americans used in the Philippines see Paul A. Kramer, *The Blood of Government: Race, Empire, the United States, and the Philippines* (Chapel Hill, 2006), pp. 198–208.

3. Carl Schurz, "The Issue of Imperialism," January 4, 1899, and "For Truth, Justice and Liberty," September 28, 1900, in *Speeches, Correspondence, and Political Papers of Carl Schurz*, 6 vols., ed. Frederic Bancroft (New York, 1913), 6:10–11, 237.

4. William Jennings Bryan, "What Next?," February 12, 1899, and "Cincinnati Speech," January 6, 1899, in *Bryan on Imperialism* (Chicago, 1900), pp. 9, 55.

5. William Jennings Bryan, "'Imperialists' See Our Duty," February 11, 1900, ibid., p. 64. For a useful overview of anti-imperialist thought see Robert L. Beisner, *Twelve against Empire: The Anti-Imperialists, 1898–1900* (New York, 1968).

6. Talcott Williams, "Cuba and Armenia," *Century*, February 1899, p. 635; Joseph B. Foraker, "Our War with Spain: Its Justice and Necessity," *Forum* 25 (June 1898): 394.

7. William McKinley, "Address at the Trans-Mississippi Exposition at Omaha, Nebraska," October 12, 1898, in *Speeches and Addresses of William McKinley* (New York, 1900), pp. 102, 104, and "Speech to the General Court, Boston," February 17, 1899, ibid., p. 196.

8. William McKinley, "Speech at Fargo, North Dakota," October 13, 1899, ibid., pp. 280–81.

9. William McKinley, "Speech at Dinner of the Home Market Club, Boston," February 16, 1899, ibid., p. 189.

10. William McKinley, "Speech at Youngstown, Ohio," October 18, 1899, ibid., p. 343.

11. William Kristol and Robert Kagan, "Toward a Neo-Reaganite Foreign Policy," *Foreign Affairs* 75 (July–August 1996): 20, 26, 32.

12. Theodore Roosevelt, *Presidential Addresses and State Papers*, 8 vols. (New York, 1910), 4:235.

13. Franklin D. Roosevelt, "Inaugural Address," March 4, 1933, in *The Public Papers and Addresses of Franklin D. Roosevelt*, 13 vols., ed. Samuel I. Rosenman (New York, 1938–50), 2:14.

14. Samuel Guy Inman, *Building an Inter-American Neighborhood* (New York, 1937), p. 9.

15. "President Participates in Roundtable with Young Leaders in Brazil," November 6, 2005, <http://www.whitehouse.gov/news/release/2005>.

16. *Congressional Record*, February 18, 1959, 86th Congress, 1st session, vol. 105, pt. 2, p. 2584.

17. *Time*, June 20, 1960, p. 32.

18. *Congressional Record*, February 26, 1960, 86th Congress, 2nd session, vol. 106, pt. 3, p. 3452.

19. Arthur M. Schlesinger Jr., *Robert Kennedy and His Times* (Boston, 1978), p. 473.

20. "President Urges Cuban People to Work for Democratic Change," August 3, 2006, <www.whitehouse.gov/news/releases/2006>.

21. "President Touches on Cuba after Castro," *New York Times*, June 29, 2007, <http://www.nytimes.com/2007/06/29>.

22. *New York Times*, May 23, 1954, p. E4.

23. Ibid., July 4, 1954, p. E2.

24. Robert C. McFarlane, *Special Trust* (New York, 1994), pp. 257–58.

25. *New York Times*, May 12, 1987, p. A12.

26. Ronald Reagan, "Radio Address to the Nation on the Situation in Central America," March 30, 1985, in *Public Papers of the Presidents of the United States: Ronald Reagan, 1985*, 2 vols. (Washington, D.C., 1988), 1:371.

27. *New York Times*, May 9, 2006, p. 3A.

28. "President Discusses CAFTA-DR," May 12, 2005, <http://www.whitehouse.gov/news/releases2005/05>.

29. Tom Barry, "Colombia: Recalling the Backyard Analogy," in Foreign Policy in Focus, *Global Affairs Commentary*, July 2001, <http://www.fpif.org>. It should be noted that the continued use of the terms "backyard" and "neighbors," often by well-intentioned scholars—even if to scorn the metaphors—validates the efficacy of the metaphors. See such works as Robert Bacon, *For Better Relations with Our Latin American Neighbors* (Washington, D.C., 1915); Oscar P. Austin, *Trading with Our Neighbors in the Caribbean* (New York, 1920); Delia Goetz, *Neighbors to the South* (New York, 1941); Edward Tomlinson, *The Other Americans: Our Neighbors to the South* (New York, 1943); Harriett McCune Brown and Helen Miller Bailey, *Our Latin American Neighbors* (Boston, 1944); Frances Carpenter, *Our South American Neighbors, 1890–1972* (New York, 1955); Donald Marquand Dozer, *Are We Good Neighbors? Three Decades of Inter-American Relations, 1930–1960* (Gainesville, 1959); Martin Diskin, ed., *Trouble in Our Backyard: Central America and the United States in the Eighties* (New York, 1983); Tom Buckley, *Violent Neighbors: El Salvador, Central America, and the United States* (New York, 1984); John E. Findling, *Close Neighbors, Distant Friends: United States–Central American Relations* (New York, 1987); Oliver Trager, ed., *Latin America: Our Volatile Neighbors* (New York, 1987); Harvey Summ and Tom Kelly, eds., *The Good Neighbors: America, Panama, and the 1977 Canal Treaties* (Athens, Ohio, 1988); James D. Cockcroft, *Neighbors in Turmoil: Latin America* (New York, 1989); Elaine Pascoe, *Neighbors at Odds: U.S. Policy in Latin America* (New York, 1990); William M. LeoGrande, *Our Own Backyard: The United States in Central America, 1977–1992* (Chapel Hill, 1998); Ana Covarrubias, "Mexico: The Challenge of a Latin American Power in the U.S. Backyard," in *Latin American and Caribbean Foreign Policy*, ed. Frank O. Mora and Jeanne A. K. Hey (Lanham, Md. 2003), pp. 13–30;

Mary Louise Pratt, "Back Yard with Views," in *Anti-Americanism*, ed. Andrew Ross and Kristin Ross (New York, 2004), pp. 32–46.

30. Woodrow Wilson, "Democracy and Efficiency," October 1, 1900, in *The Papers of Woodrow Wilson*, 69 vols., ed. Arthur S. Link et al. (Princeton, 1966–94), 12:18.

31. Nadine Gordimer, *Get a Life* (New York, 2005), p. 100.

32. Theodore Roosevelt to Hermann Speck von Sternberg, July 12, 1901, in *The Letters of Theodore Roosevelt*, 8 vols., ed. Elting E. Morison (Cambridge, Mass., 1951–54), 3:116.

33. Sumner Welles, *The Time for Decision* (New York, 1944), p. 185.

34. "Y" [Louis Halle], "On a Certain Impatience with Latin America," *Foreign Affairs* 28 (July 1950): 570–71.

35. Robert A. Hurwitch, *Most of Myself: An Autobiography in the Form of Letters to His Daughters*, 2 vols. (Santo Domingo, Dominican Republic, 1990–92), 2:264–65. Emphasis in original.

36. See Robert E. Peary, *Northward over the "Great Ice,"* 2 vols. (New York, 1898), 1:483, 492.

37. *Brooklyn Eagle*, February 12, 1899, p. 4.

38. *New York Times*, May 6, 1951, p. L9.

39. Michael Sullivan, "East Timor Violence Subsides after Days of Unrest," *Morning Edition*, National Public Radio, June 1, 2006.

40. Thomas L. Friedman, "Our New Baby," *New York Times*, May 4, 2003, p. 4.

41. White House Press Secretary Ari Fleischer told reporters in April 2003 that "the North Korean way of dialogue is often to engage in as bad a behavior as they could possibly engage in, with the expectation that the world will reward them for ceasing their bad behavior. That has been their previous actions. And the President has made clear that the United States will not reward bad behavior." Former U.S. ambassador to the United Nations John Bolton objected to direct negotiations with North Korea in 2007 because it violated "the principle that President Bush followed during his first term in office that we don't reward bad behavior." See "White House Calls Talks in Beijing on North Korea 'Useful,'" April 25, 2003, <http://italy.usembassy.gov/viewer/article>; "Nuclear Deal Rewards N. Korea for Bad Behavior, ex-U.N. Envoy Says," March 5, 2007, <http://findarticles.com/p/article>.

42. "Transcript: Senate Foreign Relations: Wolfowitz, Armitage Testify before Senate Panel," May 18, 2004, <http://www.washingtonpost.com>.

43. "Newsmaker Interview," *The News Hour*, Public Broadcast System, September 13, 2006.

44. *New York Times*, December 3, 2006, p. 1A.

45. Senate Foreign Relations Committee, "Iraq in the Strategic Context: Session 2," Testimony of Lieutenant General Brent Scowcroft, February 1, 2007, 110th Congress, 1st session, <http://www.senate.gov/~foreign/hearings/2007/hrg070201a.html>.

46. "Mixed Progress in Iraq amid New Offensives, Possible Anbar Handover," Online NewsHour: Analysis, PBS, January 11, 2008, <http://www.pbs.org/newshour/bb/middle_east/jan-june08/iraq>.

47. Francis W. Shepardson, "American Guardianship of Cuba," *World Today*, November 1906, p. 1197.

48. Murat Halstead, *Pictorial History of America's New Possessions* (Chicago, 1899), p. 134.

49. *New York Times*, April 9, 1960, p. 1.

50. Ibid., August 8, 1960, p. 1.

51. Ibid., October 7, 1960, p. 20.

52. Andrew J. Goodpaster, "Memorandum of a Conference with the President, White House, Washington, DC," March 17, 1960, in U.S. Department of State, *Foreign Relations of the United States, 1958–1960* (Washington, D.C., 1991), p. 861.

53. U.S. Department of State, *Cuba* (Washington, D.C., 1961). See also Theodore Draper, "Castro's Cuba: A Revolution Betrayed," *New Leader* 44 (March 27, 1961): 3–27.

54. Van Gosse, *Where the Boys Are* (London, 1993), p. 109.

55. Quoted in Patrick J. Haney and Walt Vanderbush, *The Cuban Embargo: The Domestic Politics of an American Foreign Policy* (Pittsburgh, 2005), p. 35.

56. "Discurso pronunciado desde el balcón de la Sociedad 'El Progreso,' de Sancti Spíritus, Las Villas," January 6, 1959, <http://www.cuba.cu/gobierno/discursos/>.

57. George Orwell, *1984* (New York, 1990), p. 263.

Index

Morgan, John Tyler, 54, 56; and Cuban proximity, 50; on U.S. occupation of Cuba, 192, 194
Morgan, W. R., 163
Mundt, Karl, 224
Musgrave, George, 78, 248

National Relief Association for Cuba, 80
Neighbor/neighborhood, as metaphor for Cuba, 32–38, 41, 46–47, 53–54, 55, 58, 65, 67, 90, 93, 104, 265–66
Nelson, Hugh, 30
Nelson, Wilford, 100
Newlands, Francis, 92, 101
Nichols, Francis, 188
Nitze, Paul, 254
Nixon, Richard, 241, 254; and communism in Cuba, 253
Norweb, R. Henry, 218
Noyes, Thomas, 114

O'Hara, Barratt, 223, 240, 241, 266
Olney, Richard, 42, 99
Orwell, George, 274
Ostend Manifesto, 26, 27, 29, 34, 36, 230; and metaphor, 53–54
Ozick, Cynthia, 116

Parkman, Francis, 108
Pasco, Samuel, 50
Payne, Sereno, 104
Peary, Robert, 269
Permanent treaty (1903), 124, 127, 227
Pershing, John, 208
Pettigrew, Richard, 101
Philippine Islands, 145, 201, 259, 264, 265
Phillips, Henry, 206
Phillips, Ruby Hart, 223
Pierce, Franklin, 34, 41
Pillsbury, Arthur, 92; and Cuban self-government, 114
Pinker, Steven, 52, 140
Planters Association, 198
Platt, Orville H., 194; on Cubans as chil-dren, 118; on Cuban independence, 184, 194; and Platt Amendment, 190
Platt Amendment, 21, 127, 152, 153, 163–64, 190, 195, 213, 218, 219, 222, 227, 242; and Cubans as children, 165; and Cuban gratitude, 189, 191
Political gravitation, and metaphor, 29–30
Polk, James, 41
Polk, Thurston, 30; on control of Cuba, 231
Portell Vilá, Herminio, 217
Power, and metaphor, 13–14, 16, 17
Pratt, Julius, 9
Pugh, George, 35
Puerto Rico, 145, 201, 259

Quitman, John, 36

Ramsey, Henry, 244, 245
Reagan, Ronald, 267; and the Cuban American National Foundation, 273
Reid, Harry, 270–71
Reid, Whitlaw, 246, 269; and Teller Amendment, 98
Remington, Frederic, 113
Renan, Ernest, 109
Reno, George, 232
Rhodes, James Ford, 31
Richardson, George, 109
Richardson, Leon Burr, 93
Rieff, David, 33
Rivers, Mendel, 223–24, 247, 254, 256
Robertson, Samuel, 166
Robinson, Albert, 115
Rodríguez, José Mayía, 183
Rodríguez Acosta, Ofelia, 213
Roig de Leuchsenring, Emilio, 217–18
Roosevelt, Franklin D., 266
Roosevelt, Theodore, 225, 268, 89–90, 153, 173; and 1906 Cuban rebellion, 103, 152, 153; and U.S. intervention, 187; and Cuban independence, 192, 195, 227; monument to, 207

Vandenberg, Arthur, 9, 195
Van Leeuwen, Theo, 130
Verrill, Hyatt, 206
Veterans of Foreign Wars, 200

War: war of 1898, 5, 6, 7, 9, 10–11, 43–
    94, 96–99; Cuban independence war
    (1895–98), 5, 10, 42–43, 176–79, 182–
    83; Ten Years War (1868–78), 5, 34; and
    William McKinley, 10–11, 45, 50, 92,
    211–26
Welch, Richard, 225
Welles, Sumner, 268
Westermarck, Edward, 180
Weyl, Nathaniel, 252
Weyler, Valeriano, 69–70, 206, 225
Whitaker, O. W., 65
White, Trumbull, 69, 178–79
Whitman, Walt, 28
Wiley, Alexander, 267
Williams, Herbert Pelham, 118
Williams, Ramon, 29
Williams, Talcott, 65
Wilson, James H., 54; and Teller Amend-

ment, 98; and Cuban independence,
    197
Wilson, Woodrow, 268; and war of 1898,
    8–9, 93; and self-government, 104–5;
    and colonized people as children,
    119–20
Wolcott, Edward, 56
Wolfowitz, Paul, 270
Wollam, Park F. 222
Women's Auxiliary of the United Spanish
    War Veterans, 200
Wood, Edmond, 40
Wood, Leonard, 140, 208, 225, 232; and
    Cuban self-government, 103, 114; and
    Cuban independence, 195, 247
Woodford, Stewart, 43; and war of 1898,
    45–46
Woodward, W. E., 81, 93
Woon, Basil, 168–69

Young, Samuel B. M. 101, 179

Zayas, Alfredo, 208
Zenor, Willam, 196